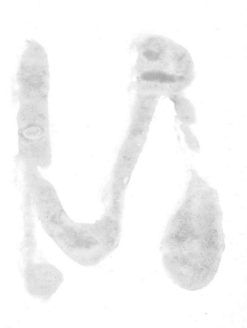

Karari Njama photographed at Nyeri on June 6, 1955, on day after his capture. Photo: Kenya Information Services.

DONALD L. BARNETT
AND
KARARI NJAMA

Mau Mau from Within

—

AUTOBIOGRAPHY
AND
ANALYSIS OF KENYA'S
PEASANT REVOLT

MODERN READER PAPERBACKS
NEW YORK AND LONDON

This book
is dedicated to all those Kenyans
who have given their lives in
the lengthy and just struggle
for Land and Freedom

Library of Congress Catalog Card Number: 65-24519
Standard Book Number: SBN-85345-135-4

First Modern Reader Paperback Edition 1970
Second Printing

Monthly Review Press
116 West 14th Street, New York, N.Y. 10011
33/37 Moreland Street, London, E.C. 1

MANUFACTURED IN THE UNITED STATES OF AMERICA

CONTENTS

PREFACE

ALL OF US who have affixed our names to the remarks that follow have in varying degrees been held responsible for the revolt popularized under the name of Mau Mau. British propaganda—and not only British—has been remarkably successful in equating the revolt of a large section of the people of Kenya with barbarism and savagery, so much so that even many Africans in Kenya are today reluctant to discuss this vitally important episode in our history with candour. This is all the more fantastic when one realizes that Kenya is today independent largely because of this revolt and the struggle of the men and women who participated in it.

During the last few years a spate of books on almost every aspect of African life has been poured out upon the world. Kenya has not been neglected in this flood. Naturally, the subject that has engrossed writers most has been Mau Mau. But virtually none of these authors has attempted a serious analysis of this movement, of its causes, character, organization and achievements. There is an obsessive preoccupation in these works with the sinister and the awesome. The very name 'Mau Mau' is an illustration of how successful propaganda can damn an entire movement to which thousands sacrificed everything, including their lives, by attaching to it an appellation that conjures up all the clichés about the 'dark continent' which still crowd the European mind.

Dr Barnett's study is, to our knowledge, the first attempt to break out of this depressing mould and present this heroic episode in our history with skill, seriousness and sincerity.

Many who participated in the Kenya Land and Freedom Army have disappeared from the political scene today. Their behaviour tends to be deliberately self-effacing and diffident. A good deal of this sense of guilt arises out of the years of 'brain washing' in the 'rehabilitation' camps of the colonial regime where they were detained. Humiliation, concentrated, continuous and consistent, was a principal element in the 'rehabilitation' process. What is regrettable and even horrifying is that some African politicians and young 'intellectuals' should think that this is as

9

it should be. Frequently, their past and the movement they created is condemned by people of stature in the politics of the country today.

Late in 1952 and early 1953, the entire leadership of the Kenya African Union, the only African political party in the country, was arrested and the party proscribed. The arrests were not confined to the higher ranks only, but also included the middle levels. The colonial government and the European settlers hoped in this way to destroy the African nationalist movement completely. The men and women who went into the forests either to fight or to seek refuge from the terror spread throughout the countryside by Government forces were leaderless in the sense that all national and local leaders were behind bars, not to emerge until recently. They had to fend for themselves and create new cadres. As Dr Barnett shows they were almost all humble men and women who felt passionately about the cause they struggled for. They were the true heroes of the years of forest fighting.

Kenya owes a great debt of gratitude to them. Anyone familiar with the political scene here in 1952 cannot fail to see the close and direct link between the political changes of recent times and the shock of the Kenya Land and Freedom Army revolt to the British government and the European settlers. Indeed, it would not be an exaggeration to say that the political consequences of their sacrifice have been felt throughout East Africa.

A remarkable feature of the personnel of the Land and Freedom Army was the absence in the forest of educated men, educated, that is, in the formal sense beyond primary school level. It is clearly not enough to say that educated men in those days were few and far between and that most of them tended to be pro-government because they usually occupied government posts. The reasons go beyond that to the wide gulf that has arisen in many parts of Africa between the intellectuals and the masses. The symbols of the revolt, as Dr Barnett points out, were traditional symbols. The educated young man of today either does not understand these symbols at all or is taught to look down upon them. They represent a way of life from which he has become increasingly isolated. Essentially, this phenomenon is yet another vicious heritage from colonialism. This is not said as a plea for a return to the old ways. Far from it. But we do have to strive for a society in which intellectuals are part of an organic whole and not merely 'black Europeans'. Not only politics and economics but also minds have to be decolonized.

Our plea to break the conspiracy of silence about the Land and Freedom Army struggle includes also a plea for a more serious study of the history of Kenya since the Second World War and more particularly since 1952. Dr Barnett deserves the thanks of African nationalists for being the first person to have seriously studied this problem. We hope that his book, valuable as it is in itself, will also help to pierce that veil of reticence which surrounds the Land and Freedom Army and go some way at least to secure to those who fought in the forests of the Nyandarua their due recognition as national heroes.

B. M. KAGGIA
FRED KUBAI
J. MURUMBI
ACHIENG ONEKO

FOREWORD

IT WAS March 1962 when I met Karari (son/of) Njama for the first time. He had been recommended very highly by two of my informants and one of the latter, Mohamed Mathu, arranged our meeting through the mails and accompanied me to Nyeri District. Karari's village was located seventeen miles off the main north-south highway and about 110 miles north of Nairobi, Kenya's capital city. It was situated atop a high ridge at an altitude of almost 7,000 feet. Across the pitted dirt road from the small, mud-and-wattle circular hut in which Karari, his wife, Nyaguthii, and their four children lived, I was confronted by a truly spectacular view. The green slopes of this and the opposite ridge, dotted here and there with small terraced gardens, descended sharply to the narrow Gura River Valley over a thousand feet below. Here, slender strips of cultivated land lined both sides of the clear, trout-laden Gura which twisted its way through the valley. The gardens, measuring an acre or less on the average, extended from the river's edge to a point fifty or seventy-five yards back where the steep rise of the slope made cultivation difficult and usually unprofitable.

The Gura, often swollen and dangerous during the long rains, was now flowing with a gentle, quiet rumble well within its rocky banks. A mile or so to the northwest the river emerged from the shadows of the vast Aberdare Range where it began as a trickle in the 11,000-foot moorland swamps, grew as it merged with other streams and tumbled down through the bamboo and 'black' forest belts and then spilled out into the valley. Miles away, in the Fort Hall District, the Gura joined the Sagana and eventually, as with most eastward-flowing rivers, emptied into the huge Tana River which deposited so much of Kenya's rich highland soil and untapped energy into the Indian Ocean some 350 miles from Karari's village.

As I was taking in this panoramic scene, Karari returned home from the sub-location primary school where he was teaching. A stocky, sturdily built man in his mid-30's, wearing khaki shorts and an open-collared sports shirt, Karari appeared at first sight much taller than his actual height of five-foot nine. His smile and manner as we shook hands and exchanged greetings was open and pleasant, lacking for the most part the uneasy restraint and suspicion I had frequently encountered in previous first meetings with Kikuyu. After Mathu's introduction, we entered the dimly lit, smoke-filled hut to drink the tea which Nyaguthii had prepared.

The wide-ranging discussion we engaged in the rest of that day and the next convinced me that Karari was an honest and very sincere human being and, moreover, one whose knowledge of Kenya's *Mau Mau* revolution was, from personal experience, very considerable. He spoke unguardedly, though in general terms, of the name 'Mau Mau', of his role in the Movement and the two years he'd spent in the Aberdares as a guerrilla leader. Fortunately, the initial impression I formed of Karari was confirmed and reinforced over the course of the next six months.

As we talked, I explained that I had already been in Kenya for nine months doing research of an anthropological nature on *Mau Mau*. Believing most of the writings on this subject to be one-sided interpretations from the point of view and perspective of the European settler and British Government, I had spent much of my time talking to Africans and collecting life-histories from Kikuyu who, in varying mode and degree, had participated in the revolt. I indicated that I had already gathered seven such life-histories and tried to make clear that my interest in the revolution was two-fold : first, I wanted to collect sufficient data for the writing of my Ph.D. thesis in anthropology;* and, second, I wanted to provide a medium through which African participants in the revolt could make their experiences and interpretations known to the outside world. My intention, with regard to the latter aim, was to make this a joint enterprise in which all contributors would share in both the work and responsibility and, if there were any, the rewards.

Before we parted, and indicating that he had wanted to record the history of the revolution ever since his release from the detention camps in December 1958, Karari agreed to come to Nairobi the following month, during the school recess, where we would

* The dissertation which resulted from this research was copyrighted in July 1963 under the title, *Mau Mau: the Structural Integration and Disintegration of Aberdare Guerrilla Forces.*

tape his life-history. The two weeks set aside for this task, however, proved entirely inadequate. Karari, somewhat inhibited by
the tape recorder, preferred to write his story in longhand. While
offering the advantage of greater control, this process was obviously much slower and confronted both of us with certain
problems. After much thought and discussion, it was decided
that Karari would resign his teaching post and come to work for
me as a research assistant while writing his autobiography. As
it turned out, this was a very fruitful and rewarding decision for
both of us.

In mid-April, Karari moved in with me and my family—my
wife Carol and our four children—and during the next six
months, living and working together, we each acquired a considerable knowledge of the other's strengths, habits and frailties.
The understanding and friendship which grew out of this working relationship, set as it was against the background of two
widely separated cultures, was for me one of the major rewards
of my eighteen months of field work in Kenya. Again, without
the degree of mutual trust and understanding we achieved, it is
unlikely that the present work would ever have come to fruition.

It might be mentioned here that while this book contains only
the single, rather lengthy account of Karari Njama, another
manuscript is in preparation which will embrace the shorter life-
histories of five other informants. Needless to say, the collective
contributions to the present work of the several persons with
whom I worked was great indeed. Without the materials contained in the life-histories of Priscilla Gathoni, Naomi Wanjiku
Kenete, Bedan Miriti Kairo, Ngugi Solomon Kabiro, Kahinga
Wachanga, John Mwangi, Karigo Muchai, Mohamed Mathu
and, of course, Karari Njama, I would have been unable to
grasp the overall nature of the revolution or prepare my contribution to this book.

Given the nature of my investigation the multiple-autobiography approach, though not without its own peculiar problems, proved invaluable. The available pertinent literature,
though on the whole voluminous, dwindled and became less
reliable as I approached—in both space and time—the conduct
and organization of the guerrilla war in Nairobi, the Kikuyu
reserves and the forests of Mount Kenya and the Aberdares. My
use of and reliance upon published materials, therefore, was

greatest in those areas of research furthest removed from the revolution proper. Thus, my discussion of traditional Kikuyu society in Chapter One is based almost entirely on works such as Jomo Kenyatta's *Facing Mount Kenya*, H. E. Lambert's *Kikuyu Social and Political Institutions*, L. S. B. Leakey's *Mau Mau and the Kikuyu*, and J. Middleton's *The Kikuyu and Kamba of Kenya*.*

Again, my interpretation of the political and economic processes set in motion in Kenya by colonization and European settlement rests to a considerable extent on the data contained in a wide ranging body of literature. Of particular value in this sphere were the works of S. and K. Aaronovitch, *Crisis in Kenya*, M. R. Dilley, *British Policy in Kenya Colony*, S. S. Heyer, *Development of Agriculture and the Land System in Kenya, 1918–1939*, E. Huxley and M. Perham, *Race and Politics in Kenya*, K. Ingram, *History of East Africa*, J. Kenyatta, *Kenya: The Land of Conflict*, N. Leys, *Kenya*, M. Ross, *Kenya from Within*, and various Kenya and British Government publications.

With regard to the underground movement and the general character of the revolution, the literature thins and becomes considerably less reliable. Though I have seriously studied works such as L. S. B. Leakey's *Defeating Mau Mau*, F. D. Corfield's *Historical Survey of the Origins and Growth of Mau Mau*, and P. Evan's *Law and Disorder: Scenes of Life in Kenya*, my analysis rests to a very large extent on the data I was able to gather from Kikuyu and other informants between June of 1961 and December of 1962.

In the area of my primary concern, the structure and organization of guerrilla forces, reliance upon published material was reduced practically to nil. While the local newspapers, Government documents and books were useful in checking and confirming key dates and events, available literature dealing with the revolution proper was, on the whole, meagre and of poor quality. Written by men who had served with the Government security forces, or based upon the writings of the latter, works such as W. Baldwin's *Mau Mau Manhunt*, Ian Henderson's

---

* In the Bibliography presented at the end of the book, those works which I found particularly useful in preparing my own analysis are marked by an asterisk.

The Hunt for Kimathi, F. Kitson's *Gangs and Countergangs*, and F. Majdalany's *State of Emergency*, are the African equivalent of most American "Cowboy and Indian" sagas. Quite naturally, these works reflected the partiality of their writers and revealed little if any effort at objective understanding. Unfortunately, even those whose training and knowledge should have dictated otherwise, such as L. S. B. Leakey, in *Defeating Mau Mau*, tended to present a one-sided and distorted view of reality—that of the *noble white man* who, fervently engaged in bringing civilization, Christianity, education and the "good life" to Kenya's backward natives, was suddenly forced to defend self and property, law and order, peace and morality, against the treacherous attack of *atavistic savages* gone mad with a blood-lust. This literature undeniably reflected the mood and perspective of most Kenya Europeans. That it failed to reflect the outlook of the vast majority of Kenya Africans, or render an adequate and balanced account of the revolution in question, is equally undeniable.

Faced, then, with the task of obtaining most of my primary data from Africans with first-hand knowledge, and having to confront the generalized fear, distrust and suspicion of the white man which the Kikuyu had acquired during sixty years of colonial rule, I had to rely quite heavily on the life-history approach. Here, working with a relatively small number of persons over fairly extended periods of time, rapport and confidence had a chance to develop. From a generalized 'European' I became an individual with specific human qualities, interests and motives. In the last analysis, the success I had in gathering life-history material was due largely to my informants' ability and willingness to accept me as an individual and accurately assess my interests in the revolution and in their own personal lives and problems.

The multiple-autobiography approach itself contained an extremely useful, built-in corroborative device. A large number of events and situations had been participated in by two or more of my informants and, though each account might reveal a given incident from a slightly different perspective, each acted as a check upon the authenticity of the others. I was thus able to abstract a considerable amount of mutually confirmed data and the shared valuations thereof. Where conflicts in the data occurred, I was usually able to resolve the issues through further discussions or interviews with other informants.

One factor which greatly facilitated the success of this approach was the essentially small-scale nature of Kikuyu society. Given the relatively high degree of mobility found among the million or so Kikuyu of the Central Province, Rift Valley and Nairobi, news and information normally spread with unbelievable rapidity. Largely by word of mouth, news could often be transmitted great distances in the space of a few hours through the informal networks of dispersed kin and neighbourhood relations. During the revolution, the paths of countless thousands crossed one another under a variety of circumstances in the city, reserve, forests and detention camps. Virtually every Kikuyu acquired, either indirectly or through personal observation, a considerable and frequently detailed knowledge of a large number of persons and events. Under such circumstances, an error, omission, fabrication or untruth on the part of an informant could not long remain undiscovered by the persistent researcher. One of my informants, for example, failed to disclose that he had served as a Government informer during his internment at a certain detention camp. This fact, however, was soon made known to me by another informant and then confirmed by two others who had likewise spent time in this camp.

Two additional factors which enhanced the value and utility of the multiple-autobiography approach might also be mentioned. Several persons who have consented to read the life-histories I gathered have marvelled, often to the point of disbelief, at the incredible ability of my informants to recall in detail events which transpired ten or more years in the past. To the Africanist who has spent time in the field this feat comes as no surprise. In the absence of a writing system the Kikuyu, as with other African peoples, were traditionally dependent upon oral history, often reinforced in song, proverb and verse, in their efforts to preserve and transmit to future generations important happenings and events. The transference of this knowledge was an extremely important aspect of the upbringing and socialization of children. Historic events of significance, along with a wide variety of other information which could not be stored in books for future reference, simply had to be remembered or stored in the human mind if it were not to be lost for all time.

The Kikuyu, therefore, even after several decades of British rule and exposure to book learning, has normally developed powers of recollection or remembrance which might be considered exceptional in societies long endowed with a written script. I should hasten to add that even in the African context, Karari Njama's recall of detail is something of an exception and, though approached, was not equalled or excelled by any of my other informants.

Related to the above is the fact that events considered of some importance to an individual will usually be reiterated by him time and time again in his dealings with other people. Upon meeting friends, relatives or neighbours Kikuyu customarily bring one another up to date on all significant happenings in their lives since they last met. This practice, which you are bound to notice in Karari's account, would obviously act to reinforce through repetition the remembrance of detail.

Regarding the credibility of the data contained in Karari's life-history, a few words are in order. As for all major events and their sequence, Karari's account is corroborated not only by the accounts of my other informants, at all points where they intersect, but by newspaper accounts, Government documents and interview material. Obviously, it has not been possible to substantiate more than a few of the minor events and details of Karari's story. I can only point out that in areas where my data converge on questions of detail, the descriptions rendered by Karari have proven accurate. While I found the internal consistency of such a detailed account as Karari Njama's very convincing, I feel the reader will be able to reach his own conclusion in this regard.

Needless to say, ultimate responsibility for the accuracy of Karari Njama's account lies with Mr. Njama himself, just as I must accept full responsibility for whatever inadequacies or errors might be found in the remainder of this book. I have endeavoured to present Karari Njama's life-history, up to the time of his capture on June 5, 1955, in such a manner as to preserve its full documentary value. It is reproduced here in its entirety exactly as originally written with the following exceptions. Where it was felt absolutely necessary to preserve intended meanings or to make clear an ambiguous statement, I have made insertions noted by the use of brackets. Minor alterations in spelling and punctuation have not been noted. My aim has been to make as few changes as possible and grammatical errors, where they were not felt to impair communication, were left as written. Finally, the breakdown of the life-history into chapters, and the titles of the latter, are my doing rather than Karari's.

It is sincerely hoped that the combination of objective, if not detached, analysis and commentary together with the personal account of a fully involved partisan will provide the reader with both an increased understanding of the background, emergence and nature of Kenya's *Mau Mau Revolution* and, through a vicarious participation, some deeper insights into the hopes, fears, frustrations and expectations of a people whose actions and outlook on life have been shaped in large measure by the double-edged sword of tradition and colonial rule.

August 1964   DONALD L. BARNETT

PART I

Background to Revolt

CHAPTER I

AN INTRODUCTION

THE revolution with which we shall be concerned in this book occurred in the Kenya Colony and Protectorate between the years 1952 and 1957. With Uganda, Tanganyika and Zanzibar, Kenya comprised a portion of what was known as British East Africa. In the twilight of the colonial period, on 12 December 1963, this colony achieved its independence after sixty-odd years of British rule. While it is beyond the scope of the present work to deal comprehensively with this historic period, I do intend here to touch upon the major conditions and processes which underlay the revolt in question. To provide, so to speak, a background against which 'Mau Mau' may be more closely and, it is hoped, objectively understood.

Let us consider, in broad stroke, the context within which 'Mau Mau' arose. Kenya covers an area of about 245,060 square miles and is bounded on the east by the Indian Ocean, on the north-east and north by the Sudan, Somalia and Ethiopia, on the west by Uganda and on the south by Tanganyika. Of this territory, approximately three-fifths is poorly watered semi-desert occupied by pastoral peoples such as the Somali, Turkana, Samburu, Boran, Masai and Kalenjin tribes. Roughly, these semi-desert areas are located in the vast former Northern Frontier Province, in the south toward the Tanganyika border and in the east between the highlands and the coastal strip. The remainder of the country, in the central and western regions, includes the Great Rift Valley with its Lakes Naivasha, Nakuru and Rudolph, the mountain plateau to the east ranging from 3,000 to 9,000 feet above sea level and including the twin peaked Aberdare Range and snow-capped Mount Kenya, and the Kenya portion of the Lake Victoria Basin to the west.

The peoples occupying these latter regions comprise the bulk of Kenya's population and its six major 'tribes': the Luo and Baluhya in the west, the Kikuyu and closely related Embu and Meru in the east, the Kamba south and east of the Kikuyu, the

23

'Europeans' in the central Rift Valley region and the 'Asians' in
Nairobi and the other towns. This region being relatively well-
watered, most of its rural peoples practise agriculture combined
with the keeping of cattle, sheep and goats.

According to the East African Census of 1948 the total
African population of Kenya numbered better than five and a
quarter million with the Kikuyu tribes comprising 30 per cent,
the Luo 14 per cent, Baluhya 13 per cent and Kamba 12 per
cent. In addition there were almost 30,000 Europeans and an
Asian population (Indian, Arab and Goan) of over 120,000.
Apart from the 9,000 European settlers of the 'White Highlands', the bulk of the non-African population lived in the
administrative and commercial capital of Nairobi—some 300
miles inland from the coast and surrounded on three sides by
the Kikuyu district of Kiambu, the ancient port city of Mombasa, or in one or another of the smaller towns of the Rift
Valley Province.

Very generally, the three 'racial' aggregates occupied distinctive positions within Kenya's caste-class spectrum. The European
community, though comprising less than 1 per cent of the total
population, constituted a kind of 'high caste', reminiscent of
long defunct European aristocracies, and occupied a highly
privileged position in both the political and economic life of the
colony. Internally segmented into a number of business, farming, civil servant, mission, professional and recreational groups,
often with conflicting interests, the European community nevertheless constituted Kenya's most unified and integrated population segment. Cross-linked through a wide variety of associations
whose memberships overlapped, and fully conscious of their
common interests *vis-à-vis* both African and Asian groups,
Europeans tended to react as a single body in the face of any
external threat to their continued existence as a privileged
minority.

Though ultimate policy and decision-making powers regarding the colony rested with the British Parliament, acting through
its Minister of State for the Colonies, Colonial Office and resident Governor, the European minority in Kenya exercised a
virtual monopoly of power in the local governing institutions.
Thus in 1948 the Kenya Legislative Council was comprised of
one Arab, five Indian and eleven European elected members,

along with one Arab and four African members *appointed* by the Governor plus sixteen official members, also European.

Within the European community, the well-organized minority of settler farmers and planters constituted a solid block. Acting through organizations such as the Convention of Associations and Kenya National Farmers Union they in large measure determined and articulated the over-all aims and policies of the white population. Despite the early and repeated formal British Government pronouncements regarding the 'paramountcy of African interests' where these clashed with those of the immigrant communities, the settlers had been successful in acquiring exclusive rights to the vast 'White Highlands' and in perpetuating discriminatory policies in the fields of education, wages, housing, cash crop cultivation, marketing and public services. The color-bar and subtle *apartheid* policies, in all their degrading aspects, bore a great and not accidental resemblance to South African practice.

Aware of the limited nature of their powers *vis-à-vis* the British Parliament, the European community and particularly the settler minority aspired to a form of self government which would both free them from British rule and interference and entrench their powers in a Kenya constitution guaranteeing continued European political dominance. The models for this line of political action lay in Southern Rhodesia and the Union of South Africa.

The Asian segment of Kenya's population occupied a middle and in many ways ambivalent position in the hierarchy of color, class and caste. Denied the right to own or lease land in the European Settled Areas and lacking the Native Land Unit of the African, the Asian was of necessity a town dweller. Outnumbering the Europeans four to one, the Asians on the whole constituted an urban middle class of traders, merchants, white collar workers, professionals and skilled laborers. It should be added, however, that while the Europeans were concentrated at the top of the economic pyramid and the Africans at the bottom, the Asians tended to be more staggered from top to bottom.

With the predominantly lower class and illiterate Arabs concentrated at the coast, the vast majority, or almost 100,000 of Kenya's socially defined 'Asians' were of Indian origin and segmented primarily along Muslim–Hindu lines into a number of religious sect and caste groupings. Among Hindus the caste system was strong and marriage across caste lines extremely rare. The primary division amongst non-Muslims was between the Gujarati segment, predominant in the commercial field, and the Punjabis, both Sikh and non-Sikh, who comprised a significant proportion of the Indian professionals and skilled workers. The dominant force among the Muslims, divided internally into a number of sects, was the Ismaili community, a Khoja sect following the Aga Khan. In addition, there were the Catholic Goans, largely white collar workers, and a scattering of Scindis, Bengalis, Parsis, Madrassis, Bombay Maharastrians, etc.

Unlike the European community, where racial identification provided a strong integratory force, the Asians of Kenya identified themselves less as Indians than as members of particular religious sects and castes. Unity, to the degree that it was achieved across these religious cleavages, was the result primarily of the lengthy struggle, which reached its height in the early 1920's, waged by the Indians for equality of citizenship with the dominant Europeans. Despite the political and commercial rivalry between 'brown' and white, however, the interests of both were in many ways closely bound up in the existing system. Indian merchants and traders, as well as white collar workers, feared the emergence of a black middle class and felt threatened, perhaps as much as the European community, by the increasing tempo of African nationalist demands. In their attacks on European supremacy and the felt resentment at being treated as second class citizens, Asians tended to share a common body of interests with the Africans on the bottom rung of the socioeconomic ladder. Their fear of African predominance, however, tended to foster the conviction that their interests might be better served if the *status quo* in black–white relations was left undisturbed. Hence the ambivalence in the position of the Asian community.

3 Kenya's African population, numbering an estimated 5,561,000 in 1952, was clearly at the bottom of the colony's socioeconomic hierarchy. The vast majority were peasants living in the overcrowded and steadily deteriorating Native Land Units 'reserved' for them and engaged largely in subsistence patterns of agricul-

ture. Another large segment of the African 'lower class' was comprised of unskilled and largely migrant laborers employed primarily on the European farms and plantations of the Highlands or in the urban centers of Nairobi and Mombasa. About a fourth of the entire African adult male population was engaged in some form of wage employment. Of this number, just under 50 per cent were engaged in agriculture, 20 per cent in Government service, 11 per cent in manufacturing and 11 per cent in domestic employment. The great mass of African labor was unskilled and the wage level, in both absolute and relative terms, was extremely low. In 1948, for example, a total of 385,000 African workers earned the equivalent of 28 million dollars—an average of $73 per worker per year, which included estimated food and housing allowances. Asian workers numbering 23,500 earned 17.4 million dollars—an average of $741 per worker per year. And European wage earners numbering 11,500 garnered a total wage of 20 million dollars—an average of $1,739 per worker per year.

These statistics, of course, reveal in only the most abstract way the degree of destitution extant among African workers in the years prior to the revolt. Though conditions have changed slightly, and not always for the better, a walk through one of the African slum locations such as Kariokor or Pumwani, would present a much more accurate picture of African poverty. It would include the thousands of Africans, not figured in the above statistics, who drift into the city as landless and unemployed peasants in search of work and sleep twelve or sixteen to a room to avoid the cold Nairobi nights. It would include the squalor and degradation which fail to seep through the lifeless tables of figures.

In addition to the peasant and worker, there was also a small but growing number of African petty traders and hawkers and an emergent white collar class of low-salaried clerks, insurance salesmen, teachers, medical assistants, etc. Competition in both of these areas between Africans and their entrenched Asian counterparts tended to sharpen the animosity and conflict between the two groups. Not infrequently, Africans expressed more bitterness and resentment toward Asians than toward the dominant Europeans. The latter were on the whole further removed from direct economic competition and interaction with

Africans than were the Asian shop keepers, traders, semi-skilled laborers and white collar workers.

Internally, the African population was segmented primarily along tribal lines. Rural areas outside the European domain were demarcated and administered by Government largely as tribal units and, with the perpetuation of traditional tenure systems, African peasant and pastoral aggregates tended to persist as tribally homogeneous isolates. Travel and trade restrictions functioned to further reduce and inhibit inter-tribal rural contact.

With the pastoral tribes remaining largely outside the cash economy and highly resistant to acculturative processes, it was predominantly the agricultural tribes mentioned earlier which entered the urban milieu where the pattern of tribal isolation was, during the post-war period, beginning to give way to broader groupings of an African national character. Thus in Nairobi, while the majority of associations continued to be based on tribal, sub-tribe or clan affiliation (e.g., the Abaluhya Association, Thukus Brotherhood Fund, Kitui Friendly Society, etc.), a growing number of Africans were entering economic, political and other associations where tribal identification was over-ridden by racial, occupational and residential criteria (e.g., the Domestic and Hotel Workers' Union, Starehe African Social Club, Kenya African Union, Labour Trade Union of East Africa, etc.). Organizers and leaders of the latter associations were by and large drawn from the small but significant segment of educated Africans. Frustrated by the severe limitations imposed upon African upward mobility in the political and economic spheres, these men tended to oppose tribal exclusiveness as an obstacle to general African advancement.

While education thus facilitated the breakdown of vertical or tribal barriers, it tended also to foster the emergence of a new horizontal cleavage between the educated and the illiterate. And with education largely in the hands of the missions, this cleavage coincided with that between Christian and pagan. For most Africans with an education beyond primary school level the European community functioned as a *reference group*, possessing various attributes of Western civilization which the educated African both aspired to and, at least in part, judged himself in terms of. More often than not, acknowledged superiority of European achievement in the areas of formal education, science and technology, material wealth and military power were projected into other cultural spheres. Thus, many aspects of African traditional belief and practice were seen by the educated as 'inferior' or 'backward' when compared to their 'advanced' European counterparts.

The illiterate peasant and worker, on the other hand, being closer to traditional customs, religion and law, was inclined to view with some suspicion and disdain the efforts of his educated brethren to become *Black Europeans*. And this distrust was reinforced by the fact that a good number of educated Africans were salaried officials or employees of the white man's Government and, especially in the case of headmen and chiefs, often found themselves supporting unpopular Government programs.

This cleavage, while significant, must not be thought of as complete or unambiguous. As we have seen, it was from amongst the educated that an elite of African nationalist leaders emerged to articulate the grievances of the illiterate peasants and laborers. The latter, in turn, normally held these leaders in great respect, sometimes bordering on reverence. Again, the illiterate prized education very highly for their children and often made great sacrifices to put a son or daughter through school. The educated, on the other hand, despite their adoption of many Western ways, retained many and frequently strong ties with kinsmen and neighbors within the peasant community. The color-bar and European discriminatory policies made it impossible for them to shed their identity as Africans or sever all connections with the illiterate masses.

Looked at broadly, then, the various rural African aggregates were formally integrated within Kenya society by a British-imposed hierarchy of governing institutions and enforcement agencies over which they had no control and little influence. The European minority, on the other hand, through its outright control or influence over these institutions, was able to sustain its position of dominance *vis-à-vis* both the African majority and the Asians of the center. The powerful settler group could thus implement policies relating to land, labor, taxation, education, etc., which, though advantageous with respect to its own calculated interests, often ran counter to those of the subordinate African and Asian groups. To sustain this inequitable and unbalanced relationship, the dominant European class was frequently obliged to compensate for its lack of popular support and numbers by the same use or threat of force and coercion required initially for the establishment of white rule at the turn of the century.

While Kenya's Africans were divided along tribal lines and faced with the new divisive tendencies indicated above, there were nonetheless strong counterforces operating to unify the African population. Regardless of tribe, all Africans were classed as 'Natives' by the dominant whites and subject as a single people to the discriminatory and degrading policies and practices of the European elite. Thus classified and treated as *one*, there was mounting pressure within the black community to submerge or play down tribal and other differences in the face of a common *enemy*—the oppressive and dominant white settler minority. The major conflict and cleavage between black and white, becoming increasingly intense and deep, operated to mitigate internal differences and foster a growing awareness of the need for African unity.

In the urban milieu of Nairobi, African groupings were emerging which sought to integrate the various tribal segments of the population under institutions of their own making and through which they could protest and contest the privileged position of the immigrant minorities. As the urban African population was comprised largely of migrant workers with one foot in the city and the other in their respective rural areas, the multi-tribal associations of the city, and especially the fast-growing African nationalist and trade union movements, tended to cross-link the many rural peasant aggregates. Where, in short, Luo, Kikuyu, Kamba, Baluhya, Giriama, etc., were joined as members of an urban association, the rural tribal groups with which these individuals maintained contact were thereby indirectly linked to one another. Inter-tribal suspicion and hostility were therefore reduced to the extent that these multitribal groups were successful in pointing out the vital interests common to *all* Africans and in working for the peaceful and friendly resolution of those conflicts which emerged.

This process of African integration outside the existing hierarchy of governing institutions was still in its early stages during the post-war years prior to the revolt. Due to a wide variety of factors, including the degree and basis of rural discontent, the extent of involvement in urbanization processes and variations in the general level of political consciousness and internal integration, the various tribal or rural aggregates were differentially involved in the process of African unification. The pastoral tribes remained by and large outside this integratory process and, amongst the agriculturists, it was unquestionably the Kikuyu who played the central and leading role, followed at some distance by the Luo, Kamba, Baluhya and Teita.

* * *

Since the Kikuyu hold center stage in this book, it should prove useful to consider some of the factors which underlay their primary role in both the African nationalist movement and peasant revolution of Kenya. Let us look first at some of the processes set in motion by the establishment of a settled European agricultural population; then at certain features and patterns revealed in the emergence and development of African associations which sought to articulate and gain a redress of peasant grievances; and lastly at certain features of the traditional society which helped shape Kikuyu responses to imposed colonial institutions.

The advent of European settlement in the years 1902–7 was to prove a determining factor in the development of Kenya's peasant economies. As a rule, the largely self-sufficient subsistence economies of Africa's indigenous agricultural tribes were brought into the exchange economy of the various colonizing powers either through the cultivation and sale of cash crops, such as coffee, cocoa, cotton and peanuts, or through the export of labor in the form of migrant wage and contract workers. It was not a matter of chance, however, which determined the particular line of development a given peasantry would pursue. Labor-exporting peasantries have thus emerged with great regularity in areas of significant European settlement, where the settler demand for land was inextricably linked with his need for cheap African labor to work it and resulted in the alienation of tribal territories, various forms of compulsory labor and taxation, and restrictions on competitive African cultivation of cash crops.

Thus in Kenya, as in other territories of east, central and south Africa, African land was appropriated for the exclusive use of

immigrant white colonists. That a good deal more land was
alienated than could be put to effective use by the settlers is
explained in large measure by the latters' need for African labor.
Lord Delamere, a leading settler spokesman, made this clear
in his appeal to the Labour Commission of 1912. In order to
force Africans into the centers of European enterprise, this
renowned settler leader urged that the land reserved for 'natives'
be cut so as to prevent them from having enough for a self-
supporting level of production. How, he pleaded, could Africans
be obliged to labor for Europeans if they had enough land to
successfully breed livestock and cultivate crops for sale. This plea
did not go unheeded. By 1934 some 6,543,360 acres of land had
been alienated for occupation by 2,027 settlers; an average of
2,534 acres per occupant, of which only 274 acres were actually
under cultivation. As late as 1940 there remained over one
million acres within the White Highlands which lay unused for
either crops or pasture. By 1952, some 9,000 settlers held exclusive rights to 16,700 square miles of land, including 4,000 square
miles of Forest Reserve, while several million Africans sought to
eke out a livelihood within their increasingly congested reserves.
Less than 0.7 per cent of the entire Kenya population, a figure
which includes *all* Europeans, held what has been estimated to
be a minimum of 20 per cent of the colony's best land.

Taxation, and its counterpart, low wages, were also employed
to stimulate the flow of cheap African labor out of the reserves.
Delamere urged quite simply that taxation be used as a means
of forcing Africans to work for wages. In 1913, an editorial in
the settler newspaper set forward some of the thinking and
rational calculations which lay behind Kenya's tax and wages
policies.

We consider that taxation is the only possible method of
compelling the native to leave his reserve for the purpose of
seeking work. Only in this way can the cost of living be increased
for the native . . . [and] . . . it is on this that the supply of labour
and the price of labour depend. To raise the rate of wages would
not increase but would diminish the supply of labour. A rise in
the rate of wages would enable the hut and poll tax of a family,
sub-tribe or tribe to be earned by fewer external workers.[1]

[1] *East African Standard*, 4 February 1913.

When one adds to the European land, tax and wages policies, the restrictions placed upon African cultivation of certain profitable cash crops, such as *Arabica* coffee, and the *kipande* or labor registration system which obliged Africans, on pain of imprisonment, to obtain the signatures of their employers when they wished to seek other work or return to the reserves, it is not difficult to understand the emergence in Kenya of land hungry, labor-exporting African peasantries.

The Kikuyu figured prominently in this process. Of the several large agricultural tribes in Kenya, it is unquestionably the Kikuyu who were affected most immediately and deeply by European settlement. As Kenya's largest tribe, occupying the rich highland regions to the east and south of the Aberdare Range, the Kikuyu provided considerable portions of the land and most of the labor upon which the European farming economy was based.

While most of the White Highlands was obtained by the British from the pastoral Masai, large sections of Kikuyuland, particularly in the rich southern district of Kiambu, were alienated for European use. This land having been densely populated, its alienation left a large number of Kikuyu families landless and homeless. In addition, vast stretches of forest land bordering the region were made part of the Forest Reserve and removed from Kikuyu use.

Between 1907 and 1938 the sporadic nibbling away of small pieces of Kikuyu land—particularly in the Mweiga area of North Nyeri and around Nairobi—combined with the 1915 Crown Lands Ordinance, which made all Africans 'tenants at the will of the Crown', and the refusal of the Kenya Government to issue title deeds to Africans, fostered among the Kikuyu a growing insecurity of tenure and distrust of the white man's motives and intentions. In addition, a rapidly expanding population, reaching an average density of 283 per square mile by 1934 in the Kikuyu districts of Kiambu, Fort Hall and Nyeri (and rising to well over 500 in some areas such as South Nyeri), led to the increased fragmentation of holdings and spread of soil erosion. Land, previously allowed a period of fallow to regain its fertility, now had to be under continuous cultivation. The result, given no significant change in agricultural practice or technology, was a low and decreasing level of peasant productivity. Under such circumstances, it is not surprising that a steadily rising number of landless and land hungry Kikuyu were forced to leave the reserve and seek employment in the centers of European agriculture and commerce.

By 1948 over a quarter of the Kikuyu population, some 273,000 persons out of a total of 1,026,000, were living and working outside the confines of their insufficient reserve. Of these, about four-fifths (218,000) were engaged as wage and contract laborers or 'squatters' on the European plantations and mixed farms of the White Highlands, while most of the remainder had entered the urban centers of Nairobi (51,475) and Mombassa (3,304) as unskilled laborers. A 'squatter', in return for a nominal wage of eight to ten shillings per 30-day 'work ticket' and the right to pasture a few animals and cultivate a small garden, was usually bound under a three year contract to work 270 days a year for the owner. All unemployed male members of his family aged sixteen or over were equally bound and women and children were obliged to work when called upon. The workers' freedom of movement was greatly impeded by the fact that written permission from the manager or owner was normally required if one wished to leave the area to visit friends or relatives, pay his poll tax or simply spend a night in the town.

A significant proportion of these external workers were peasants whose families had previously lost land through alienation to European farmers. In some cases, laborers were employed on land held by Europeans which would, under other circumstances, have been theirs through inheritance. 'Alienation', then, is a very appropriate term, for it contains the double meaning or connotation of *transference of ownership* and *losing something which nevertheless remains in existence over-against one*. It is not only the brute fact of landlessness, land hunger and insecurity of tenure which conditioned Kikuyu involvement in the nationalist movement and peasant revolt; it is also the fact that for a people who attach such sacred meaning to the land the areas alienated remained within their field of experience, unattainable yet in considerable measure unused by its new owners.

Two additional processes, set in motion by European settlement, also help to explain the emergence and development of political consciousness and organization among the Kikuyu and,

to a lesser extent, Kenya's other agricultural tribes. First, due
largely to restrictions placed on the cultivation of cash crops, the
retention of traditional systems of land tenure and cultivation,
and the dearth of economic opportunities, labor-exporting
peasantries such as the Kikuyu tended to develop as relatively
homogeneous aggregates. Lacking the economic and social
stratification characteristic of cash-cropping peasantries, the
Kikuyu were inadvertently provided with a broad base of common interests and life circumstances. It is here suggested that this
'levelling' effect of European settlement, i.e., the creation of a
relatively uniform and impoverished peasant mass, when coupled
with the intensifying struggle for scarce fertile land against the
economically and politically dominant white settler elite,
greatly increased the likelihood of unified political action among
the Kikuyu.

Secondly, the system of migrant labor set in motion by white
settlement, while it may have impeded the development of
certain kinds of cross-linking groups, such as rural credit and
marketing co-operatives, threw a large number of peasants into
an urban milieu where they often joined men of other districts
and tribes in the formation of trade unions, political associations
and other urban groups. In Kenya, as elsewhere, such associations tended to cross-link various tribes and local communities,
fostering new loyalties to larger groupings and an African
national element of consciousness. With regard to the Kikuyu,
as the major labor-exporting tribe, these urban associations also
served to cross-link the numerous previously disparate local communities and wider territorial units and hence foster a new sense
of Kikuyu identity and unity. For those who had managed to
acquire a formal education, these associations also provided an
opportunity for the emergence of an elite body of trade union,
political and religious leaders.

Just as any revolution requires a certain minimum amount of
organization, so does a people in revolt require an ideology.
Without a set of ideas and ideals, few people are willing to risk
their lives in revolutionary action. In Kenya, at any rate, it is
unlikely that the revolution would have occurred but for the
integrative ideology developed over a period of thirty-odd years
by numerous political, religious, educational and trade union

associations which articulated and brought in focus various African grievances and set forward certain political, economic and social objectives. It is not surprising that the Kikuyu played a leading role in this process.

In 1920 the Kikuyu Association was formed. Comprised largely of chiefs and headmen, it focused major attention on grievances concerning the alienation of Kikuyu land and Government's increasingly compulsive labor policies. A second group, known as the Young Kikuyu Association (YKA), emerged in June 1921. Headed by Harry Thuku, a Government telephone operator, and comprised mainly of low grade clerks, office boys and domestic servants, the YKA protested through mass meetings and petitions against (1) the Crown Lands Ordinance of 1915, (2) continued evictions of Kikuyu sub-clans and alienation of their land for European occupation, (3) the doubling of the Hut and Poll Tax from five to ten rupees, (4) the one-third reduction in African wages imposed in 1921, and (5) the *kipande* or labor registration system introduced in 1920, according to which all African males aged sixteen or over were fingerprinted and made to carry, on penalty of imprisonment, a combined identification and employment card.

During the ensuing months, the YKA gained considerable support and influence in both the city and rural Kikuyu areas. Thuku also addressed an audience of Kavirondo (Baluhya) in North Nyanza and the first signs of multi-tribal solidarity appeared with the formation of the Young Kavirondo Association. In 1922 the East African Association (EEA)—whose informal origin may date back as early as 1919—was organized under the leadership of Harry Thuku. Though made up in the main of Kikuyu, the EEA aimed at uniting all Kenya tribes around the more general African grievances. A speech by Thuku to a Kikuyu audience in February 1922, in which he accused the Government of stealing Kikuyu land, attacked the missionaries for preaching the word of the devil, expressed his hope that the Europeans would leave Kikuyuland, and urged the people to refuse to work for Europeans, was soon followed by an EEA call for all Africans to throw their *kipandes* away on the lawn of Government House in Nairobi.

Fearing the anti-European, anti-missionary and embryonic nationalist aims of the EEA, Government arrested Thuku on

15 March 1922 and held him for deportation on charges of being 'dangerous to peace and good order'. Almost immediately, and quite spontaneously, there occurred the first general strike in Kenya history. Several thousand Africans, largely Kikuyu, gathered in protest outside the Nairobi jail where Thuku was being held and demanded the release of their leader. The police, frightened and tense, perhaps, by this unexpected show of African strength, responded to a shot fired by one of their members by opening fire on the crowd. When the shooting had stopped, twenty-one Africans lay dead on the street and a much larger number were injured. Shortly thereafter, Thuku and two of his relatives were deported to Kismayu without trial and the EEA was banned.

In August 1923 a public meeting was held in Nairobi at which the speakers called for the release of Thuku and a change in the status of Kenya from Colony to British Protectorate. They also protested against Government and missionary interference in traditional marriage practices and demanded that the views and opinions of Africans be heard and seriously considered before Government undertook to modify or eliminate any tribal customs.

The following year, 1924, saw the formation of the Kikuyu Central Association (KCA), a group organized and made up largely of members of the banned EEA. For the next sixteen years the KCA agitated and pressed for reform through mass meetings, petitions and delegations to the British Parliament. They began publication of a vernacular newspaper, *Mwiguith-ania (The Unifier)*, in 1928 and helped in the establishment of sister organizations among the Baluhya (Kavirondo Taxpayers' Welfare Association), Wakamba (Ukamba Members Association) and Wateita (Teita Hills Association). They demanded, among other things, (1) title deeds to land held by Africans in the reserves, (2) the return of alienated land, or just compensation, (3) removal of restrictions on the planting by Africans of commercial crops such as *Arabica* coffee, (4) the training and employment of Africans as agricultural instructors, (5) compulsory primary education for African children, sufficient secondary and high schools, and opportunities for higher education for Africans overseas, (6) abolition of the *kipande* system, exemption of women from Hut and Poll Taxes, and removal of other measures which restricted freedom of movement or compelled Africans to leave their *shambas* (gardens) to work for Europeans, and (7) elected representation in the Legislative Council, as well as in other governing bodies, and a promise of ultimate African predominance.

The independent outlook which emerged in the political arena was soon to be carried over into the spheres of education and religion. In 1928–30 KCA led the attack against the various Christian mission societies which had earlier rejected polygamy and now required their members to renounce female circumcision and the traditional 'pagan' songs and dances. With education almost entirely in the hands of the missionaries, the latter had the power to virtually exclude from educational opportunities those girls who underwent the traditional circumcision ceremony—deemed necessary by Kikuyu and Masai for full membership of the tribe and marriage—or children whose parents adhered to customary beliefs and practices. Membership in a Christian sect, and adherence to its rules, was thus the price Africans had to pay if they wished to acquire a formal education.

As a result of this conflict, and the growing Kikuyu desire for more and better education, there emerged in 1928–9 two independent school movements: The Kikuyu Independent Schools Association (KISA) and the Kikuyu Karing'a (i.e., 'Pure') Educational Association. As education was inextricably linked in the minds of the Kikuyu with religion, KISA established the African Independent Pentecostal Church and the KKEA formed an attachment with the African Orthodox Church. Each of these separatist or independent church movements sought to interweave or syncretize Christianity—particularly that of the Old Testament—with valued and important aspects of traditional belief and practice. Thus, for example, the Old Testament refers to polygamous marriages without condemnation and nowhere forbids female circumcision. Why then, it was argued, should Africans be forced to accept European interpretations and rulings in these matters as laid down arbitrarily by the missionaries.

The independent church-school movements, standing openly opposed to any interference or intervention by the white missionaries, reflected the growing anti-European feelings of the young political leaders of KCA, whose attempts to gain a redress of African grievances through constitutional means were repeatedly frustrated by an intransigent settler elite and colonial administration.

By 1939 the KCA had a paid up membership of 2,000 (which soon rose to 7,000), a considerably larger number of supporters, and a growing influence in the independent church-school movements. They established the Teachers Training College at Githuguri, in the Kiambu District, which was open to students of all tribes, and in other ways tried to achieve African solidarity and inter-tribal cooperation. In 1938, for example, the KCA made common cause with the Kamba march of 1,500 on Nairobi in protest against forced destocking. They also helped organize a protest demonstration among the Teita, precipitated by the latters' eviction from the Teita Hills, and played an important role in the Mombasa dock and casual workers' strike of 1939 and in the general agitation of that period for the establishment of an African trades union movement.

There is no question that the power and influence of the KCA were on the rise when, in May 1940, it was declared an illegal society, largely on the pretext that it was in contact with the King's enemies in Ethiopia. Twenty KCA leaders, along with those of its Teita and Kamba sister associations, were arrested and detained or imprisoned. With its offices in Nairobi closed, its newspapers suppressed and most of its prominent leaders removed, the KCA was driven underground, where it remained alive but relatively inactive during the course of the Second World War.

In 1944, after the release of the banned KCA leaders and the appointment of Kenya's first African Legislative Council member, a new, broad-based, congress-type African association was formed. Changing its name from the Kenya African Union (KAU) to the Kenya African Study Group under Government pressure, and then back to KAU in 1946, this body's expressed aims were . . .

    . . . to unite the African people of Kenya; to prepare the way for the introduction of democracy in Kenya; to defend and promote the interests of the African people by organizing, educating

and leading them in the struggle for better working conditions, housing, etc.; to fight for equal rights for all Africans; to
break down racial barriers; to strive for the extension to all
African adults the right to vote and be elected to the East African
Central Assembly, Kenya Legislative Council, Local Government
and other representative bodies; to publish a political newspaper
periodically; to fight for freedom of assembly, press and movement; and to raise and administer the funds necessary to affect
these objects. (KAU Constitution)

Filled with the hope of democratic reform, bred by British
pronouncements during the war and accession to power of the
Labour Party in England, KAU succeeded in building up a considerable following during the course of the next six years.
Through its official Swahili newspaper, *Sauti ya Mwafrica* (*The
African Voice*), and numerous vernacular newspapers, it pleaded
the cause and case of Kenya Africans on every front, from land
and wages to increased political representation, color-bar and the
four freedoms popularly associated with the allied cause during
the war. Membership grew to an estimated 100,000 and crowds
of thirty to fifty thousand were not unknown at the public
meetings presided over by Jomo Kenyatta and other KAU
officials. The independent churches and schools flourished, the
latter numbering about 300 by 1952 with an enrollment of nearly
50,000 pupils, and the labor movement was gaining in both
strength and membership.

The East African Trade Union Congress was formed shortly
after the war by Fred Kubai and Makhan Singh and, despite
mounting Government pressure, demonstrated its growing power
in May 1950 by leading an 18-day general strike in Nairobi.

Speaking in the name of Kenya's six million Africans, KAU
leadership was drawn from all major tribal groupings and its
branches were rapidly being established throughout the colony.
Despite its nationalist character and aspirations, however, it is
not surprising that the Kikuyu, with their more numerous and
experienced leaders and generally higher level of political consciousness, should predominate in both the rank-and-file and
ruling committee of the Kenya African Union. This was true
also of the trade union movement where, as with KAU, the
degree of Kikuyu involvement was at least in part a result of
their predominance within the urban milieu of Nairobi. In 1948

this city contained 86,000 Africans of which over 55,000 were Kikuyu.

The banned Kikuyu Central Association (KCA), though retaining its own identity, was of course influential and active within KAU, the trade union movement and the independent church and school movement. In a relatively small-scale society such as Kenya, with its broad peasant base, high illiteracy rate and deepening cleavage between white and black, it comes as no shock to find a numerically small but dedicated core of educated or semi-educated African leaders assuming more or less important roles in a fairly wide range of associations. The existence of a dominant European caste and colonial regime, combined with a subordinant African population whose aspirations were growing yet repeatedly frustrated, provided a large number of African groups with a common 'enemy' or set of obstacles and, hence, a unifying base of shared interests and aims. There was thus a good deal of overlap in both the leadership and rank-and-file membership of Kenya's African political, trade union and church-school movements. This cross-linking of various African associations was tending to produce a *single movement* in much the same sense and way as the multitude of American Negro religious, political, civil rights and other groups have emerged in the 1960's within the United States as *the* Negro Movement.

With KAU being a united front or congress-type nationalist association, comprised of persons and leaders with a fairly wide range of interests and political views, it can safely be assumed that KCA members constituted the more radical element on the spectrum of moderate to militant thought. Becoming more active during the early post-war years, the KCA nevertheless remained a highly select and, of necessity, secret association whose membership was limited to tried and trusted individuals. In mid-1950, however, KCA leaders decided to radically shift their policies of recruitment. They set out to boldly expand KCA membership and to become, in effect, an underground mass movement. While the specific reasons behind this move remain unclear, it is fairly certain that it was influenced greatly by the dashed hopes for democratic reforms, combined with a growing pessimism regarding the possibility of achieving their political objectives through purely constitutional means and an increasing fear that the settler political machine was gaining ground in its struggle for an autonomous or 'independent' white-dominated Kenya on the pattern of Southern Rhodesia. The overall strategy of KCA was to forge an iron-clad unity among all Kenya Africans, beginning with the more politically conscious Kikuyu, in order to press their political demands as a single integrated body and be prepared to use various forms of pressure, such as the general strike, massive boycotts of European goods and ultimately force, if such a line of action became necessary.

In brief, then, though their aims regarding land, wages, education, the color-bar and African political predominance were the same as those of KAU, the KCA was prepared to countenance revolutionary means if the peaceful, constitutional efforts of KAU's more moderate leadership failed. This latter possibility, in fact, became a reality over the course of the next two years. Government, spurred on by the settler elite, did its best to stifle the African nationalist movement, suppressing some of the KAU and vernacular newspapers, arresting labor leaders, withholding permission for public meetings, etc., while at the same time remaining as intransigent as ever to African demands.

In summary, then, the articulation of African grievances was a vital underlying and conditioning factor with regard to the 'Mau Mau Revolution' we shall be examining. For over thirty years, and through a wide variety of African associations, a nationalist ideology was evolved which, to the Kikuyu peasant and worker, came to be symbolized in the expression and demand for 'Land and Freedom'. The tendency of this ideology to become more radical was a reflection of the intensifying struggle between a subordinate African majority, increasingly aware of its potential power, and a ruling European minority, ever fearful that its privileged position might be swept away in the rising current of African nationalism. The pattern of events in this struggle should also be clear : constitutional demands—Government repression—militant reaction.

Were there, it might now be asked, any peculiar features of traditional Kikuyu society which help explain this people's independent response and, ultimately, revolutionary reaction to colonial rule and white dominance? The answer, I believe, is in the affirmative. It centers around two closely related aspects of

Kikuyu society which were fundamentally incompatible with the imposed colonial system and conditioned an independent response to it. The first of these, a decentralized and democratic political system, fostered among the Kikuyu a deep-seated suspicion of the highly centralized, authoritarian system imposed by the British and a tendency to reject the legitimacy and resist the dictates of the latter. The second, an age-grade system wherein leadership emerged on the basis of demonstrated personal qualities such as skill, wisdom and ability, underlay the Kikuyu rejection of British-appointed 'chiefs' and their tendency to by-pass the latter and organize independent associations under popular leaders when the occasion arose to seek a redress of grievances. Let us now consider these factors in somewhat greater detail.

Prior to their forced incorporation within the British Empire during the 1890's, the Kikuyu peoples fell into four major tribal groupings—the Kikuyu, Meru, Chuka and Embu. They occupied the present administrative districts of Kiambu, Fort Hall, Nyeri, Embu and Meru, plus contiguous areas of varying extent later alienated by the British for settler use. The Kikuyu, or 'Kikuyu proper' as they are frequently termed, were divided into three politically autonomous sub-tribes, each occupying its own distinctive territory. North of the Chania River were the *Gaki* of Nyeri and *Metumi* of Murang'a or Fort Hall; south of the Chania were the *Karura* of Kiambu. A number of smaller sub-tribes of the Meru, Chuka and Embu occupied territories approximating to the current Embu and Meru districts. Though closely related both historically and culturally, in terms of language, religion, world-view and other customary beliefs and practices, neither the 'Kikuyu tribes' nor the 'Kikuyu proper' were integrated within a unitary or centralized political structure. In fact, even within the Kikuyu sub-tribes political power was held by a number of fairly small and semi-autonomous geopolitical groupings.

Among the Kikuyu proper, the largest localized kinship unit was the *mbari* or sub-clan, a land-holding group containing as many as 5,000 persons and comprised of the male descendants of a common ancestor together with their wives and dependent children. The head of the sub-clan, if not the original founder, was chosen from amongst the latter's brothers, sons or grandsons by all the adult males of the group. His selection, based on qualifications such as wisdom, tact and ability as a religious leader, was the result of a lengthy process of discussion carried on until unanimity of opinion was achieved. In this same manner, decisions were reached relating to sub-clan land (*githaka*) and other matters, religious and secular, which were the exclusive concern of the entire *mbari*. Affairs of lesser scope, affecting only the members of a given polygamous or extended family, were handled within these smaller constituent units of the sub-clan.

The territorial and political unit of which an *mbari* formed the core was the *itura* or 'village' which contained, in addition to sub-clan members, a number of attached dependants and tenants (*ahoi*). These villages were dispersed rather than compact, as the member families of an *itura* dwelled in homesteads scattered over the entire *githaka*. Disputes and other matters affecting the whole village group were handled by a village council of elders (*kiama kia itura*), which performed a wide range of judicial, religious and social functions.

A number of villages formed a 'neighborhood' or 'fire-linked unit' (*mwaki*), within which, according to Kikuyu law and custom, members could call upon one another for assistance in such tasks as house building or, if the need arose, for cooking water or hot coals to get a fire started. Each such *mwaki*, which literally means 'fire', was administered by a neighborhood council (*kiama kia mwaki*) comprised of elders representing the lower level village councils. All affairs affecting more than one village within the neighbourhood were the responsibility of this neighborhood council, which met as the occasion arose and, like the village councils, chose a 'spokesman' to act as their representative in disputes, discussions, negotiations, etc., with other neighborhoods.

The 'ridge' or *rugongo*, generally comprised of several *mwaki* and covering an expanse of land lying between two rivers and extending some twenty or thirty miles, was the largest territorial unit with fixed political institutions. In all matters affecting members of the ridge, irrespective of their sub-clan, village or neighborhood affiliations, the *rugongo* was the most important administrative unit. The 'ridge council' (*kiama kia rugongo*), made up of senior elders selected by the councils of the constituent neighborhoods, held jurisdiction over all religious, judicial and military affairs which affected the entire ridge. A spokesman or *muthamaki* was chosen from among the council members and, being responsible to the latter, carried out any talks or negotiations which might be necessary with 'outsiders' or foreigners.

While no fixed political institutions existed beyond the ridge, *ad hoc* councils of leading elders would be convened whenever matters arose involving members of two or more *rugongo*. The territorial scope of such a council, determined in each case by the particular issue or dispute being dealt with, was thus variable. The general term applied to such an area, however, was *bururi* ('the countryside'), and the council or body of elders convened for *bururi* affairs was referred to as 'the big council' (*kiama kinene*) or the 'council of the countryside' (*kiama kia bururi*). Its members would include representatives of all the involved *rugongo* and, on certain very special occasions, senior or leading elders representing all of the ridges within the territory of a particular sub-tribe.

Turning to the question of leadership within this decentralized traditional structure, it must be noted at the outset that important offices or positions of leadership, whether political, judicial, military or religious, were not, as in many African tribes, inherited or acquired by virtue of a person's geneological standing in a particular kinship group. Instead, a person's rise to importance as a leader was determined by his position within a hierarchy of age-grades and, equally important, by his ability to demonstrate to his peers those personal qualities and skills believed necessary for the natural leader. To understand this process, it is useful to consider the characteristic manner in which a leader emerged within the Kikuyu age-grade system and the political structure outlined above.

Leadership, viewed as an inherent quality or capacity, began to reveal itself quite early in the life of a Kikuyu male. While still a very small child (*gakenge*), a leader of the future would have taken charge of the games and mischief of the children within his homestead (*muchii*). His greater knowledge of the secrets of the adult world around him, his popularity and flair for leadership, made him a sort of hero among his age mates.

Before long, he would engage the child leaders of other homesteads in the village and, if he emerged successful in the clash of personalities and wits, would be the acknowledged leader of all the children within the *itura*. By this time, he would have passed beyond the status of *gakenge* or child to that of *kaana*, a young boy still too small to help in the herding of his family's goats and sheep. Soon, however, he would take up this chore and, as a *kahi* or young lad, would mix in work and play with others of similar status within the *mwaki* or neighborhood. At this stage, since *mwaki* games and dances were organized affairs, leadership assumed a more formal quality. Our future leader had to, in competition with other village leaders, demonstrate his superiority as a personality, in directing social activities and in maintaining discipline. If he did, he would automatically assume his place as the rightful leader of all the young boys of the neighborhood. Other leaders, while retaining positions of leadership within their respective villages, would defer to him in matters and activities of neighborhood scope.

With the approach of circumcision and initiation into adult status, this young boy—now referred to along with his peers as *kihi*—would join the boys' *kiama* or *ngutu* ('club') of his *mwaki*. The *ngutu*, which had its own clubhouse, charged an entrance fee—usually of one banana—and 'heard' cases involving misbehaviour among its members, performed the important functions of inculcating an *esprit de corps*, conditioning habits of obedience, discipline and mutual aid, and providing a framework for the flowering of natural leaders. If he maintained his drive and popularity, this *kihi* would have become leader of his boys' club and sat as president or *muciriri* of the *ngutu* court (*njama*). When old enough, he would be recognized as the leader of the young men of his *mwaki* who were ready for circumcision. He would play a prominent part in arranging games and dances and, generally, in organizing the social life of youths within the neighborhood.

After circumcision and the completion of the initiation ceremony, which normally covered a span of several months, this youth would have become a member of a named age-set (*riika*), comprised of all the boys initiated that year within the sub-tribe. He would also become a junior warrior (*mumo*) and, if successful, the leader of his age-set within the *mwaki* and, on payment of a goat, a member of the council of junior warriors (*njama ya aanake a mumo*). When his set advanced to the status of senior warriors (*aanake*), each youth making a payment of two goats, he would become a section leader under the command and passing on the orders of the commander of the senior age-set of his regiment, i.e., a unit comprised of all youths initiated over a thirteen year period.

In time, if he demonstrated a capacity for leadership as a warrior, he would sit on the 'council of war' (*njama ya ita*); a body comprised, in addition to regiment leaders, of senior advisors, who were no longer of warrior status, and a war magician or *mundo mugo wa ita*, who utilized his art to bless and cleanse warriors and to determine the propitious time and place for raids. In addition to its strictly military functions in offense and defense, the war council was responsible for policing the markets, preserving order within the community, carrying out and enforcing the decisions and rulings of the elders' courts, and maintaining discipline within the warrior ranks.

If, in contact and competition for reputation with his peers, a future leader was successful, his prestige and influence would spread beyond the confines of his own *mwaki*. As the time approached for his *riika* or age-set to leave the status of active warriors, he might, while retaining leadership of the *riika* within his *mwaki*, have gained an influence within his *rugongo* and earned the respect and attention of local elders as a person of sound mind and dispassionate judgment.

Upon marriage and birth of his first child, he would begin to ascend the hierarchy of elders' ranks, each marked by the payment of a goat. At first, as a *kamatimo* or elder of the lowest grade, he would be invited to attend and listen as the elders' *kiama* determined suits; in minor cases, he would sometimes be called upon to express his own views regarding the evidence and verdict. If he passed this 'test' he would be given the opportunity to advance in seniority more rapidly than his age-mates and, if inclined toward the law, train as a future *muthamaki wa cira* (leader in law). He would move quickly up the several sub-grades of junior elder.

When his first child was ready for circumcision, he would enter the lowest sub-grade of senior elders (*athamaki*) and, as his reputation for skill and wisdom in the arbitration of cases spread, he would increasingly be called upon to assist in the settlement of important disputes over a wider area After achieving the highest rank of senior elder (*ukuru*), he would serve as the spokesman and representative (*muthamaki*) of the elders' council (*kiama*) within his village (*itura*) and neighborhood (*mwaki*); and if his prestige and reputation exceeded that of other *athamaki* within the ridge, he would act as spokesman and advocate for his *rugongo* and be called upon to serve on the 'council of the countryside' (*kiama kia bururi*) as occasion necessitated.

As a *muthamaki wa bururi* ('leader of the countryside'), he might develop into a prominent political figure whose strength of personality and broad base of popular support would enable him to exert considerable influence over important legislative and military decisions in his *rugongo* and, perhaps, even within wider political alliances of *bururi* scope. If, however, at an earlier stage in his career, his bent had been more specifically toward the military or the law, he may have become a prominent 'leader in war' (*muthamaki wa ita*) or 'leader in law' (*muthamaki wa chira*). Had he neither the ability or ambition for such high rank and position, he would perhaps have remained simply a respected elder and member of the *kiama* within his village.

Positions of leadership within the traditional Kikuyu social system were thus achieved, on the basis of demonstrated skills and wisdom, rather than inherited or determined by one's status at birth. Neither, it should be added, were they positions which a person could expect to hold for the duration of his life. For within each Kikuyu sub-tribe, age-sets were grouped into named generation-sets (*riika*) which succeeded one another in 'ruling' the 'country' for a period of from twenty-five to thirty years. Toward the end of such a period, when the elders of the 'ruling' generation decided it was time to step down or retire from active political life, an *itwika* or 'handing over ceremony' would be planned. When the 'country' was at peace and all outstanding debts and disputes had been settled, this ceremony, which formally marked the accession to power of the junior generation-set, was held simultaneously at various designated places within the territory of the sub-tribe. The actual process of handing over, however, since it required the payment of a stipulated number of goats and sheep from the new to the retiring leaders, normally covered a period of two or three years.

Political authority, then, was vested in the elders of a given generation-set for a limited and fairly well specified period of time. The hypothetical leader whose career we have followed above, though his opinions and advice may have been solicited and been of considerable weight, would yield his position and the various insignia of his office to a younger and, perhaps, equally talented and ambitious elder of the new 'ruling' generation.

In brief, we have seen that the traditional Kikuyu political structure was decentralized and inherently democratic, with effective decision-making and enforcement powers resting for the most part in numerous local hierarchies of councils within each sub-tribe. We have noted, with respect to this *kiama* or council system, that: (1) councils were convened as the occasion demanded and reached decisions on the principle of 'discussion until unanimity was achieved'; (2) the particular council convened (sub-clan, village, neighborhood, etc.) was determined in each case by the scope and nature of the question or dispute at issue; (3) composition was based on the principle of 'lower-level representation on higher-level councils', with the latter owing their authority to the former; (4) the spokesman or *muthamaki* of a given council, whether that of the village or the ridge—which represented the largest fixed administrative unit—was responsible to and acted in the name and with the approval of the entire body; and (5) positions of leadership were achieved, within a system of age-grades or ranks, rather than ascribed and were limited in duration by the periodic accession to political authority of junior generation-sets.

With the imposition of British colonial rule, this traditional system was in large measure destroyed, or at least irreparably damaged. Not only were the Kikuyu tribes and sub-tribes brought within the highly centralized and authoritarian structure of the British Empire, but in this very process the age-grade system upon which their previous autonomy rested was dealt a series of rude and, ultimately, crippling blows. Military defeat at the turn of the century—a piece-meal affair made easier by the absence of a unified command and coordinated military campaign (though ultimately decided in favor of the British by the technological superiority of the Maxim-gun)—brought with it an end to the warriors' councils and age-regiments. The 'legitimate' use of force was now a monopoly of the colonial regime, and the non-military as well as the strictly military functions of the Kikuyu age-sets began to wither. The hiatus in the system of age groupings created by the dissolution of the age-regiments hastened the dissipation of the entire system. And the various sub-clan, village and neighborhood units previously cross-linked by the age-sets within a sub-tribe became increasingly isolated from one another within the British-imposed administrative system.

Furthering the confusion and breakdown of the traditional age-based political system was the fact that *itwika* or 'handing over' ceremonies were banned; a move necessitated, from the Government's point of view, by the appointment of life-term, salaried 'chiefs', whose offices were made hereditary and who were granted arbitrary, albeit limited, powers which no traditional *muthamaki* possessed. The latter, as we have seen, though possessing a degree of administrative authority in both secular and religious affairs, had little or no 'personal' power. As the spokesman of a ridge council or *ad hoc bururi* council, a *muthamaki* was not a 'chief' in either the conventional or anthropological sense. He was the chairman and representative of a body which reached decisions through discussion and consensus and owed its authority to lower-level councils.

The Kikuyu, therefore, differed from other African tribes whose *traditional chiefly offices* were incorporated within the colonial administrative structure where, taking on a highly ambivalent character (in the sense of theoretically reflecting and acting in the interest of both the colonial government and the subordinant population), they tended to act as a focal point and bottle-neck of popular grievances. The Kikuyu, on the other hand, found themselves with *no* traditionally acknowledged or legitimate institutions through which to speak or express their discontents. The appointed 'chiefs' were seen from the outset as Government officials, if not agents, with powers over but no traditional responsibilities toward their people. Thus, Kenyatta has stated that :

It has been said that the Gikuyu do not respect their chiefs, namely, the 'appointed ones'. This is perfectly true, and the reason is not far to seek. The Gikuyu people do not regard those who have been appointed over their heads as the true representatives of the interests of the community. No one knows this better than the chiefs themselves, because many of them are only able to continue in their position through the fact that might is over right. The Gikuyu know perfectly well that these chiefs are appointed to represent a particular interest, namely, the interest of the British Government, and as such they cannot expect popularity from the people whom they help to oppress and exploit.[1]

It is not difficult to understand, therefore, that when the felt need to express themselves politically arose, there was a structural tendency for the Kikuyu to by-pass 'approved' institutions, such as that of the 'chief', and seek to form others more in line with the traditional pattern and principles of leadership and organization; others, that is, which could be trusted to unambiguously represent the will and interests of the people. As we have seen, this tendency expressed itself as early as 1920 and continued unabated for the next three decades. It continues to express itself even to this day.

The reader, in later sections of the book, will be able to observe a considerable measure of continuity, at least as regards certain major patterns, between the traditional Kikuyu social system and the structure and organization of the underground movement and guerrilla forces which emerged within the colonial context. Continuities, however, are not identities and, as we shall see, these new groupings bore the stamp of modernity as well as tradition.

★ ★ ★

Turning to a consideration of the underground movement from 1950 until the outbreak of the revolt in early 1953, we might look first at some of the confusion which has arisen concerning the name 'Mau Mau'. On 31 May 1950, nineteen Africans (seventeen Kikuyu, one Masai and one Kisii) were accused, at the famous Naivasha Trial, of having administered an illegal oath binding its takers to a certain secret *Mau Mau* association. In August of the same year, this society was officially proscribed and, through its repeated and constant use by Government, press and radio, the appellation 'Mau Mau' was irrevocably linked with the underground movement and revolt which followed some

[1] Jomo Kenyatta, *Facing Mount Kenya*, p. 196, Secker & Warburg, 1953.

SUDAN

ETHIOPIA

Lokitaung

LAKE RUDOLF

North Horr

Moyale

Lodwar

UGANDA

Marsabit

Wajir

MT. ELGON

Kapenguria

Maralal

Archer's Post

Kitale
Eldoret

Kabarnet
Baringo

Rumuruti

Nanyuki

Isiolo
Meru

Kakamega

Kapsabet

Thomson's Falls

Naro Moru

MT. KENYA

KENYA

Kisumu

Eldama Ravine

Chuka

LAKE VICTORIA

Nakuru

ABERDARE RANGE

Embu

Kissi

Gilgil

Nyeri

Fort Hall

Sotik

Naivasha

Githugu

Narok
Kiambu

Thika

NAIROBI

Kitui

Magadi

Kajiado

Machakos

Tana River

Garissa

TANGANYIKA

Sultan Hamud

Garsan

Lamu

Makindu

Kibwezi

Kidini

Mtito Andei

Tsavo

Galana River

MT. KILIMANJARO

Voi River

Malindi

KENYA

SCALE

MLS 0 20 40 60 80 100

MOMBASA

White Highland:

Kikuyu Reserve:

Gen. Area of Revolt:

INDIAN OCEAN

three years later. While it is extremely difficult to avoid use of this term, the information I have been able to gather from informants and other sources points inescapably to the conclusion that it is a misnomer.

To begin with, no one seems to know precisely what the term 'Mau Mau' means, as it has no accepted literal meaning in either Kikuyu or Swahili. Some suggest that it 'really' meant *Uma Uma* (Out, Out), referring to the African desire that Europeans leave Kenya, and was arrived at through a traditional children's game wherein the sounds of common words were transposed as in our own Pig-Latin.

A few informants have suggested that one of the defendants at the Naivasha Trial used the expression 'mumumumu' when referring to the whispered voices within the darkened oathing hut and that European journalists present thought he had said 'Mau Mau'. In a similar vein, Karari Njama has recently written informing me that...

> After a long research I have come to the conclusion that the first African who disclosed the secrecy of the society at Naivasha police station told a European officer, 'I have been given *MUMA*', an oath. The European being neither able to pronounce nor spell *MUMA* correctly, created his own pronunciation... 'MAU MAU'. This error has happened more than a hundred times in this country, especially in the names of mountains, rivers and places. The correct name of Mt. Kenya is *Kirinyaga*. The Akamba people have neither the letter r nor g standing alone in their language and therefore their pronunciation for *Kirinyaga* is *Kiinyaa*, out of which the European, being unable to pronounce it, created *Kenya*.

Mr Njama goes on to indicate what he believes is a secondary meaning of the term 'Mau Mau', invented after the name had already become established. Here, the initials of the name are intended to stand for the Swahili words *Mzungu Arudi Uingereza, Mwafrica Apate Uhuru*, meaning, 'Let the *European return to England and the African obtain* his *freedom*'.

Perhaps the most plausible explanation regarding the origin of this term was given by another informant who said:

> Mau mau was not a widely known word among Kikuyu. Its only meaning was 'greedy eating,' sometimes used by mothers to

rebuke children who were eating too fast or too much. In my location of Kiambaa, in Kiambu District, however, it was also used occasionally when talking about certain elders who, when called to hear a case by the chief, were more interested in the few shillings or goats they would receive than in dispensing justice. These elders often magnified the seriousness of the case they were hearing in order to get from the guilty person a fine of a goat or lamb, which they would then slaughter, roast and eat...as if they were merely carrying out traditional Kikuyu legal practices. Earning a reputation for being greedy, these elders were sometimes called the *Kiama kia Mau Mau*, or 'Council of Greedy Eaters'. It is my belief that the man who used the term 'Mau Mau' at the Naivasha Trial was referring to the men who administered the oath as bad elders, who wanted only his initiation fee and the feast of a goat...

Though there are no doubt several other interpretations and explanations, suffice it to say here that no generally accepted meaning or origin for the term 'Mau Mau' exists. This fact argues favorably, in my opinion, for the view that the term itself and, particularly, its attachment to the underground movement and revolt were fortuitous developments.

Another, and perhaps more convincing, reason for considering 'Mau Mau' a misnomer is the fact that, to the best of my knowledge, members of the Movement never used this term when talking amongst themselves about their Society; nor was it ever incorporated in any of the oaths, songs, prayers or other ceremonials which I have come across in the course of my research. The point here is that regardless of the origin or meaning of 'Mau Mau', and despite the fact that members of the Movement knew very well that Government and the European press were referring to their association when they invoked this term, it was simply never accepted by the Africans involved in the Movement as being anything more than the white man's name for their association.

There were, however, several other names frequently used by members when referring to the Movement and repeatedly invoked in song, prayer and oath. These were: (1) *Uiguano wa Muingi*, or simply *Muingi*, meaning literally 'The Unity of the Community' or 'The Community', but perhaps better figuratively rendered 'The Movement'; (2) *Gikuyu na Mumbi*, or simply *Gikuyu*, referring to the traditionally acknowledged founders of the Kikuyu tribe; (3) *Muhimu*, meaning 'Most Important' in Swahili and very likely used as a code word; (4) *Muigwithania*, literally 'The Unifier', but also the name of a vernacular KCA newspaper; (5) *Muma*, meaning 'Oath' and used when referring to the 'Oath of Unity', *Muma wa Uiguano*, was also frequently used when referring to the Movement as a whole, and (6) KCA, or the Kikuyu Central Association.

In brief, then, while it must be admitted that detailed information is scanty and that considerably more research needs to be carried out in this area, the evidence now available seems to support the view that there never was an independent secret society identifying itself as 'Mau Mau'. And that the underground movement which most writers refer to as 'Mau Mau' was in fact a direct lineal descendant of the banned KCA which, as pointed out earlier, underwent a dramatic shift beginning in 1950 from a highly selective, elite organization to an underground mass movement. Let us now consider some of the salient features of this movement as they developed over the course of the next few years.

With its headquarters established in Nairobi, the KCA sought to expand its membership by forming a complex of local groups or cells in both the city and rural areas of the reserve and Rift Valley. The migrant labor system, in terms of which the vast majority of urban workers were obliged to maintain dual-residence in the city and reserve, lent itself nicely to this process. Organizers, themselves recruited in the city, were sent or simply went as the occasion arose into their rural areas to recruit kinsmen, friends, neighbors and co-workers. This process of recruitment involved two important factors : the Oath of Unity (*Muma wa Uiguano*) and an implicit territorial criterion of membership.

Oaths having been an important sanction in traditional Kikuyu society, it is not surprising that the KCA utilized them, as far back as 1926, to guarantee the allegiance of its members. Now, as an underground movement in 1950, it demanded strict secrecy as well as total commitment and the oath was altered to meet these requirements. With the idea that equally binding oaths would be devised for other tribes, the Kikuyu–Embu–Meru version combined features of the traditional initiation ceremony, judicial oaths and curses—modified and adapted to current circumstances and obviously more binding in their promise of divine sanction upon the illiterate—with the threat of physical punishment or death to those who refused to take or violated their vows. Following is an informant's recollection of this oath which, I believe, is typical of the thousands administered during this early period, allowing, of course, for slight local and regional variations.

One evening in February 1950, I decided to go home and visit my girl friend who was staying in the house of a relative in our village. When I arrived at the hut at about 7 :30 p.m. I found that, while she was not there, a number of people from the village had gathered and were sitting about talking, laughing and telling tales. Curiosity made me stay to find out what sort of meeting this was and I joined in the conversation. At around 9 p.m. a man entered the hut and said he was looking for a few strong young men like myself to assist him with some work he was doing in a nearby hut. Three of us volunteered to help and followed the man out into the darkness. The hut was only a few yards away and inside I saw about fifteen people. My father was there assisting some others in slaughtering a lamb. In the course of our conversation I asked one of the men what sort of occasion this was and he replied that they were awaiting the arrival of an important visitor. I knew all the people present and felt no cause for alarm; even though I felt somewhat confused by the situation.

In a matter of minutes, I was once again called outside and led with six others to a hut located beneath the black wattle trees and separated from my home by our kei-apple fence. I felt a little scared at this point because I knew this third hut had been vacated long ago and could see no point in going into a deserted house. Again, the people who were accompanying us acted as if they were guards—which in fact they were. I was also upset because my clean clothes were getting wet and soiled by the high grass made wet by the early evening rain.

As we approached the door, I saw a dim light inside and heard people whispering. But as we entered, the light went out and there was complete silence. We were all frightened at this point and entered with some reluctance on the insistence of the guards. It was pitch dark inside but I could hear the whispered voices of many people who soon began asking us, in turn, who we were and other questions about ourselves. I remember suffering a few minutes of terror while being held around the neck and arms by three or four people. Moments later, however, someone ordered the lights turned on and soon three hurricane lamps illumined the inside of the hut. What struck me first was the sight of an arch made of banana leaves and the fact that three men stood guard armed with *simis* [the traditional double-edged Kikuyu swords]. The door of the hut had been firmly bolted and glancing around the room I estimated that there were some forty solemn-faced people inside. (Later I discovered that there were also people outside guarding the approaches to the hut.)

One of the men in the room ordered the seven of us to form a queue by the arch, take off our shoes and remove any coins, watches or other metal objects we might have in our possession. It was at this point, as I relaxed a bit and saw that most of the people in the room were familiar to me, that I realized that this ceremony was probably the one I earlier wished to undergo in order to become a member of the KCA. Though the people were stern-faced and would surely have harmed any who resisted, I was unafraid from this time onward.

The man who had us remove our shoes and coins then instructed us as follows : 'We want you young men to join us in the struggle for freedom and the return of our stolen land. That is why we have brought you here to swear an oath joining you with us in this struggle. Mind you, this is no joking matter. Any who refuse to take this oath will be killed and buried right here in this hut.'

At this point, one of the persons about to be initiated said that he had never heard of such an oath and was not willing to take it. Before he had completed his statement, however, he was hit very hard in the face. This convinced him and the rest of us that this was indeed no joking matter. The man pleaded to be allowed to take the oath and have his life spared.

I had better explain now just how these oaths were arranged and the equipment used in the ceremony. I know these things not only from having taken the oath, but from having attended dozens of such ceremonies in the months following my own initiation.

I mentioned above that in the second house I entered a goat was being slaughtered. The meat was roasted to be eaten later and the skin was cut into thin ribbon-like strips which were twisted and joined to form rings. The eyes of the goat were removed together with the thorax and *ngata*, a bone which connects the head and the spinal column and contains seven holes. The eyes were stuck on either side of a 15-inch long piece of banana stalk which was hollowed out lengthwise so that it could be used as a container. Also attached were clusters of seven kei-apple thorns (from a particular tree known as *Muthuthi* or *Mugaa*) and sodom apples which were fixed to the three sides with these same thorns. This container was to hold a liquid formed by a mixture of goat's blood, soil and crushed grains, such as maize, sorghum and beans.

The arch, which stood about five feet high, was constructed of long banana stalks dug into the ground and joined at the top by tying or intertwining their leaves. On this frame were put other plants and shrubs, such as sugar cane, maize stalks, etc. The *ngata* of the goat and the thorax, or large chest-piece of meat, were hung from the top of the arch near the center.

Throughout the ceremony, each initiate wore a ring of the twisted goatskin around his neck and held a damp ball of soil against his stomach with his right hand...a symbol of the person's willingness to do everything in his power to assist the association in regaining and protecting the land belonging to the Kikuyu people.

Standing thus before the arch, I passed through it seven times while the oath administrator uttered and I repeated the following vows:

(1) If I am called upon at any time of the day or night to assist in the work of this association, I will respond without hesitation;

And if I fail to do so, may this oath kill me.

(2) If I am required to raise subscriptions for this organization, I will do so;

And if I do not obey, may this oath kill me.

(3) I shall never decline to help a member of this organization who is in need of assistance;

And if I refuse such aid, may this oath kill me.

(4) I will never reveal the existence or secrets of the association to Government or to any person who is not himself a member; And if I violate this trust, may this oath kill me.

Following this, and repeating these vows again on each occasion, I was instructed to take seven sips of liquid from the banana stalk container, seven small bites of the goat's thorax and—performing each act seven times—to prick the eyes of the dead goat and insert a piece of reed into the seven holes of the *ngata*. The administrator then had me take a bite of sugar cane, poured cold water over my feet and made a cross on my forehead with the blood and grain mixture. When this was completed, I was surrounded by a number of spectators who took hold of the skin ring around my neck and started counting. Reaching the number seven, they all pulled, breaking the ring and saying: 'May you be destroyed like this ring if you violate any of these vows!' The rest of the people repeated this curse in unison.

The oathing ceremony was thus completed and I was led into another hut with the others. A lamb, slaughtered earlier, was now roasting over the fire and we sat down to eat and talk till about midnight. Over fifty of us had taken the oath by this time and before departing we were all gathered together in a single hut to receive our final instructions. The administrator entered and told us we were now members of the KCA and linked by an oath of unity which would extend brotherhood to all members of the Kikuyu tribe. The white man, he said, was our enemy and we should have nothing to do with him. The land stolen from our people by the Europeans must be returned; and this could only be achieved through an unbreakable unity of all Kikuyu, who would act as a single man with a single purpose. We were then asked to pay an entrance fee of 2/50s. and told that an additional 62/50s. plus a ram were to be paid as soon as we were able.

In essence, then, this Oath of Unity was an elaborate initiation ceremony, with the initiate becoming at one and the same time a member of the Movement and a full-fledged, and in a sense reborn, member of the tribe. One could not, it was felt, be considered fully and truly *of Gikuyu* without taking the Unity Oath. The ceremony itself was a modern synthesis incorporating various and often modified features of the traditional initiation ceremony (e.g., passing under the arch, sipping a distasteful mixture of symbolic elements and uttering sacred vows) and customary oaths and curses (e.g., the sacred and awesome number seven, the use of the sheep's chest meat and seven holes of the *ngata*, derived respectively from the 'oath of the sheep' and the *githathi* oath, and the curses calling for divine punishment should an initiate violate his vows), together with an element of Christian symbolism (i.e., the cross drawn on the initiate's forehead) and modern political objectives contained in the vows and instructions calling for a return of the stolen lands and freedom, which were held to be achievable against a hostile white community only through an unbreakable African unity.

As a method of recruitment into the proscribed underground movement, the Oath carried with it certain logical and practical necessities, as well as certain limitations or negative ramifications. In the first place, it was necessary to prevent 'outsiders' or non-members from gaining any knowledge of the secret society, its aims or its members, prior to their own initiation. This, quite obviously, underlay the deception normally employed in getting non-members to attend an oathing ceremony. Secondly, since the society was proscribed and membership in it carried the threat of a long prison sentence, it was necessary to ensure that would-be initiates brought to an oathing ceremony became, in fact, members of the Movement who felt themselves bound by the vows of secrecy. This accounts, I believe, both for the dual threat of divine or human punishment should an initiate violate his vows and for the inherent practical necessity of killing any person who ultimately refused to take the Oath of Unity. Once in attendance at an oathing ceremony, therefore, and possessed of the knowledge which this entailed, the would-be initiate faced, and the society *had* to present him with, the alternative of taking the Oath or suffering the unhappy consequences.

While this procedure may pose no great problem for a highly selective, elite underground movement, where potential members can be carefully and intensively scrutinized before they are actually recruited, it involves serious inherent dangers when employed on a mass scale to bring an entire population within a proscribed secret society. Thus, while the vast majority of those recruited through the Oath became active and loyal members of the Movement and most of the remainder held their silence through fear of retribution, it was unavoidable that a few 'unwilling' initiates should violate their vows of secrecy. Such persons, having taken the Oath simply to save their lives, and unhindered by the promise of divine punishment (many were devout Christians who no longer believed in the efficacy of traditional oaths or curses), sought the protection of Government officials or missionaries to whom they disclosed the nature of their experiences, the secrets they had learned and, not infrequently, the names of other persons in the Movement. Again, the mass nature of the Movement and the fact that all Africans were to be enjoined as *members* through an Oath of Unity— as contrasted to an elite group which seeks *popular support* rather than a mass membership—made it easier for Government to plant informers within the organization and thus gain further information. The results of this leakage are best considered below.

The other important aspect of recruitment lay in its implicit territorial base. The primary units or basic cells of the Movement, which might contain anywhere from a dozen to several hundred members, were based, in the rural Districts of Kiambu, Fort Hall, Nyeri, Embu and Meru, on the traditional *itura* or dispersed village group. As in the past, everyone within such a village recognized his obligation to respond to a neighbor's alarm and felt free to call on others for assistance in domestic tasks such as house building or when minor inconveniences like running out of salt, water or firewood arose. In most instances, the smallest Government administrative units, i.e., sub-locations, correspond to these traditional 'villages', though in some cases an entire *mwaki* or neighborhood might be contained within a single sub-location. In any event, residence within this unit of highly interacting and diversely related persons was an implicit criterion of membership in the Reserve cells of the Movement. As the Movement expanded, friends, neighbors and relatives would be recruited through the Oath into their sub-location group or cell.

This same principle was applied in Nairobi, where the cells were comprised of individuals with a common place of origin or residence in the Reserve. Where absolute numbers allowed, as was usually the case among Kikuyu, an urban cell contained members from a single rural sub-location. With the Embu, Meru and Kamba (and perhaps the Norok Masai), the cells were comprised of persons from larger rural administrative units, i.e., locations or divisions. For the most part, these urban groups contained fewer members than their rural counterparts and, due to the migrant nature of labor, many persons shifted irregularly from their rural to their urban sub-location group.

In the Settled Areas of the Rift Valley, cells were formed within the squatter villages and on the labor-lines of European plantations and mixed farms. With travel made difficult by the work schedule, the restrictive nature of labor contracts and the Trespass Ordinance, these groups were forced to recruit members on the basis of proximity or current residence rather than, as in the city, on the basis of place of origin in the Reserve. They thus tended to be somewhat more heterogeneous in composition than their counterparts in Nairobi and the Reserve.

The structure of the underground movement, revealing the influence of traditional patterns, was based largely on the principle of lower-level representation on higher level councils. In contrast to the traditional pattern, however, and obviously a response to the contemporary colonial situation, this structure was centralized, with a hierarchy of interlinked councils integrating all of the Movement's primary groups.

In the Reserve Districts of Kiambu, Fort Hall, Nyeri, Embu and Meru, councils or committees were formed within the existing Government administrative units, beginning with the sub-location and moving up through the location, division and district. Each of the several sub-location groups within a location was headed by a council, normally consisting of nine officials, which would select two or three of its members to represent it on the location committee; each of several such location councils within a division would, in turn, select two or three of its members to represent it on the division council and, repeating the process, each of the three or four division councils within a district would choose three representatives to serve on the district committee.

In Nairobi, the same principle was applied, except that each of the urban district councils selected three to six members to represent it on the Central Province Committee (CPC), whose headquarters were located in the city. Some of these CPC members also held *ex-officio* membership in their respective district councils and, aided by the highly mobile urban African population, were able to serve as liaison officers, linking their rural and urban district committees and representing both on the Central Province Committee. Kiambu District, which surrounds Nairobi on three sides, presents a slight variation to this pattern. Here, there was only one district council, comprised of nine members drawn from both the rural and urban division councils—two each from the three Reserve councils and one each from those in Nairobi.

With regard to the Rift Valley, though the situation is less clear, it seems that local cells in the large and densely populated Nakuru and Laikipia districts were represented on the higher councils in Nairobi by a small number of organizers and liaison officers who divided their time between the city and European Settled Areas. In some areas, such as Thomson's Falls, Naivasha and Nakuru Town, it is likely that councils above those of the local cells were formed and may have sent representatives to Nairobi.

Above the Central Province Committee, or acting as an inner council within it, one is forced by the data to assume the existence of a central governing council (which I shall here refer to as the 'Central Committee') which was responsible for shaping over-all policy and directing the expansion of the Movement into other tribal areas and regions of Kenya. It is not unlikely that this group also formed the militant, though perhaps not dominant, wing of the Kenya African Union leadership.

Below, on page 64, is a chart in which I have attempted to graphically set out the major structural pattern of the underground movement as it existed prior to the Government declaration of a State of Emergency in October 1952.

Looking at the composition and functions of the various councils, we find that both 'local' (i.e., primary group) and intermediate councils normally consisted of nine elected members, referred to as 'Elders', six of whom held office as Chairman, Vice Chairman, Secretary, Assistant Secretary, Treasurer and Assistant Treasurer. While elections, usually in the form of nomination, discussion and general approval of candidates, were held at the local and all intermediate levels, many of the key organizers gained positions on the councils in virtue of their prior membership and activities in the Movement, being acknowledged as proven leaders or members of higher councils. Positions on the 'Central Committee' were, of course, non-elective and as the Movement expanded from this central core outwards, authority was often conferred upon certain persons to organize the Movement in their home areas.

There were thus two distinct processes at work in determining membership on the various councils: (1) from below, there were

Chart 1.   Hierarchy of Articulating Institutions (1950-52)

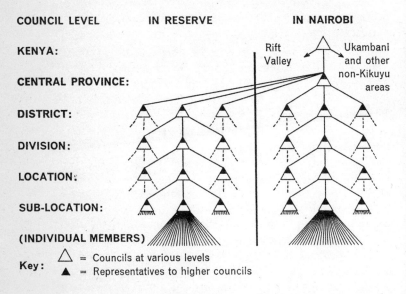

COUNCIL LEVEL   IN RESERVE   IN NAIROBI

KENYA: Rift   Ukambani
                                          Valley   and other
CENTRAL PROVINCE: non-Kikuyu
                                                      areas

DISTRICT:

DIVISION:

LOCATION:

SUB-LOCATION:

(INDIVIDUAL MEMBERS)

Key: △ = Councils at various levels
       ▲ = Representatives to higher councils

elections, held either by cell members or councilmen, to determine membership in the higher councils, and (2) from above, there was 'appointment' or the delegation of authority which, when acknowledged, entitled the persons concerned to hold office within particular councils lower than that from which their authority derived. In practice, both processes were employed on all but the highest council level, and in most instances they operated simultaneously, with persons having delegated authority being elected to leadership positions on the lower-level councils. It seems on the whole, however, that the elective principle predominated on the lower (sub-location and location) levels, while the principle of delegated authority prevailed in determining key officials at the higher (division, district and provincial) levels.

Ultimate decision and policy making powers were held by the 'Central Committee', which, though essential details in this area are lacking, presumably decided on such matters as the basic features of the oath, dues and fees, propaganda and action programs and methods of expanding the Movement. Where Government prosecution of prominent leaders was concerned, this committee also, it seems, arranged and paid for the legal defense.

Local cell councils had the authority, as well as the responsibility, to collect fees and dues from cell members, plan and hold oathing ceremonies, organize pressure against non-members to join the Movement (usually in the form of total ostracism) and plan and carry out action against Government informers. They also passed information and money to and received instructions from higher councils, kept local records, sought to spread and increase understanding of the Movement's aims and, as with all other councils, sat as a court of law whenever the occasion necessitated.

Intermediate councils, from the location to the district, served primarily as links in the chain of command and communication. In addition, however, they did a good deal of organizational work at the division or district level, such as planning and holding mass oathing ceremonies (particularly in Nairobi), arranging for attendance, transportation and entertainment at public (KAU) political rallies, etc. They also sat as courts when the occasion arose, promoted the Movement's aims through propaganda and helped implement certain action programs such as the Nairobi general strike (May 1950) and the later boycotts on European beer, cigarettes and buses.

Individual roles within the local cells centered around the recruitment of new members and participation in oathing ceremonies. It was incumbent upon every member to bring into the group as many friends, relatives and acquaintances as he could and this was usually accomplished by inviting such persons to a feast or party which turned out to be an oathing ceremony. Deception in this regard, as we have seen, was a practical necessity, since divulging the time and place of an oathing ceremony to a non-member was both dangerous to the other members and a punishable violation of the oath. In the ceremony itself, various roles were assumed or assigned ranging from oath administrator (sometimes sent from Nairobi) and assistant to guard, messenger, cook, paraphernalia procurer and general audience participant.

At this stage, the primary role of each cell was to achieve a 100 per cent membership within the sub-location, squatter village, labor-line or urban sector from which it was entitled to recruit. Though action tasks such as those mentioned above were carried out by the cells on the instruction of higher councils, it must be borne in mind that over-all strategy during this period was centered on unifying the entire African population within the Movement and being prepared for passive or violent resistance when the opportunity arose.

Government pressure continued to mount after the Naivasha Trial and the proscription of 'Mau Mau' in August 1950. Through informers and less direct leakages of information, Government gained an increasing knowledge of the Movement and was able to make numerous arrests and raids on oathing ceremonies. By September 1952 there were over 400 persons in prison for having taken or administered 'Mau Mau' oaths and several hundred others were awaiting trial. By this time, however, the Movement had grown considerably. Most of my informants, as well as other sources, estimate that somewhere between 75 per cent and 90 per cent of the Kikuyu population had taken the Oath of Unity and the Movement was beginning to spread, particularly in Nairobi, to other tribes such as the Kamba, Masai, Kipsigis and, to a lesser degree, the Luo and Baluhya.

These simultaneous processes of mounting external or Government pressure and rapid expansion of the Movement had several related ramifications which might be summarized as follows: (1) increasing membership resulted in greater leakages of information through informers and, combined with a growing external threat, led to greater security precautions, a more binding and militant oath and more severe sanctions against 'traitors' and non-members; (2) British Government intransigence to KAU's political demands plus mounting settler pressure for 'independence' and sterner action against both KAU and the underground movement led to increased internal pressure for more positive action; (3) increasing membership, the external threat and internal pressure for greater militancy made communication and effective control by the 'Central Committee' more difficult and led to a considerable *de facto* devolution of decision making power to lower level councils and individual leader-organizers; (4) the felt need for Kikuyu unity, combined with the above factors, led to an increase in the use of tribal as opposed to African-national symbols and tended to inhibit full participation by other tribes as well as by a significant proportion of semi-educated and educated Kikuyu who either remained passive or lined up on the Government side.

Closely related to the above mentioned developments are two sets of events which I believe precipitated the 1953–6 revolution in Kenya. The first, with benefit of hindsight, might generally be termed 'premature acts of violence' and included a number of isolated events such as the firing of Government loyalists' homes in the Nyeri District early in 1952 and the assassination of Senior Chief Waruhiu of Kiambu in October of this same year. Though it is quite likely that most of these incidents were initiated by local leaders, they were not altogether unrelated to the introduction around mid-1952 of a second oath which was to be administered to young men of 'warrior' age (16–30) who would then constitute militant wings attached to and under the direction of the various 'elders' councils. Below are the seven vows characteristic of this oath :

(1)   I speak the truth and swear before *Ngai* (God) and before everyone present here
And by this Batuni Oath of *Muingi* (the Movement)
Which is called the movement of killing,
That if called upon to fight for our land,
To shed my blood for it,
I shall obey and never surrender.
And if I fail to do so :
May this oath kill me
May this *thenge* kill me
May this seven kill me
May this meat kill me

(2) I speak the truth and swear before *Ngai* and before everyone present here

And before the children of *Gikuyu* and *Mumbi*

That I shall never betray our country

That I shall never betray a member of *Muingi* to our
enemies

Whether they be European, Asian or African.

And that if I do this :

> May this oath kill me, etc.

(3) I speak the truth and swear before *Ngai* and before everyone present here

That if I am called upon at night or during a storm

To destroy the house or store of a European or other enemy

I shall do so without fear and never surrender.

And if I fail to do this :

> May this oath kill me, etc.

(4) I speak the truth and swear before *Ngai* and before everyone present here

That if I am called upon to fight

Or to kill the enemy, I shall go

Even if that enemy be my father or mother, my brother or
sister.

And if I refuse :

> May this oath kill me, etc.

(5) I speak the truth and swear before *Ngai* and before everyone present here

That if the people of *Muingi* come by day or by night

And ask me to hide them

I shall do so and I shall help them.

And if I fail to do this :

> May this oath kill me, etc.

(6) I speak the truth and swear before *Ngai* and before everyone present here

That I shall never seduce the woman of another man

That I shall never take up with prostitutes

That I shall never steal anything belonging to a member
   of *Muingi*
Nor shall I ever hate or speak badly of another member.
And if I fail to do these things :
   May this oath kill me, etc.

(7)   I speak the truth and swear before *Ngai* and before every-
      one present here
      And by this *Batuni* Oath of *Muingi*
      That I shall never sell my country for money or any other
         thing
      That I shall abide until death by all the vows I have made
         this day
      That I shall never disclose our secrets to the enemy
      Nor shall I disclose them to anyone not a member of *Muingi*
      And if I break any of the vows I have today consciously
         made
      I will agree to any punishment that this society decides to
         give me
      And if I fail to do these things :
         May this oath kill me
         May this *thenge* kill me
         May this seven kill me
         May this meat kill me.

This 'Warrior Oath', later known as the *'Batuni'* or
'Platoon' Oath, though just beginning to spread at the time
the State of Emergency was declared and intended almost certainly as the initial step in long-range military preparations,
moved certain of the more restive or militant elements in the
Movement to actions the consequences of which were largely
unanticipated. It is not that these isolated acts of violence
were very numerous. Under 'normal' circumstances they would
probably not have attracted undue attention. But now, with
Government on the alert and the settler politicians clamoring
for action, they set off a chain of severe counter measures—the
second and major precipitant—which found the Movement without (1) a master plan for revolution or cadres trained in the art
of modern guerrilla warfare, (2) an adequate supply of arms,
ammunition and other weaponry or arrangements for their con-

tinued supply from outside the colony and (3) the necessary support of tribes other than the Kikuyu, Embu and Meru, which had not yet entered the Movement in significant numbers. In short, these scattered acts of violence helped precipitate, within the existing context, a 'revolutionary situation' for which the Movement was almost totally unprepared.

The second set of precipitating events was inaugurated formally on 20 October 1952 when the Kenya Government, with the consent of the Colonial Secretary, declared a State of Emergency. Within a few days, almost 200 prominent African leaders were arrested and either held for trial or detained under emergency regulations. These men included leading KAU officials, heads of the independent school and church movements, trade union leaders, journalists, businessmen, etc., as well as the educated leadership of the underground movement. In terms of the structure of the Movement, this Government move virtually wiped out both the Central Province and 'Central' Committees and, in so doing, the key institutions linking the various rural and urban district councils. Decision making powers thus necessarily devolved to intermediate councils, comprised largely of semi-educated or uneducated leaders, which were no longer structurally linked by a central committee.

The Movement thus decapitated and in a state of internal confusion, its members responded almost passively to the Government repressive measures of the next few weeks. Three battalions of King's African Rifles (KAR's) were brought in along with the 1st Battalion of Lancashire Fusiliers to reinforce the normal garrison of three KAR battalions, the Kenya Regiment and police force. Police reservists and tribal police, the latter comprised largely of Turkana and Somalis, were sent into the Central Province where curfews were imposed along with collective fines and punishment and a special levy on the Kikuyu peasants to defray the cost of extra police. 'Native' registration and pass laws were introduced along with legislation to require the registration of all societies or associations, to widen police powers enabling arrest without warrant and to shut down newspapers and lock up presses. Most of the Kikuyu independent schools were closed down, Kikuyu 'squatters' in the Rift Valley numbering almost 100,000 were evicted and sent back to the crowded Reserve along with unemployed workers from Nairobi, and peasant labor was requisitioned for the building of guard and police posts.

A significant sector of the European settler community tended to interpret the emergency declaration and legislation as promulgating a sort of 'open season' on Kikuyu, Embu and Meru tribesmen. Forced confessions, beatings, robbery of stock, food and clothing, brutalities of various sorts and outright killings were frequent enough occurrences to arouse a fear in the hearts of most Kikuyu that the intent of the white man was to eliminate the whole Kikuyu tribe. Combined with the general confusion, the partial disintegration of the Movement and the will of some to fight back, this fear inaugurated a slow but steady drift of Kikuyu, Embu and Meru peasants, particularly the youth, into the forests of Mount Kenya and the Aberdares.

Having briefly considered the context, underlying conditions and precipitants of revolt, it is legitimate at this point to ask one further question : Just when did the 'Mau Mau Revolution' begin? In answering this question, it must be noted at the outset that it is always difficult and more often than not arbitrary to select a specific date or event which marks *the* beginning of any particular revolution. Nevertheless, it is a selection which most writers, historians and social scientists find necessary, if only from the point of view of literary, descriptive or analytic convenience. In the case of Kenya, I believe it to be both useful and historically accurate to consider the beginning of the 'Mau Mau Revolution' as falling in that period, early in 1953, when several thousand Kikuyu, Embu and Meru peasants withdrew to the forested areas of Mount Kenya and the Aberdares and began organizing themselves into fighting groups with the avowed purpose of achieving their politico-economic aims through the use of force.

Prior to this period, few would question that there existed an underground movement capable of organized violence, individual acts of arson and political assassination (directed against African opponents of the Movement) and Government repressive measures predicated on the assumption that a revolt of the Kikuyu masses had already begun. What I am inclined to doubt, however, is that such factors add up to, or even necessarily eventuate in, revolution. Certainly in the Republic of South Africa today, where an underground movement, acts of violence and Government repression undoubtedly exist, there does not, as of this writing, exist a revolution. What is lacking now in South Africa, and what was equally lacking in Kenya prior to 1953, is an open confrontation whereby 'revolutionary' groups, bent on radically altering black–white relations and the political and other institutions through which such relations are sustained, break with the imposed colonial structure and pit force against force.

Contrary, then, to those writings and official pronouncements which have viewed the emergency declaration as a response to an already initiated revolution, I am obliged by the data to take the position that it was the major precipitant of, rather than a reaction to, Kenya's 'Mau Mau Revolution'.

CHAPTER II

KARARI'S HILL

KARARI son/of Njama begins his story at a KAU rally in Nyeri Showgrounds in July 1952. This event was chosen because it marked a turning point in Karari's political awareness and, in fact, his very life. From a person relatively disinterested in political matters, he emerged from this meeting fully aware that a new and very strong political consciousness was sweeping the land, and with a desire to become part of this new African force.

For the grievances and just demands expressed by the KAU leaders he found proof in his own experience. Hadn't LAND rightfully his, even named Karari's Hill after his own grandfather, been taken from him by the Europeans; and hadn't his own EDUCATION been cut short, his FREEDOM severely curtailed, his WAGES made miserably low and his pride and dignity as a man and as a Kikuyu trampled and degraded by the COLOR-BAR, by the selfish discriminatory policies and practices of the white man and the Government he controlled?

But the awareness was of more than this, for Karari had suffered the injustices of colonial rule throughout the better part of his life. He now glimpsed, became aware of perhaps for the first time, the tremendous power latent in the African masses, if only they could unite and act as one. He also noted the great similarity in ends of KAU and the Movement called 'Mau Mau', and the fact that most of the audience supported both. Like so many thousands of others, wanting to be part of this new-found oneness, Karari decided to join both KAU and the underground movement. He, to, would become of Gikuyu.

★　★　★

It was 26 July 1952 and I sat in the Nyeri Showgrounds packed in with a crowd of over 30,000 people. The Kenya African Union was holding a rally and it was presided over by Jomo Kenyatta. He talked first of LAND. In the Kikuyu country, nearly half of the

73

people are landless and have an earnest desire to acquire land so that they can have something to live on. Kenyatta pointed out that there was a lot of land lying idly in the country and only the wild game enjoy that, while Africans are starving of hunger. The White Highland, he went on, together with the forest reserves which were under the Government control, were taken from the Africans unjustly. This forced me to turn my eyes toward the Aberdare Forest. I could clearly see Karari's Hill, almost in the middle of the Aberdare Forest. The hill that bears my grandfather's name and whom I am named after. Surely that is my land by inheritance and only the wild game which grandfather used to trap enjoy that very fertile land. This reminds me of my youth life in a Boer's farm in the White Highland, but I felt that I must attend to what Jomo Kenyatta would say next.

The Africans had not agreed that this land was to be used by white men alone. 'Peter Mbiyu is still in the United Kingdom,' he went on, 'where we sent him for land hunger. We expect a Royal Commission quickly to enquire into the land problem.' He asked the crowd to show by hands that they wanted more land. Each person raised both his hands. And when he asked those who did not want land to show their hands, nobody raised.

Chief Nderi, when he took the platform, assisted Kenyatta's argument by saying that Aberdare was given boundaries which removed land from the Nyeri people. He too said that Africans had right to this unused land. This, spoken by a Government official, proved to all present that Africans had a truly just grievance on the land question.

The other point that Jomo Kenyatta stressed during the meeting was African FREEDOM. He raised the KAU flag to symbolize African Government. He said Kenya must be freed from colonial exploitation. Africans must be given freedom of speech, freedom of movement, freedom of worship and freedom of press. Explaining this to the people, he said that with the exception of freedom of worship, the other freedoms are severely limited with respect to the Africans. Freedom of movement: many Africans have been prosecuted for trespass on European land or for entering a town outside his own district. I personally faced a resident magistrate, the D.C. at Nanyuki, in December 1949 charged under trespass on a European farm. Without a fine, he sentenced me to three months imprisonment. He refused to my paying money for the sentence.

I was struck by its [the flag's] red colour in the middle of black and green, which signified blood. An hour passed without any description of the KAU flag. Most of the time I was pondering how and when we shall officially hoist that National flag to signify the Kenya African freedom. I recalled Kenyatta's words in 1947 at a KAU rally on the same ground. 'The freedom tree can only grow when you pour blood on it, but not water. I shall firmly hold the lion's jaws so that it will not bite you. Will you bear its claws?' He was replied with a great applause of admittance.

When Kenyatta returned on the platform for the third time, after a few other speakers, he explained the flag. He said, 'Black is to show that this is for black people. Red is to show that the blood of an African is the same colour as the blood of a European, and green is to show that when we were given this country by God it was green, fertile and good but now you see the green is below the red and is suppressed.' (Tremendous applause!) I tried to figure out his real meaning. What was meant by green being 'suppressed' and below the red? Special Branch agents were at the meeting recording all the speeches so Kenyatta couldn't speak his mind directly. What he said must mean that our fertile lands (green) could only be regained by the blood (red) of the African (black). That was it! The black was separated from the green by red; the African could only get to his land through blood.

'You also see on the flag a shield, a spear and an arrow,' he went on. 'This means that we should remember our forefathers who used these weapons to guard this land for us. The "U" is placed over the shield and indicates that the shield will guard the Union against all evils...'

This flashed to me a few new songs that were sung before the opening of the meeting:

Gikuyu and Mumbi, what do you think?
You were robbed of your land, you didn't sell it

Chorus : Kenyatta leads, Koinange at the rear and Mbiyu on the
        flank
        Each a good shepherd of the masses
        We have been demanding the return of African lands
        And will never give up

Dedan Mugo, friend of the Blacks, was deported because of his struggle for the Africans ... (I remembered Dedan Mugo to having been convicted for administering a Mau Mau oath in Kiambu in April 1950.)

The other song I remembered said :

My people, we have to think whether or not this land of ours
Left to us long ago by Iregi, will ever be returned

Chorus : God blessed this land of ours, we Kikuyu
              And said we should never abandon it

My people, Waiyaki died leaving us this curse :
'Never sell or give up this land of ours,' and
See how freely we have given it up !

Those of you who have been arrested and detained or imprisoned
In your struggle for freedom, don't despair !
Give up your tears and sorrows, for God will help you

The Europeans are but guests and they will leave this land of ours
Where then will you, the traitors, go when the Kikuyu rise up?

'Yes, this is a call for the return and defence of land,' I thought, 'and what about freedom ...'

Jomo appealed to unity, saying if we united completely to-morrow, our independence would come tomorrow. The four free-doms spoken of by Kenyatta could be practiced under the colonial rule. But for sure he did not mean this when he raised the KAU flag. He meant African self-government, which is often termed as freedom by the Africans. Most of the people are still illiterate or with very little education and cannot figure out by themselves the sort of self-government we all want. All the old people always think of freedom as the old lives they had prior to the coming of the European—and they go on teaching the young ones that the past would become our future freedom, while many ignorant young people interpret the freedom as casting down all the present laws with a replacement of liberty to do what he personally wishes. The trouble is that the leaders up to this present moment have failed to construe to the minds of the public the self-government Kenya is longing for.

I also noted that the meeting did not want to listen to anything about Mau Mau. When Ebrahim, the African Assistant District Officer, asked Jomo Kenyatta in the meeting what he was going to do to stop Mau Mau, he was forced to sit down by discouraging barracking [jeering]. The same thing happened to chief Nderi when he referred to 'night activities'.

When Kenyatta returned to the platform, he talked to the people about the African E D U C A T I O N, saying that it was at a very low level and maintaining that the Government should develop it in a way they were not doing. He also said that European children were getting eight times more money than the African children from the Government agencies. The Africans did not realize how much money the European community pays in tax and felt that their own money paid in Poll Taxes went to educate European children, while at the same time, Government is hindering African education with its Beecher Report.

As a teacher, I understood what was meant by Beecher's Ten Year Plan and also understood the parents' thoughts. The plan would result in most students having to leave the school after Standard 4, and gave no chance for further education except for a very small percentage. The elementary schools were so many compared to the top primaries that the vast majority of students would be forced to leave school after only four years of education. This, it was felt, was very detrimental to African children. Beecher's Ten Year Plan suggested that out of every 100 who entered school, 75% would have to leave after four years of education. Of those that continued, 75% would have to quit after two more years of education. This meant that less than 10% of all children who entered school each year would get a chance to sit for the Kenya African Preliminary Examination, the lowest exam for which Government issues a certificate. The Beecher Report was thus very detrimental to African education. Most Africans thought that the intention of the plan was to get these African children to go to work on the settlers' coffee or pyrethrum plantations after four or so years of schooling. This created a certain amount of bitterness toward Rev. Beecher and his plan and to make it worse, the man was a missionary whose ideas were already rejected by the Kisa [Kikuyu Independent Schools Association] due to their earlier difficulties with the missions. Beecher, being the leader of the East African churches, was felt to be once again trying to bring the independent schools under his control. Government supported the Beecher

Report and passed legislation in 1951 to the effect that it would be experimented with over a ten year period. This demonstrated to the African—particularly those Kikuyu attached to Kisa or KKES [Kikuyu Karing'a Education Society]—that the whole aim of the Government and the missionaries was to bring the independent schools once again under the control of the missionaries. At the same time, the plan would prevent the spread of education and guarantee an ever growing amount of cheap labour for the settlers.

The fourth point that Jomo Kenyatta talked of was the African WAGES. He said that Europeans were using the Africans as cheap labourers, as tools who were not really to be considered human beings. Treatment was bad on the European farms and they were given extremely low wages, poor houses, no education and couldn't even clothe themselves. When he talked of the skilled labourers, he said that the Africans who did exactly the same job as a European or an Asian would get less than a fifth of their wage. He demanded that colour-bar be abolished, since it existed everywhere in public services and operated to oppress the African. This being very true, there could be no argument or hesitation from the crowd in accepting it.

Taking into account the five points covered by Jomo Kenyatta, i.e., land, freedom, education, wages and colour-bar, all of them discriminated the African on a racial basis and rested on nothng but the white man's selfishness. People felt that the white community was extremely selfish, completely disregarding the African, and hindering the Africans. They didn't want the African to rise in standard; all they wanted was to retain a cheap source of labour.

Though the speakers at the meeting were supposed to denounce the evil secret society which was spreading rapidly through Kikuyuland and had earned for itself the unheard-of name, Mau Mau, the latter organization was given considerable publicity because most of the organizers of the meeting were Mau Mau leaders and most of the crowd, Mau Mau members. They were given the opportunity to circulate Mau Mau propaganda songs when both coming and leaving the meeting.

As I was pushing my bicycle uphill toward Muthuaini School where I was teaching, I enjoyed many Mau Mau songs which were sung by the crowd as they left the meeting. Here are a few verses from different songs :

If you are asked What? And you What?
Whether you are of Gikuyu?
I will raise both my hands and say :
'I am of Gikuyu'

The white community are foreigners
This land they must quit
And where will you go, their sympathizers
When all the Kikuyu will gather?

Chorus : This land of ours Kikuyu
              God blessed it for us
              And he said we will never leave it

The House of Mumbi, we are very many
We are in every place
The time is flying and never retreats
Our cry is for education
We want our children to learn
Now when there is time

[Another] song was Marari—a warriors song instigating the
ngers to fight.

om the songs, one could learn that Gikuyu and Mumbi was
ring to a new society and not to the Kikuyu tribe which we
belonged. *Muingi*, community or *Uiguano wa Gikuyu na
umbi*, Kikuyu and Mumbi Unity, were other terms that repre-
nted the name of the new society, while terms like *thaka*, beauti-
ul, *thata cia bururi*, the country's barren persons, *thuthi*, weevil
or informer, were used to refer to either opposers or non-members
of the society.

I had learnt from the newspapers that Mau Mau was a society
that had taken an oath that they will expel the white community
from this country and acquire the African freedom. I remembered
that whenever Mau Mau was mentioned in the meeting the mob
made a lot of noise that nothing more could be heard of the
speaker. I very much admired KAU's aims. This was the first
rally I'd been since 1947 and up to this point in my life I hadn't

been active or even terribly interested in Kenya politics. Now, however, a political awareness and excitement was sweeping the land which no one could ignore. I made up my mind to join KAU but was unable to make out a clear cut between KAU and Mau Mau, as I could see KAU members very much interested in these new songs which indirectly referred to another society which possibly would be Mau Mau but nevertheless I had learnt from the newspapers that Mau Mau members had taken oath that they must expel the white community out of Kenya and acquire African freedom. They were both good and welcomed by the Kikuyu. I would definitely join them. Raising my eyes to the western horizon I could see Karari's Hill, my grandfather's land, in the middle of the Aberdare Forest, still under Forest Reserve and controlled by the Government. I thought of my past life. It seemed to fall into three phases. The first found me as a young boy living on a Boer's farm on the White Highlands. The second phase involving my schooling and periods of teaching. The third was the period in which I attempted to venture the world as a businessman.

CHAPTER III

A SQUATTER'S CHILD

LIKE thousands of other Kikuyu children, Karari was born of squatter parents on a European farm in the White Highlands. His family had lost the better part of its land in 1910, when it was alienated and included within the Forest Reserve. Driven by the same shortage of land which moved so many others, Karari's father migrated to the Rift Valley to become a squatter-laborer for a Boer settler. In contrast to what it would be like in later years, the squatter's life during this early period was not intolerable. For the European, land was plentiful and labor in short supply, despite the various labor-getting techniques being employed by the settler Government. The squatter could at least cultivate as much of the settler's unused land as he could manage and pasture his own herds of sheep, goats and cattle.

Notwithstanding the tragic loss of his mother and three sisters and the absence of any opportunity for formal education, Karari views his childhood on the Boer farm as a relatively 'good time'. By the mid-1930's, however, the factors discussed in Chapter I had established the Kikuyu as a labor-exporting peasantry and the steady flow of cheap African labor into the White Highlands was beginning to catch up with the seemingly insatiable settler demand. This, plus the partial mechanization of settler agriculture (which, nevertheless, remained labor-intensive), the influx of new settlers and the fact that more land was being put to crops and pasture by the Europeans, yielded steadily deteriorating conditions for the African squatter. The restrictive regulations introduced in 1936, limiting the squatter to one acre per wife, fifteen sheep or goats and no cattle, marked the turning point in this process. For Karari, it marked also the first flickering of bitterness toward the white man and his first significant insight into the injustice of the white man's laws.

The dialogue which Karari recalls so vividly between himself and his grandfather, after he and his family had returned to the Reserve, reveals in dramatic form the fundamental grievance and attitude of the Kikuyu people toward the ruling European minority. The white man had been received in Kikuyuland as a guest and was well treated. He soon turned on his hosts, however, and conquered them with his superior weapons. With his power, and the fact that might was over right, the European helped himself to the best Kikuyu land and reduced the Kikuyu people to a degrading form of political servitude. Lord Lugard's diaries provide convincing affirmation of the basic truth contained in this Kikuyu attitude.[1]

★   ★   ★

I was born on 18 September 1926 in the Laikipia District of the Rift Valley Province of Kenya. It was on the farm of a Boer settler located about 12 miles east of the town of Thomson's Falls. I was the first born of Njama Karari and Wanjiru Wamioro. My father and grandfather belonged to the Amboi clan which was famous for its bravery, and my mother belonged to the Anjiru clan which was well known for its practice and knowledge of witchcraft.

When still very young, I realized that my father worked as a cook for M. P. Daniel, the owner of the farm. He was a big fat man—so huge that he could be thought of as abnormal. I have never seen in my life any other person as fat as Mr. Daniel and his wife.

My father had a large herd of livestock at this time, consisting of 600 head of sheep and goats plus a number of cattle which were taken care of along with the European's large herd. In addition, he had a large flock of Rhode Island Reds from which we obtained a good many eggs.

When I was about six years old, I was given the job of looking after my father's 600 sheep and goats. I would lead them down to the forest river to drink and occasionally had to fight off large herds of wolves. There were many wild animals which prayed on our herds, such as wolves and leopards, and it was my task to keep them away. Out of this herd, a sheep or goat would die almost daily and we always had plenty of meat to eat. My mother used to boil a lot of eggs from our poultry and I would take as many as two dozen of these with me to eat during the day while

[1] Lugard, Lord (Ed. by M. Perham), *Diaries of Lord Lugard, Vol. 1.* Pp. 313, passim. Northwestern University Press, 1959.

herding the animals. Sometimes, when playing with the other boys, I used these eggs like rocks, throwing them at my playmates. When I returned home from the pasture in the evening, I played with the Boer's many children. We often went swimming in the dam or into the forest to shoot birds with our slingshots or simply played and fought in the fields. The European had 12 children so there was always someone to play with. Other African squatter children spent time with me during the day while grazing or morn-

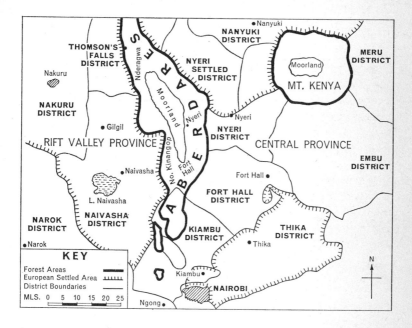

ing and evening times when they came for skimmed milk at the farm's dairy, which was near our hut and [for] which my father was responsible.

As my father had such large herds, which he could not look after himself—being in the big house with cooking and cleaning—he thought it wise to marry a second wife in 1932. By this time my mother had given birth to three more children, all of them girls. Not long after my father became a polygamist, my mother and the three sisters suddenly fell ill and died. I don't know for sure what caused their death, but according to what people said, they were victims of witchcraft—which means they died of quick-acting poison which the witchdoctors used to make sure that their curses worked.

It was a sad time in my life. A great ceremonial service was held and we who remained were cleansed so as to protect us from the evil curse which killed my mother and the three sisters. My father's second wife took me as her own son and an official adoption ceremony was held. Thereafter, I lived in my father's hut.

The owner of the farm planted wheat and kept large herds of cattle. He at first used ploughs drawn by bullocks to cultivate his fields; later, when these originally poor Boers began to make a good profit from their crops, they replaced their bullocks with tractors and bought harvester machines. My father started with Mr. Daniel as a farm labourer, driving a team of bullocks over the fields behind his plough. His employer worked in the fields at the same time and did the same job. There was not much difference between them as farmers. Only later, when African labour began to be replaced with machines, and European farmers like Mr. Daniel became rich men, that people like my father began to suffer.

Government passed a law to the effect that no African was to own cattle in the White Highlands in 1936. My father had to herd his cattle into Nyeri Reserve and sell them at a low price. Shortly after he returned, he was faced with another Government order forbidding African labourers to keep more than 30 sheep or goats. This figure was reduced to 15 almost immediately. Land, too, was reduced. Previously a man could cultivate as much land as he and his family could manage with their labour; now each labourer was allowed only one acre per wife.

My father, angered by these restrictive regulations, decided to take his large herd of sheep and goats into the Nyeri District. In June 1937 we packed all our belongings and loaded them onto our many donkeys. Wambui, my little step-sister aged two, was also carried by an ass. My step-mother carried Warau, my other step-sister aged six months. With the help of another relative, we drove the large herd of sheep goats and some donkeys covering over 70 miles in three days. Our destination was at Kagumo-ini village of Getuiga Sub-location, in Mahiga Location and in the Othaya Division.

For the rest of the year my father was kept busy selling his livestock. He charged 40s., *makumi mana*, for each billy goat and, because he never varied his price, was given the nickname *Wamana*, which means 'of forty' in Kikuyu. My father, a medium person in size, stood only five six high. His grey eyes on brown face bordered by long beard made him to look like a Sikh rather than a Kikuyu. He always smoked a pipe which he filled with native tobacco. He spoke very rarely to people and was clever in managing his business.

I was almost 11 years old when we left Laikipia. My life there had been pleasant and I had many friends. I ate well, worked with the animals and played and my step-mother treated me as her own child. Life was good though there was no opportunity for education. I had been born and raised in the Rift Valley and didn't like the idea of leaving. My resentment turned to the European farmer whose regulations about livestock and land cultivation caused my father to move.

Our new home was situated on my grandfather's land, less than three hundred yards from the fringe of the Aberdare Forest. My grandmother had died long ago when my father was still a young boy. My grandfather, who was at this time over 90 (he died in 1943 when his hut caught on fire while he slept), had three sons and four daughters of which my father was the third born and second son. He was a very brave man and had a big spear, much longer and wider than the normal Kikuyu spear, which he called *kiembo*. My grandfather, because he always kept this huge spear with him, was nicknamed Kiembo. He was a big hunter and owned big land in the forests where he used to hunt. One day I was sitting down on our homestead lawn with my grandfather warming ourselves by the heat of the sun when my grandfather pointed to a small hill in the middle of the forest just above the juncture of the Gura River and the Charangatha River and asked me: 'My grandson, do you see that hill?' 'Yes, grandfather,' I replied. 'That is where I used to hunt before the arrival of the *Chomba*—the European. That hill is still called Karari's Hill. If you went there, you could see my cooking pots in my cave. I have many beehives on that hill which would yield a lot of honey. But you see, none of my sons is interested in hunting or honey collecting. I am now old and cannot go there. Oh! My beloved beehives will rot there. I wish I were younger.'

'Why don't you tell my father to go and build on your hill so that we could collect honey nearer home?' 'Oh no, my grandson. Do you see those big blue gum trees on a line at the edge of the forest?' he asked me, pointing to some Eucalyptus trees. 'Yes grandfather.' 'Those trees were planted by your great uncle, my elder son, on his third year after his circumcision. They mark the boundary between the Native Reserve and the Forest Reserve which is under Government control. All the land west of those trees was alienated by Government in 1910. By that time we had a lot of millet growing where you see those blue gum trees growing inside the forest. Today we are forbidden to collect firewood from that forest which was ours; we are not allowed to cut even strings for tying together wood when building a hut. Do you see that small hut under the tree?' 'Yes, grandfather.' 'That is the Forest Guards' hut. It is built on my step-brother's land, Gateru. The boundary went through his land leaving him with only a small portion. Today if the Forest Guards catch a person with any forest property, he would be accused and be fined or imprisoned. We buy or work for firewood and all building materials from our former lands which the European has not planted or taken care of.

'My grandson, there is nothing as bad on this earth as lack of power. There are many Kikuyu sayings which prove this : *"Mundu utari hinya arundagwo uriri-ini wa muka,"* (meaning, "A weak person would be knocked down on his wife's bed") and *"Itari hinya kanyuaga munju"* ("A weak animal would always drink muddy water after the strong ones have quenched their thirst").

'Hee! Haaa!' he murmured and cracked his tongue in his mouth. He went on shaking his head to show his disagreement. 'I am annoyed with the *Chomba* (Europeans) for selling to me my own forest yield!' He meant what he said; I saw him shedding tears. I became terribly excited and had an ill-feeling against the white man. We both paused for two minutes or so.

'The first European to come on this ridge,' he continued, 'found your great uncle and your father grazing in the Kigumo Forest before he met any other person here. He held green grass high over his head showing sign of peace so that he would not be killed. They brought him home. When my villagers heard of a white man whom they had never seen before, very many came to my home to see him. Some warriors wanted to kill him. I preserved his life. He lived with us for ten days. He ate raw maize, sweet potatoes, arrow roots and drank our gruel. He left in peace. Those who came after him brought magic fires. They fired their magic and killed our people at great distances—three times the distance covered by a man's arrow and 20 times the distance covered by a man's spear...'

I stood and pulled out his *kiembo*, threw it eagerly wanting to know how far a man could throw a spear. I managed to throw the spear 25 feet only. My grandfather told me that a warrior could throw a spear five or six times the distance I had thrown.

'There was a great fight on the next ridge that is in North Tetu where Gakere son/of Nyingi, a great warrior, fought the white man. He was shot dead together with many of his warriors and those who escaped were chased into Nyandarua (the Aberdares). I regretted that the white man whom I saved his life went and called his brothers who came with magic fires that conquered our people. Oh! He was a spy. We found that we couldn't fight against the white man who was killing us with his magic fires and so he started ruling us and took away most of the best fertile lands. Have you forgotten the big lands you were seeeing at Laikipia full of wheat and thousands of herds of cattle and sheep and all owned by Europeans?'

'Oh, no! grandfather, that was a beautiful place to live. I used to eat meat every day, had plenty of milk that was enough to bathe in if I wanted, ate bread and butter, played with the European's children-friends of mine and I have never got any of those things here since I came about a month ago.'

'Yes, my grandson, life is very difficult here. The land is densely populated and there is neither sufficient land for cultivation nor grazing and that is why you don't have milk. The same reason has caused many people to leave this place and seek employment in the Settled Area where you were living. See the boundaries of the land I now own?' Pointing to a *muiri* tree, he showed me his land, 12 acres after survey, that was to be shared equally among his three sons. He told me that he had a share of another land about two miles east which was referred to as clan land and has never been shared to individuals. My father bought four additional acres. At this point a group of elders came and interrupted our talk.

CHAPTER IV

THE MIRACLE OF READING

KARARI's formal education began at the age of twelve; a late start, but not exceptionally so among African children of those days. The sense of urgency and dedication which he brought to the task of schooling was, and still is, characteristic of African youth. The white man's power, it was felt, lay not only in his superior weapons but also in his 'knowledge'—his books and technical skills. To a young Kikuyu in Karari's position, that book-power seemed necessary if he were to escape a life of rural poverty with its attendant misery and degradation.

In the face of increasing land hunger, education thus offered thousands of Kikuyu youth their best, if not only, alternative to joining the swelling ranks of the landless migrant worker. It also held out a promise to the successful of better paying, higher status jobs and an opportunity to fulfill family obligations and acquire at least some of the desired material goods of the dominant European minority. Only a handful could make it, however, with only three small high schools serving the needs of over five million Africans. Karari was among the fortunate in this regard, though financial difficulties following the death of his father finally forced him to leave Alliance High School after completing only two years.

These two years were nevertheless very significant in shaping Karari's outlook, for it was at the high school that he began seriously to question some of the white man's ideas and teachings which he had earlier accepted uncritically. His experiences at school, and especially within the Kikuyu student associations, made him aware of the glaring contradiction between the Europeans' preaching and practice of Christianity, and of the distorted version of Kenya History presented in his classes, where no mention was made of land alienation. The message of his grandfather was rekindled, as was the wisdom of an old Kikuyu saying: 'Between a settler and a missionary, there is no difference.'

But Karari was now caught on the horns of a dilemma which, at one time or another, confronted most educated or semi-educated Africans within this white-controlled social system. He had reached a position between two cultural worlds, one to which he could not return and another which he was not allowed to enter; and toward neither of these 'worlds' could he ever again be totally and unquestioningly committed. Though possessed of a new-found Kikuyu national pride and identity, he had already learned and changed too much even to contemplate a return to the old rural life and traditional beliefs. Again, though he now saw through the white man's deceptive teachings and religious hypocrisy, gaining an awareness of the links between Government, missionary and settler, he had learned to appreciate the advantages of European technology, which promised a higher standard of living for both himself and his people. Symptomatic of this cultural ambivalence are Karari's wavering religious views and his mixed attitudes toward the KISA school where he was employed as a teacher after leaving the high school.

*　　　*　　　*

When my father had sold all his animals, I had no work to do and it was decided that I should start school. I was 12 years old and started at Munyange School not far from our home. This school was managed by the Kikuyu Independent Schools Association. During my first year at school I did very well. I covered two years work in one year. The teachers liked me and offered me a job as their cook. In this way, instead of paying school fees, I worked as a cook's boy. This also gave me an opportunity to read all the teachers' books.

Before I learnt how to read and write, I thought that reading was a great miracle in which a person could repeat exactly the words said by another at a distant place, recording his words on a white sheet of paper. I very much admired reading. One day, on my way from school, I collected a piece of printed paper on the road and ate it so that I may have that knowledge of reading within me. I earnestly prayed God to give me the knowledge of reading.

In the evenings I never went out to play with other boys. I

always remained at home reading my first Kikuyu primer by the light of fire. We had a hurricane lamp but had no paraffin oil. My industriousness urged my father to supply me with paraffin oil regularly.

In my third year, I was made a monitor by the teachers. I attended classes in the morning and taught the lower classes in the afternoon. At this time many adults were in school as students and I was often afraid of disciplining or punishing these people much older than myself. I treated them well, however, and they liked me. When the senior boys spoke English, I carefully listened to them. I could not understand well what they were saying but I wanted to participate in their talks so I often mixed my English with Dutch words which I had learnt from the Boer's children while playing. They often laughed at me and called me Kaburu, the Dutchman. This forced me to learn English. In a short time I was challenging every student in the whole school in English, proving that I could speak good English not mixed with Dutch words.

During the third term in 1940, the school Headmaster came to Standard 2, which was my class, and asked Kiige Mbai and me to stand up. He told the class that we were clever boys and that both of us would go to Kagere School early next day where we would sit for a competitive examination with the Standard 3. He said that if we passed, we would sit for the Common Entrance Examination by the end of the year. He asked us to take our books and go into Standard 3 to do a mathematics test which he prepared. When he announced the results in the afternoon, I was second in the class of 35 pupils, some of whom were two or three years in the same class—and which I have never been in.

That night I was very happy for my success. I remembered the printed paper I had eaten. I considered that to be foolish, but I prayed God to help me to pass my exam. That night I revised my mathamatics tables and formulas. The next morning I made a long run covering seven miles to Kagere School. The test was composed of arithmatic only—both speed test and problems. The results were out in the afternoon. Only eight boys out of 35 Munyange pupils passed. I was one of the eight. The Kikuyu Independent Schools Association Supervisor, Mr. Hudson Mwangi, who had set the test said that he wanted all those who passed his test to meet him at Mung'oria School in Aguthi Location some 15 miles away from home where he would prepare all KISA students in Nyeri District for a month before they sit for the Common Entrance Examination.

On our arrival at Mung'oria School, we were distributed to different homes where we were to eat and sleep after school hours. One of the things that struck me was that the villagers, though Kikuyu, had a peculiar dialect and made a great many grammar mistakes in Kikuyu. These people grew yams, cassavas and bananas, which do not grow in our cold region. Nevertheless, after a month study I sat for the Common Entrance Examination. A month passed while I anxiously awaited for the results. At last the results were out; three boys had passed from our school. Though I had done very well in both arithmatic and Swahili, I had failed in the General Knowledge paper. Then the whole year 1941 I studied for the Common Entrance Examination, which I passed in the first division and was admitted to the Government African School, Kagumo, in the Nyeri District, together with Isaac King'ori. Only both of us passed the exam from a class of 45 in Munyange School. This was the only Government school in the whole of Central Province. The other schools were either run by the missionaries or one of the two Kikuyu independent schools associations.

On my arrival at this new school, I was first directed to the principal's office for registration and paying of school fees. I paid 45s. per year. The school rule was 5s. increment every year to the newcomers. The Principal told me that my school number was 695 and that I was to go to Standard 4A. Every door had its name written on. I was then led by one of the old boys to the school's store. I was issued with two pairs of khaki uniform, two pairs of underwear, two blankets, a plate, a spoon and a metal cup. I was led to one of the dozen dormitories of which only nine were used at that time for sleeping, each holding 30 boys. Entering the dormitory I was shown my bed—metal framework with three pieces of timber to sleep on and no mattress. In some rude manners of beating, piercing and abusive words, I was asked to put my blankets and clothes on my bed, take my utensils and follow a group of old boys. They took me to one of the two school kitchens which I dropped my utensils in the washing place. They showed me one of the two dining halls where I would be taking my meals amongst 135 boys.

I was glad to meet four old friends who had passed from

Munyange School. They took me round the school showing me the bathrooms, latrines, workshop, dispensary, teachers' quarters, school playground and school farm pens where some Native cattle, pigs, donkeys and poultry were kept for some practical work on agricultural lessons.

The dinner bell rang. One of the old boys said that we had to run in order to avoid punishment for being late. Soon we were all standing by the wooden tables in the dining hall. One senior boy whom I learnt that he was a prefect said prayers for food. We all sat down on forms, each took a spoon and the nearest plate which had maize and beans and some potatoes fried together. As we were eating one of my friends told me that the school had very many rules. He pointed out to a list of rules that governed the dining hall. There [were] duties rosters in every dormitory and in every classroom and games were compulsory. Every room had a list of its rules. Obedience, manners, punctuality, activities and cleanliness were very much observed to the standard the Government wanted the school discipline to be. The punishments for the infringement of the rules ranged from manual work through beatings by the teachers or major punishments—some canes on the buttocks under the Principal's supervision or the highest punishment of being expelled from the school. After eating we left the utensils on the tables for cooks to wash. Four pupils were selected every day according to the dormitory rosters to help the cooks to peel potatoes and bananas and to wash the utensils.

It was now twilight and the dormitory lamps were set alight. One lamp was sufficient to illuminate the whole dormitory—with the help of white-washed walls reflection; a kind of lamp I had never seen before, pressure lamp. Groups of old boys held gossips. I could hear some give account of their holidays but their whole enjoyment laid on disturbing and causing pain to the newcomers, while a few of them wanted to train the newcomers in the required school discipline. It was a bad night for me as a newcomer but I was glad the bell was rung at nine . . . It indicated lights off, everybody in his blankets and no more talking. Soon the teachers on duty came round checking whether all the pupils were in bed. I had no box [spring]. I made my clothes to be my pillow on the three pieces of timber, folded my blankets together so that I slept on and covered myself by both. As I was pondering the school rules and its beautiful stone buildings, I fell asleep.

I was awakened at six in the morning by a bell. The daily routine had commenced. This bell meant fold the blankets, bathe and dress. Everyone was required at the playground for Physical Training at 7. At 7 :15 the kitchen bell rang for breakfast—a mug of thin porridge made of maize flour. At 7 :45 the school bell rang. All the 270 pupils went into the big assembly hall for their morning prayers. The staff and the Principal sat in front of us on the raised platform. The Principal welcomed the newcomers, read a few school rules and warned us that the school aimed very high at obedience, good manners, punctuality, activities and cleanliness. He said that he preferred to expel pupils from school rather than giving punishment. He then asked us to be aware of every school rule and with that we dispersed into classes.

My class was Std. 4A. I was issued with exercise note-books for every subject, a pen holder and two pencils, and a number of text books most of which were written in Swahili. Now, though all the pupils are Kikuyu, Swahili would become the school language, both in class and outside. Now my three years curriculum has started of which I expect to have a certificate at the completion.

In my second year at school, 1943, the whole country was attacked by famine. The rations were reduced and sorghum and cassava flour, which I had never eaten before, were brought in— nasty, sticky food. The situation became worse that the whole school had to go round in the garden collecting wild edible vege- tables of the nettle family and *togotia*. Each pupil had to take to the cook a bowl of these vegetables before he could eat his meal. For two days we ate only these vegetables mixed with bananas from the school farm. Some pupils who couldn't bear this hunger ran away from the school.

By the end of the year, my father caught a disease which caused his stomach to swell up and fill with a clear liquid. During my holidays I took him to Nyeri General Hospital. The doctor re- moved from his stomach three basins full of clear liquid. Due to lack of accommodation in the hospital, my father was ordered to go home and report at the hospital once a week. Nobody in my location owned a vehicle that could carry my father 18 miles to the hospital. He had to rely on the local untrained doctors.

On 23 March 1944, at lunch time, I received the most shocking news that my father had died the day before. I couldn't eat, quickly went to the teacher on duty and asked him to give me permission to go home. He refused. As I was the only son of my father and the other three were little girls who couldn't do anything, plus my love for my father, created a necessity of my going. I ignored the school rules and went home without permission. I arrived home in the evening and found that my great uncle, Wamwere Karari, had already buried my father. I couldn't help myself from shedding tears. I had become an orphan child. There was my step-mother and her three daughters; they would now depend on me for their living. No one told me where my father kept his money—my great uncle and step-mother each accusing the other of being trusted to the money—and I knew very well that he had a lot of money. Forty shillings was all the money that could be seen from his wallet. I asked for my father's will. I was told that since he had only one son there was no question of sharing his property. All he said was that [I was] to continue with [my] education. This being spoken by a deceased person had become a curse upon me. I had to continue. How? With only 40s.? I recorded all the debts my step-mother could remember of which were only a few sheep and goats.

Now, being full of sorrow, anger and being helpless, I returned to school, arriving just a few minutes before the supper bell was rung. The prefect on duty went to report of my arrival at school after being absent for one and a half days. The teacher called me to his house and after interrogating me, he told me that he would take me to the Principal next morning. I spent a sleepless night, now worried about the Principal's punishment. I had only seven months left to sit for my last exam after completing three years. What would happen of my future if I were to be expelled from the school without a certificate? The problem remained unsolved through the night but I could see many chances of my being employed in the British Colonial Forces that were fighting in the Second World War. This being the only alternative, I had to wait until the last minute.

The next day I presented my case to the Principal. He believed that I had sufficient reasons for going home but he maintained that I had disobeyed the teacher on duty. So he asked the teacher to show me some manual work to do. He took me to the farm yard. Pointing to a compost pit 60' x 4' x 2', which had a 3-foot heap above the ground level all full of remains of maize stalks, napier grass stalks, cattle dung mixed with other rubbish, he

ordered me to empty all that into the next pit of the same measure-
ment so that the top goes to the bottom of the next pit. He told me
that I could not attend the class before I completed my work.
Three and a half days I worked on that dirty, stinking pit, with
various types of maggots climbing on my feet and swarms of flies
disturbing my eyes. When I returned to the class after completing
my punishment I just sat for the term examination. This time I
didn't do well. I was number 17 in the class of 32.

When we closed the school again in August for the second-term
holiday, I thought it was time for me to undergo the circumcision
ceremony by which members of my tribe would recognize me as a
full grown man. Being a Christian, I asked some church elders to
come and manage my feast on behalf of my deceased father. The
40s. my father left were enough for we had plenty of food in
stores and again all the village women as a rule would bring ready
food to be served to visitors. Some Christian children used to go to
hospitals for circumcision. As this was not witnessed by many
people, it created doubts whether they were really circumcised.
I thought of removing such doubts and decided to be circumcised
in the public's presence. On 17 August 1944 at 6 a.m. I went down
to the Gura River and bathed in that cold, almost freezing, water.
Hundreds of people, men, women and children, watched me being
circumcised. As all other boys and girls had been circumcised a
week before we closed the school, I was the only one remaining.
With many cheers for my bravery, I returned home escorted by
men and dancing women. Women danced wildly until midday.
For a month I was to be fed with the best food available so that
I could become strong. The last billy goat which my father left
and which was fattened in my step-mother's hut was killed for me.
The whole month was eat and play with other circumcised youths.
I was very fat and strong when I returned to school.

The third term seemed that we had completed the school's
syllabus and that we were engaged in general revision and frequent
tests. At last the examination started on 21 November, and lasted
for the whole week. For another week before leaving the school
we were engaged in manual work cleaning the school compound.

For three years I had been taught how to read and write in both
English and Swahili, do some calculation in arithmetic, little
geography, Nature Study and Hygiene, plenty of agriculture, both
theory and practical, History and Civics, Carpentry and some

backgrounds on religions. By Christianity faith and dogmas and by criticising our forefathers' ways and attitudes of praying God, and by the manners we were taught of civilized people, we were very much humiliated. In History we had been taught all the good the white man had brought us—-the stopping of tribal wars, guaranteeing security to individuals and their property, good clothings, education and religion, easy ways of communication and travel by road, railway and air and the oceans, hygiene and better medication and, finally, better jobs that would make it easy to raise the standard of living above the uneducated Africans. We were taught to honour the Union Jack, our King (the King of England and Great Britain) and our local administrators, mostly Europeans. In teaching Kenya History, the question of land was cunningly omitted. It would only be referred to as the country's backbone of economy as Kenya was an agricultural country and the white settlers as being the only people with the required knowledge of farming that kept the country's economy alive.

I then left the school thinking of the white men as good people with whom to live, from whom a better world would be created for the Africans and having no knowledge of the relationship among the missionaries, Government servants and the white settlers.

I spent Christmas time at Thomson's Falls with my uncle, King'ori Karari, on a Boer's farm—J. B. Odendaal, who had been his employer since the day I was born. He promised me that he would help me to meet half of the school fee if I passed but beyond that would only be a mere trial. Knowing that I hadn't well laid plans of obtaining my school fee, I went home. I wrote a letter to the Chairman, African District Council of Nyeri (then called the Local Native Council) asking his council to pay for my fee if I passed. I took the letter to my chief who stamped it for his approval and gave my principal a copy.

Soon the results were out. I had passed the examination and was admitted to the Alliance High School, Kikuyu. I had to pay 60s. per year, plus a 10s. deposit which would pay for any school equipment in case I lost it, while my Local Native Council had agreed to pay the balance of 140s. per year for me. I had no cash with me. It was too late for me to send a letter to my uncle, Simeon King'ori, who had promised me some money. The other uncle, Wamwere, is a poor and helpless person. I approached Munyange School elders on the last Sunday before the opening of the school.

I asked them to help me to get the 60s. fee plus my fare and pocket money. The School Committee had collected funds from the people for such purposes and two persons in the Alliance High School had their fee paid by that fund. I was instructed by the Secretary of the Committee, Jason Karimi, in the presence of the Committee that that Committee could only lend me money on the undertaking that I will refund their money after school or that they would employ me as a teacher until I paid the whole debt.

I disliked the idea for I thought that all the persons who had contributed to that fund would maintain a belief that they paid for my school fee in the hope that I would serve them for a good turn. I thought it wise to go and borrow money from a single person and so told the Committee that I could do without their money. I angrily left the Committee members, thinking that it was only helping sons of members and because my father was not a member of it again they cared little of helping me.

I walked straight to Njigori Village to the home of Kanyi Kanumbi, a great friend of my father. I had given this man a nanny goat to herd for me. That nanny goat was my New Year's gift for 1938 for being a good herdsboy which also indicated the termination of my herdsboyship. The last time I had visited the man was two days before my circumcision when I found that my goat had produced many others and that they were numbering 12 in all. I had taken five of them with me which I gave my uncle King'ori Wamioro so that he would bless me and issue permission for my circumcision.

On my arrival at Njigori, I met Kanyi grazing his herd near his home. I told him all my difficulties. I had only three days before the opening of the school and I had no money. I asked him whether I could sell some of my goats for the purpose. He told me that it was all right, though I would expect a very low price for being in such a hurry. I had then nine animals left. They all looked healthy and beautiful, resembling their mother with very many small black and white spots with its grey neck with dark brown spots. While we were arranging and selecting which animals to take to the market the next day, Nathaniel Kihara Thatu arrived. He decided to buy one of the nanny goats which did not resemble its mother. He cashed me 16s. I took that to be the average price. I had to take five animals to the market. I asked Kanyi to choose for himself one nanny goat as his gift for herding my goats well. He happily accepted. I then started my journey home.

On my arrival at home, I met two letters. One was from a great friend of mine, Emmanuel Ndiritu Theuri, by that time serving as a driver and signal and wireless operator in East African Army Commandos that were fighting against the Japanese in India. In his letter, I learnt that he had sent me 100s. to help myself. The other letter was from the District Commissioner's calling me to collect the 100s. from his office. When I read this I was very glad. I believed that God had sent me help at the right time.

Very early next morning, instead of taking my animals to the market, I walked to Nyeri. At 10 a.m. I arrived at the District Commissioners' office. His clerk told me that the D.C. was away and was not expected to return that day. Furthermore, according to his schedule he would pay such money on Mondays only. It was now Monday and if I waited till next Monday I would be a week late and probably my place would be filled by another person.

Hungry, tired and disappointed, I slackly walked home. I walked a long distance, passed many different objects without recognizing them as my brain pondered what to do. I decided to take the money receipt I had to the Principal of Alliance High School, Kikuyu, and ask him to claim the money from the D.C., Nyeri. I arrived home late in the evening and I had to say goodbye to a few friends of mine that night before I left.

Next morning, I packed my clothes in a wooden box which I'd made at Kagumo and gave it to two girl friends of mine who were to take me half-way carrying the box to Nyeri. The girls returned and I slept at Nyeri. At 5:30 a.m. on Thursday morning I caught the Royal Mail Bus which carried seven miles to Nyeri Station. I paid one shilling bus fare and pocketed the balance of my 25s. At the railway station I showed the station master my concession form. He told me that I had to pay half fare, third class, which was 4/40s. He issued me with a ticket. Soon, the big train with many coaches [arrived]. The school had booked a coach. The station master showed me to our coach. I entered with five other pupils. I found Meru students who had spent the night in the coach. One of them was a girl. It seemed amazing to me, for I had never travelled by train before. The old boys told me that I had 125 miles to be carried by the train and a miles walk to the school. Our journey would pass through Nairobi, the capital of

Kenya where there are big shops, many stone buildings and very many people. I sat near a window to enable me to observe the country as the train moved.

At 7 a.m. the train puffed and the big steam engine commenced moving and the many hundred iron wheels started rolling along the railway lines, stopping at every station. More students entered our coach. At 3:30 p.m. the train stopped at Nairobi Station. I saw many trains, people and buildings. Our coach had to be changed. We would be carried by the big Mombasa-Kampala train pulled by Mengo, the biggest Kenya steam engine. Here we were joined by pupils from the Coast Province and the Ukamba District and two half-castes. English or Swahili language has become essential for us to understand one another. At 5:30 p.m. the train arrived Kikuyu Station. The Principal, Mr E. C. Francis met us at the station. He carried many of our boxes in his small car several times. After a miles walk, we at last arrived at the Alliance High School, Kikuyu. I gave the Principal my receipt so that he could claim my fee from the D.C., Nyeri.

The buildings and the treatments are just like those of Kagumo. The school is much smaller than Kagumo, holding only 150 pupils, of whom three were girls, from all tribes of Kenya; taking in only 50 students every year. The second year 50 pupils sat for the Junior Secondary Examination while the fourth year 25 pupils sat for the Cambridge Certificate. The school was run by the alliance of the Kenya Government with the Protestant Church missionaries—which excluded the KISA and the KKES. This was the only high school in Kenya which Government had affiliated. The other two high schools were C.M.S. Maseno in Nyanza Province and Catholic Holy Ghost Mission, Mangu in Central Province, which admitted a maximum of 25 students per year who were all supposed to be Catholics. In fact, for one to be admitted in one of those high schools he must have been very clever for the reason that over 4,000 pupils competed for admittance where only less than 200 could be admitted.

The teachers were five Europeans, two Africans and an African Carpentry instructor. The studies were now much advanced. In Geometry were theorems to be proved together with the practical work I had learned before; Algebra had become a new subject; Physics and Chemistry were taught in the big laboratory; Music and Arts were new subjects to me.

I was engaged in athletics at school, playing on the second eleven in football. Every morning and evening the teacher on duty would lead prayers in the chapel which everyone must attend including the staff. Christianity was strongly emphasized, baptism and confirmation classes were taught. Different priests from various sects were invited to preach on Sundays and give sacraments. I taught Sunday school around Alliance High School. The Christian moral taught us to be polite and peaceful citizens and completely ignored the question of discrimination by teaching that all people are equal in the eyes of God no matter what colour, race or creed. It also forbade selfishness by Christ's quotation, 'Thou shall love thy neighbour as thyself'. This being the greatest commandment according to Christ's teaching, then it was obvious that the Kenya Government and the settlers did not agree with the teachings of Christianity. The school was built on alienated land, and just bordering it were some settlers' farms raising coffee, pyrethrum and dairy cattle which earned a lot of cash to them. They acquired these farms by evicting the owners, some of whom had been turned to be working tools of the farm. One could not help from admiring those Guernsey cattle, those beautiful productive farms, the good houses, the easy and high standard of life owned by the selfish settlers—the mothers of all discrimination. This resembles my grandfather's story—the settlers are no longer true friends.

In the school, there was a Kikuyu boy's association, *Gikuyu Gitungati Ngerenwa Thingira-ini*, GGNT (Kikuyu Servants—or the Rear Guards—Receive Rewards at the Elder's Hut). This was not a registered association; the masters didn't know about it. It was both political and educational in aims. It was organized by the senior boys, who taught us the need for further and enlargement of education to our people, taught history how the English people acquired their supremacy, how they came to our country, how they alienated our lands, and how hypocritical they are in their Christianity religion. We could only be equal with them if we learned up to their standards and learned how to master the various jobs they were doing in the country.

Inspired by this association, students from Othaya and North Tetu Divisions of Nyeri, together with a few from South Tetu Division, formed another association : *Kihumo kia Uiguano na Ngwataniro ya Agikuyu*, The Beginning of Unity and Co-operation of the Agikuyu (the initials, KUNA=True). I was the Vice Secretary of the association. Our aim was to deplore the differences of Christian sects. After all, they all prayed and worshipped the same God and the same Christ and yet the differences among them were so many and so great that a child had to leave a school half a mile from his home in order to attend another school 7 or 8 miles away in which his parents have been Christened.

During the holidays, our KUNA association held five meetings in which we stressed to the parents and pupils our aims, criticised what they were doing, warned them that the Kenya Government were issuing certificates to anyone who passed the competitive examinations irrespective of his religion. We told them that religion had nothing to do with the exams, hence the exam should be considered first and religion second. We appealed to them to save children such unnecessary long journeys and bear in mind that being of a different sect didn't make one become a different Kikuyu as some thought. We compared these sects with the nine Kikuyu clans, which unitedly fought against any enemy that attacked any of the clans. We preached to them that ignorance was our chief enemy, and that education was our best weapon. If we united as the name of our association forecast, it would be a true success, and if we opposed we would remain divided and defeated. We reminded them of the colonial policy—'Divide and Rule.'

In addition to this, my faith in religion started wavering. I believed in the existence of a mighty God and obeyed his ten Commandments. I took Jesus Christ to be one of the world's great teachers or doctors or prophets. I did not find sufficient proof in the Bible for Jesus to become the begotten Son of God.

The Holy Bible consisted of Middle East history, autobiographies, and prophesies which are referred to as the word of God. The Israelite history which covers almost the entire Bible is full of wars and conquering of tribes and nations who worshipped other Gods. These wars were supposedly led by Mighty God to smash other nations. This was contrary to God's peace and mercy, I thought. The Old Testament which covers the greater part of the Holy Bible is mostly Israelite or Jewish religion which in *all* respects agrees with the Kikuyu religion before the arrival of the European. This only makes a Kikuyu believe that our religion was the right one. I had a strong thought that the Kikuyu were one of the twelve Israel tribes.

The Christian sects had become so many in the world and their

differences and conflicts so great that hatred of each other had
become a common feature amongst them. It was impossible for
me to believe that they were branches of the same tree, yet Jesus
was the symbol in them all. Whenever these sects added new rules
to their churches, though they may be good for the people, yet
they each claimed that they were God's rules. This made me to
think that there was much pretence with a motive behind it.

The Christians had completely failed to practice what they
preached or believed—but more commonly acted contrary. With
these points, on the one hand, the Christianity teachings had maintained the country's peace, moral and a little bit of citizenship
and, though I kept wavering with the tide, I could not completely
abandon the church, as there were some important points of which
I could not get a substitute for them. Yet I remained critical to
the church dogmas.

Our preaching [in KUNA] was effective and I was becoming
more interested in politics. At about this time Sir Humphrey
Gilbert issued a report in Nyeri stating that the district was densely
populated and that the livestock were overstocking. He suggested
that all young persons be settled in Yatta Plains, in Ukambani,
where Government had been working out some irrigation schemes.
We were very much disappointed by his suggestions, knowing that
North Nyeri had recently adjoined to the settled area [of Nanyuki],
and probably that might be another attempt to evict Kikuyu
from Nyeri. All the Nyeri students met to discuss that report. We
confirmed his findings to be true but rejected the idea of being
moved into any other part of Kenya other than the part adjoining
Nyeri—the former North Nyeri, which was occupied by white
settlers. We then drafted a memorandum, with copies to the Chief
Secretary, Kenya Government, the D.C. Nyeri, the Local Native
Council Secretary Nyeri, and a copy to Mr E. W. Mathu, the only
African member of the Kenya Legislative Council. I with another
person were elected to take Mr Mathu's copy to his home. We
took the letter, had a talk with him in his ten-roomed stone house
and we never heard of the eviction plans any more.

The Principal wrote the D.C. several times asking him to send
my fee of which he never received any reply. I learned from my
step-mother's letter that she had received the money from the
D.C. on my behalf. I then asked her to send me the money, which
arrived just two hours before the closing of the first term. With this

money worries at home and at school, I could not do well in my studies. I was then demoted to Form 1B.

At the completion of my two years, I passed the Junior Secondary Examination in Mathematics, Arithmetic, English Composition, Swahili, Physics and Chemistry, Biology, Agriculture, History and Geography and Carpentry. Finance difficulty had become so great that employment was the only ringing sound in my mind. I felt bad for leaving the school, but had no other alternative. I thought I could do well as a teacher or an agriculture instructor. I could then help my people to learn better ways of living and farming.

Soon after I left the school, and while I was awaiting a response from the Teacher Training School or the Soil Conservation Training School, I was offered a teaching job by the Chairman of the Gachatha Kikuyu Independent School Association. I refused this offer at first, knowing that I would have to sacrifice my chance for further training. The school committee, however, told me the history of the independent schools movement and explained how they had separated themselves from the mission schools because the latter had rejected the female circumcision and polygamy, two very important features of the traditional Kikuyu culture. To marry many wives was a sign of a man's wealth and no girl could be married until she was circumcised. The leaders of the KISA considered the missionaries as the destroyers of the Kikuyu traditional and customary laws and since the missions were managed by Europeans, the Kikuyu had the feeling that the white man wanted to destroy their culture, replacing it by his own.

The fact that my parents belonged to the Kikuyu Independent Schools Association and that I myself was educated in these schools, led the committee to feel that I should accept their offer. They thought that children educated in their schools should assist in educating those to follow. They also told me how they hated to be ruled and led by the white man and how better it would be for me to lead my people up to the standard I had attained in the Government schools so that they might be in a position to lead themselves. Having heard all their arguments, I decided to accept their offer to teach at the KISA school and thus lost my opportunity for further training at the agricultural school.

Earning 140s. per month, I then became the Headmaster of the Gachatha Secondary School. At the opening of the first term in 1947, I became the classmaster of the first Form 1 in the school. I met many difficulties in my new occupation. There were no books available to the teachers for studies, no syllabuses and no scheme of work. There were only classrooms, students, blackboards and boxes of chalk. I had to go to the Government African School, Kagumo, and borrow syllabuses and copy them so as to be able to teach.

Gachatha accepted boarding students and the newly built dormitories and dining hall were built of mud and wattle. Pupils had to draw water for cooking from a stream some distance from the school. I asked the committee to buy instruction books and a small water pump. The committee was very slow in doing these things for it had no funds. It had to collect money from its members who were mainly parents of the students, who paid 99s. a year for fees and additional money for uniforms and equipment for each student. The parents were not rich and could hardly be expected to pay more. Nevertheless, the lack of funds brought about a situation in which the school failed to attain high standards in building and education. Good teachers couldn't be gotten because the schools couldn't afford to pay high salaries. As it was, teachers had often to go without salary for a number of months, until a collection was made and they could be paid.

When this occurred with me, I didn't really understand the great financial difficulties which confronted the schools. I thought the Chairman willfully failed to comply with my requests for books and other supplies and that this was hindering the progress of the school. As the Chairman had made many failing promises, I therefore decided to resign teaching. Before I left the teaching, I had a strong feeling that the Kikuyu Independent Schools Association had a heavy burden that oppressed them in the management of their schools . . . chiefly the financial difficulties. All its members paid Poll Tax to the Government and received no aid at all from the share of their money, while all the missionary schools received grants from the Ministry of Education. This was a question to be raised by the leaders of the KISA schools. I also considered their sectarian reasons, polygamy and the girls circumcision, as being unnecessary. I thought that it wouldn't be long before the country's economy forced everyone to marry only one wife with no resistance to that and also education and civilization would bring the girls' circumcision to an end in the future. I believed that girls' circumcision added nothing to them other than prejudice of pride. I also held a strong feeling that any circumcision, ear piercing, removal of incisors, or the making of any brand marks on any part of the body, though all these be traditional or customary laws, were totally against nature and perhaps they might have originated on ignorance grounds as they all aimed at making a person more beautiful or perfect.

My pupils loved me very much. When I bid them goodbye and told them my reasons for resignation, they cried tears and ran away from the school for three days and some never returned to the school. But as I was fully convinced that the Chairman was the hindrance of the school's progress and that I couldn't by any means work with him, they could not win me.

CHAPTER V

TO SEEK MY FORTUNE

DURING his brief sojourn into the world of business, culminating in a rapid retreat to teaching, Karari found himself confronted by the same barriers and vicissitudes which so effectively blocked this avenue to success for the poor but aspiring African. As a building contractor, he encountered the brute fact that in contractual relations between whites and blacks it was the former who normally set the terms and were in a position to enforce compliance. African parties to such agreements, whether in the field of employer-employee relations, crop or stock sales to European-controlled marketing boards or other areas, had little effective bargaining power and even less chance of sustaining a charge of breach of contract against a white man or firm. Though contact and a certain degree of cooperation did exist across the lines of cleavage between white and black, it was the European, from his position of dominance, who established the particular forms and terms of this cooperation. As one African leader aptly put it, it was a type of cooperation bearing close resemblance to that of a horse and its rider.

In his fling at the poultry and stock trade, Karari again met the fate of most undercapitalized African petty traders and hawkers. License fees, intense competition from established Asian dealers, Government restrictions, high transportation costs, the ups and downs of the consumer market, ill-fated ventures into illegal trade, etc., repeatedly crushed the hopes and ambitions of all but the most fortunate and persistent African aspirants to lower *petit bourgeoise* status. Karari's failure story was repeated with little variation time and time again by every informant with whom I worked. For most, however, lacking Karari's education, it meant a return to the crowded labor markets of the urban slum or White Highlands.

★   ★   ★

I left school in August 1948 and ventured into the world, this time interested in personal wealth. I held a contract with Mr G. L. P. Wedd for building a farm house and several others for clearing bush areas in the farms. After a time, a friend of mine, Karuu Gitegenye, an employee for 10 years by a Boer farmer, Mr J. B. Odendaal, who was also the employer of my uncle, invited me to a contract he had made with his employer. The contract read: 'I have given Karuu a contract to repair Leshau dam until it stops leaking and overflowing.' Signed: J. B. Odendaal.

The contract was not clear. It did not mention any payment. I met the Boer at the dam. He told me that we should measure the volume of the soil used for blocking the waterflow, and that we should dig an even level of 2 feet deep to make it easier for calculation. I asked him how much he would pay us. He replied: 'Five shillings per 100 cubic feet, and I have told Karuu the same.'

'Why didn't you put that in the contract?' I asked the Boer.

'Is orright, I been with Karuu many years and he can witness durt me always given him money widout written kondract. Is durt true, Karuu?' the Boer asked. 'Ye surr,' replied Karuu. With that the Boer, pretending to be angry, walked home.

My partner Karuu convinced me that the Boer was a trusted person. We then got working tools from the Boer's store—wheelbarrows, mattocks and shovels. We hired workers and completed the project in a month. We measured the volume of the soil we had dug and calculated the amount due to us; some 3,360s. When the Boer came to see our work, he said it was very good. He measured the volume and calculated it at 25 cents per 100 cubic feet, which came to 168s. He then deducted 3s. for hiring his implements. He told us that he would only pay us 165s.; all we had done was repair his old dam.

I was extremely angered by this and went with my partner to the Thomson's Falls Labour Office and I accused the Boer before the Labour officer, who promised to go with me to see the dam. He went during my absence, and I met him again in his office. He asked me to produce a written contract and when Karuu gave him the vague written piece of paper, he replied after reading that the money we were claiming was not in the contract. I explained him how the Boer had made a verbal promise in the presence of some of our workers. After all, he told me that there was nothing he or anyone else could do for us. He explained the law and told me to be very careful in the future to get good written contracts. He told me the following story so as to warn me of the dangers of my business.

Another Boer, it seems, had given a contract to a Kikuyu for digging a well. In the contract it stated that the man would pay the Kikuyu 5s. for every foot he dug until water was reached. Well, the man had dug 100 feet but had not yet struck water. He wanted to stop, thinking there was no water, but the Boer insisted that he keep on digging until he got water. The Kikuyu started digging again until it became so hot in the hole that they had to stop, and still no water; and also no money for the work he had done. He advised us to take the 165s. and added that he did not object to our wasting more time and money in the case, but he was certain that we could not win.

Knowing that white man was the only judge in our case, I lost hope and accepted the 165s. I requested the labour officer to speak to my workmen who were sitting outside his office awaiting for his judgement. He convinced them that we have all been deceived and while speaking on my favour he asked them not to claim more money than the Boer had paid us. Though the Boer was all the time standing trembling in the office, he didn't talk, for the labour officer advocated for him.

The Boer handed over the 165s. to the labour officer who gave me the same. After a short discussion with my employees who, though they had worked for 30 days, realized how I had been cheated and agreed that we should share the money equally amongst 35 persons and they therefore didn't demand full payment of their wages. In the end it cost me and my partner 450s. which we had spent on food for our workers over the month's period plus time and energy we had put into the labour.

The next day the Boer saw me in his farm; he pretended to be very angry because I had accused him to the labour officer and ordered me in his broken English to get out of his farm, saying that if he saw me again on his land he would shoot me. I was very angry, but there was nothing I could do. This particular Boer had less education than myself and spoke very little English. When I left, as he was instructing his workers to report to him if they saw me on the farm, he referred to me as *Mzungu wa Njama*, meaning Njama the European. He really felt that this abused me by figuring me as a very poor European [a Black European]—a poor educated person. He also told his men that anyone helping me would be immediately discharged.

This incident created in me an ill-feeling towards the European settlers as a whole. I looked at the work Africans were doing on these farms for very little wages and how the settlers exploited our energies. My uncle had been employed by this Boer for 23 years and his wage was only 22s. a month. It was impossible for me not to hate them.

Our partnership with Karuu ended and I was hired by Ol' Pejeta Ltd. (one of the Lord Delamere's estates in Nanyuki) for building farm houses. I earned 3/50s. a day. After three months, two Indians (Sikhs), a carpenter and builder employed for 22s. and 25s. a day, were discharged and I took over their jobs earning only 5s. a day, housed and rationed.

In August 1949, I left for Meru with the money I had saved to try my fortune in sheep, goat and cattle trade which had been highly recommended to me by a Meru friend of mine who would become my partner. I used to buy herds of cattle, sheep and goats from Isiolo and two other markets on the boundary of Meru and the Northern Frontier from Somali and Boran herdsmen. I would take this stock in the Tigania Division where I sold them in either whole herd or at retail. I also rented a small butchery in Kianjae market where I slaughtered all the animals that were unable to walk or were not bought alive. Trade was abundant in the area. Kahure Macharia, a young man of my location who had gone to Meru with the same objective, was a poulterer. We rented another plot with him where I would store eggs and chickens while he took the others for sale to Nairobi.

For the first three months our business flourished very well and we were very happy. The great change started. It so happened that people at this time had very little money to spend. 1949 had been a very bad year due to a severe drought and no crops had been harvested. My trade faltered with too few people around with money enough to buy my animals, many of which became weak and died. When I slaughtered them in the butchery, I still couldn't sell the meat. Finally, my business collapsed completely—but the poultry was still doing well. Kahure told me that we could make more money if we bought *miraa*-leaves of a certain tree that is planted and cultivated in Meru and which Sudanese, Somali and Boran are fond of—and take it to Nairobi; we could sell it at over six times the buying price. It sounded like profitable trade, but no one could trade with *miraa* without a license. We therefore put *miraa* inside a box and covered the top three layers with eggs. Our secret was known by some Meru who did not like to see Kikuyu business flourish. They informed the police. Since the latter trade had become very profitable, we invested most of our money in it. Kahure was ambushed on his way to Nairobi. He was caught and imprisoned for six months. All our chickens, eggs and *miraa* were confiscated—worth 1,800s.

I was also afraid that those Meru people would trap me into some trouble as they had my partner. I left for Nanyuki without money. My business had so failed as if it had been cursed.

On my arrival at Nanyuki, I went to see a friend employed in a European farm adjoining the town. The European saw me opening his gate and ordered his wild dog to attack me. I fought the dog but he tore my long trousers. The furious European came to aid his dog; he gave me a blow and the fight started. While we were wrestling, his dog and his workmen helped him. Instantly, I was taken to the police station and charged that I was trying to steal his timber. The next day I appeared before the D.C. being the resident magistrate. I proved that the European was lying. I was remanded for eight days. When I appeared in the court again, my charge had been changed to trespass. To this I was sentenced to three months hard labour. I appealed for a fine substitution, seeing friends who wanted to pay fine for me. My request was rejected and I fulfilled the white man's will.

I arrived home by the beginning of March 1950 without money after one and a half years of my attempts to acquire wealth in the world which had resulted in a complete failure. I vowed to myself not to leave my district for the next five years and see what I could do in our own little garden.

After my father's death, the man who had sold him four acres refunded our money and took his garden. The orange, lemon and loquat trees I had planted while a school boy at Kagumo were then very productful. Attracted by my former work, I made many tree nurseries. Within six months I was able to sell different kinds of fruit trees, timber and hedge trees from my nurseries in thousands and had planted over a thousand timber trees, mainly cypress, along the boundary of our land. I had started keeping poultry. My brain was then to work on land as a farmer. I had no capital and the land to work on was too small.

The new year 1951 broke with good news. Muthua-ini Secondary School (KISA), some 12 miles north, wanted a teacher. Its committee had sent an elder to come and ask me whether I would accept the job. January 15th I opened the school as the Headmaster earning 200s. a month. This school had classes ranging from Std. 1 to Form 2. The latter had five pupils only. Knowing that the class couldn't pay for its teacher, I closed it down. The lower classes, Std. 1 to 4, paid fees to the Government according to the Beecher Report and received a grant from the District Education Board, which paid the salaries of the teachers at this level and the pupils equipments. Though the higher classes were 'unaided', I had forwarded the names of all the teachers in the payment vouchers, thus enabling me to draw 140s. extra from what I was paid by the school committee.

Students had to pay 33s. per term [three terms per year] and received no equipment or clothing. A dormitory was built for students who came a long distance from their home to school. This cost 60s. extra per term and included food.

There were over 500 students in the school. The former headmaster had taken all the troubles to get syllabuses printed for the school and a few books for teachers were available. The school was better managed than Gachatha. Johana Kunyiha, former President of the KISA in Central Province and Rift Valley, had agreed to cooperate with the Government during the previous year's split [in KISA's managing committee] and was then leading only ten schools in the district while Willy Jimmy Wambugu Maina, the District Chairman, was leading all the other KISA schools [which retained close ties to the KISA-run Teachers Training College, Githunguri].

Though a scheme of work was devised, no Government approved examination could be given to students in the higher classes. Having recognized my great problem, I approached the District Education Officer, Mr Collier, who took my requests to the Provincial Education Officer, Mr Brumerly, and the latter visited my school and, after we talked, recommended that my students be allowed to sit for the Government Kenya African Preliminary Examination [KAPE] at the end of 1952. I had to build a workshop and make sure that my students had a knowledge of handcrafts which was part of the examination. This I managed to do after subscriptions were raised. I gave instruction to woodwork and prepared them for the examination by the end of the year 1952 for the Form 2 students. Practical Agriculture was another condition given to me by the education officer. The school was forced to buy more land and I spent my own money in keeping poultry and pigs for the school's practical work.

In June and July my school was engaged in inter-school sports competitions. This was followed by district and provinces competitions. My school was very successful indeed that it defeated most of the schools. Two of my pupils went to Uganda for inter-territorial races. During the sports time, I was engaged in recording the winners. The rumours that my school was to become the first among the KISA schools to be admitted to sit for KAPE the following year made me and my school to be known. By the end of the year I received many applications for admittance in the school the following year.

It was at this time, during the holidays in December, that I got married to Junius Nyaguthii, a girl teacher in a nearby school. The following year, 1952, I had to concentrate my work on the class that was to sit for the examination, but the Beecher Report which was then in practice had become a menace in education. The President, Johana Kunyiha, the School Committee and myself wanted to cooperate with the Government. In fact, we were not at all worried if the Government took control over the school's finance, but we were very much worried about the limits placed on the number of pupils per class and the number of secondary schools in the country. We didn't want to oppose the Beecher Report but we wanted it to be amended. I approached the District Education Officer, Mr Collier—the only sociable European I had ever met—and we discussed the Beecher Report. He very much sympathized with the Africans and agreed that the Beecher Report should be amended but, as a Government servant, he had no power of opposing it. He could only refer to it as the claims of the Africans. We then arranged that we would hold a committee meeting which we should invite him and other prominent elders in which we should discuss the bad points of the Report and call for a parents general meeting and also invite him in which we would claim the amendment of the Beecher Report. After all this, the education officer, Mr Collier, promised the general meeting that he was going to see the District Commissioner—who had power—on our behalf so that the Beecher's rationing system of education could be amended. In the course of his attempts to make changes for the betterment of the African children's education, my beloved friend Mr Collier annoyed the Kenya Government and was, without notice, repatriated with his wife to the U.K.

It was also time for my life planning. I had to pay the dowry to my wife's parents, which I hadn't completed by the time I took Nyaguthii, plan and build a better house and at the same time save money that would enable me to acquire a good farm on which to live with my expected family. With all these problems in my mind pulling me this way and that way, I attended the KAU rally at the showgrounds on 26 July 1952.

CHAPTER VI

THE OATH OF UNITY

IT WAS not until early September 1952 that Karari, having felt the first sting of ostracism and isolation, finally got his chance to join the Movement. It had, over the preceding two years, grown to include a vast majority of his fellow villagers and Kikuyu; it had also, particularly since the introduction of the Warriors' Oath, became increasingly bold and militant. Karari's oath, in contrast to earlier versions of the Unity Oath, reflected this increasing militancy. The vows themselves, now more comprehensive, included references to the boycott of European beer and cigarettes, the possibility of a general strike and the hiding of arms and ammunition. Again, in his instructions to the new initiates, the oath administrator made it quite clear that if reason and peaceful means failed to bring them land and freedom, they '...would not hesitate to revolt'.

The oathing ceremony which Karari attended also revealed another development. The growing need for unity and total commitment to the Movement, in the face of mounting external pressures, increasing anti-white, anti-mission feelings and the internal frailties brought about in part by the very rapid expansion of the Movement, exerted a steady pressure toward the increased use and invocation of traditional Kikuyu symbols and magico-religious practices. This fact has led many, seeking the easy satisfaction of facile classification, to regard the Movement as simply a backward-looking, 'nativistic', Kikuyu cult or religious sect which sought only a return to the old life. In actuality, as will become clear in later chapters, the secular and the religious, the tribal and the African national, the old and the new, were becoming increasingly interwoven in the complex ideological fabric of the Kikuyu peasant masses. Karari's own reflections and recollections lay bare some of the tensions and, perhaps, contradictions inherent in this developing composite ideology.

*   *   *

The Gikuyu and Mumbi underground society was becoming both popular and powerful all over the country. A song book published under the name of Stanley Mathenge Mirugi consisting of songs advertising, praising leaders and threatening opposers of the society was then on sale. The boycott on drinking European beer and smoking European manufactured cigarettes had become effective since the KAU rally at Nyeri. The vernacular papers, especially *Mumenyereri,* increased the publicity of Gikuyu and Mumbi. The unity and honesty in Nairobi had marvelled everybody. Articles such as newspapers could sell themselves in Nairobi streets and no thugs dared take that money. The reports of missing people and oath intimidation increased in the newspapers—these people were definitely the opposers of the secret society of Gikuyu and Mumbi and could only have been assassinated, or probably might have met their death by their refusal to take the oath. With this on the one hand and Gikuyu and Mumbi's aims on the other, i.e., achieve African freedom, recover the stolen lands and the expelling of the white man, [the aims] were welcomed by 99 per cent of the Africans. With this in mind, I discussed the matter with my fellow teachers and agreed that none would refuse to take the oath if called.

It was only three weeks after the KAU rally at the Nyeri Show-grounds that we had a school vacation for the second term. I went to spend my holiday in Mahiga where my wife and other relatives were living. It was time for me to erect a five roomed house. I had collected all the required building material and only the levelling of the building site stopped me from building the house I wanted to complete before the end of my holidays. It would take a person at least two months to level the ground. I decided to call my friends to come and help me to level the ground. I brewed a lot of liquor [i.e., beer] in order to entertain my friends after leveling the ground.

When the work-day arrived, I was very much shocked by the attendance. A few persons came to report that they were not available, many never turned up and the few who came never completed the work. I had learnt from some persons during the day that another villager had the same kind of work on the same day and that his work might have been attended by most of the people who did not turn up to my request. When I was told the name of the person, I could not agree. I believed that I was ten times popular to my villagers than the man.

In the evening, while we were all drinking beer sitting in a circle, I noted something queer. A 'horn of love' was passed all around, each person drank very little, spit into the horn and on his chest and shoulders as though he were blessing something and then passed it to the next person. When all had drunk of the horn, it was given to Gicuki Wacira, who stood holding the horn in his right hand and started saying prayers. He poured the remaining of the liquor in the fire, on the door frames and then went to finish his prayers outside facing Mount Kenya. In his prayers, he appealed for love, unity and the increment of the Gikuyu and Mumbi membership and power to defeat the enemy. With this we dispersed.

I anxiously wanted to see the other person's work. I was very much surprised. Over 200 people had been working all the day— leveled the ground, built the hut and the women had completed their work of mudding and thatching the hut. This only proved to me that one of the rules of Gikuyu and Mumbi was—Do not help any non-members. And that the few who had to come to help me were the only ones who thought I was a member or were non-members, if these happened to be. I felt very lonely and worried about what that society might say of me. As we entered the hut where a few persons were still drinking the remains of the liquor, I noticed another queer form of greetings—three strong hand-shakes, on the second of which the persons held each others thumbs. It was then obvious to me that nearly all my villagers had taken the Gikuyu and Mumbi oath. I did not like to stay with them; I quickly went home and slept.

The following day was a Sunday in the first week of September. After Sunday service I met Mr Samuel Ndiritu Njagi, a clerk in the Ministry of Works, a true friend and a schoolmate at Kagumo who had recently married my relative. He kindly invited me to his home. When we arrived, I learnt that he had brewed beer in his mother's hut. We spent the whole of the afternoon drinking and talking on ones job and the country's politics. A few persons came and shared the drink with us. In the evening we left toward home. On the way, Ndiritu told me that he had been invited to a feast by my neighbor, Charles Ngatia Gathitu, a pitsawyer and license holder on timber trades, situated about 400 yards east of my home.

We passed many people on the way and arrived at the house at twilight. There were some people standing outside, including Charles, the owner of the feast. He led us into one of his big huts. Inside, were many people sitting and a hurricane lamp was burning. We were told to wait there while some preparations went on in the other hut. Groups of men and women continued to come until there was very little room for anyone to sit. A few persons would be called by names and moved in the next hut. When I was called to go to the next hut, I was very pleased, but arriving outside in a clear moonshine, I could see hundreds of people standing some armed with *pangas*, *simis* (swords) and clubs. They formed a path on both sides leading to the door of the next hut. I became certain that the day had arrived for me to take the oath, and I had to face it manly, I thought.

As I led my group marching in the cordoned path, they waved their *pangas* and swords over our heads and I heard one of them asking whether there was an informer to be 'eaten'. With a reply that we were all good people from another person, we entered the next hut.

By the light of a hurricane lamp, I could see the furious guards who stood armed with *pangas* and *simis*. Right in front of us stood an arch of banana and maize stalks and sugar cane stems tied by a forest creeping and climbing plant. We were harassed to take out our coats, money, watches, shoes and any other European metal we had in our possession. Then the oath administrator, Githinji Mwarari—who had painted his fat face with white chalk —put a band of raw goat's skin on the right hand wrist of each one of the seven persons who were to be initiated. We were then surrounded [bound together] by goats' small intestines on our shoulders and feet. Another person then sprayed us with some beer from his mouth as a blessing at the same time throwing a mixture of the finger millet with other cereals on us. Then Githinji pricked our right hand middle finger with a needle until it bled. He then brought the chest of a billy goat and its heart still attached to the lungs and smeared them with our blood. He then took a Kikuyu gourd containing blood and with it made a cross on our foreheads and on all important joints saying, 'May this blood mark the faithful and brave members of the Gikuyu and Mumbi Unity; may this same blood warn you that if you betray our secrets or violate the oath, our members will come and cut you into pieces at the joints marked by this blood'.

We were then asked to lick each others blood from our middle fingers and vowed after the administrator : 'If I reveal this secret of Gikuyu and Mumbi to a person not a member, may this blood kill me. If I violate any of the rules of the oath may this blood kill me. If I lie, may this blood kill me.'

We were then ordered to hold each others right hand and in that position, making a line, passed through the arch seven times. Each time the oath administrator cut off a piece of the goat's small intestine, breaking it into pieces, while all the rest in the hut repeated a curse on us : *'Tathu! Ugotuika uguo ungiaria maheni! Muma uroria muria ma!'* ('Slash! may you be cut like this! Let the oath kill he who lies !').

We were then made to stand facing Mt. Kenya, encircled by intestines, and given two dampened soil balls and ordered to hold the left hand soil ball against our navels. We then swore : 'I, (Karari Njama), swear before God and before all the people present here that. . . .

(1) I shall never reveal this secret of the KCA oath—which is of Gikuyu and Mumbi and which demands land and freedom—to any person who is not a member of our society. If I ever reveal it, may this oath kill me! ([Repeated after each vow while] biting the chest meat of a billy goat held together with the heart and lungs.)

(2) I shall always help any member of our society who is in difficulty or need of help.

(3) If I am ever called, during the day or night, to do any work for this society, I shall obey.

(4) I shall on no account ever disobey the leaders of this society.

(5) If I am ever given firearms or ammunition to hide, I shall do so.

(6) I shall always give money or goods to this society whenever called upon to do so.

(7) I shall never sell land to a European or an Asian.

(8) I shall not permit intermarriage between Africans and the white community.

(9) I will never go with a prostitute.

(10) I shall never cause a girl to become pregnant and leave her unmarried.

(11) I will never marry and then seek a divorce.

(12) I shall never allow any daughter to remain uncircumcised.

(13) I shall never drink European manufactured beer or cigarettes.

(14) I shall never spy on or otherwise sell my people to Government.

(15) I shall never help the missionaries in their Christian faith to ruin our traditional and cultural customs.

(16) I will never accept the Beecher Report.

(17) I shall never steal any property belonging to a member of our society.

(18) I shall obey any strike call, whenever notified.

(19) I will never retreat or abandon any of our mentioned demands but will daily increase more and stronger demands until we achieve our goals.

(20) I shall pay 62/50s. and a ram as assessed by this society as soon as I am able.

(21) I shall always follow the leadership of Jomo Kenyatta and Mbiyu Koinange.'

We repeated the oath while pricking the eye of a goat with a kei-apple thorn seven times and then ended the vows by pricking seven times some seven sodom apples. To end the ceremony, blood mixed with some good smelling oil was used to make a cross on our foreheads indicating our reception as members of Gikuyu and Mumbi [while] warning us : 'Forward ever and backward never !'

We were then allowed to take our belongings, put on our coats and shoes and were welcomed to stay. We paid 2/50s. each for registration. During the course of our initiation, one person refused to take the oath and was mercilessly beaten. Two guards were crying [out] seeking permission from their chief leader to kill the man. The man learnt that death had approached him and he quickly changed his mind and took the oath.

After we had all been sworn, the house was very crowded that contained about 80 people; nearly all of whom were initiated on that night. About the same number of old members were working outside as guards. A speech was made by the oath administrator, Githinji Mwarari, and his assistant Kariuki King'ori, who told us that they had been sent from the Head Office in Nairobi to give people an oath that could create a real unity among all the Africans which would make it easier for the African to gain his land and freedom. He told us that the society was called Gikuyu and Mumbi or KCA. He remarked that the struggle for the alienated land started as long ago as 1920 by Harry Thuku and the Kikuyu who attempted to fight for the land which caused many deaths in Nairobi and the deportation of Harry Thuku to Kismayu. He said that the KCA was the society that had been struggling for the return of our alienated land. He told us that we had been initiated so as to strengthen the African struggle for the alienated land—the chief African demand. He went on : 'We have learnt that the Kenya settlers are the chief obstacles to our claims. They do not want to leave the bread and butter which they obtain from these lands at the exploitation of our blood on the so-called white paradise. Some of you here might have been fined or imprisoned under the trespass ordinance on stepping on a settler's farm while you visited your relatives under his employment or else you had gone there seeking employment only. We cannot tolerate this any longer. We are going to shout to the Kenya Government, which we know that it is controlled by the settlers, until we are heard or else their eardrums would burst. We are going to pursue our demands through reasons and if this fails we would not hesitate to revolt. We have already sent Mr Mbiyu Koinange to England to represent our case to the British Government.

'You have heard that some of our members have been prosecuted for taking Mau Mau oath. This is the same oath you have taken today. You are now members of that "Mau Mau". But don't speak as being members of "Mau Mau". If you reveal this secret the Government will imprison you and we will kill you for the breach of the oath you have taken today. Our members are all over the place, even in the Government offices. In three days time you will all learn that more than 3/4 of this sub-location have taken the oath.'

When he sat down, his assistant administrator, Kariuki King'ori, stood and taught us greetings—the old Kikuyu greetings rarely used due to changes brought about by the European civilization— such as the shaking of hands and the terminology. 'If any person wants to refer to the society he would not say "Mau Mau" as you have already been warned, but he would refer to the society as *Muhimu* (a Swahili word meaning "Most Important"), *Muingi* (meaning "The Community" in Kikuyu) or *Gikuyu na Mumbi*.'

We were warned not to talk anything about the movement in the presence of a non-member. Speaking in a group of persons, one would say that he has been bitten by a flea, or louse, or bug to indicate that there is a person [present] who has not taken the oath.

It was about four o'clock in the morning, the cocks were crowing, the moon and the stars were brightly shining. The footpaths were wet and muddy as it had rained sometime before midnight. I quickly and quietly went home and called my wife to open the door for me. Without talking to her I went straight to my bed.

Covering myself with blankets, I repeated what I swore several times. As a Christian I had undergone a contrary faith for the oath I had taken was mainly based on Kikuyu religion, belief and superstition. But the aims and objects presented by the society were so real and so essential to life that when compared with Christianity faith, of which its preachers many times failed to practice what they preach, the latter becomes strongly out-weighed. At sunrise I remembered that the next week would be my 26th birthday and that I had been born again in a new society with a new faith.

I spent the whole day in bed, partly asleep, as I had not slept the night before, and partly reciting and reasoning my vows. Reflecting on the crowd at the KAU rally held one and a half months ago at Nyeri Showgrounds supporting national demands under the national leader Jomo Kenyatta assisted by Peter Mbiyu Koinange, the cleverest Africans in Kenya—whose leadership was advertised in Mathenge's song book where Jesus Christ's name has been substituted for by Jomo Kenyatta's—and whereas the Government had taken no action against them proved to me that our true and just grievances were led by powerful and honoured men. I believed that it was an all Kenya African national movement and not a tribal one. With the understanding that African labour is the whole backbone of Kenya's economy, I believed that if all Kenya Africans went on a labour strike we would paralyse the country's economy and the white community who holds the most of it would suffer most and recognize our demands. Furthermore, our national leader, Jomo Kenyatta, had lived in England for 17 years and must have during his stay convinced the British Government of our claims.

Though the oath clung on Kikuyu traditions and superstitions, yet the unity and obedience achieved by it was so great that it could be our only weapon to fight against the white community.

Among the vows I had taken, one was to force me to accept girls' circumcision which I had rejected as early as 1947. There was no reason given for any of the vows but I thought that this vow [simply] meant to maintain the Kikuyu tradition. This tradition might be a hindrance to civilization, [but] there are thousands of educated Kikuyus who do not sympathize with girls' circumcision and who would be helped by the missionary associates to oppose it. I did not have a girl then to be circumcised; this vow might affect me personally some 20 years to come, and then it will be settled by those who are affected today.

The other vow that affected me was the Beecher Report. I have already convinced the Education Officer that it requires amendment. There are criticisms all over the country and in the Legislative Council of the Report. It must be amended, I thought, and our children would get a better education and the parents would have less to subscribe. The Government is prepared to meet teachers wages and equip the pupils at a very low cost. The parents would be happy for the relief of the heavy finance burden, with the exception of a few leaders who live on these subscriptions. Again, this vow does not affect [only] me as an individual. It affects everyone who had a child in the schools—all over Kenya. The vow rejects the Beecher Report and not the education. If it is accepted by the parents then they would not send their children to schools and I would have no one to teach. But at this stage, it seems that Kikuyu people have realized the value of education, will make the children continue to learn while their parents struggle for either the amendment or abolition of the Beecher Report.

I learnt later that, with the girl's circumcision vow, it was meant to maintain Kikuyu tradition, some of which I thought were silly. I had earlier mentioned that I was against any alteration of the human body, such as ear-piercing, scarification or the removal of the teeth. Most of the Kikuyus who were repatriated [during the months following the Government's declaration of a State of Emergency on 20 October 1952] from the Rift Valley had unhealed wounds of ear-piercing and scarification and continued to teach others to do a thing which they had abandoned for many years. In fact, a flow of going back to magic, witchcraft, seers, prophets, ceremonies and sacrifices and the old superstition had started. This happened due to (1) the failure of our leaders to explain what sort of freedom or government we were going to make. Most of our people are illiterate and have never travelled beyond their tribal boundaries making them ignorants and cannot therefore imagine of any other government other than the one our forefathers had before the coming of the European; (2) the Christianity failures; (3) the fact that Kikuyu are theists who very much honour and obey their God as they are directed by his prophets, seers, magicians and witchcraft doctors made the *Mau Mau* organizers make all the rules in the name of God who would supervise every individual as they all honoured him. This might be the cause of Mau Mau religion and superstition, on which the obedience and faith is built.

I must remind the reader here that, right from the beginning, the *Mau Mau* had been reported as 'intimidating oaths to its people'—this also happened to all its rules and policies. There were no arguments, reasonings or opposing in the movement as these could lead to betraying the movement—[they] were always settled by death. It then followed that whatever had been passed by the councils as rules or suggestions, whether right or wrong, had to be carried on.

The following day as I was going to Nyeri, I discovered 71s. in my pocket. Someone must have put the money in my pocket while we were taking the oath, knowingly or unknowingly. I thought that I would keep the money until I get the owner and then return it. Arriving at Nyeri, I took one shilling out of the money and bought a Social Service League lottery receipt, thinking that the money might have been my luck. It became true. I won 2nd prize, 726/48s. I came to learn later than Kituku Kamaitha had unknowingly put his money in my coat when we were harassed to take the oath and so I refunded it to him.

As we had been requested to induce our friends to take the oath, I cunningly asked David Wahome to accompany me to a feast some two miles away from home where I knew that an oath ceremony was held. This was very near Stanley Mathenge's home. Mathenge presided at this oath ceremony and gave a speech just the same as the one I had heard a week ago. This oath had been attended by over 200 people.

Mathenge referred to the movement as 'Our Government' or 'The African Government'. He explained to us that in the Central Province all our Administrative Officers had been elected and that they were doing their work well. He added that we should soon know them. He told us that we were to obey and respect the 'headmen' and 'chiefs' who had been elected by the African

Government. I learned later that the Colonial Government had been copied out and that the elected persons were only waiting for the day of taking over the Government. Councils started from the Sub-Location, Location, Division, District, to Central Province and, perhaps, to the Central Government. These councils consisted of nine elected persons who had powers over all plans, rules and judgements.

My school holidays ended and I went back to Muthua-ini School where I was teaching; some 12 miles from home. Being mostly busy in school working hard for my pupils to pass the Government Kenya African Preliminary Examination that was to be held in 2 months time, I did very little to help *Mau Mau* within the two months.

CHAPTER VII

THRESHOLD OF REVOLT

As noted earlier, Government's declaration of a State of Emergency on 20 October 1952, the large-scale arrests of prominent African nationalist leaders and the subsequent series of repressive measures meted out against KEM tribesmen combined to precipitate the very revolt they were ostensibly designed to crush. The implicit Government assumption that the underground and nationalist movements would collapse with the removal of their key leaders and a massive display of British military might proved somewhat faulty. While the Movement was stunned into temporary passivity and partially disintegrated by this two-pronged Government assault, it was still a long way from beaten. Leadership passed into the hands of the now unlinked district and lower-level councils of Nairobi and the rural areas and a number of militant, though semi-educated or illiterate, local leaders began moving into the forests which would become their future bases of operation. Others followed during the next few months, urged on by fear, hunger, a desire for revenge, a sense of duty or adventure, a will to strike back or a combination of these factors. The Nairobi organization, hard-hit by the arrest of Central Province and 'Central Committee' members and the repatriation of unemployed Kikuyu workers, started rebuilding—a new Central Province Committee was formed and links began to be fashioned between urban groups and those emerging within the forests of Mount Kenya and the Aberdares.

Recruitment during this period was stepped-up and an increasing number of youths and young men were, like Karari, volunteering to take the Warriors' Oath. Since it has been maintained by some writers[1] that this Second Oath was so vile and debasing as to place its takers irrevocably outside normal Kikuyu society, Karari's statement that 'it was a horrible oath, though typically

[1] See particularly L. S. B. Leakey's *Defeating Mau Mau*, p. 84–87. Methune & Co., 1954.

Kikuyu', deserves some comment. To begin with it should be noted that several features of the oath, particularly those involving sexual symbolism, were regarded as 'horrible' by each of my informants, and, I presume, by all other initiates. This fact, however, underscores their 'typically Kikuyu' character, rather than demonstrating the opposite. To understand this, one must realize that the Kikuyu are traditionally a very puritanical people regarding sexual deviancy or exhibitionism. Even minor public displays of emotion toward the opposite sex are likely to be frowned upon and few Kikuyu are willing to discuss the intimacies of their sexual life with more than one or two very close friends. Traditionally, sexual taboos were calculatedly 'broken' only within the framework of certain puberty rites and important oaths. Thus, a person accused of killing through witchcraft had to submit, if he maintained his innocence, to a public oath in which he swore, while inserting his penis in the vagina of a sheep, that he did not commit the crime in question and calling on the wrath of Ngai to destroy him if he were lying. Again, if a man were accused of having impregnated a girl and he denied it, he would have to publicly swear, while biting a piece of sweet potatoe or the tip of a bunch of bananas which had been inserted in the girl's vagina by an old woman, that if he'd ever had intercourse with the girl, the oath should kill him. Modern versions of both these oaths were common features of the Warriors' Oath.

Three conclusions can be drawn from the above. First, that the sexual acts or symbols performed or invoked while swearing an oath were calculated violations of acknowledged taboos designed, in both traditional and modern usage, to revolt and inspire awe and fear in the initiates or accused. Second, that according to Kikuyu belief, the more vile or repulsive were the acts performed while swearing an oath—i.e., the more highly tabooed such acts would be in everyday life—the stronger and more binding did such an oath become. Third, that Karari and others should have found the second Oath both 'horrible' and 'typically Kikuyu' was, in light of the above, both a normal and highly predictable response.

*   *   *

News around the country were proving that *Mau Mau* was becoming more active in eliminating persons who could not be changed in their faith together with those who were suspected that they could inform the Government about the movement, mostly Government supporters such as chiefs, headmen, police and informers.

The most striking incident occured about a month after my membership, which was the death of Senior Chief Waruhiu in Kiambu District, who was stopped while driving on the outskirts of Nairobi and shot dead on the 9th October 1952. His death was celebrated with great applause and drinking parties. I remembered that when young I used to hear a song which wished Chief Waruhiu and Chief Koinange to be buried alive. A fortnight after his death, the Government declared a State of Emergency on the 20th October. On the same night the Government arrested and detained 83 political leaders including Jomo Kenyatta, the President of KAU. Among the political leaders arrested were Kikuyu Independent Schools Association and Kikuyu Karing'a Schools Association leaders, businessmen, trade unionists and local newspaper men. Though no physical action followed the arrest of the top leaders—[a Government operation] known as 'Jock Scott'—yet it strengthened an ill-will against the Government for arresting our beloved leaders.

The following day a British Battalion (Johnnies), the Inniskilling Fusiliers, arrived here by air from the Middle East to strengthen the 3rd, 4th and 5th KAR's [King's African Rifles], the Kenya Regiment, the Kenya Police and thousands of untrained young chaps from mainly Somali and Turkana tribes. [The latter] were employed and all were distributed all over the Central Province, which is occupied by the Kikuyu, Embu and Meru (KEM tribes). Their main duty being to control oath taking and to guard the chiefs, headmen and Government servants from *Mau Mau,* who were continually gaining strength.

Two days after the declaration of the emergency, Chief Nderi of Nyeri District was informed that a Mau Mau oath ceremony was held in day time in a garden full of banana plants down in the Gura River Valley. He rushed out with his three tribal police guards armed with two rifles, a shotgun and an automatic revolver which the chief had. They were directed to a place where they were ambushed. To their surprise, they were all chopped to pieces and the gang made off with their arms.

This incident happened about five miles from the school I was teaching. When the Government received the news, a few hours later in the afternoon, many security forces were sent to the area to arrest any person they suspected that might have the knowledge of the incident. Many people fled to the forest when they saw the security forces approaching, but more than 100 were arrested for interrogation. At dawn next morning, a collective punishment of confiscating all livestock in the Chief Nderi's location (Thegenge) was enforced. The security forces performed their duty and by midday tens of thousands of heads of cattle, sheep and goats and pigs were lowing at the Nyeri Showgrounds. Many of them were butchered while others were herded to Dorobo awaiting for marketing.

No Kikuyu could claim for his animals or any property. The Government had regarded all Kikuyus as the enemy number one, the *Mau Mau*, with very little confidence in a few chiefs and headmen. The security forces, being very certain that the Kikuyu had nowhere to forward his claims, began robbing him money, clothing, beddings, furnitures, utensils, livestock, and raping girls and women. My wife fell victim to those rapers and begot a child. [This was in 1955 and resulted in the birth of Karari's second child, a girl.] It is true to say that many Kikuyu met their death while trying to prevent their property from being taken away by the security forces who had found a chance of collecting their personal wealth from the Akikuyu.

At this time the chiefs, headmen and some church elders thought that they would be killed at any time by the persons who had taken the *Mau Mau* oath and were working and walking with them as spies. They quickly searched for all the persons who had not taken the oath and sought loyalty to them. This group, later to be known as Home Guards, bitterly implemented severe beatings, different types of torture to *Mau Mau* suspects, while seeking confessions.

I eye-witnessed the beating of a person who had run away from Thegenge Location trying to escape from being arrested as a suspected person for the interrogation of Chief Nderi's death. He had fallen into the hands of a Karaihu Sub-location headman, David Mbutha, who badly beat the victim to unconsciousness. The man died on a lorry on the way to Nyeri Police Station. This headman is known to have killed more than ten people all by himself while seeking confession or eliminating his enemies, mainly his opponents.

At this time, two persons were badly wanted by Government; one of them was Dedan Kimathi, the Secretary-organizer of KAU's Thomson's Falls Branch, who had been reported by many confessors as the chief oath administrator and organizer of the *Mau Mau* movement in the Rift Valley. The second, Stanley Mathenge Mirugi, whose name and photo had been used in publishing a song book which advertised the Movement, praised the leaders, degraded and warned Africans who helped the white community and set prayers and religious hymns. To make it worse, some confessors had said that the Chief Nderi's death had been organized by Mathenge.

The police circulated advertising leaflets, one of which contained Mathenge's photo, and a reward ranging from 5,000s. to 10,000s. to the capturer, or informer who would lead the capture or to anyone who would present any of the heads to the Government. This made the two persons with their followers to run away into the forest on 1 December 1952 in order to escape their death. The police announcement made the two persons more significant figures to the people. Thereafter, thousands of confessors used Kimathi's and Mathenge's names as their oath administrators as a cover for the truth. It automatically followed that anyone who committed a crime wrote a letter calling himself Kimathi or Mathenge. In this way, the two persons became famous all over the country through the press and broadcasting informations which aimed at spoiling their names.

The arrival of Messers Fenner Brockway and Lesley Hale M.P.'s in Kenya at the invitation of KAU of 29 October, and also the tour of the Secretary of State for the Colonies in the *Mau Mau* affected areas, were used as evidence assuring people that Mr Peter Mbiyu Koinange, KAU's delegate to the British Government, had been successful in presenting the case of the African alienated land and the achievement of our freedom, and that the return of the alienated land would be announced soon after their return to England. This propaganda, which looked true, encouraged people to have more faith in the movement.

But in spite of such sweet propaganda, the situation was becoming worse and worse daily. The Home Guards' brutal methods of extracting confessions had revealed the secrets [of the Movement] and the names of members. The Government continued to strengthen its forces by bringing in U.K. battalions and by conversion. Every Kikuyu had to admit that he had taken the *Mau Mau* oath in order to ensure his life, including those who hadn't taken the oath as it had become so dangerous that a denial of having taken the oath was often replied by a bullet or a club on the head and many died before the rest yielded. With this, the Kikuyu, Embu and Meru were repatriated from Tanganyika, Uganda and mostly from the Rift Valley where over 200,000 Kikuyus had been living. Many of them had been born and bred in the Rift Valley Province and couldn't tell exactly what part of Kikuyu their parents belonged. These people, unloaded at the District Centers, had no food, were homeless and helpless.

At about the same time the Government closed over 300 schools which were under the management of KISA or KKES, thereby causing 60,000 children to loose their education. In Nyeri District, only ten of the KISA schools, under the leadership of Johana Kunyiha, were not closed, as they accepted the Beecher Report. While still teaching in one of these schools, I learnt that thousands of Kikuyu young men were returning to Rift Valley to revenge for their livestock and other property confiscated by the Kenya settlers, while thousands entered the forest to escape the Home Guard and the security force brutality; 15 years to life imprisonment had become an easy court sentence to members and leaders of *Mau Mau*.

Up to this stage, the plans and actions of *Mau Mau*, the name of the society made popular by the Government pressmen, were only known by persons who had taken the second oath. In fact, one was ignorant of the movement until he took the 2nd oath. At about 10 a.m. David Wahome, my assistant teacher, and I were knowingly led by Johnson Ndungu, one of my teachers, to an oath administrator, Daniel Muthua, about three quarters of a mile from the school. On the way I noticed a few scattered guards.

Inside the house was Daniel Muthua alone; his assistant was doing something else in the next hut. We were the only two persons to be initiated. He dipped some herb leaves in a Kikuyu gourd containing a mixture of goat's blood, its abdominal dung [i.e., the undigested stomach contents of the goat] and water, then sprayed us with it uttering words of cleansing and blessing. Each at his own time, we were initiated.

Naked, I stood facing Mt. Kenya, holding high a dampened ball of soil (damped by milk, animal fat and blood—the most important dairy products) in my right hand and the other ball against my navel by my left hand. There were five two foot pieces of the goat's small intestines laying on the ground about a foot and a half apart and I was instructed to step over these one at a time when completing the set of vows I was about to take. Then, repeating the words of Daniel, I said: 'I swear before God and before the people who are here that...

(1) I have today become a soldier of Gikuyu and Mumbi and I will from now onwards fight the real fight for the land and freedom of our country till we get it or till my last drop of blood. Today I have set my first step (stepping over the first line of the goat's small intestine) as a warrior and I will never retreat.
And if I ever retreat :
May this soil and all its products be a curse upon me !

(2) If ever I am called to accompany a raid or bring in the head of an enemy, I shall obey and never give lame excuses.
And if I ever refuse :
May this soil and all its products curse upon me !

(3) I will never spy or inform on my people, and if ever sent to spy on our enemies I will always report the truth.
And if I fail in this :
May this soil and all its products curse upon me !

(4) I will never reveal a raid or crime committed to any person who has not taken the *Ngero* Oath (*Muma wa Ngero*, Oath of Violence or Crime) and will steal firearms wherever possible.
And if I ever reveal our secrets or fail to use or turn over to our warriors any firearms I acquire :
May this soil and all its products curse upon me !

(5) I will never leave a member in difficulty without trying to help him.

And if I ever abandon a member in trouble :
May this soil and all its products be a curse upon me !

(6) I will obey the orders of my leaders at all times without any argument or complaint and will never fail to give them any money or goods taken in a raid and will never hide any pillages or take them for myself.
And if I fail in these things :
May this soil and all its products curse upon me !

(7) I will never sell land to any white man.
And if I sell :
May this soil and all its products be a curse upon me !'

I dropped the two balls of soil in a Kikuyu gourd which contained a Kikuyu knife and a Kikuyu needle. I then sat down on a stool. He gave me the well stripped chest of a billy goat, from the neck to the testicles. It had a hole in the bottom and he told me to put my penis in that hole and hold the goat's chest upright with both my arms. I then repeated the vows for a second time, each time biting the goat's chest and ending... 'May this *thenge* kill me,' and finishing by crossing the 2nd small intestine line.

He then took away the chest and brought a Kikuyu pot and kept it upside down in front of me. He then put the *ngata* [the bone, containing seven holes, which joins the head and neck] of the billy goat on the pot and gave me seven small *mugere* sticks. I repeated the oath for the third time, putting a *mugere* stick in each *ngata* hole and each time ending, 'And if I... May this *thenge* kill me !' I crossed the third line of small intestines.

He removed the *ngata* and brought an eye of the goat on the pot. He then gave me seven kei-apple thorns. I repeated the oath for the fourth time, each time pricking the eye with a thorn and ending... 'May this *thenge* kill me !' As I stepped across the fourth line of intestines, he removed the eye and brought seven sodom apples strung together on a thin hard reed and put them on the pot. He then gave me the same kei-apple thorns and I repeated the vows for the fifth time, pricking a thorn at every sodom apple and each time ending... 'May I be pricked thus if... !' and also crossing the fifth line of the small intestines.

He removed the pot and the sodom apples and picked up the

Kikuyu sword, knife and needle. Swinging these over me seven times, each time banging them down on my head, he uttered the blacksmith's curse, condemning me to death if I violated the vows I had sworn. He then brought a very small Kikuyu gourd that contained a mixture of lion and leopard fat. He dipped a reed in it and with the fat made a cross on my forehead wishing me to be as brave as a lion or a leopard and to have their personality which would frighten my enemies. He then asked me to lick the remainder of the fat off of the reed. The ceremony was over. I dressed and started back to the school with David Wahome, who took the oath before me.

On the way to the school we discussed the oath we had taken. We resolved that it was a horrible oath, though typically Kikuyu. All the vows had been militant. We had definitely been employed in the Gikuyu and Mumbi military force. 'But what would happen if one disobeyed these vows,' Wahome asked. 'Well,' I replied, 'In my opinion, though the oath itself may have no reaction, I consider that I have repeatedly vowed under God's name and that if I disobeyed the oath, my lies would anger God whose wrath might result in all the courses I have made... and most likely I would meet a death penalty from the society.'

'You are quite right,' replied Wahome. 'Remember that hundreds of people have been killed, even the well-armed European families—the Ruck family on North Kinangop and Commander Mikeljohn of Thomson's Falls. To violate any of the vows would mean to taste death. At present the Government is completely unable to control *Mau Mau*.'

'Oh! I care very little for Europeans having been killed. For many years they have killed many Africans but none of the Europeans has ever been sentenced to death by their courts of justice for killing an African in the whole 60 years history of their rule. They regard us as sykes or baboons. I wish *Mau Mau* courts had power to sentence many of them to death until they feel the result of their injustice and their hyocritical teaching "Love thy neighbor as thyself," which they never practiced. It is useless for them to teach us of the great Chinese philosopher Confucious who taught his people, "Do to others as you would have them do unto you." '

'What do you think,' I enquired, 'of *Utuku wa Hiu Ndaihu* (The Night of Long Swords)? As the rumour goes, if all the Kenya tribes are taking the oath as we are doing—which I hope they are doing —and a well-organized plot is carried out, it may be possible to kill all the Europeans at a given time since everyone of them has at least three Africans serving him, while many of them have hundreds of African servants.

'Did you note that the vows we made are of fighting plans?' I asked.

'Yes,' answered Wahome, 'that we were told frankly. But you see, the plan might have been in existence for many years and since the society is very secretive, even within its own members, it would be difficult for the ordinary person to know about it unless he was involved in the activity.'

'Now, since all the top leaders are detained, who do you think would carry on the plans?' I asked.

'Well, their lieutenants of course,' replied Wahome. 'Mathenge and Kimathi are likely to lead the war and they will soon become heroes.'

We arrived at school, took lunch and prepared for the afternoon lessons.

CHAPTER VIII

NO ROOM IN THE MIDDLE

DURING the first few months of open revolt, from February through May of 1953, Karari found himself playing a double, sphinx-like, role; one which became increasingly fraught with ambivalence and danger. As the major patterns of resistance were being established within forest, town and countryside, this dual role was becoming fixed as a way of life for countless thousands of Kikuyu, Embu and Meru peasants, particularly the women, children and men too old to bear arms. At night, or with great care and secrecy during the day, they attended meetings and oathing ceremonies, carried food and material to supply depots near the forest boundary, provided refuge and lodging for active fighters or new recruits passing through the village, purchased or stole weapons, ammunition, medical supplies, etc., for the guerrilla units, and performed numerous other tasks in support of the 'fight for land and freedom'. During the daylight hours, however, these same peasants feigned loyalty to the white man's Government and tried, under steadily mounting pressure and hardships, to carry out the normal tasks and duties of their everyday lives. Many willingly endured this ever dangerous and harsh double-life, filled increasingly with fear, anxiety, suspicion, hunger and brutality, for one, two and, in some cases, even three years. Others, whose existence was no less dangerous or miserable, endeavoured in very pragmatic fashion to play both sides against the middle, seeking to accommodate Government with one hand and the revolutionary forces with the other in a frequently vain effort to safeguard their own lives, loved ones and property. For still others, like Karari, there was no room in the middle; their situation required that they openly declare, in actions as well as words, either for or against the revolution. Karari, whose recollections reflect the ambivalence inherent in his position, decided to throw in his lot with the revolution, though this decision was ultimately made for him by the flow of events. Others faced with a similar decision, and especially those who had achieved an education equal or superior to Karari's lined up on the Government side.

*   *   *

The following week I would take my 18 pupils, who were to sit for KAPE, to the Catholic Church Mission Boys' School, Nyeri, where I would spend a week helping the [proctors] during the examination period. Soon after, we closed the school for the Christmas holidays. The holiday was very dull. Instead of the good Christmas songs, bullets echoed everywhere, [as well as] cries for the deceased, for blazing houses, for the robbing and raping; the cry of beatings and tortures in the chiefs' centers, in police and prison cells. Instead of feasts there were fasts enforced by sorrow. It had been made illegal for a group of five persons or more to be found anywhere at any time in the whole of Central Province—unless under Government supervision. Curfew orders to remain inside houses from 6 p.m. to 6 a.m. were imposed. Sadness surrounded all over. I could not go to Mahiga, my location, as a moving pass was required and worse of all, my location had been marked by the Government as the *Mau Mau* nursery in the district. I prayed and wished the New Year to come quickly and change our horror and and sorrow into happiness in which we would be victorious.

Nevertheless, the New Year did not bring any change but, instead, a mass compulsory cleansing ceremony sponsored by Government was enforced. This was performed by witchdoctors (often called Her Majesty's Witchdoctors) who were mainly *Mau Mau* members or sympathizers. In reality, they were only deceiving the Government that they were cleansing people. I attended one of these ceremonies held near the school as a spectator. As a Christian, I did not have to undergo this cleansing. Instead, I swore on a Bible at the D.C.'s office that I was not a member of *Mau Mau*. By this time the Government servants had confidence in me as a good teacher who had not taken the *Mau Mau* oath. The holidays ended and the school reopened, again with all the classes full, according to the Beecher Report, while many children still vainlessly searched for admittance.

At 10 a.m. on 21 January 1953, I received news from Consolata Catholic Maternity Hospital, Nyeri, that my wife had delivered our first born baby. In an hours time I was in the hospital to see our daughter. For the following one and a half months I took care and interest on my wife and our baby and the school.

On the night of 26 March 1953 two well organized *Mau Mau* raids took place at Naivasha and Lari. The Naivasha Raid was on a police post which was taken by surprise. After a short time of exchanging fire, the police guards ran away. Our warriors entered the camp, released all the prisoners, broke into the armoury and made off with all the arms and ammunition. According to Government's report, our warriors gained 47 precision weapons, including 18 Bren and Sten guns, and 3,780 rounds of ammunition. Our warriors claimed to have gained over 100 precision weapons from the Naivasha Raid. A young Fort Hall mute named Mungai, who had recently started speaking, was among the Naivasha raiders. His name was used spreading propaganda that he was a God's prophet and had led the raid with supernatural powers—that his little Kikuyu knife turned all the bullets into water. This propaganda was believed by many persons in the forest and reserves. After the raid the mute disappeared—dead or alive, the people in the forest could never tell, for it took them many months believing that God's prophet was in a camp somehere in the Aberdares.

This raid increased the strength and fame of *Mau Mau*. I thought they must have had good plans. The other raid was on Chief Luka of Lari and his supporters. The plan was successful. He and his wives were killed and their houses set on fire. I learnt from friends who witnessesd, that in the morning the Government killed ten times as many persons as the ones who had been killed and set more houses on fire. It was then claimed that the whole action had been committed by *Mau Mau*, in which more than 100 men, women and children had been killed. As I looked at it, there were two motives behind the Government action. The first, a revenge which, by being uncontrolled, went beyond their intentions. The second, to disdain *Mau Mau* for the mercilessly unjust killing of women and children, thereby causing the sympathizers to think that the *Mau Mau* have lost sight of their enemies and have started killed the innocent ones and that probably the following day would be their turn. This only meant to cover [i.e., hide] the *Mau Mau* aims by a horrible action to the eyes of the people.

I personally sympathized with the innocent children [who died], no matter which side killed them. But the blame cast on *Mau Mau* to the world by Government for the action was unfair and [false propaganda]. It only made me think that the British believe that killing by a gun or bomb is right, while killing with a *panga* is evil. To me, it made no difference whatsoever. But who has killed more innocent women and children, British or *Mau Mau*? I wondered whether the bombs dropped on towns and cities by the British during the First and Second World Wars—and in his many other wars—spared the lives of the innocent women and children for which they were blaming us. And who dropped the atomic bomb on Hiroshima? How many died? Compare them with the 'Lari Massacre'. Radio, press and films were used to inform the world of the barbarous, uncivilized Lari Massacre. Yes, uncivilized —but the British haven't stopped it [i.e., uncivilized killings of innocent people]. Neither have the civilized French, who have been killing innocent women and children in Algeria for over seven years, stopped it. This left me with the thought that the British were either blind in seeing their own errors, while they were bright in exposing their opponents mistakes, or they were doing it deliberately for their selfish injustices.

The Naivasha Raid marked the rising power of *Mau Mau* and was followed by a flow of thousands of young men entering the Aberdare and Mt. Kenya forests. My home, being only 300 yards from the fringe of Aberdare Forest, began to be used as a waiting place whereby the new recruits from Muthua-ini Village would await for the forest warriors to collect them, heading for Karia-ini H.Q. In this way, I was many times invited by the North Tetu Sub-location Committee. Its duties were (1) passing on of orders and instructions from the locational committee; (2) the enrolment of new members and the supervision and administration of the oath; (3) the spread of propaganda; (4) the collection of information about the opposers and informers; (5) the collection of funds; (6) the equipping and directing of recruits to the forest. I was only concerned with the latter. I was given money by the committee to buy rain coats, clothes, medicine, boxes of matches, *pangas*, etc., and distribute them to the recruits, hand them over to a guide to my house 12 miles away where they would stay for a day or two awaiting the warriors from the forest to come for them.

The sweeps and patrols in search of hiding or named *Mau Mau* increased. As my house in the school compound was never searched, we held many meetings there and it became a hideout for many

during the hours of patrol operations. Twice, after a long and tiresome patrol, the headmen, Chief Muhoya and his well-armed
askaris [i.e., police, soldiers] stopped at my house and had a cup
of tea and talked about *Mau Mau* while the very persons they
wanted were hearing them sitting in the next room. Outside my
house was the school playground filled with police, military, Home
Guards and the villagers. Chief Muhoya had ordered that every
man in his location had to join the Home Guard. Their duty was
to guard throughout the night the place allocated to each group.
It then happened that in every Home Guard group of about 50
men, only less than five were not members of *Mau Mau* and in
some groups all were *Mau Mau* members. *Mau Mau* personnel
were appointed to be headmen's guards in order to maintain a
flow of the Government plans and information. I had asked the
chief to give me a group of Home Guards for guarding the
teachers during the nights as I had learnt that many teachers
were being killed and schools destroyed in protest of the Beecher
Report. The group he gave me for guarding contained the organizers and most active members of the village, while the group
guarding the school building had only one person, the group's
leader, who had not taken the oath.

The Headman received some information that I hid the wanted
Mau Mau during many of his searches. One night, after the Headman had failed to catch two persons who had been seen by an
informer, my house was surrounded at 3 a.m. The Headman called
me. I told the two wanted persons to go under my bed. In my
pyjamas, I opened the door. The Headman spotted me with his
torchlight. He entered the sitting room, moved his torch all around
and then asked me how many we were in the house. "Me and my
wife," I answered.

He then asked for the dormitory keys. I took the keys and walked
out. Noting that the house had been surrounded by Home Guards
from another group, I greeted them and led them toward the
school dormitory. I opened the door and they entered, thinking
that the wanted persons were inside. They found nobody and left
with a great disappointment. I locked and returned to my room
and told my friends not to worry—the Home Guards had left.
Though they spent the whole day in my house, I had a feeling
that someone must have told the Headman of my activities in the
movement. I decided that I would ask the Headman what he had

in his mind when he inspected my house at night and try and gain confidence in him.

By mid-May, the *Mau Mau* strength at the Karia-ini Head-quarters—situated in the Aberdare Forest about 10 miles on the Othaya ridge in my division—was so great that the Government forces headed by military were several times killed or driven back at their attempts to reach the H.Q. In this month, Othaya Police Post and Kairuthi Home Guard Post, situated in a market of stone shops, were both raided on the same night by warriors from the H.Q. The Kairuthi Raid was successful, killing 18 Home Guards, gaining 3 precision weapons and looting the goods in the shops. I learnt later that the warrior who died at Kairuthi had been shot by one of his colleagues in mistaking him for the enemy.

The Othaya Raid was unsuccessful. The place was well-guarded. Sacks filled with soil were used to build a protection wall against bullets. A high guard's tower was armed with automatic weapons and hand grenades. The fight broke before all the warriors were in ready position as the guards had seen them. The *Mau Mau* retreated after a heated exchange of fire leaving a dozen dead warriors behind the barbed fencing wires while others were drowned by the Thuti River. I couldn't know the truth for the country had become full of propaganda from both sides. Neverthe-less, [these raids] won fame to *Mau Mau* in its propaganda.

At about the same time Gatumbiro Home Guard Post, five miles west of the school, was raided, killing three, gaining one shotgun and burning to death 17 others inside the post and suffering no casualty on the side of *Mau Mau*. Less than a mile north of this post, Bildad Giticha, Supervisor of the Church of Scotland Mission School, was attacked in his shop. He ran out in the darkness and escaped death, but his thumb and two fingers were injured by a bullet. Six neighbouring schools were attacked and equipment destroyed. Thousands of heads of cattle were taken from the reserve into the forest for the warriors' food. To follow these cattle meant death to anyone.

Bildad Giticha, with his bandaged hand suffering from *Mau Mau* wounds, was posted in my school to assist me. We arranged with him that he would be taking his lunch in my house and that he would always drive to Kamakwa at 4 in the afternoon where he was sure of security. After a week's stay with Bildad Giticha, I received a letter from *Mau Mau* unnamed leaders in the Aberdare Forest. It read :

Dear K. Njama,

We have been informed of your good activities. Many of our recent recruits praise you very much for equipment, guidance help and your wife's welcome. But there is something you should bear in mind and that is (1) You are still teaching under Beecher's Report; (2) We have been informed that our enemy Bildad Giticha lunches with you in your house and that you have been dressing his wounds helping him to recover. (3) You cannot serve two masters. We advise you to leave that job or join us or else you will find yourself in trouble.

Thaai [i.e., Peace],
AB Court No. 7

The letter upset my mind. I could not change my job. It was bad to remain jobless. The only job that Government would offer is to fight on its side against my people. 'Oh, no! I wouldn't do this!' I would arrange to meet Stanley Mathenge at home and discuss my situation with him—whether he knew of the letter or would like me to be his secretary.

Before I settled my plans, Muthua-ini Headman, Karinjoya, alias Kariuki, was raided at night. He and his daughter, who tried to help him, were badly injured by bullets and his houses and stores were put on fire. His wife and children were allowed to come out of the houses before they were set on fire. When all the buildings blazed, the gang made off, leaving the Headman's wife and her children standing outside. The Home Guards who came for help managed to take him out of the fire but he died on the way to the hospital.

The next day I took all the pupils and teachers to his funeral, which was attended by Chief Muhoya, all the locational headmen, and some Tribal Police who fired shots for the deceased's honour. In the evening I received a second strong warning that if I did not resign from that management they would take for granted that I wholly supported the Beecher Report and the Government and that they would regard me as an enemy and would not hesitate to kill me. The letter also reminded me of keeping Bildad Giticha in my house—who might be a Government informer, particularly on my activities. It also said that after the victory was

won, all the schools would be reopened under African management, but that now was the time to fight for land and freedom.
The letter was signed by Dedan Kimathi.

Worried about my security and still awaiting for a reply from
Stanley Mathenge, I collected the remainder of the school fees,
some 300s., and took it to the District Education Officer on Satur-
day morning on the 30th May 1953. He gave me a receipt and
issued me with a transfer form which notified me that I was to
commence teaching at Nduni-ini School on the slopes of Mt.
Kenya on 4 June 1953. I was not known in that area and *Mau
Mau* there was very active. I thought that I was getting into more
troubles. I could hardly think of aiding the Government and, on
the other hand, Government had failed completely to protect
teachers from *Mau Mau* attacks. The Home Guard group, up to
the moment, that had been guarding me was composed of all the
active persons who had taken the 2nd oath, and with whom I had
been collaborating in helping the fighters.

I had five days off duty according to the transfer form in which
I would make all the necessary arrangements. Pushing my bicycle
uphill toward the school, I thought of the right and the revolution
results. At that time *Mau Mau* was winning. Hundreds of Europeans were running away out of the country while others left their
farms and ran for security. All the farms within five miles from
the forest edge were left to *Mau Mau*, who drove thousands of
cattle to the forest for their food. When the Government forces
tried to follow the cattle in the forest, they unknowingly fell into
the ambushers' traps who surprisingly opened automatic fires on
them, in many occasions killing them all and gaining arms, ammunition and clothing—mainly the Government uniform which was
used by the *Mau Mau* fighters to help them to approach the
enemies deceived by their own uniforms.

On the other hand, Kenya was ripe for independence, whose
demand brought the revolt and only granting self-government to
Kenya would bring harmony again, I thought. When Kenya gets
its independence, the people who have fought against the oppressive Government would become very famous and their history
would be immortal to the Kenya African Government. 'But I have
already been employed as a warrior when I took the 2nd oath. I
am not a coward; my grandfather was a great warrior.' I remembered his *kiembo*, the story of the white man he had told me, and

cast my eyes on Karari's Hill in the Aberdare, where I believed that thousands of warriors were living and feeding on European cattle while fighting for my land. 'I will join them.' In my life, my curiosity had increased my anxiety to witness events rather than to hear them. I decided to record the Kenya revolution by witnessing the events in the forest. I made my minds to visit Mahiga the following day for my arrangements before I left for the forest.

I arrived home at 6 p.m. Feeling tired, I asked my wife to give me warm water for a bath. By 7 p.m. the group that guards me had not arrived. The new headman was conducting a night patrol with them. At 8 p.m., a gang of 21 men, armed with four rifles, three shotguns, one .22 gun, one pistol and one .44 gun, and led by Mathenge Kihuni, arrived at my house from Kigumo Forest. Three of the warriors were persons I had directed to the forest less than a month ago.

Mathenge Kihuni told me, in a friendly way, that he had been sent by Stanley Mathenge to take me to the forest for some discussion with him and his committee. I had no alternative but to go. I gave my wife 200s. and told her to take it to George Maagu, a man who had been selling me his land and whom I had [already] advanced 150s. I asked my wife to be shown a piece of land by the man which she could cultivate and get food during my absence.

Without any preparation, I tied up my blankets and some clothings, bid my wife and my little daughter goodbye and set off for the forest—leaving my bicycle to Johnson Ndungu.

It was 8 :15 p.m. when I left my house and after a short distance we stood and Mathenge Kihuni divided his gang into five groups composed of four persons. He remained in the group I was, making six persons. He ordered the groups to collect food, clothing, money, medicine, news (matemo) and the recruits from the persons in charge of the area. He told them where to meet at 1 a.m.—in a home near the forest boundary. We departed and made our way toward that home. On our arrival we met many girls who had brought food to that home, which was used as one of the forest suppliers. Inside the house were three big fat rams which we slaughtered and cooked. When the groups arrived they had 25 recruits who carried heavy bundles. We could not carry all the raw foodstuffs that the villagers had brought [and] Mathenge made a promise of coming again to collect the food.

We set off for the forest, a gang of 47 persons. At dawn, we could hear the cocks growing in the reserve as we entered the dark, cold, wet forest. Before continuing my story it is necessary to give you at least a general picture of Nyandarua, or the Aberdare Forest. As I have lived in this forest, and travelled widely there, for over two years I would certainly present you with a real picture.

From its southern reaches in the Kiambu District to its narrow tapering extremes in the north—Nderagwa, near Thomson's Falls—Nyandarua stretches some 120 miles. Its width measures approximately 50 miles in that section of the forest which separates the Kikuyu districts of Nyeri and Fort Hall from the [European] Settled Areas of the Rift Valley.

Going up the 11,000 foot height of Nyandarua from either the plains of the Rift Valley or the hilly regions of the Kikuyu Reserve, one passes through the forest fringe and into the wide belt of coniferous indigenous 'black' forest which is extremely thick in parts so that no weed can grow and contains large numbers of forest animals who drink from the many streams and rivers and feed on the forest growth or on one another. This region gradually changes into thickets of bushes all along the northern border. This is the real home of all the wild game in this forest, where you find large herds of rhinos, elephants, buffaloes, deer, bush bucks, gazelles, wild hogs, sykes, colobus monkeys, baboons, leopards, cheetahs, hyenas, and many others. (In fact, after the Emergency, this area was appointed for Royal National Park and one would enjoy the scenery and look at these animals who survived from bombing death and all sorts of air raids.) Unlike the rest of the forest, this is the only warm place and has much growth for animal food, while the cold and dense forest hinders the growth of their food in other areas.

Above the 'black' forest lies the thick bamboo forest belt which in places is more than 15 miles wide. In the maze and tangle of bamboo, standing as high as 30 feet in its middle and decreasing to mere bamboo bushes in its either ends, travel was difficult if not impossible for those who didn't know it intimately and in detail. One could hardly see beyond ten yards. The sun never shines in this area and it is extremely difficult to know east or west without a compass. The bamboos in a considerably large area are alike. In many occasions a person found himself surprisingly standing at his starting point after six or so hours of continuous walk. The only paths are those on ridges, formerly used by honey collectors who had hung thousands of beehives on the trees, or those which had been made by animals moving from one place or region to another or the aimless ones made by the animals while herding. With no signs to guide ones movement, it is easy to get hopelessly lost. Even when one knew his way movement was made difficult and dangerous by sharp cutting leaves and pointed new shoots of the bamboos on the paths and the ever-present danger of charging rhinos. Nevertheless, the difficulties and dangers of travel in the bamboo forests made them excellent places for us to set up our camps. While we came to know a given section very well and learnt to move rapidly through the dark tangle of bamboos, we knew from experience that it provided us with an extremely good defence against attacks from the inexperienced security forces.

Moving through the bamboo forest one comes to the cold grassland flat-topped area known as the Moorlands, which stretches about 75 miles in length. Here, amongst many ponds and swamps, small bushes here and there, and with patches of forest and grassgrowth beneath, life was made very difficult by the extreme cold. Clouds often cover the area very close to the ground and, combining with strong winds, make it damp and cold. During the nights, all the dew freezes to ice which would start melting when heated by the sun or in the cold months remain covered by ice near the high peaks. The [twin] peaks of Nyandarua stand a little over 13,000 feet above sea level. Though we travelled the Moorlands and used it for certain purposes, such as storing foodstuffs and trapping the animals which fed on that ever-green grass, we seldom set up permanent camps there. When strong operations were held in the 'black' and bamboo regions we occasionally moved in this area which supplied us with meat and honey and gave us chances of seeing the enemies approaching far away in the grasslands.

In addition to large rivers such as Chania, Gura and Marewa, the forests of Nyandarua are filled with many smaller rivers and streams. It is not surprising to find 20 or more such streams in an area of one mile. Usually we set up our camps near one of these cold, clear, silent flowing streams, which provided us with cooking water as well as fish from the big streams. High in the mountain these rivers and streams are extremely cold and freezing to death or drowning was a danger of which we were all aware—particularly when one of the larger rivers had to be crossed during the flooding season.

All the various types of wild animals in the forest became our friends with the exception of the rhinos, which we called 'Home Guards' because of their brutality and willingness to destroy human life. They became accustomed to our presence and smell and, after a few months in the forest, they treated us as simply another form of animal life and we in turn learnt all their habits and calls. This proved extremely useful to us in detecting the presence or approach of strangers. Security forces entering the home of the animals smelling of soap, cigarettes and laundered clothing were greeted with many danger and warning signals or calls from the animals. In many cases they were charged by rhinos, elephants and buffaloes. The deer, monkeys and *ndete* birds with their acute sense of smell and sight [respectively], were our best guards against the encroachment of strangers or enemies. Whenever we observed these animal warnings we sent out our scouts to investigate. Almost without exception, we found the warnings of our 'allies' to be accurate and because of this assistance they rendered us, we passed a strict rule prohibiting the killing of friendly animals who had kindly welcomed us into their home.

These forests then, while cold and damp and with thunder storms and heavy rains during most of the year, became the home of over 20,000 men and women revolters fighting for the Kenya African Freedom. Many, like myself, lived and fought in Nyandarua for two, three or even four years. For us, these forests became a home and a fortress as well as the provider for our most basic needs.

PART II

The Fight in the Forest

CHAPTER IX

NYANDARUA: THE EARLY MONTHS

KARARI did not enter the Aberdares, or *Nyandarua*, until May of 1953, several months after the outbreak of open hostilities. It might be useful at this point, therefore, to consider some of the major features and developments of this formative period as they relate to early forest groupings and the emergent patterns of peasant resistance. Let us briefly, then, shift our attention back to the period between October 1952 and April 1953.

It has already been noted that as Government pressure mounted during the first few months of the emergency, a growing stream of Kikuyu, Embu and Meru peasants began drifting into the bush or forested areas bordering their homes. This movement was slow, sporadic and, at least in the early stages, unorganized. It was by and large a reaction to external stimuli rather than the unfolding of a well-laid plan for revolutionary action or guerrilla warfare.

In general terms, this movement to the forests might be described as a 'withdrawal', stimulated in the main by fear of Government repressive measures and reprisals. Obviously, however, there was a considerable range of variation with respect to individual motives and specific external stimuli. Fear was frequently combined with anger, with a desire to fight back or retaliate or with a sense of mission, a dedication to the Movement and the struggle of 'right' against 'might'. As with all revolutions, less lofty motives could also be found—such as the desire for personal safety, power or material advantage. In most cases, as with Karari, a number of these factors combined in varying degree within a single individual.

Bearing this in mind, we might look at some of the more concrete conditions which led to the entrance of certain segments of the population into the forests. First, let us consider those individuals who entered the forest with the positive idea of preparing and organizing a military struggle against the adversary. Many of these men held prior positions of importance in the Movement at the district or divisional level as organizers and/or oath administrators. Some were being actively sought after by Government and two such men, Stanley Mathenge and Dedan Kimathi, entered the Aberdares in December 1952 with prices on their heads. Like others who went early to organize the fight, these men were inspired, among other things, by a personal sense of mission along with a firm conviction that their cause was just and that their God, *Ngai*, would assist them in the struggle for land and freedom.

A larger section of youths and young men entered the forests in several stages. Having taken the Warrior's Oath and being active in local militant wings, these men were a primary target of Government's security forces. At first, they remained at home during the day, carrying out their normal economic and domestic tasks, and assumed the role of fighters only at night. For many, however, this life became fraught with too much danger and they began hiding in the nearby bush during the day, returning to their homes at night to carry out raids on guard posts and Government loyalists' stock, to eliminate informers and traitors and to assist in the administration of oaths. As more and more security forces poured into the Central Province, however, and night patrols and Government raids on suspects' homes increased, many of these small groups moved into local forested areas or, where they adjoined the locations, into the forest fringes of Mount Kenya and the Aberdares. For the most part, these men shared the militant outlook of the early forest organizers. Some, however, were attracted also, and perhaps equally, by the safety and protection traditionally afforded by the forest.

Another segment of the youth were administered the Warriors' Oath and recruited directly into groups already based in the forests. The decision as to whether or not they should go was thus largely removed from their own hands. While refusal at this point, after voluntarily taking the 2nd Oath, would have been tantamount to betrayal, most needed no such threat, as the dangers of remaining in their home locations were seen as greater by far than the portending life in the forests.

A fourth element, comprised largely of urban and White Highland repatriates, were driven to the forest as much by hunger as by any other factor. Most were landless and many had lost what little stock they had possessed through Government or settler confiscation. Herded into hastily erected district centers, many were faced with the alternatives of starvation, a life of petty crime or entering the forests to fight for their food. Several thousand chose this latter course and entered the Aberdares either directly from the European Settled Areas or after spending a short time in the Kikuyu Reserve.

Finally, there are those who entered the forest primarily out of fear of remaining in the reserve. Collective punishments, forced confessions, general mistreatment by the security forces and the fears and frustrations generated by the dual role forced upon most passive supporters of the Movement, simply drove these peasants into the forests. Their flight was thus motivated largely by an urge to escape the dangers of rural life for the relative protection offered by the forest. Few realized that the struggle might last two or three years. Most were thinking in terms of a few months; they would thus 'wait it out', in much the same manner as in the past their people would have awaited the end of a Masai raid. In this sector of the forest population belong most of the girls, women and older men ... as well as some of the more frightened youth. Once there, most would participate actively in the forest struggle; many, however, continued to place primary importance on personal safety and survival.

Of the several thousand Kikuyu, Embu and Meru tribesmen to enter the forests during this early period, the educated were notably conspicuous in their absence. Karari, having completed two years of high school, was to my knowledge the most educated man in the forest forces of Mt. Kenya and the Aberdares. While some of the men had had three or four years of formal schooling and a few had completed the eight year primary course, the vast majority of guerilla fighters—youths, men, girls, women and elders—were illiterate peasants, many of whom had never been beyond the local station.

How does one account for this fact considering that the Kikuyu are generally acknowledged the most educated and 'advanced' or acculturated of all Kenya African peoples? While it is true that the actual percentage of educated Kikuyu was very low, despite their comparatively high standing alongside other tribes, this does not really explain their *total* absence from the forest. It is also true to say that virtually all high-ranking educated leaders were removed by Government before the drift to the forests began. But what of the many school teachers, clerks, journalists, medical assistants, etc., who were not detained during the first few months of the emergency? The answer, I believe, involves a number of factors which here deserve brief mention.

As previously noted, the general socio-cultural ambivalence of the educated Kikuyu yielded a highly equivocal position on the part of the latter *vis-à-vis* the underground movement. Opposed to colonial rule and generally supporting the political objectives of the Movement, the educated tended nevertheless to be against those aspects of the oath and Movement which seemed to them a degrading return to the past. During the critical months following the emergency declaration, therefore, it is not surprising that ambivalent feelings such as these led many educated Kikuyu into the position of 'moderates', wishing to wait it out on the sidelines rather than join the guerrilla forces gathering in the forests. Some joined the ranks of the passive supporters, a larger number gravitated toward a pro-Government, 'loyalist', position and many, at least for a time, played both sides simultaneously in a pragmatic effort to stay alive.

The educated Kikuyu, in addition, generally had more to lose in the way of jobs, wages, security, status, etc., than the less fortunate landless peasant or unemployed worker. Many held jobs with Government agencies, schools, hospitals or private firms that provided a standard of living which, if indeed very low in absolute terms, was considerably higher than that of most of their illiterate brethren. Not only were they thus more susceptible to Government propaganda, but working and residing as many did outside the main areas of recruitment, they were considerably less subject to the social pressures exerted upon others to guarantee their loyalty and active participation in the Movement.

Finally, it is also possible that a significant number of educated Africans were highly sceptical about the chances of resisting, let alone vanquishing, the armed might of the British with an odd assortment of *pangas*, *simis*, home-made guns and a few precision weapons. While many an illiterate peasant believed the enemy to consist of only a few thousand white settlers, the educated were in a better position to assess the actual strength of the colonial government. Though more likely an after-the-fact rationalization, perhaps it was only the uneducated peasant, spurred by a confidence in Ngai's assistance not fully shared by the educated, who could muster the courage to attempt the 'impossible'.

Let us now look at some of the general features of early forest groups. In considering this formative period, it must be realized that there was a good deal of local variation and general confusion. Nevertheless, certain generalizations can be made which apply, I believe, to the vast majority of groups which entered or were formed in the forests of Mt. Kenya and the Aberdares during the three to four month period following the emergency declaration.

Comprised largely of youth and young men who had taken the Warrior or *Batuni* Oath, and frequently including a few girls, women and elders, these early groups ranged in size from fifteen to fifty or so members. Recruitment, though based explicitly on the 2nd Oath, had an implicit territorial aspect in that most groups contained persons drawn from a single sublocation or location in the reserve or area in the Rift Valley. Organization was loose in the sense that there was no clear-cut division of labor, hierarchy of roles or differential privileges. Where women were involved, however, they normally performed their customary domestic tasks of cooking and fetching firewood and water; new recruits might also be given the more arduous task of carrying supplies from the reserve to the forest.

Though overall strategy and long-range aims were either absent or very confused during this period, most groups evolved similar tactical patterns and immediate objectives. Concerned primarily with conditions and events in their home locations, most groups established themselves in adjacent sections of the forest fringe. The fact that not all locations bordered the forest helps explain why some groups remained within the reserve, retreating to the forests only when pursued by security forces.

Hiding within the forests during the day, these groups would re-enter the locations at night to collect needed supplies, gather information, visit kith and kin, participate in oathing ceremonies, recruit new members, raid Home Guard posts or loyalists' stock and eliminate known traitors. To unify the community, both through the oath and the elimination of pro-Government elements, was a primary objective of most fighting groups since it guaranteed the greatest possible security under existing circumstances for both themselves and their supporters and facilitated the acquisition of supplies and recruits. In many instances, near or total support was achieved, with Home-Guards—as in Karari's village—and even headmen being active members of the Movement.

In structure, the forest groups of this period were quite simple. Integration existed, for the most part, only at the primary level, with relations between individual members of each group being articulated by a chosen leader. Normally, such leaders were selected on the basis of their demonstrated abilities, popularity, reputation, previous position in the Movement or some combination of these factors. The process of selection was informal, much as in pre-colonial times, and was usually accomplished through simple consensus. The responsibilities of a leader toward his followers, and their loyalty to him, were in most cases reinforced by strong kin and neighborhood ties.

The position of *leader* was not ordinarily circumscribed by any special privileges during this period; nor did those holding such a position normally possess a formal title or rank. Their decision-making powers were confined largely to camp-site selection, the allocation of tasks and tactical matters—though in the latter sphere some groups contained a seer or *mundo mugo* who, as in the traditional age-regiment system, exercised an influence in determining the time and place of raids. Regulatory and adjudicative powers and procedures were neither formalized nor consistent from group to group.

As to their relations with other groups within the Movement, the only formal link maintained by these early forest groups was with their respective sub-location or location groups and councils. We have already indicated the basic operational features of this relationship, as regards supplies, information, recruits, etc., but it is important to note the supporting role assumed by most local groups *vis-à-vis* their respective fighting groups. While the warrior-wings were originally subordinate to their local councils, the revolutionary situation tended to reverse this relationship, with elders' councils becoming increasingly subordinate to militant group leaders.

As the relation of fighting units to supporting masses is an important aspect of any guerrilla war, it might be mentioned here that the Government policy of collective punishment tended to make the local councils somewhat more conservative than fighting-group leaders. This is understandable, since a raid or killing in the sub-location often brought swift Government retaliation, the brunt of which was suffered by the civilian community. Collective fines, the confiscation of livestock, harsh forms of interrogation, arrest and internment in concentration camps were some of the punishments inflicted upon passive supporters. To avoid such repressive measures, many local councils sought to retain some measure of control over the fighting groups. This was particularly true in Kiambu, where the district council of elders prohibited the killing of loyalists or traitors without council consent and for some time retained their control over the guerrilla units.

During this early period, relations between the various fighting groups within the forest, reserve and Rift Valley were unstructured and contact between them was slight and sporadic. At the outset, few even realized that groups similar to their own existed or were being formed in other areas. A similar situation prevailed regarding forest-group relations with Nairobi groups and councils. In the city, the initial shock and confusion which set in after the emergency declaration were just beginning to clear in the early months of 1953.

A number of factors might be said to have conditioned the further integration of forest groups and the formation of large, permanent camp-clusters. Not least among these was a structural tendency toward unification grounded in the fact that all revolutionary forest groups were faced with both a common set of life-circumstances and a structurally unified enemy. The tendency here, as in comparable situations of social conflict, was for opposing groups to assume a common level of structural complexity. This tendecy was reinforced among guerrilla forces both by the shared ideological base and central-command orientation of the Movement prior to the emergency and by the traditional Kikuyu pattern whereby military age-regiments cut across and linked the various local communities within a sub-tribe.

Another, and perhaps more concrete, factor lay in the desire of many small forest groups to attach themselves to leaders of demonstrated ability and wide-spread reputation. By March of 1953, several men in different sections of the forest had gained repute through their daring in raids, organizational abilities or the strength of their particular units. These leaders tended to attract other groups and individual fighters who obviously felt their own strength and security thereby increased.

Finally, there was the obvious advantage to be gained from a concentration of fire-power. Most forest groups were very short of arms and ammunition and hence sought either to merge with other groups or establish some working relationship which allowed for the maximum concentration of arms for both offensive and defensive purposes. The prevailing military situation tended to foster this development. During the early months of 1953, the Aberdares and Mount Kenya were the unquestioned domain of the revolutionary forces. Government had established no permanent bases in either area, heavy bombings had not yet begun and security force attempts to carry the fight against the insurgents into the forest were feeble and generally ineffective. Under such conditions, the growth and integration of forest forces was both feasible and desirable, increasing security and offensive capacity and mitigating some of the more severe transportation and communication difficulties.

The small, loosely organized forest units thus began to give way toward the end of this formative period to larger, more tightly organized groupings concentrated within a number of large, permanent camp-clusters.

CHAPTER X

KIGUMO CAMP

LOCATED in the Nyeri section of the Aberdare Range, just south of the Gura River, Kigumo provides an excellent example of the large, permanent camp-clusters which began to take form in February or March of 1953. While Kiambu is regarded by most Kikuyu as the 'brains' of the tribe, Nyeri is viewed as the 'spear' or 'brawn' and has traditionally been the most militant of the Kikuyu districts. It is perhaps no accident, therefore, that Nyeri contributed 40 per cent to 50 per cent of the estimated 15,000-man-strong guerrilla force which was operating in the Aberdares by July 1953 and produced the revolution's most prominent leaders and organizers. As with so many other Nyeri products and ideas of this period, Kigumo Camp was to provide a model and example for fighting groups in other sections of the forest.

Karari's vivid recollection of Kigumo as it existed in May 1953 illustrates the major changes in structure and organization which had taken place among Aberdare groups over the preceding few months. From the small, relatively isolated and loosely organized groups of forest fighters there developed large, permanent camp-clusters within which, and largely as a product of increasing numbers, the division of labor, differentiation of roles and hierarchy of military ranks became formalized and made explicit in a number of rules, regulations and procedures. Each camp within a cluster, though retaining its own leaders and identity, now shared in the responsibility of maintaining a joint supply and sentry system and collaborated in the planning and execution of raids.

The numerical growth and integration of Aberdare groups was not a haphazard affair. Just as the small groups of the earlier period were comprised largely of persons from the same village or sub-location, so were the large camp-clusters made up in the main of persons and groups from the same location or division. Kigumo Camp, for example, was comprised with few exceptions of persons from the Tetu Location of Nyeri; a location which bordered the forest and contained a pre-emergency population of over 20,000. This territorial basis of recruitment and integration was conditioned by a number of factors, including (1) the desire of persons to unite with friends, neighbors and kinsmen, (2) the community of local interests and fears regarding family, land, Home Guards, etc., (3) the local basis of the supply system, (4) the proximity in the forest of groups wishing to remain close to their home locations and (5) the Movement's prior segmentation along territorial lines.

The formation in May 1953, just prior to Karari's journey to the Aberdares, of a Nyeri district council and army—i.e., the Utuma Ndemi Trinity Council and Ituma Ndemi Army— reflected and tended to crystalize this territorial segmentation of forest forces. Not only was Nyeri District set off from the other Kikuyu districts, but internal segmentation was based on existing administrative divisions within the district. Thus the letters in *ITUMA* symbolized 'The Warriors of Tetu, Uthaya and Mathira Divisions'.

Through the district council, comprised of all Nyeri forest leaders, formal links or relations were established between some forty guerrilla units containing almost 6,000 fighters by the end of June 1953. In this process of integration, certain decision-making, adjudicative and enforcement powers, held originally by the numerous small-group leaders, were relinquished first to camp-cluster leaders, heading informal councils of section heads, and then to the Nyeri district council.

Council officers were elected by the Nyeri forest leaders and a military chain-of-command established when the Council Chairman, Stanley Mathenge, was chosen to head the Ituma Ndemi Army and the rank of *General* was issued to six of the major camp-cluster leaders. An important principle established here was that military rank be conferred on the basis of position within the Council. Thus the Chairman of the Ituma Ndemi Trinity Council became almost automatically the head of the Ituma Ndemi Army and other office bearers were likewise given high military rank. Again, and at least in part to confirm or concretize these new ranks, positions within the military hierarchy were circumscribed by differential privileges and symbols and the highly egalitarian nature of the early forest groups was thus mitigated.

*   *   *

We continued our journey in the darkness climbing up the Kiandongoro ridge and by sunrise we were a mile inside the forest. Here, the road passes through a forest plantation of pines patulla. Thousands of acres of indigenous coniferous trees have been cleared by the forest squatters to whom an acre was allocated to each to cultivate for only three years and then the Forest Department planted timber trees, shifting the squatters into another dense forest to clear.

As we moved through maize fields, though all the crops had been destroyed by the Government so that the forest fighters may not feed on them, one cannot hesitate to admire that fertile land with its layer of black humus ranging from six inches to more than a foot in many places, on which grows such healthy and fruitful crops. We soon came to Kiandongoro, an evacuated village on security reasons, and there on the border between the dense forest and the bamboo region stood a small Kiandongoro Forest School with stone foundation, slab walls and shingled roof in which monkeys and baboons had become the 'pupils.'

After a short walk on the ridge road, we turned to the south and started descending the slopes of the Gura River which forms the fertile Kigumo valley at its bottom. We were then entering more dense bamboos measuring five to six inches in diameter at the bottom and more than twenty-five feet high. The soil could not be seen as the ground was covered by a layer of dry bamboo leaves and footprints could not be traced. The area is covered by many springs with clear, cold-running water. The leading person made a halt signal and we all stopped. He thrice whistled like a certain night bird and received a reply by the same call. This was to inform the guards of our approach so that they would not regard us as enemies. There stood six armed guards. We shook hands, reported the country news, they gave us a password, 'kilima,' and we left. After 200 yards walk we stopped again and two persons were sent to call Mutobachini, the leader of the camp. He came with three armed warriors [and] after greeting, we left a quarter of the raw food we had carried there to be stored. I learnt that was the supplies camp, though we did not see it.

At midday we sat down by one of the streams and took our lunch, which was boiled rams meat and some cooked vegetables from the reserve. Mathenge Kihuni who was leading the group knew me as a leader and treated me as his equal. We had a little rest during lunch time, through which I had a chance of observing every type of precision weapon they had and learned how to operate it and the terms used for them. *Makara* ('charcoal') meant ammunition, *Mwaki* ('fire') equalled gun, *Kamwaki* ('small fire') equalled pistol, *Gatua uhoro* ('the decider') was used for the [big] game shooting guns ranging from .375 to .450, *Bebeta* [from a Swahili term, *pepeta*, meaning to winnow or sift] equalled Sten gun, *Makombora* ('the destroyer') meant Bren gun.

After lunch we continued our journey. I noticed that all the time only one person was leading our way. He was supposed to know more about the forest on the grounds that before the emergency he had been visiting the forest for the purpose of hunting or collecting honey from both bee hives and the forest trees. A person who had such knowledge was called *muirigo*, literally meaning 'a clear forest path.'

At 2 p.m. we crossed the River Gura in Kigumo Valley about eight miles from the reserve boundary. Half an hour later we found a wide path made by our fighters which came from Kigumo Forest squatters' gardens to the Kigumo camps. The path was strategically made up through a steep rocky slope which ended on a flat natural bench at the edge [of which was] a big fig tree where the guards stood. The enemies' bullets could not catch the guards while the guards had all the chances of shooting the enemy. Before we started climbing the steep slope—the guards' challenging area—our *muirigo* gave a password, '*Hiti*,' which literally means hyena. The six guards were armed with one Sten gun, one two-barrelled .44 gun, two .303 rifles, one shot gun and the last guard had two grenades and a *simi* [a double-edged traditional Kikuyu sword]. After exchanging greeting and a little talk we entered the gate [i.e., pathway] for the first camp some 400 yards ahead.

At 3 p.m. we arrived at the camp. It had more than thirty rain shelters where these people slept. Each shelter had four poles; the first pair six feet high while the hind pair was five feet high.

[Each shelter was rectangular, measuring approximately 12 feet across the front and having a 9 foot depth.] The roof, built of bamboo splits and made to overlap a pair of joints, looked liked a tiled roof from the inside. The outer side of the roof was covered by bamboo bulks which provided a satisfactory rain proof. The walls were uncovered. The ground had been slightly levelled and bamboo leaves spread on the ground made a mattress. In the middle of the camp were two big kitchens measuring about twice the size of a hut. Two girls, a woman and three men were busy boiling some meat in two tins and a big saucepan; all the time taking much care that no smoke could be seen by an airplane. Thin dry bamboo splits were used to keep the fire burning without smoke. There were two leaders' houses seven by seven feet; the only ones which had walls to protect [against] wind and cold, this being the only difference from the others.

This section dressed in the normal clothes but seemed to have lasted more than three months without washing or changing. It was rainy season and all the area was wet and muddy. More than forty warriors wore the police uniform of black raincoats and hats. The camp had a lot of cattle beef well hanged on trees and the nine thousand foot altitude was a very good refrigerator which prevented the meat from going bad. The camp was very clean, all the bones were heaped on a bamboo table; some long split bamboos were used as pipes to bring water right inside the kitchen.

Mathenge Kihuni introduced me to the section leader, General Nyama. Then, sitting in his room, [the latter] ordered some meat for us. He said that he preferred the food we had brought from the reserve and that he would like it fried with a lot of fat. We were given a cows cold tongue which I thought was boiled the night before. After eating we were given hot soup which had a half-bitter taste of wild herbs which were supposed to increase health and remedy some diseases. When I wanted to help myself at a short call, I was given a *panga* and instructed to dig a hole and cover properly my excreta. I learned that to be one of the camp rules.

While we were talking with General Nyama, I asked him how I could see Stanley Mathenge as I had been called by him. He hesitated. 'No newcomer in this forest is allowed to see Mathenge or Kimathi until he has completed seven days. You can only see him at his own consent.' Then Mathenge Kihuni confirmed that he knew very well that I had been called by Stanley Mathenge and that he was the person who was sent for me. Nyama said that Mathenge was living at the Headquarters Kariaini and that it was very likely that he had accompanied Kimathi to Murang'a (Fort Hall). Mathenge Kihuni confirmed that they had left for Murang'a and that they would not stay long there. At this juncture the guard commander interrupted by announcing permission for the camp to collect firewood. General Nyama went out to give some instructions.

By the time he returned, he was accompanied by two section leaders, Wanjau and Githae Mugweru; the latter a person I had taken care of in hiding during a Home Guard's patrol, fed and supplied medicine to him and his friend. They had both escaped from the Settled Area after receiving severe beatings for being oath administrator suspects. He was very much pleased to see me and he invited me to his camp about 300 yards west. He also told me that Wanjau's camp was 300 yards south uphill. He asked me whether I had seen the six guards under the big fig tree. He told me that each of the three camps sends two sentries to guard the main entrance of their camps.

We arrived in his camp when all people had gathered in the center of the camp to say their evening prayers. Then, all facing Mount Kenya with some soil in our right hands, one person said our prayers :

Oh God, the most powerful! We praise thee for guarding us throughout the day. We have raised our hands to show you that the soil you gave our forefathers is now being used by strangers who have robbed us of our lands, our gift and inheritance. These strangers are killing us for our lands. God, mercifully look upon the spilt blood of our brethren and hear our call and cry. We have no weapons to fight against these people but we believe that thy sword will defeat our enemies for we are your sons and daughters, we believe that you did not create us so that we might become servants of other people in the lands you blessed to our Father Gikuyu and Mumbi.

God, close the enemies eyes so that they will not see our people who have gone in search of food and let our warriors who have set off for raids defeat our enemies by surprise. Bless our dinner, keep us, guide us and guard us from all diseases. Bless the water, honey, fruits and vegetables of this mountain so that they may become good food for us. Let all the animals in this forest become our friends.

We now remember our oppressed people in the reserve, prisons and detention camps. We pray for all our leaders, those who are leading us in the forests and in the camps. We pray you for our leader Jomo Kenyatta, guard and guide him. Grant him power to defeat the enemy so that he may lead us rightly in the land you gave and blessed to our parents Gikuyu and Mumbi.

We pray you thus believing that you will hear us, our merciful Father, in the name of Gikuyu and Mumbi.

We all ended together by saying three times '*Thaai, thathaiya Ngai thai,*' which means, 'We praise Thee oh God,' or 'God's peace be with us.'

I estimated the persons I saw to be 300. Mr. Githae introduced me to his people, most of whom knew me and asked me to give a speech. As I was tired and unprepared, I only encouraged them that we were going to win our battle. Many of them surrounded me asking [about] home news and how their relatives were. The camp had four girls and three women and a few old men who were the elders. By this time the fires were made and I moved in Githae's hut which proved to me that the two camps had been built from the same plan. We kept warming ourselves talking of different raids while we awaited for dinner. Soon a fat cow's hump, well roasted, was brought to us on a plate. We ate to our satisfaction, followed by the same kind of hot soup half bittered by wild herbs.

As we kept talking with Githae, I learned that each of the three camps had an average of 360 persons and that the recruits were distributed equally among the three camps. I also learnt that General Kahiu-Itina was the head of those camps. I knew him as an ordinary carpenter before he entered the forest and by that time he had accompanied Mathenge and Kimathi to Murang'a.

I asked Githae to teach me the signals and terminology they were using. He then went on, 'If you meet a green branch planted in the middle of a path, that means do not pass there, there is danger ahead. If you meet two green branches dropped on either side of a path or bent, that means that the camp is near and you are approaching the guards and that you should give a signal. We whistle like a night-bird which says "*Kuri heho-i ndirara ku?*"

(literally meaning "It is cold, where shall I sleep?"). The guards will also reply your call and they would then await a friend and not an enemy.

'When you come to the sight of the guards, they would shout to you "Number!" [in English]. If you replied "Seven," they would know that you are an enemy because our people would only reply in Kikuyu, "*Mugwanja,*" meaning seven. Then the guard would say "Pass!" which really did not mean that you were allowed to approach the guards as an English speaking [person] would interpret, but that only asks you to shout the camp's password or if you are from another camp, you shout the name of the camp and its leader. The camp passwords are names of trees, animals or mountains, which are changed daily.

'Short sharp whispers [e.g., hss, hss, hss] indicate the enemy's approach or something to be observed, while long [low hisses] mean quiet!'

He also taught me some terminology : *itungati* meant warriors (plural) or non-commissioned officers [the meaning here is actually unranked fighters]; *Ihii cia muhitu* meant 'forest boys' or warriors [as did] *njamba cia ita; nyomu nditu,* 'the heavy animal,' meant *Mau Mau; Kiama Kiria Kiracoria Wiathi* meant The Council which is Searching Freedom [i.e., The Freedom Seeking Council, a name used briefly by the new Nairobi leadership]; *mbuci* meant camp [pronounced bushi and derived from the English 'bush']; *kariiguri,* 'it is up,' meant an airplane is approaching; *Gatimu* ('small spear'), *Gatheci* ('sharp instrument') and *Gathugo* ('a throwing weapon') meant Home Guard and was derived from *itimu* meaning large spear [stemming from the fact that Home Guards were initially armed with spears]; *Kenya Ng'ombe* meant Kenya Regiment personnel [*ng'ombe,* meaning 'cow' in Swahili was the Kenya Regiment emblem], and *icakuri* (singular, *gicakuri,* 'a heavy pitchfork') was used to mean any Government military personnel.

It was interesting to hear all those names that the forest people had invented. He also told me some of the camp rules :

(1) Everyone must wake up before dawn, just the time when birds begin their morning songs (which were regarded as their prayers) and all together say our morning prayers.

(2) Everyone must hide his belongings—clothes, blankets, cup,

plate and spoon, etc.—and the persons responsible for the camp's utensils or such must also hide them.

(3) The Guard Commander at each camp would select two sentries every morning who would be replaced at mid-day by a second group that would guard the camp's entry till sunset. As darkness was one of our guards, only a few persons were requested to pay attention to any approach while the others rested or chatted around fires.

(4) The Guard Commanders would check arms and ammunition always when new sentries were to take over.

(5) Nobody was to light any fire during the day for the purpose of warming or cooking without the Guard Commander's permission as its smell and smoke could betray the camp to the enemy.

(6) Nobody was allowed to go out of the camp without a written pass which he would show the guards while leaving or entering any camp.

(7) Nobody was allowed to eat any food before it was shared [i.e., distributed] by the head cook.

(8) All food must be kept by the camp storekeeper, who issued out the daily ration every evening according to the number of people in the camp and the [available] supplies in his store.

(9) Nobody was allowed to stay in the kitchen if he were not a cook.

(10) Nobody was allowed to make any noises or cut down trees around the camp before 6 p.m.

(11) No sexual intercourse was allowed as it was believed that it would bring calamity to the camp. [A traditional Kikuyu belief according to which sex was thought to weaken and bring disaster to active warriors and was hence tabooed.]

(12) Every person must bury his excreta whenever he or she goes to a short call.

(13) Nobody was allowed to go to [i.e., enter] the leader's house without his knowledge and consent.

(14) The camp's records must always be up to date in (i) Registration, (ii) How many people are out of the camp and what are their names, (iii) The sentry duties records, (iv) Raids and spoils records, (v) The arms and ammunition record.

(15) All the fires must be completely covered if an airplane roared during the night.

(16) The Guard Commander must inspect the sentries at any time to ensure that they were alert and that they had not fallen asleep. Guards were warned that death was the best punishment for a guard who was found asleep during his sentry hours but caning was the only one imposed.

(17) Everyone must obey the camp rules without question or hesitation.

Having learned a bit of signals, terminology and camp rules, I was getting sleepy for I had gone for a very long journey all the day long. Githae called a girl and asked her to make a bed for me in his hut. The recruit who had been carrying my blankets was called and asked to give them to the girl. The altitude, the shelters' structures, the bamboo-leaf mattress on the cold wet soil and the insufficient beddings made my first night extremely so cold that I wrapped myself with the blankets leaving no entrance for air. The night was cold and silent. At about three in the morning colobus monkeys started a roaring which continued all over the forest for a time. At 4:30, thousands of birds started their morning prayers which they presented in a very sweet music with different notes and pitches from different types of birds. We were all awakened for the morning prayers followed by the Guard Commanders' roster calls for the day's sentries.

I noted that some wore two or three pairs of clothes at the same time, while others had their blankets folded and hung over their shoulders under their raincoats. This was to provide them with warmth and the safety of their belongings in case the enemy took over the camp, would search for any hidden property and destroy or take them. I also noted that only the leaders had hot roasted meat and hot soup for breakfast while others went without. [Each warrior received rations only once a day.] They warmed themselves with the last night's charcoal covered by ashes and could not make fires as this was against the camp rules. The sun does not shine at any time under these tall thick bamboos and the area always remained wet and cold.

I wanted to know the strength of the camp, and so I asked Githae how many arms they had. He told me that his camp had twenty-nine rifles, five shotguns, two .22 guns, three pistols of which he kept one, a grenade and a dozen *banda* or homemade guns. 'The other two camps have almost the same amount because we share everything equally, but each has a Sten gun with the exception of my camp. But we always arrange our raids, camp guards and food transporting together so that we can have sufficient arms.'

At 10 a.m. we visited Wanjau's camp about 300 yards south uphill. We were escorted by two armed warriors. We didn't carry the pass letters for the leader was known and respected and the distance was very short. One of our escorts gave signals to the guards and we passed. Like the others, the guards' houses were built some sixty yards away from the camp and beside the path that led to the camp. All the houses were of the same plan. This camp had a place with sunshine where we found all the people warming themselves. We met Generals Wanjau and Nyama discussing a cattle raid for food. They resolved that they would raid Ihithe Village the following night. I expressed my wish to get to Kariaini Headquarters and they promised me some escorts the following day.

The cook was sent to prepare lunch for the leaders—some well-fried meat. I came to understand that they would not eat maize or beans, which could be stored for a long time without going bad, while they had meat which could not be stored for as long a time before it went bad. This must be the reason why I have eaten only meat in these camps.

I wanted to know whether the leopards and hyenas ate their meat which they hung on trees. Wanjau told me that all the animals had become friends and that they would neither attack anyone nor eat that meat. He went on, 'We pray for these animals who have kindly welcomed us in their homes and who have been put in our category by the security forces—in other words they regard us as animals. The rhino is our only enemy here inside the forest. We call him 'Home Guard' as he resembles those who did not take the oath. But there are no rhinos in the Kigumo Forest. We take it for granted that all the rest of the animals have taken an oath of allegiance. They have stopped running away from us; in fact the monkey and ndete bird are our guards. They tell us the approach of an enemy by their alarms.'

Because these animal alarms were often true, it made it easier for many to believe that God had given them such powers so as to help us to defeat the enemies approach. This led to the passing of a rule prohibiting the killing of an animal as it was thought that if we made these animals angry, they would probably fight against us and chase us from their home. The birds, mice, rats would come right in the kitchen to eat any food that might have fallen as though they were tamed. *Gituyu*, a type of big rat, as big as a cat with a two-foot whip-like tail, were so daring that they would eat maize from a person's hand and were not at all afraid. They broke their allegiance, [however] by going into our stores. They would eat as much maize as they could and carry as much as they could, as many trips as it were possible for them, to fill their stores in which they buried our maize. They were therefore killed.

The sun went behind the western mountains and we were back in the camp saying our evening prayers, after which fires were lit to warm ourselves. Githae proceeded on telling me of the formation of the Ituma Ndemi Trinity Council. He said that on the 25 May, all the leaders sat where we had spent the day and elected the leaders of the Ituma Ndemi Army. ITUMA is a name made from 'I'—from *I*tungati, meaning the warriors, 'T'—representing North and South *T*etu Divisions of Nyeri, 'U'—representing *U*thaya Division of Nyeri, and 'MA'—representing *Ma*thira Division of Nyeri. Then the three divisions makes the Trinity of the Nyeri Army. [*Ndemi*, literally "arrow head," referred to an early generation-set which was believed to have invented the art of metal-working and the first metal-tipped weapons.]

I was told that Stanley Mathenge was elected as the Head of Ituma Ndemi Trinity Council—hence the Head of Ituma Ndemi Army—and Dedan Kimathi as his Secretary. A few others were elected as Counselors. After the election all the top leaders left for Murang'a and probably I would meet them at H.Q. Kariaini on their way back. At this stage the dinner came, nice pieces of well-roasted meat stuck on short sticks sharpened at both ends. Taking out his small pocket knife to cut the meat, Githae told me that every person in the forest was entitled to have a sword, a knife and a box of matches which would enable him to live alone for some days if he happened to lose the others. Some more boiled meat was followed by hot soup. Everyone ate to his satisfaction.

After dinner, we arranged that I had to leave the camp for H.Q. Kariaini early the following morning, since my escorts had to return to the camp by three in the afternoon so that the arms they had could be used in the cattle raid that evening. We then fell asleep.

CHAPTER XI

KARIAINI HEADQUARTERS

KARIAINI is significant in that it represents the only permanent H.Q. camp to be established in the Aberdares as well as the largest and most developed of the camp-clusters which typified this period. In structure and organizational pattern it was similar to Kigumo Camp, though the military hierarchy of roles tended to become more formalized and symbolic status differentiation and privileges more pronounced after the formation of the district council and army. Under the leadership of Stanley Mathenge and Dedan Kimathi, Kariaini was to attract many Nyeri leaders and guerrilla units and became the major center for new recruits in this sector of the forest.

The rapid increase in numbers along with the development of a central command tended to diminish, though not eliminate, the importance of territorial segmentation among forest groups. The main H.Q. camp included persons not only from various locations in Nyeri District, but also numerous North Nyeri and Rift Valley people as well as several Fort Hall and Kiambu Kikuyu, a few Embu and Meru and even four Luo from the Nyanza Province. In addition, with many leaders acting in a concerted fashion to coordinate raids, maintain the security system and allocate supplies, the bonds between those of near or equal rank tended to become strengthened. The relevance of this factor will perhaps become clearer if we focus attention on certain features of the newly formed Ituma Trinity Council.

As indicated earlier, much of the decision-making and adjudicative power previously held by individual section and camp-cluster leaders was transferred to this district council which, approximating the pattern of traditional Kikuyu elders' councils, was to meet as the occasion required in order to hear cases, formulate rules and policies, and coordinate military planning and tactics. Though endowed with certain powers, however, it is important to note that the Council lacked what we might term an independent enforcement arm. Thus, while its leader-members voluntarily surrendered to it *rights* to formulate policy, reach judicial decisions and pass rules binding upon themselves as individual section or camp-cluster leaders, they failed to provide the Council with a *force*, independent of their own, to guarantee that its decisions and policies were carried out. Whether or not the Council's rulings were implemented, therefore, depended in large measure upon the willing compliance of its leader-members.

Closely related to this is the fact that the authority of each leader, while now *legitimized* by Council recognition, still rested primarily upon the loyalty he commanded from his own warriors. The latter, in turn recognized the authority of the Council primarily because of their own leader's membership and participation in it, rather than the converse. It is important to note while reading Karari's account, therefore, that while leader-leader loyalty within the Council was strengthened by the latter's power to issue military ranks, by the *esprit de corps* generated through the Leaders' Oath and by effective concerted action, this 'horizontal' loyalty between leaders was still secondary to the 'vertical' loyalty binding leader to followers and, conversely, followers to their leader.

So far, we have confined our discussion largely to Nyeri guerrilla forces. By June of 1953, however, there were numerous smaller and less well-organized forest groups operating out of the Fort Hall and Rift Valley sectors of Nyandarua. Contact with some of these groups was established in late May by Nyeri leaders and at least partial success was achieved in coordinating their efforts for the June 25th 'all-out raid'. While the relations thus fashioned were as yet informal and unstructured, they constituted an important prelude to the wider integration of Aberdare guerrilla forces.

Outside Nyandarua, some 5,000 fighters, mainly from the Embu and Meru Districts and the eastern locations of Nyeri, had established themselves in the forests of Mt. Kenya. A Nyeri leader, Waruhiu Itote, who later became widely known as General China, had been sent to organize the Mt. Kenya fighters in March by Dedan Kimathi. Only minimal contact was thereafter maintained between these leaders, however. For the most part, Mt. Kenya forces evolved their own organizational patterns and pursued an independent course of action throughout the revolution.

As previously indicated, other groups remained in their reserve districts, keeping out of sight during the day, carrying out raids at night and entering the forest fringe only as the occasion demanded. Sporadic contact was made by Ituma Ndemi Army sections with some of the guerrilla units operating in the Nyeri District, but none at all with groups in Fort Hall and Kiambu.

In Nairobi, the Central Province Committee had been reconstituted by June and militant units operating under the various urban district committees were formed. Less disciplined groups also emerged, some engaging in 'revolutionary activities' primarily for personal profit. Contact between Nairobi and forest groups had been established by this time, though no formal relations existed whereby policies, strategy and tactics could be unified or coordinated. Nonetheless, a fairly sophisticated supply and recruit system, operating largely at the district or location level, linked forest groups with their urban counterparts and a small but increasing amount of arms and ammunition, medical supplies, clothing and money were being sent into the forest along with the new Nairobi recruits. One of my Nyeri informants, Mohamed Mathu, who was then working as a draughtsman for the Nairobi City Council, described his role in this system as follows:

> My main task on the location committee was to fill in cards for the new recruits who were about the enter the forest. When meeting fighters from different areas, this card would identify the man as a comrade and remove suspicion of his being a Government spy. I also assisted in distributing the necessary equipment to newly formed fighting groups. Late at night, in an area of Bahati African Location called Far Bahati, shoes, raincoats, shirts, pants and jackets were issued to the men and they were escorted to our arms depot at Kassarani. About five miles from Nairobi, near the rock quarries and the Spread Eagle Hotel on the Fort Hall road, these recruits were issued guns, *simis* or *pangas* and were instructed for a day or two on the use of firearms. These weapons were being stolen or purchased in the city. On several occasions I helped escort these men to Kassarani. After turning them over to our permanent

guard for instruction, I would return to Nairobi in the early
hours of the morning. The new fighting groups, usually numbering one to two hundred men, would then be escorted in
small groups, first to Thika, then to Murang'a and finally into
the forest. Every night the men would pray facing Mt. Kenya
and then set off through the bush into the darkness. During the
day they would sleep and remain in hiding, being assisted with
food by our members in Thika and the reserve.

In summary, viewing the entire revolutionary movement as
of June 1953, we have noted the existence of four major zones
of guerrilla activity, i.e., in Nairobi, the Kikuyu Reserve, Mt.
Kenya and the Aberdare Range. In each of these zones, as well
as in areas of lesser importance in the Rift Valley and smaller
forests, the revolutionary forces operated with relative autonomy.
Unification or integration at this stage was confined largely to
guerrilla forces operating within each zone, and even here its
achievement was not yet fully realized.

*   *   *

After morning prayers, four armed warriors, one of whom was a
guide, were told to escort me to H.Q. Kariaini and another man
was asked to carry my luggage. We had breakfast and left the
camp at 8:30. On the way to H.Q. Kariaini I could see places
where bombs had been dropped and had ground the bamboos into
thin threads. When we arrived at River Thuti, we met the path
from the reserve to the H.Q. It was big and wide as a road;
thousands of cattle and people had for many months been using
it. There was no trouble of hiding footprints; in fact the warriors
enjoyed to ambush anyone who followed the cattle.

    After climbing a steep hill we came to a small flat grassland
patch. Our *muirigo* whistled the signal and after replies, we went
right across the grassland toward the guards whom we could not
see standing a hundred yards in front of us. There stood 20 well-
armed guards with five automatic weapons. We shook hands and
gave out our pass. I came to learn that the grassland area was
semi-circled by guards whom we did not see and who could only
attack when the head guards gave signals by either shooting or
sounding a bugle. There was no chance for the enemy to escape,

for even if the enemy retreated there were still guards along the path for 200 yards distance.

As we entered the camp, we first met a dozen of the guards' huts. These were rain shelters measuring 10′ by 8′ with sloping roofs thatched with *ithanji* reeds. The uncovered walls could neither protect [against] wind nor cold, but gave the guards the chances of seeing all directions and a quick way out. There was a fire place in every hut and at least a hundred guards slept here, about a hundred yards from the main camp. Over 200 such shelters made up the main camp, which had a cold, clear running stream across it. Three big kitchens with gabled roofs and measuring 20′ by 8′ were erected at suitable distances for their supplies [i.e., conveniently near the main clusters of shelters]. As I passed near one of them I could see tins and big saucepans boiling meat at 11 o'clock in the morning; taking care of the smoke, lest it be seen by an airplane. The camp was not at all afraid of land forces. As I approached the leaders' houses, I noted that they were built differently from the others. They looked exactly like European tents, with doors, and had a partition inside separating the bedroom from the fireplace. I also noted that the leaders had a private kitchen. Inside the camp I could see over a hundred well-armed men awaiting the signal from the guards. The rest of the people had gone to warm themselves by the heat of the sun over the hill.

The camp was located half a mile within the bamboo zone and built at the bottom of a steeply rising hill which had formed a natural bench on its northern end. To the south, the hill formed a tall wall, more than 1,000 feet above the head of a person standing inside the camp. To the southeast fell a steep cliff making a narrow ridge direct east which was the camp entrance. To the northeast, a continuation of the slope from the natural bench [descended] to the River Thuti, which drains many streams running from this hill. About a mile to the west was the great thicket of bamboo which, due to its old age, had all died and fallen to the ground making it impassable.

As all the top leaders had gone to Murang'a, I found Kihara Kagumu, Gicuki Mugo and Njau Kiore leading the camp. I did not know any before. My escort introduced me to them and, after a short time, left, returning to Kigumo Camps. When I was telling those leaders about the country news, two other leaders arrived; they were Gicuki Wacira and Thiongo Gateru (known as Watoria), both my relatives whom I was very glad to meet. Kihara ordered for lunch and quickly hot fat boiled meat was served on plates followed by the same soup. As we were eating, Gicuki Wacira asked me whether I had received Mathenge's message asking me to visit him in the forest. He told me that he was one of those who wanted me to go and help them and he was glad for my arrival. I then told them of how I had received the message and about my journey. Gicuki gave me a letter to read to the leaders. It had come from Mathenge stating that he would arrive the following day.

After eating, they invited me to their camps a quarter of a mile east at the edge of the cliff and located close to one another. The buildings are alike, the camp is a small one with 15 shelters and little more than 100 warriors. Gicuki's wife and her daughter came to greet me. There were many relatives and neighbors in the camp. Gicuki told me that Wacira Gathuku, another relative, was in charge of the H.Q. Hospital situated half a mile west of the H.Q. He warned me, however, that no persons were allowed to visit the hospital and advised me to write a letter to him asking him to come see me at H.Q.

I returned to H.Q. in the evening, during the prayer time. I was surprised to see more than 2,000 people (to my guessing) in the camp. Many of them dressed in the ordinary clothing while about 800 of them wore different Government uniforms which must have been acquired mainly from the dead security forces. A few had long and shaggy hair and beards. Some had woven [or braided] their hair like women while others had wool braided in with the hair to imitate the Masai. In fact, they could approach any Government force without being suspected. Nearly half the people were armed with swords or *pangas* while the rest had various types of European guns and more than 600 homemade guns. I could guess their ages; most of them were between 25 and 30 years old. There were a few old ones, well over 60 years. The leaders could quickly be recognized. They all tied turbans around their heads, looked more clean and healthy than the rest, wore shoes or boots, possessed either a wrist or pocket watch and carried a hidden pistol and a walking stick.

I was very much astonished by seeing nearly 1,000 youths who stood armed with only a sword or a *panga* and were ready to fight against the Government tanks and cannons of the Royal Field

Artillery Forces, the machine guns and the bombers. This was exactly what was prophesied some ten years ago [i.e., earlier] and reminded me of a youth dance called *Muthuu*. The dance was invented in 1942 by boys between the ages of 10 and 14. I was sixteen then. We tied rattles on our legs. The rattles were made of small tins in which we had put small stones and then pressed the opening so that the small stones could not come out. When these rattles were shaken they gave sharp rhythmical notes. On our heads we put long birds' feathers which were waved as we danced. In our hands we held a well-carved wood in the shape of a *panga* or sword which we called *muiko* or G. North ('genos')—the trade name on the *pangas* which were produced by G. North Co. in Nairobi. When dancing we referred to ourselves as Germans or Japanese and proclaimed that we did not care where the war might come from—'If from the air, we will fight; if from any side we will fight.'

Our prophecy had been fulfilled. Most of the people in the forest were those who had danced *Muthuu*. I came later to recognize that the seven months imprisonment we prophesied revealed itself to be seven years. More than 100,000 people, including Jomo Kenyatta whom we very much praised in our *Muthuu* and *Mucungwa* dances—though none had ever seen him—served an average of seven years in prison, detention or the forest, or in two put together or in all three categories. Prior to this, *Mihuni* songs created in 1939-40 by youths between the ages of 18 and 25 had prophesied unknowingly the scarcity of food and property, bravery and death in the thousands. One of the songs said : 'This mourning you have for the death of just one person; in our village 3,000 have died and I feel nothing. Having a knife and a walking stick, there is no thicket into which I wouldn't venture.' At last all the prophesies became true.

I did not take much time considering how a *panga* could fight against any of the jet bombers with their machine guns. Moved by emotion and will, I quickly believed that the time had come for all prophesies to be fulfilled—for such had turned out to be common gossip. The prophesy of the Kikuyu's honored witch-doctor, Chege Kibiro, who foretold the coming of the whitemen, the building of the railways and the going of the whitemen out of this country. I remembered the star that brilliantly shown in 1946 and moved from southwest to northeast which was claimed by witchdoctors that it indicated their departure and showed the whitemen the way home.

Our victory would just be a miracle, I thought. I believed that God was the most powerful, the creator of the world, who laid down the great oceans and rivers as boundaries and gave each race its own land. The Kenya Highland is our inheritance from the Heavenly Father Ngai. God did not create us so that the whitemen may have cheap labor from starving servants. God, whose name has been used by our people as the symbol of achieving our ends, would avenge for the gross injustice done to the Kenya Africans by the British Government under the influence of the Kenya Settlers. We had to defeat the Europeans, I continued to reason. There were 60,000 Europeans against six million Africans. Each European had to fight against 100 Africans. It did not matter if he killed half of them and finally be killed himself, making sure that the survivors would share the land that had been used by the European, cast down the colonial rule and form an African Government... which would accept European instructors, in technique, trades and industries. Their obedience and respect of the African Government would be the most important qualification for them to stay in Kenya.

My knowledge had been swept together with the thousands of ignorant warriors whose focus was only the Kenya Settlers. I had ignored the fact that the colonial system from U.K. was the source of our exploitation which we were determined to eliminate.

Night came and the fires were made. Kihara Kagumu invited me into his hut. While we sat down around the fire warming, I asked him several questions. First I wanted to know how many people were in the camp. He told me that there were 2,600 people of whom 124 women. 'Forty warriors and a dozen females,' he went on, 'are taking care of some 26 patients most of whom were injured during the Othaya raid. Wacira Gathuku, whom you wrote this morning, is in charge of the hospital. Harrison Gathinji and Muhindu are the doctors there.' I commented that I knew Gathinji.

'The camp has 450 European weapons and some 650 *banda* (homemade weapons). A group of 100 well-armed guards whose huts you saw a hundred yards away guard the camp entrance and they are the only ones supposed to be ready at every minute of the day or night. Njau Kiore, the tall black man who wore the police raincoat, is the leader of the guards section. His camp is four miles away, just one mile from the fringe of the forest. He has 300 strong guards who guard the entrance to Kariaini. If the enemy were seen entering the forest, the fight would start there and they would be unable to approach us up here. There are four other camps surrounding the H.Q. at less than a mile distance, each having an average of 300 people.'

He told me that though there was a supply of cereals from the reserves, the Chief food was beef from Native cattle. The policy had been to eat only the Home Guards' [i.e., loyalists'] cattle, but since all cattle were put together in pens which were strongly guarded, then we had to fight for them and keep records of food-stuffs, so that at the end it could be reported how many bags of maize, beans, wheat or potatoes, etc., we had used. It would be required to know how many heads of cattle, sheep, goats and pigs we had used. How much or how many belonged to the enemy and how many belonged to our members and how much to a particular individual would be due to him for compensation. 'You see,' he went on, 'our Government had asked us to fight but has not sup-plied us with any arms, food or clothing; whatever we spend then our Government would be responsible for compensation.'

The dinner was ready; well-fried meat with nice thick gravy and some doughs [i.e., fried corn-cakes] followed by soup. As we were eating, I raised a question on the Othaya Raid. He told me that about 400 people from H.Q. raided Othaya Camp at night time with the intention of releasing prisoners and acquiring more arms. About the same number of persons had to raid Kairuthi and Ihuririo at the same time. (Kairuthi raid was successful as I had reported; Ihuririo group failed to raid and the leader gave the excuse of being late right from the starting.)

'The Othaya Camp was well-protected with barbed wire fences,' he continued. 'The guards were laying in fortified covers behind soil sacks which had built a wall impassible by a bullet and in tall guards' towers which enabled them to see far away and secured their positions. The guards saw our people approaching the barbed wires and then opened fire before our people were ready. Some reported to me that they were over 300 yards behind when the fight broke and a heavy rain started pouring almost simultaneously. The Kenya Police inside the camp threw mortar [i.e., flares] in the air which shone better than the moon and changed darkness into light, making every one of our warriors visible. As our warriors were laying together along the barbed wire fences, they were badly beaten by grenades from the guards' tall towers above their heads. Though they managed to cut the barbed wires when one person was blowing a bugle, they did not enter the camp as they noted that many of their people were falling down dead. There were several cries, "Come to the Bren gun, I'm shot!"

'They retreated and ran away leaving behind the dead and the dying; taking with them only the ones who managed to walk when held. It was still pouring as they left and the River Thuti less than 200 yards behind them had so swollen that it wanted to swallow everybody who tried to cross it. The Bren gun was drowned with its owner, Kambo Wamwere, who had reported that he was shot.'

I told him that Kambo was my cousin. He replied that Kambo was a very brave warrior.

As all the raiders had not come from the H.Q.—some had come from different camps in that region and as far as Location 14 of Murang'a—each returned to his camp after the raid. No person in the forest could tell how many enemies or warriors were killed in the Othaya Raid. Each could only give an account of what he had seen or heard others say on the way back to their camps. None could tell the truth about the absenties. Some guessed that they might be in other camps and kept waiting for them. Later on I learned that 16 warriors had died; the drowned and the missing ones from H.Q. alone were 16 other warriors. Eighteen patients in the H.Q. hospital were mostly suffering from grenade shells while more than a dozen had received light injuries in the same raid. Most of the warriors claimed at least a dozen of the security forces might have died.

After dinner, the whole camp rejoiced in songs of praise to the country and warriors' leaders, songs of prayers, propagating the Movement, degrading and warning the Africans who helped the Government. The whole forest echoed in the dead night's silence. It was a great entertainment which cast away all worries and increased courage.

Here are a few of the songs we sang that night. I learnt later on that it was one of the only entertainments we had after dinner. We made a new song to record every event. We therefore could report our activities in songs.

NDERAGWA AREA

Kamwamba

Thiongo

Makanyanga

KARATHI'S MOTHER'S
× Kimbo
Ndungu

Mt. Sattima
13,104

Ngara

Amboni R.

Mweiga

Mburu Ngebo Army

Gati's Cave

Kiaruchibi

Kingora

Gathee

MWATHE
×

Wambararia

Kenya
Levellation camp

Jericho

Abdulah

MIHURU
×

CHIENI
×

Nyaga

Kahiu-Itina

Chania R.

NYERI

NYERI

RIFT VALLEY

KIPIPIRI
FOREST

Ituma Ndemi Army (1)

Kenya Levellation Army

Gura R.

KIGUMO
×
Kabuga Mathenge
×
KARIAINI H.Q.
Karunga

Ituma Ndemi Army
(2, 3, 4)

NO. KINANGOP AREA

12,816
Mt. Kinangop

N. Mathioya R.

Kenya Inoro Army

Gikuyu Iregi Army

KARURI
×
NGAMUNI

S. Mathioya R.

Maragwa R.

FORT
HALL

KEY

Gen. Aberdare Forest
guerrilla army areas: ○—○

Major forest camps: ×

Some minor camps: •

Rivers;

MLS. 0 1 2 3 4 5

(1)   God created Gikuyu and Mumbi
And kept them in Gikuyuland.
They were deceived by Europeans
And their land was stolen.

Chorus: I'll never leave Jomo
I'll never leave him.
I've been solemnly promised
The return of our lands.

Kenyatta stood at Ringuti and said :
'Vagrancy and laziness
Do not produce benefits
For our country.'

Chorus: I'll never leave Jomo
I'll never leave him.
I've been solemnly promised
The return of our lands.

Sorrow and trouble came
With the white community.
When we accepted them
They stole our land.

(2)   When our Kimathi ascended
Into the mountain alone,
He asked for strength and courage
To defeat the white man.

He said that we should tread
The paths that he had trodden;
That we should follow his steps
And drink from his cup.

'If you drink from the cup of courage,
The cup I have drunk from myself,
It is a cup of pain and sorrow,
A cup of tears and death.'

We are tormented because we are black,
We are not of the white community;
We do not share their blessings,
But our own God is before us.

Don't fear to be exiled
Or detained in the camps,
Or to lose your belongings or life;
For still is our God before us.

Even though our hearts are troubled
Jomo will never desert us.
Just as he was never abandoned,
Oh God, at Kapenguria by Thee.

You must display his perseverance
In the face of trouble or death;
Knowing that you belong to
The Kingdom of Gikuyu and Mumbi.

(3)   The day Kenyatta was arrested,
      Which was on a Monday,
      He was taken to the airport.

      Chorus: They mocked him, saying
                  'Jomo, you've defended the blacks
                  Now defend yourself and we'll see!
                  If you can win we will accept you.'

      When Pritt heard the news
      He felt a strong sympathy
      Seeing the Kenyans in trouble.

      Spear-bearers (i.e., Home Guards)! We'll never compromise.
      You had us, your brothers, put in prisons
      And revealed the secrets of the blacks.

      When they heard the news they were surprised
      To learn that the witnesses were
      Their own Kikuyu sisters and brothers.

The lawyer asked a girl, Peninah Wanjiku,
'Are you sure Jomo was there
When the oath was administered?'

When all the chaos is finished
We'll return to our homes and our land
And many spear-bearers will commit suicide.

(4) The children of Gikuyu live in the forests,
Under the pouring rains;
With much hunger and cold
Because we want land.

Chorus: Woeee! Woeee! Woeee, Ayahee!
Would you bear death, troubles and imprisonment
Because you want your lands?

Who are those singing aloud,
Living beyond the ocean;
Praising Jomo and Mbiyu as
The seekers of right and justice?

Some Gikuyu separated themselves
And betrayed the others because
They thought we could never win.
Our House of Mumbi, We will win!

(5) Mother, whether you cry or not,
I will only come back when our lands are returned;
When I obtain our lands and African Freedom!

These songs continued until late after midnight. With a lot of
excitements, I wrapped myself in blankets and fell asleep. This
area being of higher altitude than Kigumo and also being exposed
to strong winds, was much colder than Kigumo.

After morning prayers, the sentries were posted and we took
breakfast. I noted that nearly everyone had a kitbag (*gitumbeki*)
containing at least three ready meals. Kihara told me that we had
better go up the hill and expose ourselves to the sun. Here, most
of the people spent the day in small groups of at most twenty,

discussing and taking great care lest we be seen by an airplane.
A few people were sent out to collect honey. A few dug hiding
holes, while others [simply] went under the big trees when the
Harvards dropped their 50-pound bombs.

At 10 a.m. Wacira Gathuku arrived, aged 55, resembling much
to my father with a white turban on his head and long beard,
dressed in a grey suit, a wrist watch and a walking stick and a pair
of gum boots. We were both glad to meet each other. We talked
of the current news, my journeys, his job, the hospital and the
patients and such. At lunch time, Kihara called his attendant who
brought his kitbag, out of which we ate roasted and boiled cold meat.

Soon after lunch Stanley Mathenge with three other leaders—
Kahiu-Itina, Ngara Gitegenye and Gategwa—arrived from
Murang'a with two dozen warriors, all well-armed, and ten carriers
including a girl, who all carried food and other belongings.
Mathenge, six-feet-tall brown man of medium thickness with little
beards on his chin and black moustache, wore a woolen grey beret
on his head, a red-spotted colored scarf around his neck, a khaki-
colored rain- and cold-proof coat with leather buttons, a long pair
of black trousers and a pair of black shoes, a wrist watch, a walking
staff and an automatic pistol hoisted on a waist-belt. We were very
happy to meet each other. Mathenge asked me whether I had
received his letter. He thanked me for going to the forest, adding
that he would be able to speak to the Government through me in
writings and he would be certain that all records were properly
kept. He told me that I had no case to answer, he only wanted me
to go and work with him in the Land and Freedom Army. He
refused any further discussion on the issue and promised me that
we would have the discussion privately in the evening while warming ourselves by the fire.

He called his personal secretary Ndungu Mathenge, who was
nicknamed Achieng Oneko [the KAU Secretary tried with Kenyatta and four others at Kapenguria], and ordered him to write
letters addressed to all the leaders in the forest between Rwarai and
Muringato streams—Rwarai marks the Nyeri/Muranga boundary
and Muringato marks the Nyeri/Northern Rift Valley boundary—
telling them to attend a leaders' meeting at H.Q. Kariaini on the
11th of June 1953 without fail. Mathenge asked me to help his
secretary in writing copies of the letter. As Mathenge did not know
how to write, I had just to put down his name for signature. The

three leaders who had accompanied Mathenge from Murang'a were responsible for the letters' delivery. They left for their camps and Mathenge gave us a short account of his journey.

He said that Murang'a people were very brave fighters but they lacked fighting tactics. He said that they were conducting day battles in the villages which were resulting to the deaths of many women, children and the old persons who are generally found in the battlefield, as the security personnel would always avenge on them. He also said that a part of a sub-location had fled into the forest with their animals, women and children for hiding purposes. He told us that he left Kimathi organizing them [i.e., the Murang'a fighters] and that he may continue his journey as far as Kiambu. 'I have come to arrange a plan which I am sure will shake the Kenya Government. It will show our strength and ability.'

It was getting cold as the sun was sinking behind the western mountains. Mathenge asked Gathuku to go to the hospital with four of his carriers, one of whom was a girl, and show them where to peg out his tent while he would go and greet the warriors in the H.Q. I accompanied Mathenge to the camp. After prayers, when all were seated, Mathenge gave a short account of his journey, encouraged the fighters, introduced me to them and asked me to speak to the people. I read two verses from the Holy Bible which I had selected:

Lamentations. Chapter 5, verses 1-9.
1. Remember, O lord, what is come upon us: consider, and behold our reproach.
2. Our inheritance is turned to strangers, our houses to aliens.
3. We are orphans and fatherless, our mothers *are* as widows.
4. We have drunken our water for money; our wood is sold unto us.
5. Our necks *are* under persecution, we labour, *and* have no rest.
6. We have given the hand to the Egyptians, *and* to the Assyrians, to be satisfied with bread.
7. Our fathers have sinned, *and are* not; and we have borne their iniquities.
8. Servants have ruled over us: *there is* none that doth deliver us out of their land.
9. We gat our bread with *the peril of* our lives because of the sword of the wilderness.

Ecclessiastes. Chapter 4, verses 1–3.

1. So I returned, and considered all the oppressions that are done under the sun : and behold the tears of *such as were* oppressed, and they had no comforter; and on the side of their oppressors *there was* power; but they had no comforter.
2. Wherefore I praised the dead which are already dead more than the living which are yet alive.
3. Yea, the better *is he* than both they, which hath not yet been, who hath not seen the evil work that is done under the sun.

After reading, I closed the book and began my speech. 'My countrymen, I'm glad to be with you this evening. I am also pleased with your bravery and your efforts in this hard struggle. It is only four days since I left the five hundred children I was teaching in order to join you, and I am glad that you who are listening are five times as many as those children. I have just read two verses to you in Kikuyu language which I am sure that you have all understood. The first was the Lamentations of the prophet Jeremiah of Israel for his people. Did you find it to be true with us today?'

'Yes, quite true,' replied the mob. 'This wood is sold to us and if we don't buy, it would only rot here,' said one person. 'We die for our own food,' said another.

'So, you agree with the prophesy of Jeremiah?'

'Yes, we do !' they replied.

'Then don't be worried of what has become of us, saying that this is strange news you had never seen or heard of before. You have already heard it from the Israelites. It has happened to many other races and nations. It is History and History repeats itself. It is our turn now. All you have to do is persevere and fight bravely. There is no playing with either arrow or gun. Whenever you pull the trigger or release the arrow from the string, you can not stop it by any means from hitting the object you aimed at. This means that we have started our fight for Land and Freedom; whether you like it or not, whether you surrender or not, our aim must at last be achieved by either you or your children.

'My countrymen, the question is "Are you ready to fight till we get our Land and Freedom or are you going to leave the fight for your young children?" '

'Oh, we are going to fight!' they exclaimed. 'We are going to win,' shouted another person.

'You can fight and win in actions but not in words. Remember the saying, "Actions speak louder than words." Goodbye.'

Mathenge thanked me for the speech, asked the people to cheer for me three times by clapping their hands, then commented on my speech. He told them that he had called me to go and help them in the land and freedom struggle and that he believed I would be of much help—stating that I had given a very courageous speech on my first day. He then bid them goodbye and we left H.Q. toward the hospital escorted by four armed warriors, the person who carried my luggage and his secretary.

We arrived at twilight and I could see ten living shelters and a kitchen, two leaders' houses, Mathenge's tent and the leaders' kitchen. The only difference in the buildings was that all the walls were completely covered in order to protect the patients from the severe cold. The camp was within scattered bamboos and under big trees. The nearby stream made a swamp covered by long *ithanji* reeds. It was too cold for mosquitoes to breed in the swamp.

After exchanging greetings with the patients and their guards, we moved into Gathuku's hut. I was glad to meet Dr Harrison Gathinji and I was introduced to Muhindu his assistant. Gathinji went on telling me how he was treating the patients and that they were recovering well. Some had bullets healed in them. I told them that I was a Scoutmaster and that I had two First Aid Certificates and a Red Cross emblem which proved that I was fit to aid patients especially the ones suffering from loss of blood.

'You see Gathuku,' Mathenge commented, 'we have now got a very important person—Mr Njama. He is a teacher and has given a very courageous speech at H.Q. which I would ask him to repeat tomorrow morning. You have heard again that he is a very good doctor. He would be working with you, Gathinji, and I think you will all be of great help to our patients. He is a brave warrior, Scoutmaster and will teach our warriors how to spy, hide and signal. I remember I was with him in 1947 when he received praiseworthy letters from His Excellency the Governor for saving an old man's life. I hope you will do much more than that for your people. Again, he is a very well educated person; he can write and speak English. I do not know to read, how can I speak to the Government while in this forest? You will be writing all I want to say in any language you wish (pointing at me) and I will be sending it to the Government. You will be my Secretary; that is why I called you. Though without education, all those who have offered their lives in the course of fighting for freedom would surely have some priority in the African Government, while people like you with education would rise to the top of the Government Departments.'

At this stage the dinner was ready; well-roasted ribs of a fat cow, pancakes and a thick gravy, diluted honey followed by hot soup. As we were eating, Gathinji remarked that plenty of food was the best medicine they could give to the patients. I emphasized that statement explaining how the food we eat provides for growth and the repair of our bodies. After dinner, Mathenge claimed that he was very tired from the long journey and went to sleep. I noted that all the girls were sleeping in one hut and that no warrior was allowed to sleep with a girl. I was told it was a rule that even in the H.Q. all women slept alone. Gathuku had a big room which he slept in alone but it was generally used as the sitting room. My bed was made here and I fell asleep. The area was a bit warm and I had a good sleep.

The following morning I gave the same speech. I attended the patients and noted that the greatest difficulty was an operation whereby it would be necessary to remove a bullet from either abdomen, chest or head. Not even one of us had surgical knowledge, though we had some apparatus. All we could do was to treat the wound and let it heal with the bullet inside. Many cases were light and we removed it [i.e., the bullet].

I spent the day in a private place over the hill alone with Mathenge and Gathuku. Mathenge told me of his visit to Nairobi in March; how he was arrested and taken to a police station. He could see the posters selling his head and his photo on the notice board as he entered the charge room. The police did not recognize him and he was soon released and returned to the forest via Murang'a.

He also told me of a fire bullet incident. He said that when they were on a journey with Kimathi in Murang'a they were all sitting warming around a fire one night when a bullet exploded in the fire. 'The bullet passed near me and I escaped death very narrowly. God didn't want me to die. We tried to find out who had put that bullet in the fire, but all in vain. I suspected that

Kimathi might have put the bullet, or his agent, aiming at eliminating me so that he would become the chief leader. He was not at all pleased when I was elected to be the head of Ituma while he was elected to be my clerk. He thinks that his education makes him more clever and important than myself. But, you see, all the leaders proved that that was not true by electing me in his presence. I decided not to accompany him for the rest of our planned journey and chose to return here to prepare for an all-out raid. I would pray God to punish the evil one who had put the bullet in the fire.'

In the evening, we found Kihara Kagumu awaiting for us at the hospital. He reported that there were three cases to be heard under the chairmanship of Mathenge. 'The cases,' he continued, 'were : (1) under the leadership of Gen. Nyama, our warriors have robbed Joram Muchanji's shop at Ndunyu Market. The owner is a great comrade who supplies us with all the shopping goods. It is a very bad act to a friend. It may cause a hatred to many people. (2) The second case is of raping. Some warriors in Ngara's section have been accused of raping girls. (3) The third case you can remember; Gacuhi shot dead his fellow partisan and took off his gun at the Kairuthi Raid. It is still to be proven that he shot him knowingly for the purpose of acquiring the gun.'

Mathenge became very angry with Gen. Nyama. He said if such a thing happens again he would split the H.Q. into sub-location sections and order each section to have [i.e., acquire] its supplies from its own sub-location only. He asked me to write a letter to Kigumo leaders and all leaders around H.Q. asking them to attend a meeting at H.Q. June 9th to discuss the three serious cases. The June 11th meeting remained unchanged. After writing all the required copies, I handed them to Kagumu for dispatching. This report by Kihara made me think that there were different segments amongst the fighters; and probably they might have different motives for entering the forest. I had already noted that there were women and old men who had come into the forest for the sake of hiding or to escape the security force tortures...and this might be true of some warriors.

The following day we visited three camps surrounding the H.Q. Our intentions were to get information from different places about the current news and the reports on camp activities. At midday we were at Watoria's camp and were listening to his assistant Kahinga

Wachanga reporting about the camp when we saw puffs of smoke all along the forest boundary. It quickly spread and began to be clear to us that thousands of houses were being set on fire by the Government. We became worried and kept looking at the increasing fires. In a short time fog and clouds of smoke became so thick that we could no longer see the reserve. We sent out scouts, who returned in the evening reporting that all the houses between one and three miles from the forest boundary had been burnt. They did not see any civilians in that area, only security forces.

The following morning we got the correct information. The Government gave people six hours notice to remove all their belongings and livestock; then Government forces followed harassing them and taking away whatever pleased them—furniture, clothings, utensils and money. At the expiration of the six hours they set all houses on fire, even the Home Guard houses. All the people were told to meet at some selected centers and were warned never again to step in that area. 'Any person seen in the area would be shot without question,' they said. 'Forget your gardens as you have forgotten your houses. That area is our battlefield with Mau Mau. It will be called a SPECIAL AREA. You have now lost both house and garden for helping Mau Mau. We promise you that you will lose more if you continue to help Mau Mau. If you have a friend who can accommodate you in his house you can go; if you don't, you will sleep just where you are.' All the livestock were put together in one herd at every center and armed Home Guards were to herd them all the day and guard them during the night so that we will not be able to get any more food.

We were annoyed by the Government action. Mathenge told me to write another letter to the leaders ordering them to raid all the cattle centers as quickly as possible, before pens and guarding forts were established, and to bring to the forest as many cattle as possible and try to dry the meat for preservation. 'Make sure that you ambush all those who would follow the cattle at the right place and that you strike at the right time,' [I wrote.]

On the morning 7 June each of the six groups that were sent out of H.Q. for cattle raiding returned with an average of 100 head of cattle. We had plenty of meat but, though we tried to dry and preserve it, some went bad. The fight started at 7 a.m. when many of the groups which followed the cattle fell into the hands of our ambushers near the fringe of the forest. When the Govern-

ment forces found that they were overpowered, they signalled for
airplanes to help them. They asked them to drop bombs a few
hundred yards in front of them thinking that they would fall on
our people. The result was what they never expected. The air
forces sighted two of their groups, then the twelve airplanes
dropped their bombs on their own people, killing 42 of them. When
they sent strong forces to check the airplanes work, they were
surprised to see that they had killed their people.

Our warriors, being unable to combat the Harvard bombers,
withdrew and arrived H.Q. safely. They reported to me that they
were frightened by the bombs which were dropped near them but
it seemed as if the airplanes had spotted their own people for they
were bombing on the same place.

Two days later, I received the following news from three of
our H.Q. warriors : 'Yesterday evening on our way to the reserve
we passed where the airplanes were bombing trying to help their
people. We were very excited by the bombed area, in which about
4,000 square yards had been cleared as a garden. We saw many
lumps of blood, torn pieces of flesh and clothes, food tins, some
ammunition, etc. We were then very certain that the airplanes
must have bombed their own people. When we arrived in the
reserve, we were told by the villagers that they were exhibited some
42 badly damaged corpses which Government claimed were the
Mau Mau killed by bombs; but they had noted that most of the
corpses were not of Kikuyus.'

After attending the patients, Mathenge, the leaders in the hospital and myself, escorted by six armed warriors, set off for the
meeting place on the hill about a mile from the camp. On our way
we noticed one of the sentries only when we were ten yards from
him. He said that he'd seen us while we were a hundred yards
away; he also said that the other guards who encircled the meeting
[place] were seeing us but we could not see them as they did not
expose themselves. As we approached the meeting place, we could
see leaders sitting down on the little grass which grew under the
big trees some 150 yards in front of us. On our arrival, they stood
for Mathenge and after exchanging greetings we all sat down in a
circle.

All the twenty-seven leaders were from Nyeri. Many of them
were new to me and curiously focused on me their long shaggy
hair and beards on black and dark brown faces with their pro-

truding dark brown eyes. These bloodshot-eyed leaders, or most of them, were armed with different types of pistols; three had Sten guns and three others big game shooting guns. Figuring out that all the powers of law and order were vested in the hands of those people and that their decision was final, I felt uneasy.

The meeting started with prayers. We all stood facing Mt. Kenya with soil in our hands while Mathenge said the prayers. Then only Mathenge remained standing in the center of the circle. Taking a small stick about a foot long from a pile of them, he proceeded to curse the traitors: 'Let any leader who would reveal confidential matters to the warriors or to anyone else not entitled to the matter, let the person who creates hatred between others, the witchdoctor who kills people by poison to enjoy his practice, etc., etc., be destroyed along with his entire family and vanish from the earth.' We all had to repeat the curse after him and he threw away a stick into the bush after the completion of every vow.

One person enquired whether all the persons present had taken the Leaders Oath. I said that I had not taken it although I had been working as a leader. I was then asked to take the Leaders Oath.

With a little worry about the oath I was going to take and a little pleasure of my promotion, I stood in the middle of the leaders facing Mt. Kenya, raising my hands high over my head with soil in my left hand and a piece of goat's meat in my right, I repeated the vows after Mathenge:

I swear before Ngai and all these people here that...

(1) I will never reveal the leaders' secrets to a warrior or any other person who is not a leader.

(2) I will never run away or surrender leaving my warriors behind.

(3) I will never abandon the leadership of my people but I will go wherever my people would send me and do whatever they ask me to do in my country's name.

(4) I will never disdain [i.e., degrade or criticize] any leader in the presence of warriors.

(5) I will never by any means cause or plan the [injury or] death of another leader.

I ended each vow by chewing some meat and a little soil and

saying : 'If I fail to do this, may this oath kill me. If I lie, may Ngai kill me.'

At the completion of my oath, I was asked to take my books and sit down with the others and start recording the minutes. I whole-heartedly accepted the vows I had taken. Mathenge went on to introduce me to the leaders as his secretary. He then informed the leaders that he had called them to hear and decide what was to be done to three accused fellows whose actions had brought much shame on the whole of our Movement. He gave the names and the allegations against each. He said that any leader may question the accused or comment on his views. One would apply for permission to speak in the usual way of cracking [i.e., snapping] finger against thumb and raising his hand. The permitted person would then come in the center and take a bunch of sticks that would indicate the points he was to speak. Mathenge ordered for the first accused King'ori Gitegenye, to be brought; then he sat down along with the others.

King'ori Gitegenye was brought, guarded by three escorts. He stood in the center of the circle and was sworn by Gicuki Mugo that he would not lie before God or that court. Gicuki went on to tell him that he was accused of raping a girl in the reserve about a week ago when he, with others, were sent to fetch food. The defendant said that he did not expect such reports for the girl was his friend. He remarked that other warriors who saw him with the girl that night must have misreported him intentionally. He was then asked to go away.

As he and his escorts disappeared, Gicuki read a letter from the sub-location leader in the reserve accusing the defendant of raping a girl. A warrior witness was called. After being sworn he said that he had left King'ori with that girl about 100 yards from the home he had entered to collect food. He heard the girl crying and quickly went there. He found both standing. 'The girl reported of the incident saying that she was raped and beaten. When King'ori heard, instead of defending himself, he continued to beat the girl until I separated them and took the girl to the home where we left her. We then carried our food and started our journey.'

King'ori's brother, Ngara Gitegenye, the leader of that camp, was the first leader to speak. He said that he had questioned King'ori before and was convinced that he was guilty. [After a number of others had] commented on the witnesses, it was resolved that King'ori was guilty. 'According to our customary laws,' said one, 'he would pay seven rams to the elders, an ewe for cleansing the girl and brew some beer; but now none of these can be afforded in this forest. We have to substitute it with what we have; either money for fine or strokes on the buttocks.' Since warriors did not possess any money, the latter punishment was to be imposed. During arguments on how many strokes, Gathuku remarked that raping should be considered as a capital charge, for it either resulted in destroying a girl, causing her to be barren or causing a hip dislocation; and in some cases the raper kills the victim while defending himself from shame and fine. It was then resolved that King'ori was to receive twenty-five strokes on his buttocks. He was brought again and the sentence was carried out on the spot.

Though I did not raise my hand to speak—I was very busy recording the speeches—I had been convinced that the case was well conducted.

The second accused, Gen. Nyama, who sat among the other leaders, stood and after swearing said that he did not order any robbing of our associates [i.e., supporters]. He sent them to rob the Home Guard shops and said that they had local guides who knew Ndunyu Market very well. As he sat down, Mathenge ordered that those guides be brought in.

One of the guides stood in the center and said that just three days ago they were ordered to plunder as many cattle as possible, irrespective of associates or Home Guards, and the orders had come from our chief leader, Stanley Mathenge. 'I could see no difference between the taking of ones cattle or goods in his shop. I thought that we would record his goods the same way as we have recorded his cattle and [he would] await for compensation. We ransacked all the shops. I thought that if we left his shop [untouched], that would betray him as our helper and his goods and his life would be under the mercy of Home Guards...which would have been worse than what we did.'

The guides were asked to go away together with Nyama, and after a short discussion the case was withdrawn. After a short time they were all called and warned never to commit any action that would anger our associates; causing them to feel bad on us and probably leading them to turn against us.

In that case I learnt that Mathenge was confused in what to do and what to leave in the taking of our associates property.

The third accused, Gacuhi, was brought strongly guarded. After the guards had inspected him, he was sworn. Gicuki Mugo proceeded on reading his accusation, saying that on the night of the Kairuthi Raid he shot dead his comrade and took his gun. Gacuhi, full of fear and sorrow, admitted that he shot the man, whom he thought to be an enemy, but very much regretted when he realized that he had killed his friend.

The three witnesses who were heard said that ... 'After defeating the enemies, we entered the shops in order to take out goods. When we were leaving the shops we spotted a figure outside coming toward us. Gacuhi who was in front of us, without asking a question, opened fire and the man fell twenty yards before us. As Gacuhi ran there to take the man's gun, we heard other sentries asking, "Who is that shooting at us?" We then realized that one of our people was dead.'

Answering a question whether they thought that Gacuhi wanted to kill the man, each said that they were all working with Gacuhi inside the shop and when they came out he surprisingly fired at a figure which he did not know, but excitement had caused him to think that it was an enemy and he had right to strike as quickly as possible before he was struck. The witnesses remarked that he was innocent.

After a short discussion, there was no proof at all that Gacuhi wanted to kill. It was therefore regarded as an accident and Gacuhi was set free with a warning to take much care next time.

The meeting was postponed [i.e., adjourned] to the following morning when it would resume for the making of some rules and regulations brought about by the cases. When the meeting resumed the following day, I continued my job and recorded these rules and regulations, which were resolved [i.e., passed] after some arguments :

(1) That raping is an offence as old as the Kikuyu tribe and that any further cases of that sort would be regarded as capital charges.

(2) Since women were the source of calamity and would cause conflicts amongst our warriors in camps, and as they were not engaged in fighting, they should be kept in their separate camps where they would be guarded and fed. That the follow-

ing day a group from H.Q. would go and build a women's camp at Mumwe stream.

(3) That warriors were entitled to take by force any foodstuffs in the gardens and livestock concentrated at any Government centers irrespective of whether they belonged to friend or foe.

(4) That foodstores of known supporters were [to be considered] the property of the owners and that we could only ask them to help us.

(5) That our warriors were allowed to take or destroy any enemy's property;

(6) That the supplies of foodstuffs, clothes, medicine, money, arms, etc., were to be organized in the sub-locations [i.e., on a sub-location basis] and that the forest organizer of a sub-location was the only person who would write a letter to the other organizer in the reserve so that he could hand over the supplies for transport to the forest.

(7) That whenever any supplies have arrived in a camp, they should be shared by all the members of that camp and not [allocated] on a sub-locational basis.

Before the meeting adjourned, it was agreed to write an apology letter to Joram Mucanji, whose shop had been robbed. I wrote the letter and told him to keep a record of all his lost property awaiting for compensation when we achieved independence. I asked him to send us a copy of his record of the lost property.

The leaders were asked to bring plans for raids that would shake the Government for discussion on the following day. The meeting dispersed.

On the 11th June 1953 a dozen more of the expected leaders from Mweiga Settled Area of the Northern Rift Valley arrived at the meeting place at 10 a.m. After exchanging greetings, Mathenge reported that since the leaders we had been awaiting had arrived, we were to start the meeting.

The meeting commenced with the usual prayers, all standing and facing Mt. Kenya. Then, all sitting down in a circle, Mathenge stood in the center and asked whether there was a warrior in the meeting and requested every person who had not taken the leadership oath to raise his hand. I noted that there were three people who had not been promoted to leaders status. They were asked to move in the center of the circle and were sworn in by the oath.

After that, these three new leaders were informed by Mathenge that they were not invited to the meeting as he had sent an invitation letter to every leader and that he did not know anything about them. They would have to go to the camp and wait for their companions. Mathenge then went on to utter a curse [binding all the leaders to secrecy] in the same way he had done the day before. Like a newspaper reporter, I recorded the meeting's first speech.

Mathenge told us that the matter we were to discuss was of great confidence and importance and that everything must be kept in secret until the plans had been carried out. 'We made the plan with Kimathi at Murang'a,' he continued, 'and agreed that he was to carry on the plan for Murang'a and Kiambu, Mbaria Kaniu would organize the whole of North Kinangop while Ndungu and Kimbo will organize the Northern Rift Valley. The most important thing is that the raid should be carried on over all the country on the same day and exactly at the same time. You need not worry about date and time; I would give you twenty-four hours notice of the date and time. All you have to do today is to know what, where and how to raid.' He gave me a letter and asked me to read it aloud to the meeting. It read :

(1) Every camp must seize and bring into the forest as many livestock as possible.

(2) Destroy all the roads, railways, bridges, electric and telegraph wires in your area.

(3) Kill as many enemies as possible in your area.

(4) Raid your nearest trading centers for clothing, and all goods in the shops.

(5) Raid your nearest dispensary for the medicine [and medical supplies] only and bring it in the forest.

(6) Put on fire as many enemy houses as possible.

(7) Raid all water pipes on the farms and bring sizes 1/2 to 3/4 inches in diameter for the making of guns.

(Signed by) Dedan Kimathi

'Those are the raids,' continued Mathenge, 'the next thing is to allocate areas to be raided by different camps. It is now the leaders duty to know how many bridges or enemies or houses etc., are in his area. This will enable you to determine the number of groups into which you would divide your section; and hence how many warriors would go into each group. I would give you four days only for preparations as from tomorrow. Thereafter you must be ready at all times throughout the month. Any leader who fails to carry on the raid will be demoted to a regular warrior.'

When Mathenge sat down, a few other leaders commented on their support of the idea. We spent the rest of the time allocating the areas to be raided by different camps in proportion to the number of warriors in the area. At this stage I learnt that Nyeri had 5,800 warriors in Nyandarua, of whom 1,800 were new recruits who had entered the forest within that week. The Government action of burning and evicting people all along the forest boundary, declaring their farms to become 'Special Area' and forcing all men to become Home Guards and fight against their people in order to prove their loyalty to the Government made so many men flee to the forest in order to escape the Government punishment imposed to non-loyalists. This only increased our number in the forests; more fighters joined in this month than any other.

The meeting ended and the leaders returned to their camps.

CHAPTER XII

THE PROPHETS OF 25TH JUNE

KARARI'S account of the 25 June raid and, more specifically, of the failure of Kariaini forces to carry out their part in this 'all-out attack', focuses attention on the role and influence of the seers among Aberdare guerrilla forces. It also provides a striking illustration of the seeming incongruity, in the context of a modern-day revolution, of prophets, omens and magico-religious beliefs. To understand this phenomenon, it is necessary to view the role of the *mundo mugo* in term of both continuities in Kikuyu culture and ideological reactions to contemporary events.

The traditionally important role of the *mundo mugo*, as a member of the Kikuyu War Council with numerous military duties and functions, has already been alluded to in an earlier section and it is easy enough to view his role within revolutionary forest groups of the 1950's—e.g., advising on raids and other military matters, using his war magic against the enemy, conducting cleansing ceremonies, transmitting messages from Ngai, usually received in dreams, to the guerrilla leaders, etc.—as merely an extension or continuation of traditional belief and practice. This, however, would be to overlook the importance of contemporary pressures, internal and external, and their affects on the complex and developing ideology of the forest insurgents.

To provide a context for this discussion and, as ideological matters will be of continuing concern, a framework within which future developments can meaningfully be considered, it might be useful here to address ourselves to the general question of *Mau Mau* ideology. It must be noted at the outset that many writers have attempted to characterize this ideology, and not infrequently the entire revolutionary movement, in terms of one or another general and comprehensive category or label. *Mau Mau*, it has variously been asserted, 'was in fact a religion',[1] or, rather than a religion, 'a self-conscious return to tribalism...

---

[1] L. S. B. Leakey, *Defeating Mau Mau*, p. 41, Methuen & Co. Ltd,, 1954.

based on synthetic paganism',[1] 'a wholly tribal manifestation aimed at tribal domination, not a national liberation movement',[2] 'a form of millenarism',[3] or 'a pseudo-religious cult ... of the golden age'.[4]

I must confess that I find all such attempts to 'fit' the ideology of Kenya's revolutionary movement into a single, neat category wanting in both historical accuracy and utility. Unfortunately, the Movement issued no manifesto and all who address themselves to its ideology are obliged to make inferences from a wide array of songs, prayers, oaths, etc., which, in their variety, can be used selectively to support any number of sweeping generalizations.

My own investigation of *Mau Mau* ideology, viewed as the unifying set of aims, interests and beliefs of the Movement, has shown it to be a rather complex phenomenon containing at least four major aspects or components; namely, secular, moral-religious, African national and Kikuyu tribal. The weighting or importance attached to these several aspects, as we shall see, changed over time and varied from group to group. Nevertheless, it will be useful at this point to consider the general characteristics of each component as part of the total ideology.

Developing largely out of the manifold politico-agrarian grievances directed against European rule and white settler occupancy of alienated African land, the *secular* aspect of *Mau Mau* ideology was revealed most clearly in the oft-repeated demands of the Movement for higher wages, increased educational opportunities, removal of the color-bar in its variety of discriminatory forms, return of the alienated lands and independence under an all-African government. As a reflection of the developing relationship of inequality between black and white in Kenya society, these secular aims were, in their political dimension, an expression of African nationalist ideology—i.e., a demand for African 'Freedom' and self-determination. ('You cannot build on the work of a foreigner. His word should be drowned in deep waters by God. His rule should be brought to an end. In this country of ours, Kenya, let the black people govern themselves alone.'

[1] F. B. Welbourn, *East African Rebels*, p. 133, SCM Press Ltd., 1961.

[2] F. Majdalaney, *State of Emergency*, p. 70, Longmans, 1962.

[3] L. P. Mair, *British Journal of Sociology*, Vol. 9, No. 2, p. 175, 1958.

[4] F. D. Corfield, *Historical Survey of the Origins and Growth of Mau Mau*, p. 9, Her Majesty's Stationery Office.

'If you look around the whole of Kenya, it is only a river of blood; for we have our one single purpose, to lay hold of Kenya's freedom.')

Within the revolutionary forest context, this secular-African national aspect was reflected and symbolized in the demand for 'Land and Freedom'. As will be noted, 'freedom' was seldom if ever viewed as a specifically Kikuyu or tribal objective, but rather as the end-product of a successful African struggle *vis-à-vis* the European adversary for independence from colonial and white settler rule. ('Mother, whether you cry or not, I'll only return when our lands are recovered; when we obtain land and African freedom.')

With respect to 'land', however, the objective was more often than not seen in tribal or specifically Kikuyu terms. Thus, in song and prayer, the common reference is to the land left to the Kikuyu by Ngai or the mythical ancestors of the tribe, Gikuyu and Mumbi; and its recovery from European hands is viewed as a Kikuyu objective. ('O God, the most powerful! We praise Thee for guarding us throughout the day. We have raised our hands to show You that the soil you gave our forefathers is now being used by strangers, who robbed us of our lands, our gift, our inheritance. These strangers are killing us for our land.' 'I'll never leave Jomo, I'll never leave him; since I've been solemnly promised the return of our land.')

The secular aspect of *Mau Mau* ideology, then, had both an African national dimension, centering largely around the aim and concept of 'freedom', and a tribal dimension framed in terms of specific Kikuyu claims to alienated land. The revolution's political frame of reference was thus African national, its agrarian frame of reference, Kikuyu tribal.

The non-secular or sacred aspect of *Mau Mau* ideology was framed largely in terms of moral-religious precepts, according to which the secular aims of the revolution were seen as sanctioned and legitimized by a higher, supernatural power. Most important among these precepts were the following, repeated over and over again in song, prayer and oath. (1) *'We have been wronged by the Europeans; our cause and struggle are just and right.'* ('God created Gikuyu and Mumbi and placed them in Gikuyuland; they were deceived by the Europeans and their land was stolen.' 'Sorrow and trouble came with the white man; when we accepted them they stole our land.' 'We are tormented because we are black; we are not of the whites and do not share their blessings, but our God is before us!') (2) *'God is just and powerful; right will prevail over might.'* ('Please, O God! Look mercifully upon the spilt blood of our brethren and hear our call and cry. We have not weapons to fight against these people, but we believe Thy sword will defeat our enemies; for we are your sons and daughters and do not believe you created us to become servants of other people in the land you blessed and gave to our ancestors, Gikuyu and Mumbi.' 'Have no fear in your hearts, God is in heaven. Be brave, God's power is here and the Europeans will be driven out.') (3) *'A just cause must nonetheless be fought for; God helps those who help themselves.'* ('Warriors of Gikuyu, awake! Ye who cannot see that the old man grows older. If you sleep the foreigners will seize all our wealth and then what will the children of Mumbi feed on?' 'You of the House of Mumbi, even if you are oppressed do not be afraid in your hearts; a Kikuyu proverb says "God helps those who help themselves".')

Combined with a reaffirmation of certain common traditional values and customs, precepts such as these provided the Movement and revolution with a 'moral force', a conviction that the struggle was just and a belief that right would prevail over might. It is quite likely that similar convictions have formed an integral part of all revolutionary ideologies.

Together with their incorporated secular aims, these moral-ous precepts and beliefs also performed an important unifying or integratory function, linking in common cause and brotherhood a vast majority of the previously dispersed and frequently conflicting Kikuyu, Embu and Meru groups. To the extent, however, ıt this was achieved through the use of specifically Kikuyu symbols, persons of non-Kikuyu tribal affiliation tended to be excluded, if not alienated, from the revolutionary movement.

Though the religious aspect of *Mau Mau* ideology contained a syncretic quality, with various aspects of Old Testament Christianity found interwoven with their Kikuyu counterparts, it was framed largely in terms of traditional beliefs and concepts. Christianity, particularly in its institutionalized form as represented by the missions, was avowedly rejected. In the black-white struggle, it was viewed essentially as just another aspect of European domination. ('Between a missionary and a settler, there is no difference'—a Kikuyu saying.)

We are now, I believe, in a better position to understand the role and ideological implications of the *mundo mugo* among Aberdare guerrilla groups. Largely isolated within the forest and without the direct participation of their more highly educated and cosmopolitan leaders, the peasant forces of this period tended to place considerable weight on the specifically Kikuyu aspects of their composite ideology. Kenya African nationalism, though by no means disappearing, was forced into the background by a strong sense of Kikuyu 'nationalism' or tribalism. The felt need for tribal unity—no mean achievement in its own right and in large measure accomplished by mid-1953—led to emphasis being placed on the more specific grievances of the Kikuyu peasantry, particularly those centering around land and the dominant position of the European settler. And the increasing anti-white, anti-mission feelings, together with an equally strong desire to recover the lost dignity, the surrendered 'manhood', of the tribe, conditioned the reaffirmation of certain aspects of traditional Kikuyu law and custom.

It is in this light that we must view the role of the *mundo mugo*. With the rejection, for the most part, of Christianity, went a reaffirmation of the merits and credibility of the old religion and its legitimate 'professional' practitioners. Traditionally, however, magical and religious beliefs were interwoven within a single system of thought which, particularly among the illiterate peasantry, had been supplemented rather than displaced by Christianity over the preceding fifty years. The magico-religious beliefs prevalent within the ranks of the guerrilla fighters, therefore, and the widespread acceptance of the legitimate military role and prophetic powers of the *mundo mugo*, are best understood as continuities in traditional Kikuyu culture which were both reinforced and, to a considerable degree, reshaped by the forces operating within the revolutionary context of 1953.

As we shall see, the actual powers of the seers in determining or influencing military policy and tactics varied considerably from group to group, depending in large part upon the importance attached to magico-religious beliefs by the individual leaders. There was, in addition, considerable variation over time in the role and importance of the *mundo mugo*. Though the 'moral strength' derived by the forest fighters from their beliefs in the prophesies and magical powers of the seers is difficult to assess, it must be objectively noted that the seer's role was of dubious military value and a source of both stress and internal conflict within the revolutionary movement.

★   ★   ★

The following day, after cleansing and dressing my patients' wounds, of whom many were almost healed, I climbed up the hill with Mathenge and other leaders to spend the day warming by the sun's heat. At about 10 a.m., four Harvards started bombing the H.Q. area with much stronger bombs than before. The bombing lasted fifteen minutes, followed by five minutes of firing from their machine guns. During the bombing I saw a few persons run into their holes, while many others, including myself, ran under big trees and lay down on our stomachs with our noses almost touching the ground and held soil in our hands amidst the horrible thunders of exploding bombs, which echoed as death hoots to me, and the frightening earth tremors. In the fainting breath, each said his own prayers, asking God to save his life and to avenge against the injustices of our strong enemies.

After the departure of the Harvards we were very much anxious to know whether they had caused casualties. They had dropped one bomb right inside the camp and another at the edge. Luckily there were no people in the camp at the moment for they were all on the hillside where the airplanes could not bomb successfully. Though there was no person injured, the day was referred to as 'the first heavy air raid.' We suspected that a captive—for there were no surrenderees by then—had pointed out to the Government the site of H.Q.; but since these airplanes went on bombing other areas in which there were no camps we concluded that it was a mere guessing of where the camp could be and our warriors continued to live in the H.Q.

On the 21st June, under the authority of Mathenge, I wrote a letter to each leader notifying him that the 'all out attack' would be on 25 June 1953, commencing at 7:30 p.m. I also wrote a propaganda letter to the Government saying :

The June 25th raid is an example of our planned series of attacks. The Europeans and Asians who are with us are very much engaged in the making of guns and plans. We are certain that our next all-out attack will make you flee our country or commit suicide. The more you punish the civilians in the reserves, the more they hate you and the more they join our forces. We are glad that you are spending thousands of pounds daily paying pilots' wages, oil and bombs which kill hundreds of buffoloes, elephants, deer, etc., and only supply us with plenty of meat right here in the forest. Whatever worst you do against us, God changes it to be our best help.

Yours Victoriously,
General Stanley Mathenge

After reading to Mathenge the propaganda letter I had drafted, he was very pleased with me and said that the letter should be posted as it was near Munyange Police Post. All the other letters were dispatched the following morning and all the messengers were to report at H.Q. on the evening of the 24th that they had delivered the messages.

When Kihara Kagumu visited the hospital on the morning of the 25th he reported to Mathenge that the H.Q. camp had selected 1,600 warriors who would participate in the all-out attack in 32 groups of 50 men each. He said that each group was to be led by a lieutenant or an appointed warrior and that they would all leave H.Q. at 4 p.m. so that they could see the security forces going to their guarding positions by 6 p.m. and then mark the ambush places, they would then separate, each group heading to the place it would attack.

The following morning an injured warrior was brought to the hospital at about 7:30 a.m., his calf being badly torn by a grenade. I quickly applied a pad on the pressure point to stop bleeding and cleansed and dressed his wound. Meanwhile, hot soup was being prepared. As he was drinking the soup, he reported the [previous] night's raid to me, saying that they arrived at the forest fringe before 6 p.m. and saw over 800 Devonshire personnel assisted by military and Home Guards taking their positions at all possible paths. They became frightened. They could pass their ambushers and carry on the plan, but they thought that the Devons would block their way back in such a way that they would either be killed on their return journey or would remain in the reserve and continue a day battle which had not been planned.

The other reason [i.e., for their failure to carry out the raid] was the superstitious beliefs which were being taught by the witch-doctors that if a deer or a gazelle passed across the path of a group that was going to raid, it indicated bad luck and the warriors should abandon their plan. Twice a deer and a gazelle had crossed our way. This [belief, he said,] was supported by many warriors who said that they disobeyed the same rule when they were going to raid Othaya and the result was very bad, as the seers had fore-cast. This caused their decision to put off the raid.

Two of the groups of 50 understook the risk and decided to fulfill the plan, while the rest awaited at the forest border. The patient was in one of the two groups that attacked a guard post and took away very many head of sheep and goats, of which some were lost in the darkness and only 160 arrived at H.Q. The other group managed to bring 40 head of cattle. The patient continued that he was one of the guards who remained behind to fight the enemy who might follow the livestock. 'When we passed the Devons' ambush we were all happy about our success. We started talking loudly as we approached the forest but we did not know that the Devons had heard the first group and had followed it to the forest edge, and that they were laying there waiting for us. We unknowingly entered their ambush, which we realized [only] when they opened fire on us. We were so near them that they used grenades, [one of] whose shells injured me. I think we must have lost some of our people there.'

The raid report was very disappointing. The seers had ruined our plans. It seemed to me that most of our warriors, including many of their section leaders, were under the command [i.e., influence] of the prophets. This was one of our great dangers I thought. If Government used these seers to help them, they could either lead our warriors into Government ambushes or induce them to sur-render claiming that they had been directed by God to convey this message to the people. I talked the matter over with Mathenge and found that he also believed in witchcraft. I kept on thinking of a way which could turn our people from the prophets, but this was impossible until their messages were realized as a danger. I quickly learnt that my attempts to make our warriors turn against the prophets were interpreted as urging them to disobey God's messengers and thus disobey God's instructions.

By nightfall, the report from H.Q. was that two armed warriors were still missing. It was suspected that they were casualties of the Devons. A group of people was sent out to search for them in the ambushed area near the forest edge while another group was sent in the reserve to find out the current news about the raids.

The following day we received the news from the reserve messengers saying that they were told that when the day broke, the Devons with some Home Guards (who reported the story to our messengers) went to check how many people they had killed. When they arrived at the place where they had opened fire, they did not see any corpses but there were blood trails. They followed the blood track thinking that it would lead them to some corpses. They unknowingly approached two injured warriors who opened fire killing two Devons. They were then both killed and their guns fell into Government hands. The corpses were exhibited to the reserve people.

Though the H.Q. camp failed to raid on June 25th, the report in the reserve and from Government information through radio and newspapers indicated that the forest fighters were well organized, many in number, scattered everywhere, and that the raids had incurred heavy losses on the Government side in a single day.

Up to this date, the H.Q. had an average of two raids a week on either military, police or Home Guard centers, followed by ambushes in which Government attempted to enter the H.Q. It just serves here to say that the Government had four and a half months of trial and error in which it lost many of its forces [as well as] arms and ammunition which increased the strength of our warriors. The road from the reserve to Kariaini H.Q. was as wide as many of the vehicle roads today in the reserve and had been known by the Government forces as 'the road to death.' I think that an account of some of our early successes would make the reader [better able] to figure out a bit of the fight in the forest.

It was about 10 a.m. on May 5th, before my arrival, when our watchmen reported that they had seen about two thousand men and women led and guarded by military, Home Guards and some Europeans marching toward Kariaini Forest squatter gardens with the intention of uprooting *nduma* (arrowroots), potatoes and all the remaining foodstuffs so that our warriors would not get any more food from those gardens. Our guards were strengthened and set off to meet them in the gardens with a warning to take care not to shoot the civilians. As soon as our warriors were ready, they sounded bugles at different positions which indicated the opening of fire. When the civilians heard the bugles they ran away. Five military persons fell dead while the others made off following the civilians. They were quickly followed [and our fighters succeeded in] killing three more and capturing one Home Guard, thirty old men and fifty women. A few warriors were left guarding the captives while the others chased the military right inside the reserve. Two military persons dropped their guns at Ihuririo about a mile from the forest fringe. Our warriors collected the guns and returned to the forest, releasing all the captives who wanted to go back. A dozen old men and eight women, who wished to join us, were taken to H.Q. Our warriors gained two Sten guns and nine shotguns in that unprepared fight.

Our enemies ignorance of things in the forest was their great disadvantage. When we saw them coming, and knowing the path they would have to follow—for we used to stay at the forest fringes, observe and count the enemies before they approached the forest—we would then deploy ourselves along the path, out of sight, and when their last man passed our ambush we would open fire, killing some and forcing the rest into the depths of the forest. Once caught in the heart of the forest it was very unlikely that they would escape; often they would run into others of our fighters or be killed by the wild forest rhinos or buffaloes.

When, as sometimes happened, one or two Government soldiers escaped from the forest and returned to his camp, reporting about the ambush, reinforcements were often rushed to the spot where the fighting had occurred with the intentions of collecting guns and their injured comrades. Knowing these reinforcements were coming we would usually move a mile or two from the place of ambush toward the reserve and deploy again along the paths we suspected the Government forces would follow. Not suspecting that we would come closer to their base and the reserves, these forces often walked straight into another ambush similar to the first.

Another way in which our fighters trapped the security forces was to go out of the forest and then march single file singing back into the forest, leaving a very clear track for Government to follow.

They would then circle back and lay in wait for their trackers and forces to come along the path which they had prepared for ambush.

Many encounters were those in which the Government forces followed livestock thinking that the camp would be far away inside the dense forest and perhaps that they would find us slaughtering the animals and even making a lot of noise which would make them detect our presence. We always had our ambushers in such tracks for a distance of at least five miles from the camp.

In successful such encounters indicated above, we gained a great deal of arms and ammunition. The other sources were raiding camps and posts and ambushing individual personnel in the reserves and towns, raiding European homes stealing guns, buying from police, military, Home Guards and from Europeans and Indian traders and opportunists. Among the Government servicemen were our members and sympathizers who supplied us with ammunition free of payment. When our members were issued with arms and ammunition by the Government in order to join the Home Guards, some of them fled to the forest with all their supplies. Bullets had become token payment [from security force personnel] to prostitutes who later sent them to our warriors.

The Government reaction against our June 25th raids was very bad. The survivors [i.e., peasant civilians] were forced to rebuild all the roads and bridges, and construct new roads so that military vehicles could move more quickly and easily from one place to another. That was the beginning of the daily communal fatigue [i.e., labor] under the supervision of armed Home Guards, in which all able bodied civilians in the reserves were forced to spend all the day constructing new roads which would have taken a century to construct. Contour and bench terracing was the other project, and building police and Home Guard posts and digging trenches to surround those posts for protection. [Later, the peasants were forced] to build new enclosed villages. Personal tax was increased to 75s. so that Government could get more money for maintaining its forces and partly to repair the damage caused by our warriors on the all-out attack.

All the Kenya Europeans were mobilized to strengthen the Kenya Regiment. With their arrival in the reserves the brutality of shooting civilians in cold blood increased. Their motto was 'The only good Kikuyu is a dead one.' During this month [June] in my location, Richard Gituro, Itong'e Gicuhi, Rong'o Kibico and Juma Muteru were called out of their houses, taken to Kamoko Home Guard center where they were badly beaten, [it being] alleged that they had helped *Mau Mau* with food. Each was then taken out of the camp in turn and shot. Irungu Mukuru had been shot on the same day on his way to Ndunyu Market.

[There was also an] increase of inhuman torture in the local camps, e.g., men castrated, beatings aiming at fracturing a limb, putting *thabai* or *hatha*—poisonous stinging plant leaves of the nettle family which causes great pain and swelling for half a day— in women's vaginas, pressing hard breasts or testicles with pliers. At this time, Ihururu Center in the North Tetu Location of Nyeri had been exercising all those tortures. By the same time Simba Camp (*Kambi ya Simba*) in Thomson's Falls District and another camp in Bahati area of the Rift Valley on the farm of a well-known settler named Felth were reported to be the worst in torturing. Hundreds of persons who fell victim of these tortures can be seen anywhere in the country or in towns as crippled beggars having lost one or both legs or arms or suffering other deformities. I have come across six castrated men, one of whom, Kamau Njoroge, was nicknamed *Mapengo* [toothless] due to the absence of his front teeth in both jaws which he lost at Simba Camp. He lived with me in Athi River and Lodwar detention camps.

In addition to the killings, beatings and torture, starvation was accelerated in which thousands of children and old aged persons died. This was started by the repatriation of many many thousand Kikuyu from the Rift Valley and Nairobi into the reserves followed by the repatriation of forest squatters in both Mt. Kenya and the Aberdares. Thirdly, the eviction of people from a one to two mile strip all around the mountains in early June. This decreased the areas of food production and caused over 250,000 people to be homeless, landless, jobless and helpless; in addition to this there were strict curfews and they were forced to work on communal fatigue all days getting no food and no pay and losing time to attend their gardens where they could get something to keep them alive. To make it worse, in late July an order was issued in many parts of Fort Hall and Nyeri for cutting down all maize plants (our chief food)—just at the point of their bearing—bananas, sugar canes, etc., thus losing the whole harvest. It was alleged that *Mau Mau* were hiding in the gardens and therefore all the gardens must be cleared. The motive behind it was to accelerate hunger. It is now possible to figure out the conditions of the hungry, exploited and homeless peasants where, in the nights, at an altitude over 6,000 feet, the heavy long rains join the winter months of June, July and August when thick mists and showers continue most of the time and the temperature falls down to an average of 55°F. and more than a fortnight can pass without seeing the sun.

Much later, in 1955, after thousands of children and old aged persons had died, the International Red Cross came to aid the survivors. It was reported to me that a group of the old aged persons were taken from my village to the Chief's Center to be fed by the Red Cross; none of them survived. It is worthwhile mentioning here that children suffered most due to the absence of their parents, being either killed, detained or in the forests. Our warriors were taking much of the foodstuffs in the gardens and livestock into the forest and the security forces were feeding on the remainder. The starvation caused the peasants to eat any edible leaves such as sweet potato leaves in order to live, while disease in the unsanitary villages [a forced villagization program was begun at the beginning of 1954] killed its share. In fact, the whole situation had become [i.e., by the end of 1955] the destruction of wealth and health.

CHAPTER XIII

THE BREAK-UP OF THE KARIAINI H.Q.

AS PREVIOUSLY noted, Government, during the first half of 1953, was unable to make effective or sustained contact with the guerrilla forces operating within the forests. Its strategy, therefore, was concentrated on breaking or at least neutralizing the popular base of the revolt among the peasant masses in the Kikuyu reserve. In addition to curfews, movement restrictions, new pass requirements, collective fines and punishment, 'cleansing' and counter-Mau Mau oathing campaigns and severe methods of interrogation, Government launched a strong anti-*Mau Mau* propaganda campaign, raised personal taxes and introduced a 'communal' or forced labor scheme whereby damaged roads and bridges could be repaired, guard and police posts erected and new agricultural schemes enforced without cost. The Kikuyu reserve was made a *Special Area*, wherein a person failing to halt when challenged could be shot, and the forests of Mount Kenya and Nyandarua were proclaimed *Prohibited Areas* in which all unauthorized Africans were to be shot on sight. Added to the latter area was a 100-mile strip of land, from one to three miles in width, lying between the forests and reserve. Here, all huts and graineries were burned, peasants evicted and crops slashed in an effort to prevent the flow of supplies into the forests.

With the arrival in June 1953 of a new Commander-in-Chief, General Erskine, a somewhat revised strategy became apparent. Government troops stepped up their attacks on the forest guerrillas considerably. Five tracks were cut into the Aberdares by an imported team of Royal Engineers and forced Kikuyu labor, battalion-strength bases were established within the forest fringe from which sweeps and cordon operations were launched, and Lincoln heavy bombers began flying regular missions over the forest. To implement this new offensive strategy, security force strength was greatly increased and, by September, included the

39th Brigade of Buffs and Devons, the 49th Brigade of Royal Northumberland and Inniskilling Fusiliers, the East African Brigade of six KAR battalions, the Lancashire Fusiliers, the Kenya Regiment and two East African units, an armoured car division and a squadron of Lincolns—a total of eleven battalions and over 10,000 soldiers. In addition, the police force was increased to 21,000 men and the Kikuyu guard units to a somewhat higher figure. During the third quarter of 1953, then, the British and Kenya Governments were employing a force of well over 50,000 men against the *Mau Mau* insurgents.

This shift in Government strategy obviously affected the military situation of the forest guerrillas. For one thing, the increased bombings and enemy bases within the forest made large concentrations of guerrilla fighters increasingly unfeasible and, combined with other factors, led to the eventual break-up of Kariaini and the other large camp-clusters. As Karari notes, many leaders and their followers had already shifted to the Rift Valley side of the forest by the time Kariaini H.Q. was overrun and its forces dispersed by the enemy on 11 July. Some believed it sounder policy to base themselves on the western side of the range where they could both direct their attacks against European farms and stock and gain some relief for their hard-pressed civilian supporters in the reserve. Supply problems had also exerted pressure on the large camp-clusters. The concentration of forest fighters tended to limit the area in the reserve from which supplies, and particularly food, could effectively be drawn, thus placing severe burdens on relatively few Kikuyu locations. Again, the new rule requiring each forest unit to obtain supplies from its own sub-location obliged many sections to set up camps closer to their home areas in the reserve. For the Rift Valley sections, being without reserve sub-locations, this ruling increased their desire to leave the eastern sector of the forest for the more familiar regions bordering the Settled Areas.

The continued Government operations in the area bordering the reserve, and the resultant dispersal of forest forces, also greatly reduced the effectiveness of the Ituma Ndemi Trinity Council. No meetings could be convened and contact between the leaders was greatly hampered. Another consequence of the dispersal was to reaffirm the territorial basis of section recruitment. The smaller Nyeri forest camps established during this period were comprised almost exclusively of persons from one or two sub-locations, while Rift Valley sections were composed largely of fighters from the same general areas or districts of the 'White Highlands'. Finally, the break-up of Kariaini and the other large camp-clusters led to the establishment of numerous small groups of men wishing both to escape military discipline and avoid clashes with the security forces. These groups spent most of their time hiding in the forest fringe or reserve bush. Their thefts of peasant crops and occasional raids on supporters' stores and shops tended, of course, to alienate rather than win the respect of the peasant masses. These men were referred to by the organized forest guerrillas as *komeraras*, a term normally used of persons or criminals in hiding from the law.

*   *   *

By June 30th, 1,000 warriors had moved from H.Q. to the Rift Valley in three groups and there were still 2,500 left. This number had to be reduced so that the supply of food would be even to other areas [i.e., so that other areas might contribute their share of food and other supplies]. The sub-locational food supply system which was introduced then angered the Rift Valley leaders and almost caused conflicts. The leaders in the H.Q. had been unable to keep an eye on all the warriors and it was reported from the reserve that our warriors were robbing both food and money from our associates [i.e., supporters]. For these reasons, Kamau Githongo, Gicuki Mugo, Kabuga Njogu and Gikonyo Kanyungu were to be given 300 people each and were asked to start their own camps by July 1st, leaving H.Q. with only 1,300, including those in the hospital.

During the first week of July, a meeting was called for the Nyeri leaders to report on the June 25th attack. The meeting was held at the same place and organized in the same manner as the last meeting. All the leaders, with the exception of the H.Q., reported their successes as it had been planned. Though the H.Q. leaders were criticized for handing over their responsibility to warriors, no punishment was imposed on them; but they were warned not to do anything of that nature again. Each camp spent [i.e., retained] its own spoils with the exceptions of medicine, that was to be shared to H.Q. hospital, and more than three miles of water pipes which were to be shared to the camps who had none. Gun factories were to be erected and the necessary tools were to be obtained from our people in the reserves, e.g., hack-saws, files, door bolts, springs from rat traps, screws, chisels, hammers, etc.

My knowledge of the situation then [prevailing] in Kikuyu reserve made me think that it was absolutely wrong to make the Kikuyu reserve our battlefield. Our warriors were taking a good deal of food and the rest was being plundered by the security forces. I then addressed the leaders meeting appealing to them to withdraw completely from all the forests adjacent to the Kikuyu reserve and move to the Rift Valley side where there was plenty of settlers' fat cattle, merino sheep, pigs, poultry, big wheat stores, maize meal stores, etc., which belonged to our real enemies. If we moved there the Government would also withdraw its forces from the Kikuyu reserve following us and our people would be greatly relieved and also have more to eat. All those who lived in the Rift Valley supported me while those who did not know the Rift Valley opposed, giving their reasons that they did not know where to get food and, as this was done during the night, they couldn't figure out the way in that unknown country. When I pointed out to them that they would always have a person who knew the areas well [with them], they replied that our absence from the reserves would give the Home Guards much freedom to do what they liked to our women and children and also it would be reported as our defeat in their propaganda.

I understood from their replies that they wanted to remain in the area they were familiar [with] and that they wanted to eliminate the Home Guards as they regarded them as our chief enemies. With this I noted that our people were losing sight of the enemy and that the enemies were creating enmity between [i.e., within] the Gikuyu tribe so that they would kill each other while the enemy would stand to restore peace after our tribe had been reduced to the number he wanted.

I was disappointed by Mathenge for not supporting my suggestion. He said that it was alright for some people to move to the Rift Valley, while others remained to discipline the Home Guards. The meeting then dissolved. Nevertheless, as a result of my speech, a few groups moved to the Rift Valley side of the forest thus decreasing the strength of the H.Q. to around 800 warriors.

Due to Government's regular attacks on H.Q.—on one of

which the Devons were seen by the guards just a few hundred yards from the camp very early in the morning before the sentries had started their duty—Mathenge decided to move to Mumwe stream near the women's camp about six miles north, near the border of bamboo and black forest. We left H.Q. Kariaini on July 7th, escorted by twelve armed warriors and a young girl who acted as Mathenge's cook and carrier. We spent a night at the women's camp, enabling me to talk to my step-sister, Wambui, who was living there. She had earlier been Mathenge's assistant in the reserve and had automatically moved with him into the forest. I learnt that only twenty-two women were in the camp while many other girls and women continued to live in different camps with their lovers against the rules. I understood the reason was that the leaders themselves did not obey the rules for each continued to keep a girl in his hut.

I did not like the women to stay in the forest; in fact I was very unhappy to see my step-sister in the forest. I decided to make arrangements for her to leave. I discussed the matter with Gicuki Wacira who was then the incharge of the women's camp and he agreed that his wife and daughter would also leave the forest. We sent them to Thegenge Location, Gacatha, and asked a friend of mine to take care of them. Though the man turned to become a Home Guard, they found other helpers till the end of the emergency.

The following day, we moved to our new camp of six persons— three warriors, Mathenge, his girl and me. Though our food supply was from the women's camp, only Gicuki knew the whereabouts of our camp. Mathenge had arranged a post [i.e., rendezvous] where we would meet our food and had warned all of us never to reveal our camp's situation. Nevertheless, the camp was situated about a mile east within scattered bamboos bordering the black forest under a big camphor tree which had fallen making a cave with sufficient room for about ten persons. Mathenge and his girl slept in a tent.

On the fourth night in our new camp, which was the 11th July, we were all awakened by fire [i.e., gun-] shots at about 3 a.m. After listening carefully, we were certain that the H.Q. was in danger. We had earlier received information that the mobilized Kenya settlers under the leadership of the Kenya Regiment had entered the forest on the morning of 7th July in small groups of about a dozen people.

The following morning we received reports from Gicuki Wacira that the Kenya Regiment incorporated with the Devons captured the H.Q. just at the time we heard the shots. He said that fifty warriors and seven girls had then arrived in his camp from H.Q. and that the person who could report [personally] about H.Q. was at the food's post. We went there with one warrior and found Samuel Wahihi with three other warriors. After greetings, Wahihi went on, 'We had received a message from a seer saying that we should not sleep in the camp as Government would raid it during a night. Many people who believed in prophesy left the camp after dinner and went to sleep on the mountain while a few slept in the camp. The enemies entered the camp without being noticed. We were all awakened by their shots. We could not return the fire. Our best risk [chance] was to run away as quickly as possible. I cannot tell how many people have died, but from experience, I would say that it was very difficult to run away as the dense bamboo had made a great wall in the darkness which knocked everyone down after every five yards or so.'

'Why did you disobey the seer?' Mathenge enquired angrily. 'I had no faith in them, but now I believe they have power,' said Wahihi. 'You should have known this long before,' said Mathenge. To prove his faith, he showed us his Lucky-charm—a small leather pouch which he carried in his pocket—that protects him and has power to frighten others. He said that all military, police and Government officers had the same talisman commonly fixed in their belts or just put in their pockets. He said that he was in the Second World War where he learnt this fact.

Wahihi said that they had two persons wounded in their legs and a third one in the forearm. He affirmed that none had any fracture but there were many others who had been hurt by stumps, thorns or the dried bamboos. I went with them to dress the patients. I always carried some medicine in my kitbag together with the record books. When I arrived, I found that they had all been well dressed as every camp had a dresser. After a little talk with them, I returned to our camp. I told Mathenge that the patients were not badly injured and that they would soon recover. He sent me to the hospital to bring his belongings and tell the hospital to move to a new site and spy whether the enemies were still in H.Q. or had left. He asked me to observe and assess the damage in H.Q.

On the morning of 13th July, I started my six mile journey

toward H.Q. with six armed escorts from the women's camp. On our way we could see the enemies' foot marks returning [i.e., leading away] from the H.Q. We were afraid to follow the main path, so we made our way through the bush and on our arrival at H.Q. we noticed that some huts were still burning as the enemy had set many of them on fire while knocking down others. We looked for corpses but did not see any; though we saw lumps of blood and two bands of fifty rounds of ammunition each. We continued our journey to the hospital and found that all had moved safely, leaving two guards for us as Mathenge had told Gathuku that he would collect his belongings on that day. The two guards told us that the enemies did not see the hospital as they were misled by our many paths up the hill leading only to where our warriors spent the day warming by the sun's heat; but they saw Wacira's camp on their way home and found nobody there as everyone left safely while the enemies were still firing at H.Q.

'We spied on the H.Q. yesterday afternoon after the enemy's departure,' continued one of the guards, 'and were surprised by the big fire of the burning huts. We found five corpses; each had one hand cut off at the wrist. We took them out of the camp and buried them. We could not tell, though, how many warriors died as the rest dispersed in many areas; but many corpses were seen later around that area and it was believed that many collapsed unseen. Thereafter, the four other guards left us and followed the patients to Kigumo and then to a new camp site near the Chania River about 35 miles to the northwest. We were ordered to wait for you for three days. If you failed to come, we would go to the women's camp and ask for some warriors who would carry the [i.e., Mathenge's] luggage.'

They then showed us where they had hidden the luggage and we hurriedly carried them and started return journey. Arriving at H.Q. ruins, we were spotted by two warriors and a girl who had spent almost two days without knowing the whereabouts of the others. They joined us and freed our warriors by carrying their luggage. Leaving H.Q. we could see some smoke from the Kenya Regiment base four miles inside the forest. One of our companions remarked that that was the place they had killed twenty-eight head of cattle on 11th July when they found that the Kenya Ng'ombe had blocked their way.

On our way, I spotted a group of Kenya Ng'ombe sitting down

taking their lunch under the bamboos about fifty yards from me. I signalled to my group asking them to retreat. Four of them ran away when they saw the white forces. We followed a *muirigo* [path] on a ridge leading into the heart of the forest which had been trod by many enemies a few hours past. After a short distance we arrived at a place where another enemy group had taken lunch. They had left some opened tinned food which we thought were poisoned, a new panga and a knife tied to a thin green wire and connected to a buried grenade. One of my companions was about to pull the panga when I shouted to him to stop. I told them that it was a mine trap and would kill us all if it exploded.

We changed our direction and moved northward across hills and valleys and many streams. At each stream we found a big track of the Kenya Regiment moving upstream. I began to wonder whether we would ever meet the camps we were heading for. There were echoes of shootings in many areas and the enemy's method of searching out a camp was unknown to our warriors. By following a stream, the enemies would enter our camps unseen, while the sentries would be guarding the camps' entrances. Their distribution seemed as if they were covering the whole forest. We had lost our way and I was leading my group according to my thinking whereabouts the camp might be. When we arrived at a bamboo section that was clear enough for anyone to see at least a hundred yards in every direction, I told my people to rest and have lunch. While we were having lunch we spotted our four persons who had run away. One of them lost his luggage and they were not certain of the direction they were moving.

At 3 p.m. we continued our journey, arriving at an enemies' deserted camp; they had cleared it by cutting down trees which had been thrown as if they were building a fence. They had buried everything, even their fireplaces, leaving the camp very clean. At about 4 in the afternoon, airplanes started dropping food to their forces and we could then learn whereabout their camps were that evening and learnt that they had passed us.

We arrived, safely and tired, at the women's camp at 5:30 p.m., though having many scratches of strawberry [thorns] on our faces, arms and legs. Gicuki told me that some guards had seen a group of 15 Kenya Ng'ombe passing along the *muirigo* on the ridge behind the camp. He added that sentries had been posted in every possible direction for the enemies to enter the camp. I learned that he had not posted any guards down or up stream which I instructed him to do the following morning. After arranging with him that Mathenge's luggage should be brought the following morning to our post store, I left with one escort to our [camphor tree] camp. I then reported my journey to Mathenge, after which he commented that it was difficult for us to fight against Government forces on any unplanned fight and the best we could do was to hide our footprints and if they missed us they would go out of the forest and we would plan our attacks. 'I shall go with you tomorrow to the women's camp to instruct them how to hide their footprints,' [he concluded].

The following day we were at the women's camp; Mathenge went on instructing the warriors how to hide footprints by moving on their toes or heels, straightening any fallen weeds behind, stepping on the dry leaves or on hard soil, moving backwards when crossing a road or path so that the footprints may mislead the trackers. He told them to pray hard and to obey the seers' instructions, remarking that those who had obeyed the seers were not in the camp when H.Q. was raided. He added that the dead ones must be the disobedient ones. He suggested that no one should leave the camp until the enemies had left the forest and that rations should be reduced to keep us longer. He bid them farewell and deceived them [by saying] that we were leaving for Mt. Kenya.

When we went at Gicuki's hut for a meal, he reported that he was faced by a great difficulty of defenseless and helpless women in his camp. He supposed that if all women were in his camp as our rule suggested it would result in a failure for [there would be] more food consumers than food carriers to bring the food and [not enough warriors to] defend them. He asked what would happen if the camp was dispersed by the enemies whereby a group of ten women found themselves without a man or with one or two men. He pointed out that our rule referring to women should be reviewed and amended. He remarked that most of the warriors and mostly the leaders had not observed that rule and if they took the responsibility of their lovers the better for us. Mathenge promised that he would call a leaders meeting as soon as the enemies left the forest. We returned to our camp to hide ourselves for the rest of the month.

On the way I considered how our warriors were dispersed and how they would be contacted again after establishing several camps; how it would be difficult to get them again in one camp; how Mathenge had left H.Q. in the hands of a group of leaders of almost equal rank though Kihara Kagumu was the only one bringing reports to Mathenge regularly; how Mathenge had started to hide instead of taking leadership and command in his hands; how he was controlled by superstition beliefs. I began to wonder how much he could do for the leadership he was responsible. I became worried whether Kimathi was of the same type and before reaching any decisions I arrived at our camp.

During the [next] two weeks, our warriors were confronted by the diehard Kenya Regiment. The difference between the Devons and the Kenya Regiment was that the latter wanted to kill us while the Devons wanted to capture us. Two warriors reported different tales to me. One was chased by a group of Devons and when his raincoat was grabbed [i.e., caught in a bush] he took it off and managed to run away. The Devons did not fire any shot at him. Another was found in a tree taking honey from a beehive and was asked by Devons to come down slowly. Full of fear and almost certain of his death, he landed on the ground and ran into the bush. He told me that they did not fire at him or chase him, but [instead] he heard them laughing.

The Kenya Ng'ombe wanted only to kill as many Kikuyu as possible. As the sons of settlers they showed no mercy. It was reported to me later by our warriors who made contact with them that they never left behind their arms or corpses, unless they were all dead. One of our successful sections which managed to kill a dozen of the Kenya Ng'ombe told me that they believed the Regiment's motto was to maintain their Bren gun. 'Whenever we shot their Bren gun man,' [they said, 'he] shouted "Johnny, come to the Bren gun, I've been shot by a bloody fakin Mau Mau," and another one moved over to operate it. We were in a position that we could see them all; they were descending a deep valley and we were on the next ridge. The distance was about 200 yards. When the last man fell from the Bren gun, we did not stop firing. We took time to aim at their corpses until we were certain that they were all dead as we had learnt that their injured ones pretended to be dead and had [earlier] killed eight of our warriors with grenades. It took us an hour to get there. We collected one Bren gun, two Sten guns, two Patchet guns, three rifles, two shot guns, three automatic pistols, two dozen grenades, ammunition, clothes, food and medicine. We took their telephone wireless and signalled to Kangima center reporting that we had captured one of their sections and that we wanted the Government to send food by air for their people at the source of Mathioya River about ten miles west of where we were. But the Government dropped bombs instead of food. We then destroyed the telephone wireless.'

One of the Kenya Regiment's achievements was to disperse our warriors into many small sections out of which grew many incapable self-styled leaders whose leadership was [concerned with] how to get food and how to hide. We called these groups *komerera*. Once they found that they were masters of themselves, they cast aside many of our rules, took the law in their own hands and fulfilled their pleasures. They robbed and disturbed our associates in the reserves, acquired money from our members at gun point, abducted many girls to the forest, raping some, and administered some absurd and illegal types of oaths. Some established themselves as leaders in the reserve while others claimed that they were the top leaders' messengers. The *komerera* leaders had no priority to [i.e., clearly defined roles or privileges *vis-à-vis*] their warriors other than to be called leader; while they acted and lived as equals in their camps they became very popular to their warriors. They all [i.e., many] didn't like to be ruled again and started to hide from us the same way as they hid from Government forces. We had a great deal of trouble hunting these outlaws and disciplining them again; a threat of shooting them if they refused to return to their former camps under the recognized leaders was issued and there was no resistance once they were caught—but it was difficult to find their camps. Eventually, most of them returned to their recognized leaders.

The bad weather helped us to drive the Kenya Regiment and the Devons out of the forest, which enabled Mathenge to call a meeting of the leaders in Kigumo and Kariaini areas to amend the women's rule by the end of July. The meeting was held near the women's camp, [attended by] thirteen leaders and Mathenge in the chairmanship. I continued my job to record the minutes. After a long discussion it was resolved that :

(1) A girl or a woman should be regarded as a regular warrior.
(2) Their work in camp should be fetching firewood, cooking

and serving the whole camp, cleaning utensils, mending warriors clothes and washing leaders' clothes.

(3) Every girl must be married and each woman must live with her husband in their hut or tent as they liked.

(4) Each camp leader must announce these marriages in the presence of all people and the party concerned could inform their parents in the reserve if they wanted.

(5) Either of the couple, or an outside warrior, would receive 25 strokes if found guilty of seducement.

It was agreed that the lost small groups of warriors be searched and brought to the camps and that further plans of attacking the enemy would be considered after resettlement. The meeting ended.

As I was growing dissatisfied with the deficiency of plans and ideology, I decided to talk to seven of my location leaders including Mathenge. I started by pointing out how children and women were starving of hunger in the reserves and how we continually grabbed the little food they had to keep them alive. 'We are able to go anywhere we like,' [I said,] 'and take whatever we want by force; but our children, wives and parents have no alternatives other than to wait for their death either of starvation or the enemies' stroke. I think that if we moved to the Rift Valley we could get plenty to eat and leave what we are using now to the starving ones. In addition to this, our location is on the Government's blacklist as the Government believes that everyone in Mahiga has taken the oath—which is almost true; only twenty-three persons have not taken the oath, of whom about half have already been killed. Government believes that it is the home and nursery of Mau Mau; why don't you want to preserve it as our home supply [base]?'

'We want to, but how?' one replied. 'By shifting our battlefield from our location to the Rift Valley,' [I answered.] 'You must be aware that whenever we kill or burn a Home Guard's house, their revenge is between ten and twenty times on the same object. It is true that we lose more and give the Government a chance it wants for killing our people; for even the Home Guard himself is a part of our tribe and population. If we could get him to work for us [it would be] better than to lose him. [We should] fight our enemies in the forests, in the Special Areas, in their camps and at any other place of contact, avoiding fights in the villages and assassinations in the villages in order to safe[guard] the civilians. If we could destroy the settlers' homes, livestock, plants and stores, they would lose hope in this country and decide to quit.'

Kabuga Njogu, the first supporter, continued to point out what works our prisoners, i.e., Home Guards, could do to develop our country, especially the road making, [after we were victorious.] Ngara Gitegenye, the first opposer, did not favor the idea of sparing the Home Guards. He suggested that our warriors should fight only the enemies in their [home] areas. Mathenge, who spoke last, supported my idea, adding that some people should remain in that area in order to check the enemies lest they construct permanent camps in the forest during our absence, which would be difficult for us to drive out. The rest supported my idea wholeheartedly and we resolved never again to commit an action in Mahiga Location that would cause Government to revenge on the civilians. Though our sections moved to the Rift Valley and returned several times, we kept our resolution to the end of the emergency and thus decreased the direct killing of our people in the reserve by the Government forces.

Mathenge, as the chief leader and oath administrator in the reserve, had collected a great deal of money in Nairobi, our location and division and some other divisions. We had little to buy with money apart from clothing, as most of our supplies were from spoils. When I enquired of him what he intended to do with the money he told me that he would help those who are in need. I pointed out to him some widows with orphan children. We selected 30 women, including his wife and my step-mother, whom we granted 20s. each, and 20 more women whom we granted 10s. each. We appointed Kabingu, King'ori and another warrior to distribute the money to the owners.

When the Devons and the Kenya Regiment left the forest, they spent the next two weeks making a line of ambushes all along the forest edge throughout the night. They stationed armoured cars with caterpillar wheels [i.e., tanks] on many ridges which continued shooting propelled shells or cannons and mortars at intervals, covering three miles distance inside the forest. Sometimes they used strong machines which shot more than 25 miles in the forest. All these forces started firing from the forest edge at 4 p.m. and continued at one hour intervals in order to frighten our warriors. As our warriors—150 from H.Q. and the women's camp had set up another camp near ours at Mumwe—learned that our enemy's were more prepared during the nights than in the days, they decided to raid the Home Guard herds in the Special Area at 2 in the afternoon. After a short exchange of fire, the Home Guards ran away and our forty warriors brought 130 head of cattle. They passed by our camp without knowing. When we saw them we asked them to give us one fat bullock which we slaughtered at our camp. They took the rest to the women's camp and shared it to other camps.

CHAPTER XIV

THE MWATHE MEETING

IN MID-AUGUST of 1953, after almost eight months of open revolt, a general meeting of Aberdare fighters was held near the banks of Mwathe stream on the eastern edge of the moorlands. In the present chapter Karari vividly recalls his journey to the moorlands and the many events, great and small, which occurred there during the five-day Mwathe meeting. Of primary importance was the formation of the Kenya Defence Council, a body comprised of all recognized forest leaders and headed by Dedan Kimathi and six other elected officers. The Kenya Defence Council represented the first attempt by Aberdare leaders to bring the guerrilla units operating in the four major regions of Nyandarua (i.e., Nyeri, Murang'a, Nderagwa and North Kinangop) under a unified military command and to integrate all of the revolutionary forces both within and outside the forest under a central governing council. At Mwathe a number of steps were taken to accomplish this task: eight Land and Freedom Armies were named, together with their commanders and areas of operation; formal military ranks were issued—following the British pattern; an overall military strategy was agreed upon, as well as a uniform set of rules and regulations; and a unified record system was devised and men assigned to administer it.

Though the specific powers of the Kenya Defence Council were never spelled out in detail, they were generally conceived to be those necessary for the overall planning and coordination of the military campaign. Like the Ituma Ndemi Trinity Council, however, the Kenya Defence Council was granted a considerable measure of policy- and decision-making power by its leader-members, but very little in the way of administrative and enforcement machinery. Its rulings, tactical policies and organizational programs were, to a large extent, left to lower-level leaders to administer and enforce. That so much authority was delegated to, or left in the hands of, individual section leaders is best understood as reflecting the actual distribution of effective power among the various forest leaders, each of whom possessed his own following and forest sphere of influence. The Kenya Defence Council, and the formal military hierarchy it created, thus tended to legitimize rather than alter the positions previously held by the guerrilla leaders. Later we shall examine some of the advantages, frailties and ramifications of this relatively weak central council and the loosely knit organization of guerrilla forces over which it held nominal control.

The thunders of war and revolution invariably upset the established familial patterns and sexual norms of conduct of a people. Within the forest, the role and position of girls and women—who traditionally played no part whatever in Kikuyu military affairs—was highly ambiguous and tended to shift as the battle lengthened. At the outset, as we have seen, the tendency was for women to assume their normal domestic duties and tasks despite the radically altered conditions of life and military setting in the forest. For a time, the traditional taboo on sexual intercourse for active warriors was upheld, thus reducing the potential strain and conflict inherent in the numerical discrepancy between males and females—i.e., women never comprised more than 5 per cent of the total forest population. But the sexual taboo operative in the olden days of brief Kikuyu raids and defensive encounters against the Masai could not be maintained as the revolt stretched from weeks into months.

The violation of the taboo on sexual intercourse, and the conflicts engendered thereby, led to an early ruling by the Ituma Ndemi Trinity Council according to which women were to be segregated from the men and sustained within camps of their own. This ruling, however, was never fully implemented or enforced. Many of the warriors, and particularly the leaders, refused to comply with the rule and be separated from their wives or sweethearts. Again, those women who were gathered together in women's camps constituted too heavy a burden for the warriors who had to feed and protect them.

The revision of rules pertaining to women made by the Ituma council were approved and added to by the leaders at Mwathe. The primary aim was to establish more realistic rules and norms of conduct between the sexes and thereby reduce the possibilities

of friction and conflict. To ensure the permanence of forest liai-
sons, 'marriages' were to be publicly announced and registered,
and leaders were not to interfere in the women's selection of
spouses. Again, acknowledging a shift in the role of many
women, the latter were to be issued ranks up to that of colonel
on the basis of their abilities as warriors—which they were hence-
forth to be considered, along with the men.

As we shall see in later chapters, the problems and conflicts
generated by the presence of women in the forest were never
completely resolved despite the many and varied rule changes.
Karari's account of his conversations with one of the camp
women at Mwathe warmly reveals some of the dimensions of
this problem, as well as his own conflicts and personal, if not
typical, solution.

★ ★ ★

On the third day of August, Kimathi's messengers from Murang'a
arrived and handed a letter to Mathenge which he asked me to
read to him. It said:

Dear Mathenge,
I have called a general meeting to be held at *Nguthiru* (Moorlands) on the banks of Mwathe stream. I am coming there with
all the leaders from Fort Hall, with many of their warriors. I
expect to meet you there with all the Nyeri leaders and warriors.
I have written a letter to every leader I know and have sent
them to North Kinangop of the Rift Valley and Nderagwa for
the Laikipia District. In short, I expect all the leaders in
Nyandarua Forest. The meeting would start on 16/8/53 to the
20th. You should therefore carry sufficient food to last you more
than a week.
As this would be the first general meeting for all the warriors
in Nyandarua Forest, I think we should:
    (1) Elect a Kenya-wide Council,
    (2) Make rules and regulations,
    (3) Instruct our leaders and warriors,
    (4) Make plans on raids,
    (5) Issue out ranks,
    (6) Discuss any other arising matter.

Convey my sincere greetings to the leaders and warriors. Work hard and pray.

Thaai (Peace)

Dedan Kimathi Waciuri

He listened carefully as I read the letter to him privately. As was his habit, he had some ground native tobacco in his mouth which made him to spit often. After a long pause of thinking he said, 'Who is the chief, Kimathi or me?'

'I do not know well, for I have only recently learned that you were elected as the chief of Nyeri warriors and Kimathi as the secretary; but the Government advertises Kimathi as the leader of all the warriors in Kenya.'

'That may be the reason why he tried to kill me by putting a bullet in the fire so that he would become chief leader. Leadership is a gift of God. I will take my share and he will take his.'

'Yes, that is true,' I replied.

'I am the man to call Kimathi to a meeting; he is only my clerk (Mathenge, like most others, did not know the difference in duties between a clerk and a general secretary). With whom did he arrange that meeting? All the Ituma counselors are here in this district.'

I explained to him the difference between a clerk and a general secretary and warned him that it might be possible that Murang'a, North Kinangop and the Nderagwa might have their councils just like our Ituma in Nyeri but these counselors have never met and when they meet, they will elect one leader. 'The leader would be either Kimathi or you. You should then attend the meeting for many people would not support you during your absence.'

'I will make up my mind when I see the other leaders around here,' he said.

By this time leaders and warriors from other divisions had left Kariaini, leaving behind only Othaya Division warriors. I accompanied Mathenge to visit all Mahiga Location camps and two of Othaya. In each camp he had a private talk with its leader. Whenever I asked any leader after their talks whether he was to attend the Nguthiru meeting, the reply was doubtful and leaning to Mathenge's decision. One of the leaders, Kabuga Njogu, told me that he had been asked by Mathenge not to attend Kimathi's meeting; but in spite of that he would go because the motive behind it was jealousy on chieftainship. Watoria (Thiongo Gateru), assistant of Gicuki Wacira in the women's camp, told me that he would attend the meeting, after which he would move to Nderagwa where he would continue fighting with the settlers and their property. We started planning our journey. I had 170s. in my wallet of which 120s. was from boarding fees at Muthaini School. I sent 20s. in the reserve ordering six yards of calico for 15s. for making my tent, five pounds of wheat flour for 3s. and a dozen boxes of matches for 2s. My order was successful and I wanted to know Mathenge's decision. He told me that he was not attending the meeting. I asked him to write Kimathi and explain his reasons for not attending. He refused to write a letter but sent me [instead]. He asked me to tell Kimathi that he was very busy searching warriors who were badly scattered by the Devons and the Kenya Regiment last month in their strong operation.

On the evening of 14th August I bid Mathenge and my companions goodbye and went to spend the night at the women's camp with other warriors who were willing to attend the meeting. During the night, our *safari* food was prepared—roasted meat for all and some pancakes for Watoria and me. Gicuki Hinga was appointed as my luggage carrier. Very early the following morning, we all prayed together, asking God to bless our journey, keep and guide us all the way. We set off, a group of twenty-eight warriors. The weather was bad; great mists, wet cold leaves in narrow animal paths. Sometimes we had to make our new path in thick bushes, our feet sinking in the damp cold soil saturated with water for at least two months.

We arrived Kigumo and were joined by Gen. Makanyanga's (Kariuki Mathinji's) gang of a hundred and twenty-eight warriors, including a dozen women. We found that the Gura River had swollen up and the best crossing place we found was two and a half feet deep. The able warriors used a staff to help them and held the hand of a weaker person. We all managed to cross that cold, strong and swiftest river in the Nyandarua Forest. We changed our direction to northwest and started climbing a mile steep hill of which its first part was in the black forest and the other in the bamboo zone. On our arrival at the top we found a deserted ruined camp. I learned that it was one of Kahiu-Itina's old camps captured by the enemy. I could see torn pieces of clothes and damaged utensils.

We moved on flat land covered by thick bamboos across which a big road from Nyeri to the Moorlands via Kiandongoro Forest Station was under construction. Armored cars and tanks with many machine guns managed by military and assisted by Home Guards supervised the civilians who were forced to make the road which would enable the Government to transport its forces quickly some thirty miles inside the forest and which they would use to encircle or cordon us in certain areas.

We sat down and sent scouts to check whether there were enemies along the road. During this time I learned from Makanyanga that he had twice sent scouts to [spy on] the road constructors and the reports were that though difficult to defeat them, our warriors could manage to disturb them; but we were afraid that they [i.e., Government forces] may kill the civilians and allege that they were killed by *Mau Mau* or that the civilians fled to join the *Mau Mau*. When our scouts returned, they reported that we could cross the road and must do it quickly lest we are met by the enemy's Land Rovers which moved to-and-fro checking our movements. On arrival, we found that we had to climb over a five feet high fence of the fallen bamboos and walk on them like monkeys for forty feet, then cross the road, thirty feet wide of well-cleared soil by tractors, on which our footprints could be seen. We had to move on toes and circle the leg [i.e., twist our feet] so as to hide any human mark and start climbing on those fallen bamboos on the other side of the road. For a few hundred yards we continued to hide our tracks and after scattering to further mislead any pursuers, found ourselves moving in scattered bamboos and bushes with patches of grass which fed large herds of buffaloes and we could see the morning tracks of rhinos and elephants here and there. It was not long before we were challenged by a furious rhino who passed across our path dispersing the men.

It was already half past one and we sat down for lunch . . . cold roasted meat. We continued our journey, stopping twice on the way in order to get honey from forest trees. The honey was diluted with water and each drunk a cup of the cold sweet drink to quench our thirst after a long journey and a fatty lunch.

By four o'clock we started descending gradually the slopes of the River Chania. At sunset, I found myself lagging with four warriors; I could see the last man about a hundred yards in front under the dark bamboo cover. I was almost exhausted and could not increase any speed. Without seeing anyone, we followed their tracks. The darkness increased so that we could no longer see their tracks. We had hope that they had not encamped far away. I could smell smoke from the camp and guessed the direction for a few hundred yards. Our movement became very difficult and we continued stumbling down over the rough terrain. I signalled with the call of the nightbird to check whether they could hear us. Luckily, the guards replied my signal. I shouted that we were lost and wanted help. The guards met us and showed us the way. We could see camp fires some 300 yards away but to get there was very difficult; cold had increased so that we were shivering and often falling on that slippery steep slope.

At 7 :30 we arrived in the camp, cold and tired. I was glad to meet Wacira Gathuku and (Shumali) Gathura Muita, the in-charge of the general hospital. This is where the patients were moved when H.Q. was captured. I met Mathenge Kihuni for the second time. He told me that he had brought food for the patients and that he was also going to the meeting with some 87 other warriors. We talked of what had happened but as soon as I became warm I began to feel sleepy; I could not even wait for dinner. Wacira showed me where to sleep and soon I slept.

The following day we continued our journey in a caravan of 244 persons. As we approached the Moorlands, we found a dead elephant. The hyenas had eaten all the meat leaving the hard bones and the three-feet-long ivory. We carried the tusks and moved direct north along the bushes bordering the Nguthiru grass-land so that we would have somewhere to hide if an airplane flew over us. We crossed the rivers Chania and Gikururu; the water is very cold up here within the altitude of 11,000 feet. Mist became our ally, protecting us from being seen by an airplane. We changed direction due west and were moving on burnt grassland. I learned from one of our warriors that an airplane had accidentally crashed while bombing the forest, setting the fire which burnt grass over about ten square miles.

At two in the afternoon it started pouring hailstones. These frozen stones struck hard on us causing us to freeze. The ground had not sufficient heat to melt them and they caused our feet to freeze. We couldn't go further and so made our camp on the bank of a small stream running across small bushes. We pegged tents, some using blankets to make tents. There was no difference between smoke and mist, therefore we made big fires at 4 p.m. It was so cold that I was unable to straighten my fingers. Some hot strong coffee was prepared for the leaders while soup was made for all. After eating, drinking and warming, it was still so cold that we had all to smear our bodies with animal fat. Some leaves and grass were cut and dried with fire in order to make mattresses on the frozen ground. I hardly slept that night.

The following morning, I was very much surprised to see that the dew on the grass, on our tents and blankets and some water that was left in a *karai* (metal basin) had all frozen. We continued our journey on the frozen grassland which melted by 10 a.m., when we had a little sunshine, but we never felt its warmth. We arrived at Mwathe stream about one in the afternoon, where we sat down for lunch. I and eight other warriors started fishing with safey-pin hooks, string and bamboo fishing rods. I caught sixteen fish within less than an hour; the small stream had very many fish. I learned that Government had sent thousands of young brown trouts upstream which fed on the smaller type of fish that were originally found in the stream. One elder amongst us named Wandare was one of the men who had taken fish upstream in 1925 according to his memory.

We continued to climb a small bushy hill on a wide old animal path which led to Mwathe Camp. At two miles distance, we could see cleared areas which looked like big gardens. When I enquired of what that was, I was told that that was the area in which grass had been cut for thatching the camp's huts. On my arrival at the guards' camp at 4:30 p.m. I guessed the cleared area to be five acres. I could see more than thirty guards' huts built of different sizes and shapes; round, gabled roofed, and the familiar type of shelters. Either branches with many leaves or grass had been used to cover the walls; an attempt to check the extreme cold.

Some two hundred yards west lay the Officers' Camp. All in-comers and their supplies were stopped here and after some checking and recording, the supplies were handed over to the storekeeper who took them to an underground store some three hundred yards north of the camp. The meat was hung on trees where the altitude of almost 12,000 feet served as a refrigerator. Our elephant tusks were taken to the store and we were told that we had touched an unclean dead animal. [Traditionally, the eating or touching of

single-hooved animals was tabooed among the Kikuyu.] We were
then ordered not to mix with the others until we were cleansed.
Some leaders, including Kimathi and Wang'ombe Ruga, his witchdoctor, came to see the elephant tusks and say hello to us. Kimathi
told us that we had a lucky journey and that the ivory were great
wealth; and added that we had to be cleansed, introducing his
witchdoctor, Generals Macharia Kimemia, chief leader of
Murang'a, Mbaria Kaniu, Kimbo and others.

We made a long queue of two hundred and forty four persons
facing Wang'ombe Ruga the witchdoctor and passing by him he
would smear a little sheep fat, which is believed to be anti-calamity,
on both hands, face and feet, then dipped his fly-whisk made from
the tail of a cow into half a gourd which contained a mixture of
the rumen content of a hyrax (used as substitute for a sheep) which
had been dried, water and some wild herbs, one of which was
mwembaiguru—a creeping plant which produces milky sap, very
sweet-smelling roots used to sweeten soup, and is regarded as a
lucky plant. He then sprayed us saying, 'I cleanse you of all the
calamity and evils you might have contacted.' After the cleansing
ceremony, all the warriors were told to go to a camp that was
vertically opposite us; some two hundred yards of grass southwards separated us from that camp. To get there one had to cross
one of the Mwathe's cold-running tributaries. The camp, under
big trees with grass undergrowth, looked like a big nomads' village.

To the west lay the main camp with hundreds of huts of different
types, shapes and sizes. The leaders were welcomed to the officers'
camp and were led to the officers' mess room—25 feet by 12 feet,
with gabled roof and all the five-foot walls covered. As one enters,
he would see two long [rough wooden tables, covered with soft
cedar bark,] separated by a four foot wide corridor which ends at
a table at which Kimathi, Macaria, Kahiu-Itina and Kimbo sat.
There I had coffee with some other fifty five leaders. Each table
was occupied by twenty-six leaders, of whom the two who sat at
the ends acted as prefects who ordered food and organized the
kitchen.

While still taking coffee, Kimathi went on introducing the leaders
who had arrived. Though he had heard of me we had never met
before. All he could say of me was, 'He has been headmaster
Muthuaini School and has earned reputation for helping many of
our warriors and we are glad to have such an educated person.'

'Mr. Njama, yesterday we raided your school and captured many exercise books for our records and a radio from your former house,' said Kahiu-Itina.

'I hope you will tell me all that in detail.'

'How was your journey and how is Mathenge?' asked Kimathi.

'We had a three-day-long and tiresome journey, mountain climbing and bad weather being our chief obstacles. We didn't see any enemy traces on the way but we were lucky to collect elephant tusks which has made me to undergo a cleansing ceremony which reminded me of the last cleansing ceremony I underwent some twenty years ago when I was about seven years old.'

The others fell into a laughter at this, and I heard some saying, 'We have made you anti-Christian.'

'Mathenge is all right,' I went on. 'I have been his secretary for the last two and a half months. He asked me to greet all the leaders and asked me to tell you, Kimathi father/of Waciuri, that he will not attend the meeting. He told me that he was busy collecting *itungati* who were dispersed by the Devons last month.'

'And what about the other leaders, Njau, Ngara, Gicuki and the rest from Kariaini who have not attended?' asked Kimathi.

'They are in the same boat with Mathenge and will not come.'

'I believe that he has only refused to come,' said Kimathi, 'for the excuse he has given is a very weak one. There are many leaders who can carry on orders for searching the lost *itungati*. We had been expecting Mathenge today, but now our meeting will continue without him. One thing I am certain of and that is that whatever good we do here will be supported by all the people, even the unborn.'

A whistle was blown. 'Prayers! Prayers! Prayers!' shouted someone outside, calling all people to attend the evening prayers. We all went out. After prayers, Kimathi invited me to his room, which had been very well protected from cold and a fire was burning to keep it warm. As I sat down, two warriors brought two animal skin kitbags full of honey they had been collecting all the day. Kimathi ordered one of them to fill a big mug with honey and give it to me. He told me that he would brew beer with the honey for ceremonial prayers. While I was eating the honey, Kimathi asked me what I had left Mathenge doing. I told him that for more than a month Mathenge and I had been hiding under a big camphor tree and that he was not at all concerned with the searching of *itungati*; he simply didn't want to attend the meeting because he felt that he should have called the meeting or you should have arranged the whole matter with him before advertising the meeting. 'The other leaders wanted to come but were stopped by him. Kabuga Njogu who disobeyed his boycotting of the meeting may tell you what he was told.'

'He has already told me the whole story,' said Kimathi, 'but Mathenge has lost a great chance of being known to many of our *itungati* from Murang'a, North Kinangop, Nderagwa and even the Ituma Ndemi Army of which we elected him to be the chief leader. I hope he is not suffering from megalomania. I would certainly attend any meeting he would call me to. I would like to meet him and resolve our differences and the suspicions which might have arisen from a fire-bullet incident at Murang'a. Nevertheless, I would postpone nothing due to his absence...though I would always call him to my meetings and place his chair in front of the present leaders all the time during his absence.'

'Officers' mess! Officers' mess! Officers' mess!' shouted a voice outside. I asked what that meant. Kimathi told me that it was a call for dinner and that all the officers should sit together in their messroom. He called for Captain Ngiriri, a brown, handsome, five-six man and a great joker. Imitating a KAR, he stood alert and saluted. Kimathi then told him, 'Mr. Njama and I would like to have dinner here.' He went out shouting to the kitchen girls. He returned escorting two girls who brought us pancakes in a plate and a thick gravy of meat and potatoes. As we were eating, Kimathi told me that those potatoes were brought from North Kinangop and that a few warriors who were left behind roasting some were followed by some Kenya Regiment who opened fire on them at close range. 'Five of our warriors are still missing and two of the gang are suffering from hysteria. They are voiceless and still shivering, though unhurt.'

'Yesterday night,' continued Kimathi, 'we launched one of our surprise attacks on *Muitwo na Higi*, alias Kagunduini Center. General Kahiu-Itina's section had collected one of the 50 lb. bombs dropped by the airplanes. We decided to explode it in one of the Home Guards' plots. I sent some 600 *itungati* under General Kahiu-Itina and ordered them to carry all the goods in the twelve Home Guards' shops. With them, I sent 150 warriors to bring food from our depots in the reserve and three groups of fifty strong each to plunder their cattle. All of them were very successful. After looting all the shops, Kahiu-Itina and a few others were.... Oh! Let me call Kahiu-Itina so that he would give you the first hand account. Captain Ngiriri!'

'*Abandi*,' [replied the captain,] a term derived from '*Effendi*,' the KAR's title for 'Sir,' originated from Turkey. He actively stood at attention and saluted.

'Tell Gen. Kahiu-Itina to come here.'

'*Ndio Abandi*' ('Yes Sir'). The speedy man rushed out and returned within two minutes with Gen. Katiu-Itina. '*Timamu Abandi*,' meaning 'finished, fulfilled, done, or complete Sir.'

'*Mzuri* ['Good'] Captain.' The man saluted again and left. In a laughing tone, Kimathi said, 'I want you to tell Mr. Njama how you conducted the *Muitwo na Higi* attack. Commence just at your arrival in the reserve.'

'On our arrival at the forest border,' started Gen. Kahiu-Itina, 'the 150 food carriers dispersed in the various food supply centers. From the three cattle groups I took ten *itungati* from each forming another group which I sent to raid Wairagu's aviary. He is a notorious Home Guard. I ordered them to bring all his poultry and their eggs. One of the cattle groups had to raid near the plot while others went to Chania. Out of the 600 *itungati* I had, I sent sent twenty of them to your school and told them not to hurt any of the teachers or make any damage to the school, but [to bring] this radio from your former house and all the exercise books from the headmaster's store so that we can have record books for our sections. I told them that since they had no one to fight against, they should fire a few shots in all directions so as to frighten the Home Guards—also giving the teachers an excuse that their survival was due to their escape in the darkness before our warriors entered their houses—and quickly return to the place of our departure and wait for us there.

'Arriving at the plot [i.e., market center], I sent three groups of 20 guards each to guard the three roads that might bring helpers on vehicles. Since only Nyeri could send strong helpers, I added 20 more warriors to that road. I entered the plot with 500 *itungati*, opened fire and soon learned that no one was returning our fires, but we could hear them running away. We broke shop doors and windows and entered. We found that the owners had escaped through the rear doors. Our warriors became busy in packing the luggage. Since there were very insufficient empty sacks, we used blankets and other cloths for tying our bundles of clothes, cloths, medicine, sugar, salt, beans, flour, exercise books, etc., etc. In the Tusker beer shop, we broke all the bottles and poured the beer. Our warriors, heavily loaded, started moving to the forest. I sent someone to call the Nyeri-road guards and ordered them to follow our warriors and urged them to hurry up before we set the bomb on fire.

'I was left behind with a dozen others. We put the bomb in the middle of the center shop. I sent some warriors to my former workshop and asked them to bring the carpenter's plane rubbish [i.e., shavings] and the others collected waste paper and the small paper containers. We covered the bomb with the stuff and poured four tins of kerosine oil on the rubbish, set it on fire and ran as quickly as possible. After five minutes or so we were more than a mile from the plot. We saw a big flash of lightning followed by a thunderous horrible noise accompanied by earth tremor. The falling and crashing of the stone of big shops continued for several seconds. We saw the Nyeri lights go off and the whole area became dead silence under the influence of the dreadful alarm. I think all the shops were destroyed.'

'I would be very grateful if you destroyed more than that,' interrupted Dedan Kimathi. 'You see, Mr. Njama, the Government has closed trading centers which were under our people and those Home Guards had some privileges because of torturing our people and forcing them to confess. Surely the Government has been very unfair. It has closed our schools, as part of punishment, stopped all our vehicles from moving while Home Guard vehicles are still moving.... Gen. Kahiu-Itina, make arrangements tomorrow for some *itungati* to ambush Shadrack's omnibus. Tell them not to return in the forest until they destroy that bus and the owners.'

'I am glad that you have closed one Home Guard trading center and have taught men, women and children the experiences we are getting about these bombs. That bomb's destruction, which is now open for all to see, would be a fair proof that when the Government is dropping thousands of bombs in this forest and Mt. Kenya it aims at destroying us the same way. How many warriors have been destroyed by these bombs up to date?' I asked.

'In early March,' continued Dedan Kimathi, 'nine squatters from the North Kiningop fled with their large herds of livestock through this forest heading for Murang'a. They knew that if they were repatriated they would lose their livestock. They were spotted by a Police Air Wing plane on Nguthiru grassland soon after crossing the river Gura. They tried to hide in a very small cluster of bamboo but unfortunately they were beaten with grenades and machine guns to their death. Some of their survived livestock were collected by our warriors, the rest were eaten by hyenas, leopards and their families.

'The other incident was in Murang'a towards the end of the same month. Our warriors had made fire during the day and its smoke was sighted by the small patrol planes. There were more than 300 warriors in that camp but our greatest luck was that the enemies had not started using bombs by that time. They dropped several grenades in the camp amidst the people. Nine were killed and eighteen were injured. We then learned to hide smoke during the day and fires during the night. Ever since, the airplanes have never contacted our people, though they have been dropping bombs aimlessly. Sometimes, when their foot forces enter our *mbuci*, they later on direct their air forces who heavily bomb the vacated camps. Whether they think that we might have returned in those camps or they merely want us to see their strength is a thing I can't tell.'

'Since our enemies are using strong bombs,' I commented, 'our warriors should be strongly warned to take much care about smoke during the day and fires during the nights. Why did you choose this place for the camp while we are surrounded by large tracts of grasslands and the warriors have cleared more than five acres of grass which I sighted when I was two miles away and which can be seen by patrolling planes from a great distance?'

'My reasons,' said Kimathi, 'are, first, this place is the center of Nyandarua and all our warriors would have to travel equal distances. The second reason is that since we have never made camps up here, the Government would not suspect us to be in this cold region. The third is that it is so misty that no airplane can see us. Moreover, we have only three more days and we shall disperse.'

'How many people are in the camp?' I asked.

'A little over four thousand and six hundred,' replied Gen. Kahiu-Itina.

'By the way, Gen. Kahiu-Itina, did you say that you raided my school because you wanted this radio and some exercise books?'

'Yes, that's what I said.'

'I remember that there were two radio sets in that center; Jeremiah Ngunjiri had a bookshop and kept much stationery and there were all types of exercise books in every shop. Couldn't those satisfy our wants without disturbing the children's education?' I eagerly asked.

'We could, Mr. Njama, but you see our aim is to cause losses to the Government in all possible ways,' continued Gen. Kahiu-Itina. 'Now the Government would buy another radio for the school and supply new books.'

'It worries me very much, father/of Waciuri....'

'He is called Field Marshal Dedan Kimathi,' interrupted Gen. Kahiu-Itina, 'and the other leaders will receive their official ranks tomorrow.'

'Thank you very much, General. It worries me very much, Field Marshal, to hear that so many teachers have been killed and so many schools destroyed by the people who are seeking freedom... the same people who are [now] singing of praise and cries for education. Listen to them singing!' (Outside, our warriors just finished singing the first song below and were starting the second.)

(1) Neither your unsatisfied wants
    Nor your difficulties will kill you.
    Without eyes to see the tears of the children
    It matters not whether one is foolish or clever.

    If Mumbi's children are not educated
    Then neither the European
    Nor the Asian will lose sleep
    Worrying about how to satisfy their needs.

    This is a time for sharing.
    Kikuyus arise!
    Let us help the children with their difficulties
    For they are the ones who will take our places.

    The need for a spear is gone
    Replaced by the need for a pen.
    For our enemies of today
    Fight with words.

Parents, give us pens so that we might advance
And assist our Kikuyu Heroes.
For it is we, your children,
Who will have to aid you in the future.

(2)   If it were Ndemi and Mathathi
Father, I would ask you for Kirugu
Now, father, I only ask you for education.

Today's heroes, father, sing only of education
Isn't Mathu for education, father?
Will I ever be proud of my education?

Today's heroes, father, have all gathered
In order to protect the land
Haven't you that same thought?

This good land of ours, Kenya
Was protected in the past by warriors
Who carried spear and shield.
Did ever cowards win cattle?

As our warriors continued to sing many other songs, as they
usually did after dinner, I asked Field Marshal Kimathi whether
he understood that our deeds in the schools were being interpreted
as meaning that we did not want education and that our aim was
directed to barbarism, witchcraft and superstition; and that our
actions being contrary to what we sing are enough to convince
even our supporters, who are really urging for more and better
chances of education.

'I was not aware of that,' replied Kimathi, shaking his head.
'Though I very much feel the need for education, I greatly oppose
the Beecher Report and have objected to it being put into practice.
For I know that practice forms a habit. I first believed that all
people hated the report as I do and that we could fight it by our
biggest weapon of boycotting it; but when I learned that the
people at the schools led by the missionaries did not oppose it and
that they were helping the Government to defeat us, I then thought
these loyalists might even have consulted the Government to close
all the schools that are not organized by the missionaries so that

they could have the control over the education and continue to ration it as medicine. You know well that all these missionaries are Europeans. Even Mubia (a Catholic Italian Padre) has said several times that there is no difference between him and the others of the white community. He has also claimed that he has warned the Europeans, "*Nindakwirire utige kunora mukuha na mbari cieri, ugagutheca.*" ("Don't sharpen the Kikuyu needle at both ends, for it will surely prick you.") Meaning that the Europeans should not give the Africans any education that might endanger their [i.e., the white man's] paradise.

'Of all the teachers who have been killed and schools which have been destroyed, very few [are due to] orders from me; in fact, none for the killing of teachers. But I have ordered the destruction of some schools for the demonstration of our objection to Beecher's Report, as you have learned from Gen. Kahiu-Itina raiding your school. The rest [of the raids have been carried out by supporters and *komereras*] from mere bitterness to that harmful plan which has led to the closure of about 300 of our schools. The interpretation doesn't matter much, for one can interpret anything in any way he likes. If I were to speak to the people I would tell them the Government doesn't want us to be educated and that is why it has closed our schools; it wants us to continue witchcraft and superstition for after closing the schools it has given us no substitute other than collective punishment without trials, and many innocent people are punished. Don't you think that the people would agree with me?' asked F. M. Kimathi proudly.

'They would surely agree with you,' I replied. 'Did you start the meeting yesterday as you had said?' I asked.

'Oh, no! Our first sitting commenced today at 10 a.m. We didn't do much as we spent most of the time in the formal discussions and since it was the first time to meet we wanted to know each other better so everyone had a time to speak, especially the ones whom I could say very little about in the introduction... they had to introduce themselves. All we have done is to form and elect officers of the Kenya Defense Council, of which I was elected President, Gen. Macaria Kimemia (Murang'a) Vice President, Gen. Kahiu-Itina Treasurer and Brig. Gathitu Secretary. We elected seven office bearers altogether, including myself, and all the leaders are members of the Kenya Defense Council. This Council would be responsible for plans and organization.'

'Thank you very much, Field Marshal, for the information you have given me. I'm feeling tired and sleepy and I would be glad to be shown where to sleep.' Captain Ngiriri was called and on his arrival was asked whether he had made arrangements for my room. He replied that he had prepared everything. I thanked Kimathi for his kind invitation and followed Capt. Ngiriri. He led me into a seven by five foot gabled room with four-foot walls well protected from the cold. A bright fire was burning; with its light I could see my bed in which a lot of grass had been used to make a mattress, a heap of firewood and the room attendant, a girl not less than five feet eight inches, fair brown, healthy and dressed in calico sheets. We shook hands and the jocular captain commenced his introduction.

'Mr Njama, this is your *kabatuni*,' he said, pointing at the girl.

'What is *kabatuni*?' I asked.

'I mean that this is your "small platoon" that you will have to command. She must be with you in this room all the time. She will take care of you; make your bed, take care of your beddings, warm your bathing water, clean and mend your clothes, fetch firewood for keeping you warm, and it is her duty to entertain you in any way that pleases you. Do you understand that you *kabatuni*?'

'Yes (*Eeei*!),' replied the girl.

'This is Mr Njama, and this is Miss Wangui. If you have any troubles call on me. Sleep well. Good night.'

The girl placed a piece of log near the fire and asked me to sit on it. I sat down, deeply thinking about this surprising procedure. Wangui went and quickly returned with some water in a *karai*. She put it on the fire in order to warm the freezing water. We kept quiet for some minutes as I continued to weigh how our warriors could live with women in such a situation. 'To feed and defend women [I thought] is an unnecessary burden to our warriors. Sleeping with them would bring calamity to our camps, weaken our *itungati* and, probably, they would become pregnant and would be unable to run away from the enemies, and they would be killed. No child can survive in this condition. For generations, women had been a source of conflicts between men. Wouldn't some of these girls, the ones brought into the forest against their wills, surrender and give the Government much information about us? I wished I could get them all out of the forest and let them face their fates in the reserves like the others.'

'Mr Njama, the water is warm. Wash your feet,' said Wangui in a pleasing tone.

'Thank you,' I said, taking off my boots. 'When did you enter the forest' I asked.

'I entered the forest one month and three weeks ago.'

'Why did you want to come?'

'I did not want to come. I had taken food to the supply center with four other girls. Then we contacted a group of eight warriors. They asked us to help them to carry the food to the forest border and, arriving, they refused to let us return. We slept two nights with them before arriving at Gen. Nyaga's camp, where we found some 28 other girls. The *itungati* reported to their leader that we wanted to come to the forest and that we were badly hunted by the Home Guards. We did not [try to] prove that they were lying as their leader welcomed us and we feared saying his warriors had lied. I have since been living with one of the warriors until we came to the meeting. We were then selected to serve the leaders. Each leader has a girl attendant and there are 20 girls in the kitchen awaiting for distribution to the leaders who will come.'

'Do you know how many women are in this camp?'

'They are well over 450.'

'Do you like your job?'

'Yes, I think so. It is not much different than the work I did at home, and the only work I know how to do. Wherever I might go under the sun, I think these same duties would follow me.'

'How do you feel about being forced to sleep with a man you have not chosen?'

'There are different ways of forcing a girl; which one do you mean?' asked Wangui anxiously.

'I mean what you have been instructed by the captain.'

'Each girl and woman has her own different view. Some girls are annoyed for being parted with their lovers and forced to seek some new ones. I am not in their group for I have no lover here in the forest. Generally, I would think of sleeping with a man as an individual concern. Here, it seems to me that the leaders consider this as part of the women's duty in the Society. I believe that since I could not do any other better service to my people, I would then willingly accept it as my contribution to the Society [i.e., Movement].'

'If you are given permission to go back to the reserve, would you be happy?'

'Oh no! The Home Guards are merciless and I wouldn't want to meet them. I would rather remain here with you warriors up to the end.'

'Thank you very much, Wangui. I am glad that you have openly and sincerely spoken to me. Where do you usually sleep?'

'In the kitchen, with some other girls,' replied Wangui politely.

'I have to thank you again Wangui. Go sleep well and remember to come early in the morning. Good night Wangui.'

I entered in my blankets and in the darkness stared, reflecting on all that night's discussions. An ill feeling about approaching a woman at any time while still engaged in the fight grew strong on the top of my head and I therefore vowed to myself not to play with women till the end of the fight.

The following day broke with a change in the weather; we could see the snow cap of Mt. Kenya while saying our morning prayer and eagerly staring at the sacred Home of God asking Him to guard and guide us. Though I did not believe that God *lived* there, I believed it to be a holy place. Firstly, this traditional belief, which had begun with the creation of our tribe, must have originated from something to do with God and not from nothing. Secondly, God's guards, the ice and snow, capture any being, insect, bird or reptile, that steps in the whole place and remains forever a dead captive, yet [one which] will never rot so as to become a warning sign to the others not to go there. Thirdly, it had been reported by the mountain climbers that it was absolutely difficult to climb to the top of Mt. Kenya. Fourthly, it had been rumored for many years that no airplane could fly across the top of Mt. Kenya as it was all the time driven by a strong wind causing it to pass just at the side. Fifthly, Mt. Kenya is on the equator, where it should be warm enough to melt the whole ice, but it never melted. Sixth, the history of the Jewish religion, which corresponds to the Kikuyu, is full of prayers and sacrifices on the mountains; and the great religious teachers, Sidharta Gautama and Jesus Christ, went on the mountains to pray. Since my tribe had chosen the top of this mountain to be God's home and did not believe that God lived on any other mountain, it had to be respected as the churches, temples or mosques of other peoples' religions.

At 9 a.m. on the 18th of August 1953, fifty-six leaders from all parts surrounding Nyandarua, with the exception of Kiambu, stood up for the opening prayers under the Chairmanship of Field Marshal Dedan Kimathi inside a meeting room 25 by 12 feet. On the stage were a bamboo-stick table placed in the middle and two other tables on either side. These tables were covered by bark of cedar trees which substituted for the table cloth. At the middle table sat Gen. Macaria Kimemia (Murang'a), Kimathi in the center and Gen. Kahiu-Itina. At the right side table sat Brig. Gathitu Waithaka, the Secretary Kenya Defense Council, Mwangi Giciinu (Murang'a's Secretary) and myself as Kimathi's secretary. (He had invited me to record minutes of the meeting for his own files.) On the other table sat Brig. Kirihinya—Gen. Kimbo's representative for the area from Nyeri to Thomson's Falls, Mbaria Kaniu, representative for North Kinangop, with their clerks. The rest sat on forms [i.e., benches] like a gathering in church.

Our first job was to name our armies. [Below is a listing of the eight armies agreed upon, together with their respective numbers, names, areas and leaders.]

(1) *1st Army:* ITUMA NDEMI ARMY—Nyeri District warriors, under Gen. Stanley Mathenge (even though he was absent). (*Ndemi*=an old Kikuyu ruling generation, the founders of smith work. *Ndemi* means arrowhead.)

(2) *2nd Army:* GIKUYU IREGI ARMY—Murang'a District warriors, under Gen. Macaria Kimemia. (It should be called 'Gikuyu' because our legend instructs us that the tribe originated in Murang'a. *Iregi*=one of the Gikuyu ruling generations which reformed laws and regulations. *Iregi* literally means rejector or innovator in reference to a generation group.)

(3) *3rd Army:* KENYA INORO ARMY—Kiambu District warriors, under Gen. Waruingi, whom none of us had met but only heard of. (*Inoro*=a stone used for sharpening knives, swords, spears, etc.; referring to Kenya Teachers College, Githunguri, in Kiambu, which was sharpening Kenya's brains.)

(4) *4th Army:* MEI MATHATHI ARMY—Mt. Kenya warriors, under Gen. China, (MEI was derived from *M*eru, *E*mbu and *I*kamba. *Mathathi*=one of the ancient ruling genera-

tions that found red ochre and used it to paint their hair, shields, etc. Literally, *thathi* means red ochre.)

(5) *5th Army:* MBURU NGEBO ARMY—all the Rift Valley warriors, under Gen. Kimbo. (*Mburu,* derived from MBUtu cia RUguru, meant 'Army of the West,' or 'Rift Valley Army.' *Mburu* itself literally means an age-group in Kiambu only; [it was also a term used when referring to] Dutch settlers. *Ngebo* = 'level' and was invented to mean to lie level to the ground when fighting so that enemies' bullets cannot catch one. So [i.e., the implication was that] the army was supposed to fight as strongly as the Dutch settlers in the Kenya Regiment and the Kenya Police Reserve.)

(6) *6th Army:* THE TOWNWATCH BATTALIONS—all our fighters in all the towns; most of them at this stage did their normal work during the day and attacked during the nights or at any time they had a chance. [This was simply a name given in respect to town and city fighters who had no overall commander or unitary organization.]

(7) *7th Army:* GIKUYU NA MUMBI TRINITY ARMY—any person or persons, wherever he or they lived, provided that they sympathized, helped us in any way or fought on our side. We felt that we were *one* in the union of Gikuyu and Mumbi, [following the Catholic notion the 'Trinity,' the union in one God of the Father, Son and Holy Ghost].

(8) *8th Army:* KENYA LEVELLATION ARMY—all persons fighting in the reserves, [in Nyeri] under Gen. Kariba. This army was not in existence until much later towards the end of the year, [and even then it lacked an overall commander, with outstanding individual leaders emerging within each of the various districts.] *Levellation* was derived from 'level.' Informers and Home Guards were regarded as stumps and to get rid of them meant to *level* the country.

Having completed the naming of our armies, Kimathi went on to instruct the leaders how to keep a camp register. He emphasized that all the fighters must be registered and that each leader must be able to answer any question with regard to his *itungati*—how many alive, dead, captured, injured, etc., etc. He said that big exercise books should be used as registers and columns be drawn vertically and each titled as follows: (1) Index Number;

(2) Warrior's Name (including father's name); (3) Date of Entry in the Forest; (4) Warrior's Clan; (5) District of Residence; (6) Division; (7) Location; (8) Sub-location; (9) Village; (10) Duties; (11) Rank; (12) Date Injured; (13) Date Surrendered; (14) Date Captured; (15) Date of Death; (16) Remarks.

He added, 'Those warriors who are determined to persevere, bear cold, hunger, heavy rain while dressed in rags, unarmed by the state, and who are ready to die so that all the Kenya people, irrespective of their tribe or their help, may get freedom and land to cultivate, [should be rewarded and remembered]. Some are dead and more will die, but whether living or dead, the fact remains that all those who are fighting anywhere have offered their lives as the price of Land and Freedom. If you die, your heirs would take your share of land and enjoy the freedom you died for. Big memorial halls in memory of those who died for freedom shall be built in all the towns and these registers bearing all the names of our warriors, recorded as I have instructed, shall be put in these halls for future generations to see. I would suggest that the names of the leaders should be printed on the walls of those memorial halls. Make sure that these registers are properly kept up to date; they should not be stored in the camps but should be stored far away from camps in beehives, caves, inside trees with big holes or in underground well-built stores, well preserved from rain or ants...'

'Lunch! Lunch! Lunch!' came the cry from outside, and we all went to the Officers' Mess for lunch—some fried meat.

When the meeting resumed at 2 o'clock in the afternoon, we started a general discussion on the women's role. A few leaders stood up to speak, laying their emphasis [on the fact] that there was no difference between a girl and any other warrior, though their works were different. They pointed out some girls who had killed KAR's or policemen and had brought their guns to the forest. They added that the girls were very good spies of every camp where the Government forces had taken them, and also that they were excellent bait for trapping Government forces one or two at a time. The evidence given placed the girls in the same category as any other warriors and proved that girls had a right to come to the forest.

When I stood up, I pointed out that some of the former speakers had used a few cases in order to achieve a sweeping statement. I pointed out that seven out of ten of all the women in the forest had been either lured or abducted by our warriors for their mere pleasure. Some leaders knew that well, while others believed the invented stories that all the girls were badly wanted by the Home Guards and that they came to the forest for their security. I compared gains from the women's work in the camps with the conflicts and difficulties arising in feeding and defending them and the possible conflicts between our warriors. I mentioned that it was alleged that Kiriugi Muciri had been killed because of a girl.

'No! That is a false accusation,' shouted Kimathi. 'Do you know who killed Kiriungi?' Kimathi asked me.

'No, I do not know,' I replied.

'Do you know why he was killed?' Kimathi asked me.

'No, I do not know, but from what I have heard, the people in Kigumo and Kariaini areas believe that his death was caused by jealousy of the girl he had!'

'I heard his case,' said Kimathi, 'and appointed a committee to find [i.e., investigate] the case before the decision was reached. I know that such allegations would mean to scandalize my name, for I am very much concerned with that case. I know that you had not entered the forest by that time and your statements depend on hearsay about the case.'

'Back to what I wanted to say,' I continued, 'never mind whether that case is true or not, but I would prophesy that a few would meet their death right here in the forest due to conflicts brought by the girls. Believe me or not, all types of brains are amongst our warriors, even the rhino brains.'

I then went on to mention the rules we had made at Kariaini and how we amended these rules at Mumwe. Many leaders supported these Mumwe rules and they were confirmed with the addition of the following :

(6) Every camp leader shall interrogate every girl joining his camp in the future and if he finds that the girl was either lured or abducted to the forest, the warrior concerned shall be beaten 25 strokes and the girl be returned to the reserve.

(7) Girls shall get ranks [up to that of Colonel] as other warriors according to their activities in their camps, and their former activities would also be considered.

(8) Girls in the camps were to be given freedom to chose the men they wished to live with, and the leader should not indulge

in the matter until the couple comes to him for registration as husband and wife.

(9) Once registered, death would be the only thing that could cause divorce in this forest.

Having done away with the [question of the] women's role, we turned on to issuing ranks. 'We shall issue ranks,' Kimathi began, 'from the lowest to the highest in accordance to individual activities and try to encourage our *itungati* to seek the next rank. We must make these ranks to be a real life [i.e., of real significance] in the camps. You must see that all the ranks are respected and given some privileges so that they would be admirable. We have different jobs apart from fighting such as clerks, doctors, cooks, store-keepers, *mundo mugo* (witchdoctors), blacksmiths who make guns, some elders who give us some advice and hear small camp cases, etc. If all these are given the same rank, that means that they are all equal, even the girls who happen to be of that rank. These ranks should show each warriors keenness and industriousness and must be respected after the war. Many of the best farms are owned by ex-army officers in both world wars. I think that these farms are their gifts as pensions, apart from the high salaries they were given. I would like to see my officers taking over all those farms as their pensions! (Applause.) Though we do not have money to give our fighters, every rank we give out must be accompanied by some money, no matter how little, that would be to indicate that if we had money we would be glad to pay our warriors sufficient salaries and that we lay this debt to the first African Government.'

Many leaders stood up to comment and support Kimathi's impressing ideas. In fact, we were all interested and admired to see the ideas accomplished. When Kimathi stood up again, he asked leaders to prepare a list of twelve persons in each camp who would be issued with ranks from a Lance Corporal to a General. The fifty leaders gave a list of 600 names. After a long discussion on how to allocate money to the ranks, it was resolved that the lowest ranks would get 2s., 5s., 10s. up to 100s. by 10's. This amounted to at least 28,000s. Kimathi requested each leader to contribute some 600s. from oathing fees, dues, raids, etc., which totalled to 30,000s. For the rest of the time, the clerks were very busy writing names, ranks and amounts on the envelopes to be presented to the owners, while Kimathi's table put the right sum in the right envelope.

It was 5 o'clock when we left the meeting room heading to where all the warriors had gathered in the open cleared-grass area. On our arrival all the warriors stood up and saluted. Over 200 selected and well-instructed guards of honor presented arms while the rest stood at attention and sang Kimathi's song : 'When our Kimathi climbed the mountain alone. . . .'

After the song, the rest sat down, with the exception of the guards. The leaders stood in front of the people in a straight line and Kimathi in the center. I stood next to him on the left, then Macaria Kimemia, Kahiu-Itina and Mwangi Gicimu, who arranged the envelopes in their order and passed them to the right. I called out the names and ranks—this started from the lowest to the highest—written on the envelope and passed the envelope to Kimathi. Then the person called would come in front, salute and shake hands with Kimathi, receive his envelope, salute again, and go back to sit down with the others. There was great noise of cheering all the time when one received his envelope. When all was over, Kimathi repeated his speech about ranks. He received many applauses when he made promises that our warriors should be rewarded for their service.

It was almost twilight when he ended his speech and we felt badly cramped by cold when we stood up and turned toward Mt. Kenya to ask God's blessing and protection, after which the men dispersed singing songs of praise for the leaders and quickly lit fires for warming and cooking. The singing and composing of new songs continued until late after midnight.

I was one of six leaders who were not issued with ranks that day on the grounds that we had only recently entered the forest and that [while] our past activities had placed us among the top leaders, the forest activities were the chief concern in the ranking. Moreover, the leaders in that meeting were new to me and none of them could recommend me as I did not belong to his camp; and as I had not worked with Kimathi before, I couldn't get recommendation for a rank—though I was given respect.

During the night I visited many warriors' huts to see how they were behaving. I talked to them and learned that they were not fed enough and that some had started hiding food as they approached the camp in order to increase their ration. Some complained that the leaders had three meals a day while the *itungati* who risked their lives in order to get that food had only one insufficient meal. Later, I went to visit Kimathi. We talked till 3 a.m. on many topics.

I went back to my hut and found that Wangui had made a nice fire. Cap. Ngiriri came to see me and asked whether Wangui had disobeyed. I replied that she hadn't and that she was doing her work very well. He queried why she had not slept in my hut the previous night. I replied that I had given her permission to do so. I added that I liked Gicuki, my former carrier, to take care of my luggage during the day. The Captain agreed and left. After washing my feet, I entered in my blankets and wished Wangui goodnight. She left and I fell asleep.

The following morning at 8 :30, the storekeepers reported that some *itungati* had stolen food from the camp store and all the remainder could be issued in the evening for one sufficient meal or served as half-ration for two days. That morning we expected Thiongo Gateru who had gone to raid settlers' cattle in the Wanjohi area. He arrived at 9 o'clock and reported that he and his gang had managed to bring 78 head of cattle to the Moorlands about 10 miles from the camp, but the Devons who ran in their Land Rovers in order to block them sighted them with their big lights.

'We were lucky,' he said, 'that we had crossed their jeep track when they saw us. We drove the cattle in a small depression and maimed them by cutting their hind leg tendons. We then climbed up far and watched. They were directed by cattle lowing and when they spotted them, they opened fire, thinking we were there. When they stopped firing, they had killed many cattle. They all stood up to check how many people they had killed since they hadn't seen anyone running away. They lit their big torches and when they learned that they had not killed anybody they gathered together and started discussing about the cattle and laughing at our running away. We all aimed at their group and together opened fire on them. We saw them falling down, whether dead or alive we do not know. We kept firing for a minute. When they started to return our fire we made off. We were so cold and hungry that two of our warriors were left behind, being unable to walk, and they lit a fire just at the border of the forest and the moorland.'

'Do you think that the enemies can follow your track up to here?' asked Kimathi.

'No,' replied Thiongo. 'We have walked on rocks for a mile's distance and then another mile in long grasses and each person moved in his own track taking much care of the grass behind and again we followed the top ridge *muirigo* in which our guards could see an enemy approaching as far as their eyes could see.'

'Captain Ngiriri!' called out Kimathi.

'*Abandi*!' He came running and stood at attention and saluted.

'I want the Guard Commander here right now!' said Kimathi.

'*Ndio Abandi*.' The Captain flashed out of sight.

'Storekeeper! Get many of the leaders in the yonder camp to help you inspect the warriors' kitbags and check whether you could find any *gitungati* who stole food from the store. Do you understand that?'

'Yes Sir,' [replied the storekeeper.]

'*Timamu Abandi*, here is the Guard Commander,' said the captain.

'Go and check all the guards,' said Kimathi, 'and warn them not to make any fires today even if they freeze from the cold. Tell them to keep their eyes opened. Start with the north ridge *muirigo* and tell them that enemies may follow Thiongo's gang's track. Tell the *itungati* not to go that direction in case they go to collect honey. Report to me that you have fulfilled that as quickly as possible.

'Gentlemen, get in the meeting room so that we can start our meeting,' said Kimathi. Soon after we had all sat down, Kimathi stood up and said, 'Since we are running short of food and we are far away from all food supplies, we should try and finish our meeting today so that we can disperse tomorrow. I would like all the leaders to instruct all our *itungati* that to destroy enemy's property is almost the same as destroying the enemy himself. Make sure that *itungati* do not destroy our supporters' property, which would cause them to turn against us, but instead encourage them that they would be compensated [for their losses.] I think it is a good idea to record all the losses that every member and supporter has suffered from the Kenya Government. These records should include all the Government's damage and should be recorded in columns resembling our registers: (1) Index Number, (2) Name (including father's), (3) District of Residence, (4) Division, (5) Location, (6) Sub-location, (7) Village, (8) Money lost in Cash, (9) No. of Cattle, (10) No. of Sheep and Goats, (11) Pigs, (12) Poultry, (13) Donkeys, (14) Value of House and Belongings Burned, (15)

Crops Damaged in *Shambas* (acres), (16) Crops Damaged in Stores (bags), (17) Shop or Plot Losses, (18) Vehicles, (19) Contributions to our Warriors, (20) Timber Mills or any other losses.

'Do you agree with the recording of the lost properties?' asked Kimathi.

'Yes! We do,' replied the leaders.

'Have I forgotten something to be added to the loss columns?' queried Kimathi. After a few minutes of pausing, Kimathi continued. 'The next record we should prepare should tell us how many people died during the freedom struggle who were not fighters. This would mean to record the names of all the persons who died from the date of the emergency declaration to the end of the revolution, no matter whether this was a young child or an old aged person. Many of them are dying of starvation brought about by the Government or diseases in the unsanitary villages or other conditions created by the Government; but there is no difference between death by hunger or hanging.

'The other register should be for the names of our enemies, i.e., Home Guards, informers, Tribal Police, whether dead or alive, and how many are dead in each area. This book, like the others, should be recorded thus : (1) Index Number, (2) Name of Person and his father, (3) District of Residence, (4) Division, (5) Location, (6) Sub-location, (7) Village, (8) Date of Death. It is interesting to see that the *Kamatimu's* (Home Guard's) book has only eight columns, which indicates that they should die. Each camp leader should collect these data from the villagers by sending our *itungati* for the required information.

'Every camp leader must keep a Cash Book that will show how much money he has collected and how much he has spent and the balance thereof. The other record you should keep is the Camp Store Record that will show how much supply your camp has spent either from plunder or charity from our associates. One more important record that you should keep is a History Book in which all the camps' daily events are recorded. And lastly, there is the Hymn and Song Book, the Hospital Record and the Duties Roster. In summary, each camp must keep the following books : (1) Register, (2) Individual Loss Accounts, (3) *Kamatimu* Records, showing the enemies of Freedom and hence national traitors, (4) Death Record Book for the civilians, (5) Cash Book, (6) the Supplies Record, (7) History Book, (8) Hospital Records, (9) Hymn and

Songs Record, (10) Camp Activities, showing every individual's activities. Do you find that to be an easy job?' queried Kimathi.

'Oh no!' replied the leaders. 'It is a very hard job and in fact it requires very educated people to run it,' said Macaria Kimemia.

'I and Mr Karari Njama planned all that last night and we did not sleep until three [hours] after midnight,' said Kimathi.

'You must really have worked hard,' said Kahiu-Itina.

'Yes, we worked hard; but we must work much harder than this in order to achieve our goal,' I commented.

'We want five educated persons,' continued Kimathi, 'one for Ituma Ndemi Army, another for Gikuyu Iregi Army and two for the Mburu Ngebo Army, who would move from camp to camp instructing how these records should be kept and collecting all these records which should be given to the fifth person who would record them in the final books. The fifth person would be our Chief Secretary. I think Mwangi Gicimu (pointing at him) is the most educated man Gikuyu Iregi Army has and I do not think there would be any objections in appointing him for Murang'a.'

He paused to wait for comments and with the approval of Murang'a people, Mwangi Gicimu was then elected. Kimathi pointed at me and asked me to stand up. 'That is Mr Njama of Ituma Ndemi Army,' said Kimathi. 'The most educated and capable man we have all over the Nyandarua Mountain. I have no doubts that he should be our Chief Secretary. Do you approve of that?' All the leaders raised their hands saying '*Ei*,' [i.e., 'Yes.'] 'Sit down Chief Secretary, I am certain that you know your job,' said Kimathi laughingly. He pointed at Brig. Gathiitu Waithaka saying, 'You all know him, our Kenya Defense Council Secretary. I think that his duties are only when the Council meets and I would suggest that he would work for the Ituma Ndemi Army.' This was approved. I learnt later that we had many more qualified people than him. Nevertheless, his popularity had qualified him.

Casting our eyes on the Mburu Ngebo Army we could hardly get any educated person among those brave fighters. It was then necessary to post two people from either Nyeri or Murang'a so that the job could be done correctly. I suggested that Aram Ndirangu who had been a teacher in my former school was a person whom I trusted that could do that job well. Being supported by Gen. Kahiu-Itina, who knew Aram before the emergency, and the fact that he was a clerk in one of Kahiu-Itina's sections made Aram to be called on. When he arrived, there was no objection and Aram was told that the following day he would accompany Gen. Mbaria Kaniu to North Kinangop to record the things he would be instructed about. As Aram left we went on to look for another person to record the accounts in Nderagwa between Mweiga and Thomson's Falls.

Gen. Kahiu-Itina suggested that since I had nothing to record at the time it would be better for me to fill the remaining vacancy after which I would start my job as the Chief Secretary entering all data brought to me together with what I would have collected from that area. Kahiu-Itina's suggestion was supported by many people and it was resolved that I would start my work in the Mburu Ngebo Army, making Gen. Kimbo's camp as my head office. Kaburu (alias Mathenge Gathiru) was appointed as my guide and in charge of my permanent bodyguard of three armed warriors and a carrier.

To end that subject, Kimathi said : 'We have to write letters to the Nairobi Central Committee and inform them how to keep these records we have been discussing, and another letter to Gen. China for the Mt. Kenya warriors. We have to send Gen. Matenjagwo, who speaks Kikamba fluently, to Ukambani to mobilize the Akamba warriors. I will personally go to the boundary of Murang'a and Kiambu and awaken the Kiambu people. It is too late up to now to find that their warriors have not entered the forest. If I could get [i.e., make contact with] the Kiambu warriors, I would be able to send our message to the Masai warriors. Meanwhile, as I am on that *safari*, I would ask Mburu Ngebo Army leaders to send out a few warriors into the small forests such as Nyandundo, Dundori, Bahati, Longonot, Thomson's Falls and Mau Summit.

'The other thing that I would stress is the making of guns. I want to see every warrior with a gun and you must work hard to achieve this in as short a time as possible. You must collect dues from our members, as much as you can, and spare the money for buying ammunition, medicine, clothing, stationery and guns-factory equipment. It has been reported to me that an excellent blacksmith has entered the forest in the Ruthaithi area and that he can make guns with no difference from the manufactured ones. We would be very glad and if this proved to be true we would require a smith from every camp to get together and be taught by him. I hope that this would improve and quicken our supply of arms.

'You must also continue to make hand grenades and even bombs. Cut the bullets into two equal parts. Put half the gun powder into an empty bullet case; then carefully fill the other half with small stones of shotgun balls size or sharp heavy pieces of metal about the size of the shot itself and try [to see] whether you can make two bullets out of one. This was suggested to me last night by Mr Njama and we have not yet experimented it.

'Now, as you can see, we are very late for lunch,' said Kimathi, changing his tone. 'As you are aware of our store being stolen, I very much doubt whether we would have any lunch today. Anyway, we better have half an hour break. In the afternoon we shall discuss about the laws and regulations or any other rising matter. During that time Mr Njama will take the camp clerks and instruct them how to keep the records we have been discussing. Make sure, Mr Njama, that you see and sign a specimen copy of every type of record for all the clerks.'

I promised him that I would do as he wanted. We then left the meeting room.

I saw a group of people outside Kimathi's hut. Some of us went there to see what had happened. I was very surprised to see three warriors who had stolen food from the store badly tied like a bundle and urged to tell the names of the other participants. Their hands and heads had been pushed between their legs in such a way that knees touched ears. Kimathi asked them whether they had stolen food and they pleaded guilty. When they were asked to mention the other companions, they said that they were only three. Kimathi said that they should be beaten till they give out the names of the other thieves.

I sympathetically addressed Kimathi. 'Field Marshal, these *itungati* have admitted their theft. I feel that they should be punished because of their theft only. I feel it both unfair and unwise to punish them for the other thieves. I think that many different gangs stole the food at different times. Moreover, even if two or three groups met at the store it would be difficult to know one another in the night's darkness for the fact that they do not know each other even during the day. Please, remember that all these *itungati* have come from different areas, Murang'a, Nyeri, Kinangop, Nderagwa, etc., and they do not know each other. I also think that the pains they are now getting for being tied like that is a sufficient punishment.'

'For how long have they been tied,' asked Kimathi.

'For a little more than two hours,' replied the storekeeper.

'Untie them,' said Kimathi.

The guards started untying them.

'These are Home Guards living with us,' said one of the leaders, 'they care only for their bellies.'

'You ate to your satisfaction last night, didn't you?' asked Gen. Kimemia.

'We did sir,' replied the *itungati*.

'I would then satisfy myself by beating you until I feel that you have had enough pain!' said Gen. Kimemia.

'Give them twenty strokes each for me,' said Kimathi as he entered his hut.

The three *itungati* received twenty canes each on their buttocks from Gen. Kimemia. They were then set free.

Finding that there was no lunch, I called Captain Ngiriri and told him that I wanted all the camp clerks to be gathered at a place where I would be able to instruct them.

As soon as these clerks were gathered, I started instructing them. I drew all the columns, titled them and filled the first line for illustration. I gave them the first record to copy out while I was drawing the second. When I completed seven records, I started checking every individual's work. I made the necessary corrections and signed the correct pattern. When I finished checking sixty-three clerks' work, I started teaching them how to record the battle history of the camps. I warned them to take much care in cases where murder had been committed; never to record real names of our warriors concerned. I suggested that it would be better to use the unknown nicknames or to create new names or letters for substitution which only the clerk can understand. I warned them that if the Government ever catches these books, there should be no evidence whatsoever for convicting any of the warriors in these record books. This would be exactly the same way in writing out the camp activities. They were to write in such a way that only we could understand it—by using the forest terminology and code words. [They were] never to record that so-and-so was sent to kill so-and-so. In these cases, they were to write down the date and the place to remind themselves and then write that 'when our brave warriors showed the enemies our strength, they returned to the forest victoriously singing.' The camp activities should be written only after discussions between the camp leader and weighing each individual's activities.

'While making songs you can use our nicknames for brave warriors and for their brave actions while fighting against the Government forces, but never use these names if the action happened to be on or in a civilian's home, whether he or she be the worst informer or traitor.'

When all was over, I appointed Mathitu and Dan Gacau to assist me to collect data. I went with them to Kimathi after the evening prayer and after reporting my duty. I requested him to allow me the two assistants. He first checked what they had copied as patterns and was very pleased with their work. After interrogating them he told them that they would work under me.

When I asked Kimathi what rules they had made during my absence, he replied that they did not make any new ones but discussed the old ones and emphasized that all the leaders must see that all the rules and regulations are obeyed. Then Kimathi took a short horn and with it drew some beer from a big gourd in which he was brewing. He gave it to me and asked me to tell him whether the beer was ready.

'It is ready now. If it stays until tomorrow it will be as bitter as pepper,' I said.

'Yes, it is because I have put in a lot of bitter honey,' said Kimathi. 'The bees here collect the juice from bitter trees such as *mikorobothi* and *mithukuroi*. By the way, what is your ruling generation group?'

'I am of Mwangi generation,' I replied.

'You are then my father,' said Kimathi, 'and you cannot participate in public ceremonies because you are not of the present ruling generation of Irungu-Maina. And what is your clan?'

'I am *Mumbui* of the great *Wamagana*, now known as *Mbari a Kaboci*,' I replied, giving him the empty horn.

'Oh! You are of my clan. Have another horn!' said Kimathi.

I took a little sip out of the horn and then asked him whether he had written the letters to the Nairobi Central Committee and to Gen. China.

'Oh! Finish off that horn. You will help me to write the letters,' said Kimathi. He told me that I was to write Gen. China and inform him about the formation of Kenya Defense Council and ask him to organize the Mt. Kenya Branch; how to keep all the records; to try and increase his arms by all means; to maintain discipline over our warriors, and to send a report on Meru and Embu warriors and their leaders.

With the light from a fire, I drafted the long letter, enclosing the patterns for all the records and the necessary explanations. When I finished, I gave it to Kimathi. After reading, he stamped it *Land and Freedom Army*. I was very surprised to see that beautiful stamp. He told me that it had been prepared in Nairobi and that he had just ordered a Kenya Defense Council stamp from Kamau, the general Secretary of the Nairobi Council, and would send it along with a copy of the letter. When we finished writing the letters, Macaria Kimemia and Kahiu-Itina arrived. They said that they wanted to taste the beer.

'The beer is for ceremonial prayers,' said Kimathi. 'And the prayers must start before the birds start their prayers; that means that every person must wake up before four in the morning. This should be announced to all the camp inhabitants.'

Captain Ngiriri was called and asked to announce the time of prayers. Kimathi took the horn and gave us all in turns. Then Macaria Kimemia and Kimathi continued to plan their journey to Murang'a. Kimathi said that soon after prayers we should pack our luggage and at seven all the warriors should assemble there and we would wish them goodbye.

'Mr Njama, I expect to meet you in September in Location 8, Fort Hall, at Karuri Ngamune,' said Kimathi. 'If I am able to contact the Kiambu warriors, I would then spend the rest of my time with them till we meet there. I hope that you will all collect that data that would be useful to our independent government.'

'I will do my best, Marshal,' I promised. I then wished them good night and went to my room. Though the ration had been reduced, the little beer I had taken caused me to fall into a very deep sleep.

I was awakened by a noise of someone who was calling out people to assemble for prayers. I went out still covering with blankets. It was a clear night and all the stars were shining brightly. The morning star was brilliantly shining a little over Mt. Kenya. The birds started prayers. I was interested to see what Kimathi was doing. I stood near the door and watched Kimathi inside. He drew beer with a little gourd (*ndahi*), poured a little on the fire so as to extinguish it at equalateral point representing three

kitchen stones while saying : 'As the fire goes out, so may all the
evils go out of us; as these charcoals run cold, so may our enemies,
and let peace remain.' He poured a little on the frames of his
doors so as to cleanse his house. When he came out, he stood
facing Mt. Kenya and poured some beer on the ground, saying :
'God! We give thee only what we have, honey, animal (domestic)
fat, cereals (a mixture of different kinds of millets).' Pouring a little
of these on the ground, he said : 'That is yours, our Father Gikuyu,
and that is yours my father Waciuri.' Then, pouring a little [more]
beer and the mixture he had on the ground, [he spoke the following prayer.]

God, we beg you to defeat our enemies and to defend us from
them; close their eyes so that they will not see us.

Our Father Gikuyu used to pray you with these things I have
in my hands. On all occasions you heard him and fulfilled his
request. We are his sons and daughters. We claim that the
highland grazing plateau you gave us and all the fertile land
you gave our Father Gikuyu has become foreigners' plunder. We
beseech Thee our Heavenly Father to restore our stolen land
and drive away these strangers who have turned out to be our
enemies. They have taken their strong firearms against an
unarmed nation. Oh God! Be our arms. We are certain that
even if they pour fire on us from their airplanes you will still
protect us from their wrath. God, we request Thy peaceful and
merciful eyes to look upon the blood flood flowing in our
country, and hear the cries of the perishing lives demanding Thy
help.

We are certain that you are the Mighty One, and no nation
can defeat You with its earthly weapons. Our Father, our
Leader, our General, we have confidence in you that we shall
come out of this forest victoriously and that you will bring our
enemies, the white strangers, under our heels. We want to rule
our country and to enjoy all its produce.

Oh, Lord God, we kindly beg You to bless the fruits of this
forest, the water we drink, the honey, the leaves and vegetables
and the animals we live with, so that all in this forest may
become our food without infecting us with any disease.

When we cast our eyes in the reserves we are very sorrowful
seeing our parents, wives and our children, widows and orphans,

starving. Our homes have become ruins and foxes dwelling places. Our sons and daughters are shot and raped in the eyes of their parents. What a great woe! Oh God, we are suppressed, our cries for help have not been responded to. Oh God, hear our prayers!

We pray you God to protect our associates and leaders in the detention camps. Turn the enemies to be their friends. We sympathetically ask You to defend our leader, Jomo Kenyatta, in his trial. Give him power and wisdom to defeat the enemy and to be able to lead our nation.

We pray Thee, Oh Lord, for the dead. Keep their lives [i.e., spirits] in peace and help their names here to become immortal national heroes.

Please, Oh God, bless our today's journey and all the journeys of our warriors. Bless all our warriors, wherever they may be.

Kimathi then moved forward and approached a burning fire and poured all that was remaining in his hands on the fire saying: 'As this fire goes, so be it with all our evils. As the wood and charcoal run cold, so may the war run cold and peace prevail. As we bury the fire, so may all the evils be buried and never rise up.'

Then all the people followed with a bit of any food in the right hand and a handful of wet soil in the left hand, threw these on the fire, then raised their hands high facing Mt. Kenya. By the time the last man threw what he had, there was no fire but a big heap of soil. We all together said the Christian's Lord's Prayer and ended our prayers by saying '*Thaai, Thathaiya Ngai, Thai*' three times.

'Go and pack your luggage and come back here at seven o'clock. Those who do not want to leave the camp may remain. It is advisable that you leaders wait for your *itungati* who are on *safari*. They would bring you food.'

We all dispersed. I went to see Gen. Kirihinya, who had been sent by Gen. Kimbo, so that he would lead me to their camp. On the way, Thiong'o saw me and told me that he wanted to accompany me and that he had to wait for a dozen *itungati* who had gone to raid cattle in the North Kinangop. He went with me to Kirihinya and after a short discussion we decided to wait for those *itungati* because of the arms they had carried.

Returning to Kimathi's hut, I found that a group of leaders were drinking the remaining beer. I was welcomed and joined them. Though the beer was very bitter, the drinkers were very many so that each person drank only a little, insufficient to make him drunk, but causing a little effect. When we had finished drinking, all the warriors were ready and waiting for us. We went out and after standing up to respect Kimathi they sat down trying to expose themselves to the morning sun rays.

Kimathi stood up and addressed the mob, saying that he was very glad because of the good work done by our *itungati* in the past fights and raids and in carrying the food for a very long distance, though some hungry *itungati* had stolen food from the camp store which was a very bad manner, for all of us had sworn never to steal anything belonging to our members. He frightened the warriors that those who had stolen the food had broken part of their vows and would meet great misfortune for this. He warned us to bide with our vows or else we would make our God angry and cause him to pour his wrath on the breachers.

He told them of the Kenya Defense Council and that it had elected four secretaries to record all their losses caused by the Kenya Government and record all the matters that would cause our names and our work to be known to our Government and the world. 'These are our secretaries,' said Kimathi, calling us to stand in front. He gave each of us a closed envelope. When I opened mine, I found a hundred shilling note and the original copy of a letter to each of the four secretaries. My letter read :

TO ALL SECTION LEADERS IN NYANDARUA :
The bearer, Karari Njama, is our Secretary. He will instruct your clerks how to keep our records and collect all the necessary data referring to Registers, Loss Account Records, Civilian Death Records, Kamatimu Register, Hospital Records, Supplies Record, Cash Books, History, Camp Activities, Hymns and Songs.

Help him with all his necessities, food, clothing, etc. Lead and escort him from your camp to the next camp. He is an officer and may help you in plans and organization.

Yours,
Dedan Kimathi
President, Kenya Defense Council
LAND AND FREEDOM ARMY
20 August 1953

When we had all received our letters, Kimathi gave the other leaders two minutes each to speak to our warriors. Macaria Kimemia, the first speaker, stressed about our laws and regulations and emphasized obedience. The second speaker, Kahiu-Itina, talked on what and how to raid. The third speaker, Gakure Karuri, encouraged our warriors and warned them never to surrender. The fourth speaker, Mbaria Kaniu, talked about camp activities and promised our warriors that they will share the Kenya Highlands. When I stood, I told our warriors :

Many people took oath with you. You are the only ones that God has selected to deliver our country out of colonial exploitation and the settlers' slavery. Your weariness, starvation, perseverance of cold, pains and in some cases your blood or life would be the ransom [i.e., payment] for the liberation of all the people of Kenya—and even the game animals—no matter whether they took the oath as you did or not.

It is of great importance then to note that if you do not bear these difficulties you can neither free yourselves or anybody else. If we can endure all these difficulties, we shall certainly set our nation free and we shall come out of this forest as victorious national heroes. As we learn of the legend of Gikuyu and Mumbi, who lived thousands of years ago, so will our heroes' names become forever immortal. If you want the nation to make your name immortal, you must be prepared to die for the nation. I think that all of you here are prepared and determined to make your names immortal. Our God is in front of us and I have no doubt of winning. I think it advisable for me to read a few verses from the Holy Bible. They are words of the great wise prophets of ancient days.

'For all this I considered in my heart even to declare all this, that the righteous, and the wise, and their works are in the hands of God : no man knoweth either love or hatred by all that is before them.

'All things come alike to all : there is one event to the righteous, and to the wicked ; to the good and to the clean, and to the unclean ; to him that sacrificeth, and to him that sacrificeth not : as is the good, so is the sinner ; and he that sweareth, as he that feareth an oath.

'This is an evil among all things that are done under the sun, that there is one event unto all : yea, also the heart of the sons of men is full of evil, and madness is in their heart while they live, and after that they go to the dead.

'For to him that is joined to all the living there is hope : for a living dog is better than a dead lion.

'Whatsoever thy hand findeth to do, do it with they might; for there is no work, nor device, nor knowledge, nor wisdom, in the grave whither thou goest.'

I have read the verses in Kikuyu and without adding a word of my own. I would give the final message as it is found in the Revelation, Chapter 22, Verses 12–14 :

'And behold I come quickly : and my reward is with me, to give every man according as his work shall be.

'I am Alpha and Omega, the beginning and the end, the first and the last.

'Blessed are they that do his commandments, that they may have right to the tree of life, and may enter in through the gates into the city.'

Two days ago, none of you knew that he or she would be issued with a rank. Your leaders came without your knowledge and ranked you according to your work. This is a true symbol of the last message I have read to you.... 'to give every man according as his work shall be.'

Kimathi stood up for his final message and closing down of the meeting. He said :

You are my warriors and disciples, followers and pupils. When Jesus parted with his disciples, he sent them to teach and preach to all nations and baptized them in the name of the Father, and the Son, and of the Holy Ghost. The same message I convey unto you all. Go all over Kenya (raising high his walking stick in his right hand) and preach to all African people and baptize them in the name of Gikuyu and Mumbi and of our soil. If you die for the soil that will never perish, our future generations which will use that same soil you died for will ever rejoicingly maintain your name and fame. Work hard and pray ! Goodbye all !

Swinging his walking stick and standing alert as a person ready for his photo to be taken, Kimathi smiled as the crowd cheered him, wishing him the best luck on his journey as they dispersed.

At this stage, I very much wanted to take Kimathi's photo but alas, since I had left my camera at home, I opened both my eyeballs and locked his photo behind my retina.

Kimathi, aged 33, stood almost six feet, strong and healthy; his long self-woven hair hanging over a fair brown oval face; his big grey-white and brown eyes protruding below black eyebrows separated by a wide short flat nose. A very little mustache grew above the thick lips; his large teeth with a wide natural gap on the center of the upper jaw and a wider gap on the lower jaw in which two middle incisors had been customarily removed; his oval round chin covered with little beards; his long neck shooting out of his wide shoulders, dressed in a suit of whitish-grey corduroy jumper coat, on which three army stars were fixed on both shoulders, and long trousers. Three writing pens were clipped on his top right hand jumper coat pocket, a heap of exercise books in his left hand, in which the ring finger had been cut off at the second joint, an automatic pistol hoisted at his leather waist belt, a metal bracelet on his right hand wrist—which he told me had been given him by Paul Njeru Gicuki, a close friend and Thomson's Falls KAU official who had been captured and detained several months earlier. His L-shaped curved brown walking stick, touching the ground, stood vertically and parallel to his trousers. His black shoes prevented him from feeling the damp frozen soil.

Kimathi turned left, gave the exercise books to his carrier and started for Murang'a at 9 a.m. His group went on singing the previous Murang'a journey song :

> June 5th we left Mbaria's
> Heading for Tuthu to see our warriors
> And when we arrived at Mathioya River
> We found many difficulties, rain, cold, mud
> And hunger throughout the night.
>
> In the forest we lived under many difficulties
> Of heavy rains and many days of hunger
> The ice had become our food
> And we persevered for three days. . . .

The rest of the crowd dispersed singing :

The House of Mumbi has no enmity with anybody
And does not think to make enmity with anybody
He who hates it, may God destroy
He who loves it, may God keep him well. . . .

I remained standing with a few leaders looking at the long marching lines of our warriors dispersing, while a few were just returning to remain in the camp. When they had all disappeared, I asked Thiong'o and Kirihinya to make arrangements for posting sentries as there were no sentries. I also asked them to think whether we would shift into a new camp nearby or remain in that old camp. After our short discussion, in which we invited other leaders concerned, sentries were posted and we resolved that we would remain there for at most two days awaiting for our warriors.

I called my assistants and told them that we had to start work there and then recording the individual losses of the persons we had in the camp. We walked uphill and after passing some rocky areas we came to a flat top area with scattered growing big trees, many old fallen trees, some of which had more than 30 feet in circumference, and grass grew everywhere. This is where our warriors had gone to spend the day when they understood that the camp was not well guarded. We spent the whole day there working. The weather had changed. It was a fine clear day. In the evening we went back to the camp. It looked like a deserted village with only about 400 inhabitants of different sections. Some sections had left two or three persons to lead their warriors where the others had gone. The whole management of the camp, with its joys and noisy songs, had gone away. The hungry warriors sat by their fires drinking honey, which they had collected during the day, diluted with lukewarm water.

Kirihinya's section had roasted and preserved meat to last them for three days more and were willing to share some to our warriors who had joined them. I called my luggage carrier, Gicuki Hinga, and asked him to bring the packet of wheat flour I had brought. I gave it to Kirihinya who asked his cooks to make us some cakes. After dinner we fell asleep.

The following morning, August 21st, was still a fine clear day. After morning prayers, many warriors scattered in the neighboring forest in search of honey. Leaders, girls and a few warriors went uphill to spend the day.

At 10 a.m. I was still recording loss accounts of some individuals when airplane roars reached my ears. As the roaring increased, I closed the books and climbed up on a big fallen log in order to see which direction the airplanes were heading. To my surprise, I saw six Harvard bombers from Mweiga Aerodrome aviating directly to our camp. I shouted to the people to hide very quickly, jumping down to take my cover under the big log. The airplanes started dropping bombs at the guards' camp about a mile away before all people had gone to their hiding places and [they] were forced to lie down on very small bushes. Two airplanes passed over our heads and dropped two bombs about two hundred yards to our west. The cleared grass area and the camps could be clearly seen by a person from the airplanes [and there] each plane unloaded a score of bombs. They then aimlessly started dropping bombs to the scattered forest areas surrounding the camp. One of the bombs fell about a hundred yards from us. This caused a horrible death hooting noise, strong winds, earth tremors and much fear. As the damp soil or twigs blown by the bomb fell on some of us, I thought that we were spotted by the airplanes and then with great regret for our inability to shoot the airplanes, the love of my country and people, fear and sorrow of death, caused me to grab soil in my both hands and with a true faith in God ask Ngai's protection. My faith in the Movement had made me almost an optimist with a belief that all things will end well on our side.

After ten minutes of bombing, the airplanes continued firing from machine guns for another ten minutes and then departed. When the airplanes left, I thanked God very much and moved around to see whether there was any casualty. I saw two girls and a warrior trembling because of fear. Thiong'o, Kirihinya and I went to the camp to see what the airplanes had done. I saw many pools of water in the holes made by the bombs. On our arrival at the camp, I was very much surprised to see that the camp had been ruined. At least each airplane had dropped ten bombs right inside the camp. Many huts had collapsed and some were completely buried.

In Kimathi's hut we found two warriors eating roasted potatoes. They had unknowingly smeared their faces with ashes and looked very hungry and ugly. I asked them where they were when the airplanes dropped bombs. They told us that they were all the time inside that hut. They told us they could not move anywhere without being seen by the airplanes and therefore had decided to wait

for death right there. Each had some patches of mud thrown by
the bombs on his body. We could see holes made by the mud in
walls of the hut. They told us that they had found some potatoes
hidden in a bush. We did not agree with them for we suspected
that they had stolen the potatoes from the store. Nevertheless, we
made no effort to find out. We believed that the two warriors were
blessed and saved by God.

We then went to see the guards. We found that they were all
well. They told us that they had run away some two hundred
yards from the camp during the bombing period and they felt as
if the bombs were exploding among them. I told them that some
itungati might have been captured or surrendered, for the airplanes must have been directed by someone who knew where the
camp was. I urged them to watch for land forces who might be
brought by lorries to the Moorlands to check the airplanes work.

Some other two warriors arrived calling their sentries and reporting that they were leaving that moment. We also decided to leave.
On our return, we crossed the stream in order to see the other
camp. We noted three bombs near the stream which had not
exploded, but they were deep in the mud. We were afraid that they
may explode at any time and we hurriedly moved away to warn
all our *itungati* not to return in the camp.

Arriving where our warriors were, we were glad to hear that
there was no casualty to our warriors. Only one *gitungati* had
been hurt a little on the right leg by a small stone thrown by the
bombs. We collected our belongings and were ready to leave for
Karathi's Mother in the Nderagwa region. Some *itungati* had gone
to collect honey and we could no longer wait for anyone. We
thought that they would follow us or stay in any other camp they
would find and they could be told whereabouts we were.

At midday we started our safari of eighty-one persons, moving
due north on an animal track which seemed as if it were the laid
boundary between the Rift Valley and Central Province. From
here one can see any part of the country in any direction, looking
at it from above. I used three different types of binoculars which
had been obtained from the Tree Tops Hotel to check how far
one could see using them. It was possible to see clearly a man or
an animal in the Rift Valley but it was difficult to see clearly a
person in the Nyeri area. I could see well buildings in camps and
Government forces' tents.

CHAPTER XV

TOURING THE FOREST CAMPS

D URING the remaining months of 1953, the Kenya Defense Council secretaries and those few leaders who, like Dedan Kimathi, were almost constantly on the move, visited most of the Aberdare Forest camps. The roles assumed by these representatives of the Council were, in fact, those of organizers and liaison officers. In their tours, as we shall see from Karari's account, they attempted to help in the planning and execution of raids, give instruction to leaders on general tactical procedures, introduce the new record book system, set out the broader aims of the revolt in speeches and gain recognition and support for the Kenya Defense Council from leaders not present at the Mwathe meeting. It is difficult to assess with any precision the measure of success achieved by these men, though my data suggest that it varied considerably from camp to camp and area to area. In general, their greatest effectiveness seemed to be with sections whose leaders or their representatives were present at Mwathe. These leaders, on the whole, accepted the authority and legitimacy of the Kenya Defense Council and were making an effort to implement its rulings and policies. Less effective were the efforts to organize the smaller sections under leaders who did not attend the Mwathe meeting and/or were reluctant to acknowledge the authority of the Kenya Defense Council and the leadership of Kimathi. Little if any effective influence, on the other hand, could be exerted on either the very small *komerera* groups or on those sections of the Kenya Levellation Army which established semi-permanent encampments within the forest fringe.

Though, on the whole, Kimathi's efforts to bring Kiambu warriors into the forest organization were unsuccessful, he did manage to contact Kiambu elders in the reserve and learn the whereabouts of certain guerrilla sections. The Kiambu District Council elders had retained considerable control over their fighting groups and were relatively successful in enforcing their ruling against reserve raids. This is borne out by Government reports of relative 'quiet' in Kiambu during this period and is illustrated by one of my Kiambu informants, Karigo Muchai, in the following passage : [1]

In late September 1953, I was sent on another mission; this time to the European Settled Area of eastern Kiambu where I instructed Gen. Gitau Kali to shift his forces from the Settled Area to Narok. As we talked during the night in his hut, we were attacked by a small group of Special Branch men and their *askari*. We returned their fire and when the hut went up in flames under the Sten guns, we separated and disappeared into the bush. None of our men were injured, but as we had fled in different directions, I was obliged to return to Limuru that night without an escort.

Three days later I learned that Gitau Kali had shifted his force to the area around Kikuyu Station, only eight miles from his original position. Here, he was acting in violation of District Committee rules, attacking Home Guard and police posts indiscriminately and giving Government an excuse to badly punish all of the nearby villagers. We could not allow these attacks in the reserve to continue and a message was sent to Gitau Kali ordering him to appear before the Kiambu District Committee. When he arrived from Kikuyu Station, he was severely reprimanded. In order to discipline him for not obeying our ruling against fighting in the reserve, we agreed that he should receive fifty strokes and be hung by the wrists for an hour from a tree. After being punished, Kali was ordered to lead his fighters to Narok immediately. This order he carried out promptly.

Kimathi's scouts, while learning of the existence of several Kiambu fighting groups in the southern Aberdare region (officially designated the Kikuyu Escarpment Forest), as well as in the Mau Escarpment, Suswa Hill, Melili Forest, Mt. Longonot and the Narok area, failed to make contact with these groups or learn much regarding their activities or organization. It might be useful at this point, therefore, to interrupt Karari's account and hear a little more from Karigo Muchai regarding the situa-

[1] This passage, and the one which follows, have been translated into English from the original taped account of Karigo Muchai, which was recorded in Kikuyu.

tion in Kiambu. As we shall see, these Kiambu guerrilla units lacked a central military command and were linked together only loosely through their common base of supplies in Kiambu and their relation to the Kiambu District Committee of elders.

As the repressive measures of Government increased, with sweeps of the villages becoming more frequent and with beatings, arrest, theft of property and the rape of our women becoming the order of the day, many of our fighters were leaving to join their comrades in the forests. Three camps had been set up in Narok, two in the Longonot area and three others in the southern Aberdares. Apart from the investigations I was carrying out on Government atrocities, I made several trips into these areas acting as a messenger, delivering guns and ammunition and escorting new fighters from the reserve and Nairobi into the forests.

In June 1953 a new Kiambu District Committee was formed. It was to consist of 24 members and remain hidden in the European-settled area of Limuru. I was elected along with another man to represent Kiambaa Location. Two members were elected from each of the three divisional committees and two from each of Kiambu's nine locations, making a total of 24 elders on the District Committee. Our people in Nairobi also sent two members to sit in on important meetings.

At this time, as movement became more difficult and meetings in the locations harder and more dangerous to hold, all of the lesser committees in Kiambu were disbanded and the locational representatives on the District Committee were empowered to act on behalf of their people in the various locations and to maintain communications with them through messengers. Most of the members of the District Committee were housed by our fighters in the Limuru area.

Soon after this reorganization, when the need arose for a man to represent our fighters in Kiambu, I was selected for this post by the District Committee and given the rank of Field Marshal. Our fighters were organized on the sub-location, location and district level. Representatives from each lower group would be sent to the next highest committee with the result that our District Committee of fighters consisted of 19 members: two from each locational fighting unit and myself as chairman.

My main job was to act as representative of the fighters on the District Committee of elders, where I would put forward the requests, suggestions and grievances of the fighting units as well as passing on to them the directives of the elders. I was, in effect, the link between the District Committee of elders and the fighters of the district, as well as the link between the forest fighters and our people in the reserves.

A man named Waruingi, who was later killed by the security forces, was one of our most successful and daring leaders in the Kiambu bush and it was my responsibility to maintain contact with him and to supply him with arms, food and men when needed. The Kiambu people in Nairobi were our main source of arms, medicine, clothing and other necessary supplies. These would be delivered to me and I would take the supplies directly to Waruingi or to one of our other leaders in Narok, Longonot, Ngong or the southern Aberdares.

In July, Government, apparently getting some information from its informers, sent out a group of tribal police to arrest me. I was in my house late one night when I heard footsteps outside. Quickly, I grabbed a few of my belongings and made my way out through a window, disappearing unnoticed into the darkness of a cornfield. My wife and aged parents were interrogated for some time by the police as to my whereabouts. But as all had sworn an oath of secrecy, they simply kept on repeating that they didn't know where I was.

From this time onwards I decided to remain in hiding with the District Committee of 24. Here, I had the protection of 36 fighters and could more easily carry out my work for the Movement. With Government repressive measures mounting and our fighters operating more and more out of the forests, the Kiambu District Committee concerned itself increasingly with the welfare of relatives of killed or detained members. Collections of money were arranged for their care and assistance. And money was also collected to pay the legal fees of men accused on capital charges, such as the possession of arms or ammunition. It was a favourite game of some of the European Special Branch men to place a bullet or two in the pocket of a man they were searching during a sweep. They would then 'discover' the bullets in the presence of witnesses and charge the man of being in possession of ammunition. Several men were tried and hung as a result of tricks such as this.

I also continued assisting the committee in its work of investigating Government atrocities. The findings were sent to the Central Province Committee in Nairobi, where attempts were being made to bring these facts before the eyes of the world through the press and a few sympathetic Europeans...

Our forest fighters from Kiambu were not, at this time, integrated within the main body of fighters located in the Aberdare Forest adjacent to the Fort Hall and Nyeri Districts. When news reached our District Committee that on two occasions some of our men had been attacked and disarmed by Fort Hall fighters under the command of Gen. Kago, it was decided by the elders, and agreed upon by the Central Province Committee in Nairobi, that Kago should be contacted and an attempt made to set matters straight.

In August 1953 I was sent with three elders and an escort of four fighters into the southern Aberdares to meet with Kago, who was operating in the forests around the Fort Hall-Kiambu border. When we met I told him our grievances and handed him a letter from the District Committee setting out in detail the two incidents in which his men were involved. I explained to him that it was stupid for us to fight one another in order to gain firearms. We were all brothers engaged in a war against the Europeans and should act in unity whether from Fort Hall, Nyeri, Kiambu, Embu or Meru. Kago replied that he had already learned of the incidents and that they had been carried out by some of his men without his knowledge. He said he had already punished the men involved and guaranteed us that such mistakes would not occur again in the future.

Though Kago could have been held responsible for the actions of his men and punished, I must say in his defense that this type of incident was often very difficult to avoid in the early months of the fighting. In many cases the guards posted around the camp of a group of forest fighters wore stolen Home Guard uniforms and when seeing strangers approach would signal them in a manner requiring a special response. As sometimes happened, new recruits just entering the forest would not know these signals and hence could easily be taken for enemies and ambushed. On the other hand, if they spotted the guard before he saw them, they might in ignorance open fire on what appeared to them a Home Guard and so initiate a battle. Later, incidents like this became very rare, but in mid-1953, with the organization of the forest fighters not yet adequate to prevent them, they did occur. And this was particularly so with the Kiambu fighters, who entered the Aberdares several months after our people from Nyeri and Fort Hall had already established themselves there.

During this same month of August it became necessary that I deliver arms and food to our fighters in Narok, who were under the command of Generals Nubi and Ole Kisio. I set out with 20 men and armed with 12 rifles and 6 homemade guns. It was about 5 a.m., as we moved from our hideout in Limura toward Narok, that we ran into a Government ambush near Kikuyu Station. By the time we realized it we were completely surrounded by security forces. Being in a bad position and greatly outnumbered by the enemy I decided that we should try and make a run for it rather than engage the Government forces in an open battle. I directed my group to aim all of our guns at one point in the circle around us. When I gave the signal we all opened fire and ran through the hole which our bullets prepared. Once we made our move, Government forces returned our fire and three of my men fell to the ground, dead or injured. The rest of us continued into the bush and lost our pursuers. Without stopping we continued on toward Narok, arriving the next day and turning over the supplies we had brought to Gen. Ole Kisio.

After discussing our business and spending the night in one of the Narok camps, it was necessary that I return with my 17 fighters to Limuru. We were provided with an escort of 50 additional fighters and set off through the bush during the day, making sure not to reveal ourselves to the enemy. While traveling I noticed a Government reconnaissance plane overhead, but felt quite confident that they hadn't spotted us. After a day's tiring journey, as we were sitting on the ground eating, one of our guards ran up excitedly and told me that we were being surrounded by a large force of Tribal Police, Home Guards and military units.

With a force of 67 well-armed fighters and being in a position well chosen for its defensive cover, I decided to deploy my men for battle. Government forces soon opened fire and a fight began which lasted till dark. One of my fighters was killed but we managed to capture 12 enemy rifles. It is difficult to say just how many men the Government force lost.

Not knowing where the security forces had withdrawn to for the night, it was unwise for us to continue our journey. Instead, I sent a couple of my men back to Narok to ask for reinforcements. By the following morning, 300 additional fighters arrived at our camp; Government, of course, had also built up its forces. A day-long battle began, ending at night-fall with a loss of 11 of our fighters. We had captured no enemy guns and it was decided that we should move out of the area.

Midnight found us in the Mt. Longonot forests where we met with a group of fighters under the command of Gen. Waruingi. We were led to Waruingi's camp and planned to rest there for three days. At the end of the third day, as we were making preparations to leave, we were spotted by a military plane which started to bomb the mountain. Soon after, Government ground forces began to attack on our position. Our own force, in addition to the men who had come with me from Limuru, consisted of 300 fighters from Narok and about 400 of Waruingi's men. After a long and gruelling battle we took stock of our position. None of our fighters were killed, though six had sustained injuries. Arrangements were made to take the injured men to the Aberdares for treatment and during the darkness of night I started off with my men and an escort of 150 fighters toward Limuru via Kijabe and Lari. When we arrived at Kijabe the fighters from Longonot and Narok bid us farewell and we were provided with a smaller escort by the local leaders for the remainder of our journey. The next day we finally reached our Limuru hideout. Our escort left us but unluckily ran into a Government ambush and lost 25 men.

*　　　*　　　*

At two o'clock we arrived where Thiong'o had maimed cattle. We were surprised to see that the Kenya Ng'ombe had poisoned all the seventy-eight carcasses. They had bayoneted them at the ribs so as to enter the poison inside the meat and had put some in the mouths. Though hungry, we laughed at their fatty bait and thought they were foolish. They thought they would kill many of us by the poisoned meat but instead they urged us to raid more cattle. If they hadn't poisoned those cattle our warriors would have stayed for a fortnight feeding on them. It was a pity to see that even hyenas had not eaten that poison.

We changed our direction to be northeast and we were climbing over 13,000 feet, the highest peak of Nyandarua. I and a few others climbed up the peak. Though the sun was still shining it was extremely cold. Most of the area is covered by grass and scattered cactus family plants grow on this frozen soil. Some places are just bare rocks. From here we could see all the villages in which rivers flow from this mountain in three directions : east, north and west.

We continued our journey, this time descending towards small bushes then into fertile land with many scattered big trees with grass undergrowth. The more we descended the more the animals increased.

The sun set when we started entering the bamboo region. Here we could see our peoples' tracks. It was almost twilight when we arrived at General Kimbo's *mbuci*. Kimbo was glad to see his representative Gen. Kirihinya, his warriors, and other new persons.

There were no huts in this camp. All the warriors slept in tents made of calico sheet. Gen. Kimbo had a European *safari* tent, another manufactured big tent was used by several warriors who did not have tents of their own. My tent was set up and the fires were lit. The leaders' fire was under a big tree where some eight leaders sat around it.

Gen. Kirihinya reported that we were hungry and we would like to eat our fill. Soon some dried meat, *ngarango* (fried fat crisps), and the ready cold meat they had all the day was issued to all those who had been on *safari*. While we were eating, other meat was being roasted and cooked. Each of us was served a whole rib of a big fat cow. I guessed it to be about ten to twelve pounds. We ate as much as four pounds each.

'All the sections living in this region live entirely on meat,' said Gen. Kimbo. 'We are trying to dry and preserve meat in any possible way. We don't ration meat here; everyone eats his fill.'

While we were eating, we reported to Gen. Kimbo all about the Mwathe meeting. Kirihinya reported about my job. Kimbo was very much pleased with the piece of work allocated to me. He told me that he had a small typewriter and that I could use it if I wanted. He told me that his gang had evicted five settlers, [the latter] leaving behind their livestock, houses and property. He told me that he had personally attended a raid on one of the old aged settlers and asked him to give the keys of the house. After taking out all they wanted from his house, he gave him a notice to leave the farm if he didn't want to die.

Gen. Kimbo, a young black tall [man of] medium thickness was dressed in a KAR Libyan cloth suit. His head was covered by long black wool woven into his hair, falling below his shoulders. He had a pair of gum boots and carried a small revolver and a double barrelled .44 gun (*gatua uhoro*).

We felt quite warm down there and being tired from the long journey we had gone, felt sleepy. I was asked not to go to bed before I drank soup. Soon the soup was brought in a big mug. It looked like milk because of the fat put in it. This area is supposed to be the richest in herbs, which they had embittered the soup with, and [they] claimed those herbs made them strong. After drinking, I started sweating and thought that it was due the soup's heat; but I came to realize during the night that it was the herbs effect that had generated so much heat.

The following day, August 22nd, I typed five eviction notices and addressed each copy to a particular settler living nearby. I gave each seven days notice to pack his belongings and then quit our country or else recognize our people as equal humans and have full understanding that they [i.e., the Europeans] are foreigners and that they can only remain here under the Africans' consent in a friendly cooperation. It would be quite impossible for the Europeans to live like masters and the owners of the country as servants.

I warned them that unless they changed their selfishness, superiority manners, color discrimination and monopoly there would be no room for them in Kenya or anywhere in Africa. They would either accept our citizenship or go back to their densely populated islands or discover an uninhabited planet and colonize it.

I reminded them that many of them are ex-army officers and they must remember very well that our people helped them to fight against the Germans who were bordering us in Tanganyika and the Italians who also had colonized our neighbors in Somali. 'Many African people died in order to defend you,' [I wrote]. 'You were given the land you have today as a pension for your service in that

war while our people were given KIPANDES (identification registration cards) as their gift for [service in the] First World War. The
same thing happened in the Second World War; after helping you
to defeat your enemies, our people were forced to dig contour and
bench terraces as the gift.

'That unjust period has gone by. A good turn deserves another.
We have twice helped you not to be enslaved by the Germans and
Italians. Our real fight has come. Come then and help us to
achieve our independence. Your help would better our relationship
and you would be here to stay.

'We are not fighting against the white community but we are
fighting against your bad policy and system. We want to be free
in our own country, organize an African Government and utilize
the land you have, including the unproductive [i.e., unused] land
you have reserved for your future generations while millions of
Africans, the real owners of that land, are starving.

'Kenya African Government must prevail at any rate, under all
costs and in spite of all your military strength. You may think it
is a dream, as you all believe, but the realization would reveal it
to be a miracle. If you want to live in Kenya you must help us
now when we need your help. If you are against us then pack and
quit. We shall not need your help after achieving freedom.

'I shall send General Kimbo Mutuku, whom you all know well,
to check whether you have gone by the expiry of this notice...
Your New Kenyan, Karari Njama, Chief Secretary, Kenya Defense
Council.'

I gave Gen. Kimbo the letters to arrange for their distribution.
We agreed that our warriors would take the letters to the laborers
employed by each settler who would then plant the letter in small
bamboo [tubes] just outside the front door of his house. We also
agreed that our warriors should visit these farms on 9 September
or as soon as these settlers became tired of waiting for us and
dispersed being convinced that we had lied in the letters.

During this time my associates were busy recording. I learnt
from the register that that section had 288 warriors, of whom a
dozen were girls. Kimbo told me that he had another group of a
hundred *itungati* which lived near the borders of the forest mostly
engaged in storing cereals from raids for future use. He told me
that the dried meat in his stores was starting to go bad, i.e., to be
covered by white fungi on the top layer after two months stay in

the store. I told him that that was the effect brought about by humid air. We found that we could store meat for a longer time only in dry places. I suggested that if the store doors were completely covered in order to prevent any more air to enter, the meat may last longer. We arranged that I should demonstrate what I was telling them the following day in one of the filled up stores.

Having completed my work in Kimbo's camp within ten days, I decided to visit Ndungu Gicheru, a famous leader who had shot down an airplane. I left with a group of nine warriors, descending through small bamboo bushes and then into thorny bushes. We saw many large herds of buffaloes who ran away when they saw us—some remained staring at us until we disappeared. Large herds of elephants, which neither ran away or attacked us, would stand collecting our smell by moving their long trunk and amazingly observe us. The rhinos, mostly living in pairs or in threes where the third one was young, though in many occasions they ran away, they always warned us with a loud hissing not to approach them and often challenged us. Here we saw very many types of animals. We thrice stopped on the way to collect honey. One beehive gave us sufficient honey to eat and drink.

We arrived Ruhotie stream at noon. The camp was situated in small bushes near the forest edge. There were no huts built. This section much resembles that of Kimbo's; they all used tents or when there is no rain just slept in the open. All the warriors seemed very fat, looked strong and healthy. Their clothes were no different from those of garage men; they all looked black and dirty due to the fat spilt on their clothes and on their bodies.

I talked to Ndungu of the job, which he knew well for he had spent a night with me at Gen. Kimbo's. He told me that he was prepared to shift his camp near Kimbo's the following day. He told me that one of his fighters named Cie, who had encamped two miles west would remain there with some fifty warriors and store as much cereals as they could.

I made arrangements that my assistants would visit the subsections and I would return with Ndungu's gang and work for it until they came. In the evening, after prayers, we waited until it was dark before fires were lit.

'It would be dangerous to light fires here where the smoke can be seen by persons in the settlers' farms,' said Ndungu. 'Sometimes they come with their armored cars and tanks just very near us and after setting them up, they fire over our heads far away. They could not think that we were living so near. When we steal cattle we first drive them right inside the forest and mix the cattle tracks with the buffaloes' tracks and then bring our cattle here. Whenever they follow the cattle we have stolen they often follow buffaloes tracks and have never found our camp.

'My camp, apart from raiding cattle, plans how we could trap one or two of the enemy forces and acquire their guns. The repatriation of our supporters from this area has created much difficulties. Most of the workmen in this area are Turkana and Kipsigis and they very much help our enemies.'

'Let me tell you, Mr. Njama,' interrupted Kamwamba, one of his junior officers. 'You know Leshau very well. After repatriation, we visited Landsburg farm at night and found that Gacari's daughter had been married by a Kipsigis man. She treated us well at first, gave us food; and when she went out she locked us in her house while she went to call some *askaris*. When they were ready, one of them shouted : *"Toka yote na farua ya furotakis na vipande!"* (All of you come out of there with your poll tax receipts and *kipandes*!) We thought we were finished; quickly broke the door and opened our Sten gun swinging it in all directions. Though they opened fire on us, we could hear them running away. Four of us managed to escape but three of our warriors died there. One of them is your relative, Mwanu Njama. We planned a revenge on that village. It was successful and we killed many of the villagers and burned their houses. That is why we have to rob these workers in many occasions.'

'Why don't you give them an oath and instruct them on our aims and try to make them have confidence in us?' I asked.

'You see Mr. Njama, these are very foolish people. They wouldn't understand what is freedom; all they can understand are the things they can see, touch or feel. Mind you, they are not farmers that they need land to cultivate; they are poor people and never had they livestock which starved due to lack of grazing land. The settlers satisfy their hunger by giving them *posho* and a little money which is used for buying tobacco, their only luxury. They do without clothes or soap. Three yards of calico satisfies one in clothing for the whole year and. . . .'

'We have to send many missions into the reserves of these

people,' interrupted Ndungu, 'and open many schools for them in order to educate them.'

'At present they are all deceived by the Europeans that our aim is to employ them and give them worse pay and treatment than what they are getting from the settlers. In all areas the Government is using all sorts of dirty propaganda, some of which would be difficult to wipe out of their minds.'

At this stage dinner interrupted our talk and turned our minds to the sweet fatty well-roasted beef. When we were eating Ndungu told me that his section had 184 *itungati* of which four were girls. Two of them were very brave and had trapped a KAR man, killed him, and brought his gun to the forest. He also confirmed that all the girls in Kimbo's and his section had been taught how to use any weapon.

As Ndungu became busy in selecting *itungati* who would go to raid cattle in settlers' farms, we ended our talk and I went in my tent to sleep. In this warm area there were many hyrax and their loud cries, almost similar to the gun's burst, was the only poor music of the night.

The following morning we set off for Kimbo's with some 150 persons. My two assistants were directed to the other two camps. A group of 40 *itungati* was left in that camp so that they could raid cattle and follow us at Kimbo's the following morning.

We arrived at Kimbo's in the afternoon and Ndungu's *itungati* made their *mbuci* just the opposite bank of the same stream. As soon as the *itungati* finished clearing the camp site, I started recording their losses and instructing their clerk. In the evening we prayed together; it was the beginning of a coalition management. While we were sitting around a burning fire warming, I reminded the leaders of the notices I had written to settlers some twelve days ago. After a long discussion, it was agreed that we must wait for Ndungu's *itungati* who had gone to raid for cattle and then send out our scout three days after their arrival.

Heavy rain started pouring and we dispersed into our tents. That night we ate our dinner in darkness. Great flashes of lightning frequently shone, followed by horrible thundrous noise. September had begun and the heavy rain was clearing all the mist and saying goodbye to us. We were entering a fine sunny month.

The rain poured throughout the night at intervals and continued the same the following day. At 9 in the morning we heard shots and suspected that our *itungati* were fighting against the cattle trackers. This was quite true. At one o'clock half of our *itungati* arrived with 37 head of cattle. They told us that they managed to drive almost a hundred head of cattle from a big herd grazing in the bushes about half an hour before sunset.

'We noted that we would be seen driving them to the forest,' said one *gitungati*, 'and so we herded them until it was dark. We then commenced our journey. Inside the forest we several times came across large herds of buffaloes and charging rhinos that dispersed the cattle. In this way we lost about thrice the cattle we have. Heavy rain had become another obstacle. We decided to make fire and guard our cattle until morning. In the morning we drove our plunder, leaving 20 *itungati* to ambush the cattle trackers just where we had slept. Later on we heard them fighting but we were far away.'

'How is your track? Can the enemies follow it up here?' queried Kimbo.

'Oh no!' replied the *gitungati*. 'Since they were fought they cannot come any further. Moreover, they would find the lost cattle and return with them claiming that they have beaten *Mau Mau* and got the cattle back. In addition to that we hid our footmarks well and in some cases exposed our footmarks to buffaloes' tracks which they would follow.'

Meanwhile all *itungati* were busy killing the cattle, but instead of removing the hides they would cut pieces of meat with the hide. The hide had become a good cover and could be eaten during food scarcity. Kimbo ordered the guard commandant to post some strong sentries about five miles from the camp on the cattle track who were to keep watch until six in the evening.

At 7 p.m. all the guards arrived and reported of their fight with the Kenya Ng'ombe. They could not tell any detail of casualties on the other side but believed that their first firing must have knocked some Kenya Ng'ombe down. That night we enjoyed fresh meat.

For the next five days, I continued my work and was rejoined by my assistants. I told them that we had to finish our work within two days and start our journey to Murang'a on the 12th September. The same evening our scouts returned saying that all cattle had been moved some 20 or 25 miles from the forest edge. Many homes within the region of five miles had been deserted. Government forces had been posted to guard some homes. A few homes at different centers had kept cattle as baits at their strong centers. There was no other work done on those farms apart from herding livestock.

'Could we raid any of those homes?' asked Gen. Kimbo.

'No,' replied one of the scouts. 'The owners and their families have gone away with their belongings, but most of them have joined the KPR [Kenya Police Reserve] and returned; their duty is to guard these homes and farms. They do not sleep inside the houses but they keep ambushing us outside throughout the night. We learned from Gakuu's scouts that those who guard livestock sleep right inside the herd and that those guarding merino sheep wore sheep skins. When Gakuu's *itungati* approached, the sheep ran away from them leaving behind the armed forces in sheeps' skins. When they moved to catch the remaining sheep, the sheep opened fire, killing seven and capturing four. It is quite dangerous to raid any place unless it is well spied.'

We talked much about the enemy's tactics, finally my suggestion was accepted of spoiling their water pumps and using the water pipes for making guns. We also agreed to destroy all the bridges that were in use near the forest and to cut down wire fences and telegraph [lines].

The following day some 250 *itungati* left for the raid. When they returned they brought 16 wagon bullocks and reported that they had successfully fulfilled what they were required to do. They had hidden the pipes far away in the forest and guessed that the pipes could make 10,000 guns.

We completed our work on the four sections and arranged to start for Murang'a on 12 September. The following morning special prayers for our journey were made, after which we started our journey comprised of twelve *itungati* including Lieutenant Kamwamba, armed with six rifles. My carrier, Gicuki Hinga and Mathitu my assistant asked permission to remain there. Though I was given another carrier, I couldn't get another assistant. The Government rarely contacted those gangs. They had plenty to eat and life seemed smooth to them.

We decided to make our way through bushes bordering the Moorlands. We started moving due south. At about 10 o'clock we crossed the river Amboni (Honi). I noticed a swarm of bees moving to and fro over an old fallen log. We paused to see whether we could get honey. We agreed that it must be an old home of bees and might have honey. We made fire and split the log. To our surprise we collected a lot of honey that increased our luggage.

At midday we were about to cross the Nyeri-Kabage road. About a mile's distance we could see an enemy's camp, [made up of those] who were constructing the road. I took out my binoculars to enable me to see clearly. I saw one tank, three armored cars, two lorries, a Land Rover and two tractors. There were as many as thirty tents; a group of KARs and Home Guards were guarding some civilians who were clearing some small clusters of bushes. We had to go a bit deeper inside the forest to avoid contact with these enemies. After passing them we returned to the open grassland.

At three we crossed the Kiondongoro road and then the Charangatha River on an old bridge on the Nyeri-Kinangop foot track. Soon we arrived at Karari's Hill where we found large herds of buffaloes and their families grazing. We stopped and discussed about the animals. We resolved that though it was very cold it was possible to graze milk cattle and sheep for wool. The grass growing around and some wheat seeds which had been dropped by our warriors were a fair proof that wheat could do well in the altitude of 10,000 feet.

We made up our minds to search for Kigumo sections on Karari's Hill on the steep side descending to the Gura River. By five o'clock we crossed the Gura River just below its big waterfall. We started climbing the steep slopes in the thicket of the tall bamboos. Our progress became difficult; we were tired and had not come across other fighters tracks. It was six o'clock when we arrived at a big *pondo* tree whose branches had become a nice rain proof and its base a pig's dwelling. We cleared the pigs' dung and encamped there for the night. After prayers, we roasted meat, warmed water and diluted our honey which we drank. Though we did not make our tents, we spent a warm night.

The following day we continued our journey changing our direction due east at Muthuri's Hill. We were very much surprised to see that the Government had made a new vehicle road as far as there. Being afraid to follow the road, we changed our direction to southeast, heading for Mumwe camps. On our arrival, we visited many old camps that I knew and found that all had been deserted, but we could not find any recent tracks. In the evening, we encamped near the forest edge.

As we were eating dinner, I told my comrades my plans. 'To-morrow we shall move southwards,' I said, 'right across the Kariaini gardens, where I hope we shall be able to find other fighters' tracks from the reserves which would lead us to their camp. We shall then be able to get a guide to the nearest Murang'a camp where we would be given a guide to Karuri Ngamune. The five days we have are enough to meet Kimathi on the 18th September.'

After our morning prayers we continued our journey. When we came to the Kariaini vehicle road that was used for transport-ing camphor timber, we found that much weed had grown on the road but some people had passed along it previously. We followed the road. At midday we found a great deal of ripe strawberries on either side of the road. My comrades became interested in the berries and started eating, talking loud to one another.

We were suddenly stopped and dispersed by Sten gun fire at very close range in front of us. We were forced to make our paths through the thicket of berries which scratched our faces, hands and feet. When we stopped running, I found that I had only two armed warriors and two carriers. We sat down for lunch and in great silence listened whether we could hear our comrade's signal or movement. Though we didn't hear them, we didn't think that we could have suffered any casualties for the great bushes pre-vented the enemy from seeing us.

In the afternoon we crossed the Kariaini gardens, but failed to see any tracks. When we came to the river Thuti, we walked down stream now searching for a crossing point of our fighters. Luckily, we saw a track in which foot marks were cleverly hidden. We followed it and to our surprise we entered a small camp on the bank of a very small tributary. There was a rectangular kitchen and four other small circular huts. Though there was nobody in the camp we could see fire well covered and believed that that must be one of the *komerera's mbuci*. We thought that they had gone to hide themselves and that they may run away if they see us. We therefore decided to wait for them in the camp.

In the evening, their scout came to spy whether the enemies had seen their camp. When he saw us, he started running away. I shouted for him to come back. He halted and asked me who I was. I told him my name. He came and we shook hands. He told me that he knew me when I addressed them at H.Q. Kariaini. He told me that there were 21 other *itungati* including Thogithi their leader. He told me that they always spent the day hiding far away from the *mbuci* since the enemy dispersed them at H.Q. He signaled for the others to come. They came carrying firewood. After exchanging greetings, some went to their store where they had potatoes and arrowroots to keep them only two more days according to the storekeeper's report. These black, weak fighters had only one rifle and four *banda* with two bullets for each.

They admiringly looked at us. We looked very healthy and fat. I ordered my carrier to give them some meat so that each could have a bite. We told them of our journey and their leader told me they had broken away from H.Q. when it was captured by the enemy. When I asked him whether he knew where the big camps could be, he replied that there were no big camps in Kariaini area. 'Mathenge split them into small groups of about twenty people so that we can be able to hide our tracks.'

'Do you know where Mathenge's *mbuci* is?' I asked.

'Yes,' replied Thogithi, 'it is at Karunga.'

'Where is Karunga?' I asked.

'Just on this ridge, less than an hour's walk. I will take you there tomorrow,' promised Thogithi.

'What important raids have you made since I left?' I enquired.

'When did you leave?' demanded Thogithi.

'Today makes it exactly a month.'

'We have made no raid at all. It became difficult to raid cattle, but we could manage to get one or two rams that are being fattened in the homes of those who have not yet shifted to the new villages. Our chief food now is potatoes, arrowroots, raw bananas, sweet potatoes or any other crop growing in the gardens. Last week we started eating raw maize from the Muhuru region. I am planning that we will all go for maize tomorrow.'

'Would you leave the camp empty?' I asked.

'Unless we have a sick person we would all go,' replied Thogithi.

The boiled mixture of potatoes and arrowroots was ready and was served for our dinner, after which I went to my tent to sleep.

In the morning after prayers, I noted that they had thrown away the system of posting sentries and became disgusted by those *komereras*. I asked Thogithi why he had not posted guards. He replied that it was absolutely useless to post unarmed persons as sentries. I warned him that the enemies may enter their *mbuci* during their absence as we had done the previous day and trap them all. I advised him to keep guards who could blow a whistle or quietly run to inform the others that the camp had been seen by the enemy.

We then climbed up hill behind the camp in the black coniferous trees with no undergrowth. Layers of dry leaves had been shed by those trees making it impossible for the foot marks or tracks to be seen. Here in an open space they generally spent the day eagerly looking for the sun to warm them.

We left the camp heading to Mathenge's *mbuci* and moved due east. We soon came to an open space which showed that a few people used to spend the day there. Casting my eyes onto the reserve I could see Kamanda (Kihome) Home Guard Post less than two miles' crow fly built on Mahiga-Othaya boundary.

'How are the *kamatimo* in that post?' I asked.

'They are very cruel,' replied Thogithi. 'The European officer in the camp, nicknamed Kibithi (literally, the hairy skin of the buttocks), is a mad man. He has collected the village boys aged between 14 and 16, supplied them with a brown-green uniform, fed them well, supplied them with European beer and *bhangi* [a drug], and has trained them how to use every kind of weapon. He uses these audacious children as his soldiers to fight in the forest and in the reserve. During the night they dress like ourselves and knock at the doors of our wives or mothers. Once they are in, they quickly ask for food and money and claim that they have been sent by the known local forest leaders. They ask for the names of the Home Guards who are troubling the civilians and whom they would like to see exterminated.

'Having trapped our wives and parents these foolish youths, under the influence of alcohol, monetary rewards and the good treatment they receive, either shoot and burn them in their houses and pretend a fight with Mau Mau outside, opening fire and blowing whistles and shouting, or beat them till they confess, after which they are prosecuted or detained. These boys make fun when they point out a tree, a dog, a cow, a sheep or a man to be their target. Sometimes they fight with guns and kill one another and then laugh praising the hero. They eat livestock of their choice and...'

'*Eei ni muru wa Njama?*' interjected Mathenge not far away.

'Yes, it's me! Hello Mr. Mathenge, I am glad to meet you again.'

'How are you, Mr. Njama?' requested Mathenge, leaning on his five foot man-head-carved walking staff.

'I am very well,' I replied.

'And how is your journey?' asked Mathenge.

'Not very bad,' I replied, 'with the exception that my *itungati* were dispersed yesterday at midday by enemies on that road yonder.'

I moved to greet his *itungati* including his *kabatuni*. Then Mathenge called me to go sit at a private place where we could catch a little warmth from the morning sun. I started telling him of my journey to Mwathe and all that had happened at Mwathe General Meeting.

'Your report,' said Mathenge smilingly, 'confirms much of what Kabuga had told me, but his *itungati* generally described the whole matter of Mwathe as being "the *mbuci* of great discipline and hunger."'

'That might be true,' I replied. 'You know how difficult it is to ration food for nearly 5,000 *itungati*.'

Mathenge remarked the meeting as a great success, beyond his estimation and that Kimathi had greatly benefited from his absence in the meeting. I reminded him that I had forewarned him.

'Though Kimathi has been officially established as the head of all the warriors,' I said, 'no person has been pointed out as his deputy for many people have your name in their minds for that post.'

'What rank were you given?' demanded Mathenge.

'I wasn't given any rank,' I replied.

'Shall I be given a rank by Kimathi?' queried Mathenge discontentedly.

'No,' I replied. 'The Kenya Defense Council, of which you are a member, will decide your rank; but you must remember that the qualification for ranks are based on personal activities and capability and not according to one's wish.'

'Yes, I now agree,' said Mathenge, 'that a group of people is wiser than the wisest man. Your speech now will make me bide with all that you passed at Mwathe. I had been thinking that Kimathi dictated all that he wanted.'

'Oh no!' I replied. 'If you want to confirm this you better accompany me to Karuri Ngamune in Murang'a where another leaders' meeting will be held in which reports from our armies would be heard. The meeting will commence on 9 September, three days more. I would be very glad if you could send your *itungati* to Mumwe and Kigumo camps to find out whether my *itungati* who were dispersed yesterday might be in any of those camps. If they are found they would be better directed here.'

'I will try and send out some *itungati*,' said Mathenge, 'as you requested, but I do not think that it would be possible for you to get to the meeting. I would like to go with you but I am not prepared. You see it is bad to start such a *safari* without sufficient food. Right now none of us knows where any of the Murang'a *mbuci* is situated; and if we went and missed their *mbuci* we would then use our food before we could return here.'

'That is why I demanded my *itungati*,' I said. 'Four of them carried nothing but *safari* food, mostly dried meat and fried fat crisps.'

I called on my food carrier and asked him to give us a little meat and warned him that that was the only food we all had to take us to the meeting.

'This meat must have come from the Rift Valley," said Mathenge admiringly. 'Which part of the Rift Valley did you visit after leaving Mwathe?'

I told him how we remained in the Mwathe camp and how we were bombed; our *safari* across the Moorlands to Kimbo's *mbuci*; my visit to Ndungu's camp and the camp life of the *itungati* who lived in Nderagwa area. I emphasized the *itungati* there were very fat; that they had plenty of meat, all the excess of which they dried and stored. I told him that the enemy have never found any of their camps, that the only contact with Government would be only a planned raid or ambush. I told him how settlers had quit, leaving behind their livestock.

Mathenge became very much interested and decided that he would spend Christmas in the Rift Valley. He told me that most of the Ituma *itungati* had gone to Rift Valley as I had suggested and that there were fifteen *mbuci* of about twenty *itungati* each living in Kariaini. He told me that his camp had thirteen *itungati* including his *kabatuni*.

I asked him where those camps were situated and he told me that they were very near. We set off for a common place where *itungati* from those *mbuci* met.

'Why haven't you raided that Kamanda Home Guard Post?' I

asked, pointing at the post. 'I have been told of its cruelty and brutality by Thogithi.'

'We would very much like to destroy that horrible institution but we have run short of ammunition. The little we have spared would be used for means of living only. It has become difficult for us to get food from the reserve unless we fight for it, even from the gardens.'

We arrived at a place which those *mbuci* used as their meeting place. Many of them were lying on their backs exposing themselves to the sun. They stood up for Mathenge and they were surprised to see me. After exchanging greetings, we all sat down. I was glad to meet Kihara Kagumu, Gicuki Mugo, Elijah Kihara Gatandi and Kibira Gatu and many other leaders. Mathenge asked those leaders to point out some *itungati* who would go to search my lost *itungati* at Mumwe and Kigumo camps. I drafted a letter to the leader who might be keeping them in his *mbuci* and handed it over to the *itungati*. We asked the *itungati* to return the following day with their report.

I spent the rest of the day repeating my story to those leaders. In the evening, I went with my four *itungati* to Mathenge's *mbuci*. I saw a rectangular kitchen and two other warriors' huts roofed by *mahindu* leaves of a banana family plant. These are waterproof when they are green and untorn, but when they dry up they wrinkle and shrink and become torn and then leak. My tent was pegged a little farther from Mathenge's and my *itungati* were accommodated in the two huts. Mathenge used to warm himself in the kitchen and so we both went to warm ourselves in the kitchen. I criticized him and pointed out that he should have a private fire even though he was the only leader in the camp and enjoyed the company of others in the kitchen.

We were served with two maize cobs well roasted while some other maize was being boiled. I asked my *itungati* to give out some meat so that each could have a bite, after which we slept.

The following day the messengers arrived at ten in the morning reporting my *itungati* were all safe and had slept the night before at Kabuga's camp, which was situated at the sources of Mumwe stream. I read a letter from Kabuga telling me that my eight *itungati* lead by Kamwamba left his *mbuci* on the previous day, returning to Kimbo's.

Having no food nor guide to Murang'a, with only a day before the meeting started, it was then impossible for me to get to the meeting and so I abandoned my *safari*.

For the rest of September I remained with Mathenge, entering data already collected by his clerk, Ndung'u Mathenge. During my stay there, no raid took place. Our warriors were bush harvesting maize from Muhuru region and storing for the future use. The Home Guards, Devons, Police and KAR troops spent the nights in the maize fields ambushing our fighters. In most cases our warriors met death while looking for food rather than in battlefields. Nevertheless, there were so many gardens all over the country that the enemy were not able to cover them all. Our fighters were very good at spying and detecting the enemy through hearing, a nervous [i.e., intuitive] sense of danger and smelling. The latter sense had grown strong in such a way that our warriors could smell the enemy at more than 200 yards away; notably soap and any form of tobacco.

I left Mathenge in the first week of October, guided by his *itungati* to Kabuga's *mbuci*. On our arrival at Kabuga's *mbuci*, we were astonished to find it so badly ruined by the foe. Luckily, we were seen by four *itungati* who had come to spy whether the enemy had gone, so that they could get food from the camp store, and whether the hidden camp utensils had been seen by the enemy.

They told us that great calamity had befallen their camp. One of them, in great fear and worry, said: 'On the previous day, the enemy opened fire on us in this camp, killing two of our fighters and injuring four others. When we ran away with our casualties, we arrived at a place where we selected a site for our new camp. The girls were sent to cut *ithanji* reeds for thatching our huts in a swampy open area. The girls had spread some clothes in that open area to dry. Then four Harvards which were passing over our heads saw the girls and their clothes and quickly unloaded their bombs on us. We all ran away from that area but four fighters, including a girl and our leader Kabuga, were injured by the bomb shells. Kabuga and another *gitungati* were both slightly injured at their right forearm.

'We built a new camp and a hospital that evening. Yesterday afternoon, the enemy forces arrived at the bombing area in order to assess how many people they had killed. They did not find any corpses but the blood trail led them into our hospital where they finished off four of the patients. Two of the patients survived and came to our camp because they knew where it was. We then moved into a new camp near the sources of the Thuti River. We have run short of food and have lost much property in those harassed moves. That is why we had come to check whether the enemies saw our food store, but for good luck, they didn't see it.'

'We believe that women have brought all this calamity to our *mbutu* (group),' commented another *gitungati*. 'Last week, Kiruthi Gikuri abducted a woman named Wamu who was only recently married to Kamotho, the great witchdoctor in Mahiga Location. We suspect that we might be bewitched by Kamotho or else that [trouble] would be the punishment for our intercourse with women inside our camp against the taboos.'

'That is a very sad report,' I commented, shaking my head. 'Do you have any more food in the store that we can help you carry?'

'Yes,' replied the third *gitungati*, introducing himself as Kanji, the storekeeper.

We all went to the store and carried as much maize as we could. We then moved direct west and arrived at the camp at 4 o'clock. Here, I was glad to meet Kabuga. His wound had been smeared with M.B. 760 powder [a form of aspirin] and left undressed according to his personal advice. I asked his assistant Harrison Gathinji why he had allowed himself to be directed by a patient who didn't know better than him. He replied that he found it difficult to argue with his leader.

I instructed Kabuga on the necessity of covering a wound. I told him how dirt and germs are dangerous of infections by entering the body through wounds. I cleansed and dressed his wound.

He then told me the whole story of his camp's misfortune which confirmed all that I had been told by his *itungati*. He told me that Kiruthi Gikuri was to be tried the following day for abducting the wife of Kamotho the witchdoctor, who might have cursed all the camp's calamity. Wamu, the woman concerned, had been in that *mbuci* for a week. When Kiruthi heard the camp's gossip was full of anger and disappointment with him, he ran away into the reserves where he was arrested and detained.

I stayed in the camp for a week collecting all the necessary data. I then went to Ngara's *mbuci* situated at Gacamba Hill, which is separated from Karari's Hill by a deep valley in which the river Charangatha flows.

I remained in the camp for a week collecting data from about

150 warriors. During my stay in this camp I thrice went fishing, since about two dozen people were always down at the Gura River fishing under the leadership of Gacungi Waicahi. The fish were not rationed, though they could catch as many as 300 in a day, for there were some who did not eat fish. [Fish were not a part of the traditional Kikuyu diet.]

On the second day of my stay in the camp, the *itungati* who had gone to harvest maize brought a report that a missing girl, Gathoni Wagege, had decided to surrender and on her way to the reserve—having cunningly passed the camp guards by deviation—met the enemy about two miles from the guards point and was shot dead. The guards waited for the enemies at their ambush but the enemies didn't come.

The following day at about midday the enemy, who had followed a well-worn track to the *mbuci*, unknowingly fell into our guards' ambush. They exchanged fire some five minutes after which the enemy retreated without causing any casualties to our fighters.

The following day one *gitungati* named Ngatho Kio arrived in the camp from Gilgil. He said that he had spent three days all alone and without food or fire. He said that about two dozen *komerera* on the small bushes of Gilgil rocky areas, under the leadership of Kirigu Ikinya Theuri, were badly dispersed after stealing a cow in one of the neighboring farms. He said that they could not fight the enemy and they were in great danger of being cordoned by the foe in the small *lelishwa* bushes which are surrounded by miles of grasslands and settlers' homes.

'Why did you go there?' I asked him.

'We had gone there,' replied Ngatho, 'in order to avoid this horrible bombing and frequent contacts with the enemy. Since our fighters go to raid cattle so far from the forest, they [i.e., the cattle] are not guarded at all. We would then enter the cattle pen and select one of the very fat bullocks and slaughter it inside the pen and each *gitungati* carries as much meat as he can. We would then move some five miles and roast meat that would last us three days and then walk some five miles and hide ourselves near a settler's home in very small bushes—a place where the enemy would hardly think of. They would then try to search for us in any of the nearest forests. Though we could manage to hide in this way, there is no hope of surviving whenever our hideout is found by the foe.'

'If I saw Kirigu now, I would just shoot him,' said Ngara angrily. 'You see, Mr. Njama, that man ran away with 35 of my *itungati* and you hear that he has now taken them to be slaughtered by the merciless Kenya Ng'ombe.'

'How many were you when you were attacked?' demanded Ngara.

'We were 24', replied the frightened *gitungati*.

'Where were the other 11 *itungati*?' queried Ngara.

'They had been killed within the two contacts we had with the Kenya Ng'ombe,' replied Ngatho shamefully.

'How many enemies has your gang killed?' asked Ngara.

'None,' replied Ngatho.

'How many head of cattle do you kill when you enter in a cattle pen?' I asked.

'We kill only one for we cannot carry more than that,' answered Ngatho.

'What other losses has your gang inflicted to the enemy?' I asked.

'None,' replied Ngatho.

'And for how long have you been there?' I asked.

'Almost two and a half months...'

'Shut up!' interrupted Ngara angrily. 'You are one of those who came to hide and fill your bellies. I am sure you will all perish.'

'Ngatho, you have become a silly idiot,' I said, shaking my head. 'You can neither help yourself nor anyone else and you do not know what you came to do here. I would advise you to remain under the leadership of recognized leaders who would show you what service you would render to our country. Do you understand me?'

'Yes,' said Ngatho.

'If you had killed all the cattle in all the pens you had visited, I said, 'you would have struck the enemy a heavy blow. There is little difference between destroying property or the owner. That property is his strength. His heart is with his property.'

'If you knew where the others were I would have you lead us there now. You have not been serving the country since you left me—you have been foolishly serving yourselves. Do you understand?' shouted Ngara.

'Yes,' replied the humiliated *gitungati*.

'Then don't do it again!' concluded Ngara.

Though Ngara criticised Ngatho, he himself had become a weak leader in the camp's management. He had allowed many *itungati* to abduct girls to the *mbuci* as they desired. He himself had ordered Wakarima, daughter of Manyara, to be brought to him so that she would become his third wife. Some *itungati* had refused to carry food from the reserve for nearly thirty women, other men's wives, who were in the *mbuci*. They had suggested that each *gitungati* was responsible to carry his wife's food and that those who had no women would no longer share their food to these women. That led to the dissolution of the camp store, [which was] replaced by individual or group stores with individual or group kitchens respectively. Each *gitungati* on arrival from fetching food, which they did cooperatively, had to give his leader two big size tins full of maize which he took in his store which was managed by his assistants, Githinji Ngecu and Ndeithi Kinyua, the Guard Commandant.

A group of some cowards who thought that it was dangerous to get food from the reserves had started trapping animals and birds and fishing, thus getting their food right there in the forest and to them there was no need any more of going out of the forest.

I discussed the matter with Ngara, criticised and pointed out his failures and the dangers that would result. I told him that he was unknowingly leading the worst type of *komerera* gang I had ever met.

He felt that I had insulted him and started proving to me that all his *itungati* obeyed him and that they were capable of managing their own affairs.

'Your acceptance to [i.e., allowing] your *itungati* to manage their camp affairs is your greatest failure,' I remarked.

He then went on telling how he had discussed the matter with his *itungati* and had failed to solve the problem of the women in the camp or to stop more from coming. I told him the rules we had passed at Mwathe on behalf of the women. He replied that Mathenge had warned him and some other leaders not to obey those rules passed by Kimathi and his friends in the absence of Mathenge, the elected leader of Ituma Ndemi Army.

I told him that I had been with Mathenge for a fortnight in his *mbuci* and had cleared all his doubts. In fact, that Mathenge had appreciated and accepted all that was passed at Mwathe General Meeting.

Ngara agreed with me but found it very difficult to alter what he had agreed to in the discussion with his *itungati*. He was afraid that his *itungati* might revolt against him.

I proposed to him to move to the Rift Valley with all his *itungati* where he could conduct a cattle raid. I told him that if his section could bring a herd of cattle so that everyone would have plenty to eat, he would then be able to reorganize the camp store and common kitchen without any opposition. He promised that he would move to the Rift Valley within a week's time.

On 29 October I left the camp for Chania to meet Kimathi. Of the four *itungati* I had, none know the whereabouts of the Chania *mbuci*. We had to rely on tracking them. After crossing the Kiandongoro road, we turned east until we came to Kiandongoro Forest Station, where we saw KAR troops on guard. We quickly changed our direction due north and started descending the Chania steep slopes. At two in the afternoon, we arrived at the river Chania where our warriors used to cross the river on a fallen log. One of the *itungati* suggested that we should not cross the river on that log because the enemy used to ambush our fighters there and would not open fire until our warriors were on the log. 'Kimathi's brother, Daniel, was killed right here on this log,' concluded the *gitungati*.

We then turned due west up the river and followed an old track of our fighters. At sunset we were climbing the Mutangariua Hill and had not noticed any sign of a camp, but we were certain that the track led to one of our fighters' camps. We made our camp in some bamboo clusters amongst the black forest. At night we could see a fire burning on the opposite slope across the river. We heard a gun shot which we were certain had been exploded by the owners of that fire. We suspected that it might be the enemy's camp fire and so we covered our fires facing their direction.

The following morning, after prayers, we followed the track uphill and at nine we had fallen into Brig. Gen. Kahiu-Itina's guards. They laughed at us when I told them where we had slept. They told us that we were only about one and a half miles from the camp and that we could have reached the camp if we knew.

When I told them of the fire we had seen, they told us that the fire was in Gen. Nyaga's *mbuci* where Kimathi stayed. They added that Kimathi had left their camp at four on the previous day. We left the guards and entered the camp. I was glad to meet Kahiu-Itina, Ndiritu Thuita and his brother, Dr. King'ori, a qualified dresser, and Kibuku Theuri, the Muthuaini sub-location organizer.

Kahiu-Itina told me of their Murang'a-Kiambu *safari*. He told me that though they had reached Locations 1 and 2, just at the boundary of Murang'a and Kiambu, they did not see any Kiambu fighters; but they sent their scouts both in the forest and the reserve. The former reported that there were no Kiambu warriors in the Nyandarua forest, while the latter reported that the Kiambu elders kept control of their *itungati* and had stopped them from fighting in the reserve. Nevertheless, some small *komerera* gangs under General Waruingi were still operating in Kiambu reserve. The ex-Rift Valley persons of Kiambu disobeyed the elders' boycott call on the fight and moved from Kiambu to the Rift Valley under Gen. Joseph Kibe Kimani. Their sections were on Mt. Longonot and Suswa Hill. Others were in Melili forest in the Mau Escarpment under Gen's. Kibutu and Ole Kisio. Some went as far as Narok in Masailand, while a few of them were stationed at Naivasha.

'When we heard all that,' said Gen. Kahiu-Itina, 'Kimathi wrote a letter to the Kiambu elders telling them we believed Kiambu was the leading district and we had honourably named its army as Kenya Inoro Army. It was a pity, [he wrote] to see that instead of their leadership, as we expected, they were helping to delay our independence. We promised them that we would supply them with leaders and instructors until their army was strong enough to lead itself. We complained in that letter that our supplies from Nairobi were coming through Murang'a instead of Kiambu, which was nearer the forest.'

Kahiu-Itina and his colleagues left me alone in the hut and attended a report from a returning gang which had been sent to the reserve. It had been dispersed by the foe, losing two and two others injured.

I was very much disappointed with the news. Kiambu, the most advanced and educated district, seemed to have abandoned the revolt, I thought. Likewise, all the educated people had not fully supported the fighters, not one who equalled my own education. I began to wonder why they had not joined the fight. 'Could they all be cowards? Or is it because they hated the hard forest life, or do they think that we should not fight for our land and freedom, or did they wish to get the illiterate peasants into the fight and expect to reap the harvest thereof while during the fight they stood as onlookers who would fit themselves well into the winning side?' These thoughts puzzled me for a time.

'Jomo Kenyatta and his colleagues are suffering the same consequence, [I thought]. The Kenya African Union leaders and all the top country leaders who are in detention camps are classified in the same category with the fighters. Peter Mbiyu Koinange, the most educated African in Kenya and our delegate to the British Government on our land and freedom claim, has not abandoned our aim. It is only the white collar, the *tie tie* men who work for the Europeans, who have become spectators or European helpers. Their percentage in the country is very small, and they can do little harm to the country, but the biggest blow now would be lack of leadership. The Kiambu people are the originators of the oath and all the ideas behind the Movement; why should they surrender when it is red hot? Wouldn't they like to harvest the fruit they planted?'

There are four Kikuyu sayings that answered my questions. '*Kiriti gitigunaga muni.*' ('The land does not benefit the pioneer' [i.e., the one who first acquires it.]) '*Murimi tiwe murii.*' ('He who cultivates does not always reap the harvest.') '*Hia ciukaga thutha na igakira matu.*' ('Though the horns grow after the ears, they are longer.' And, '*Maari mbere macokire thutha.*' ('Those who were in front, turned out to be the last.')

The Kiambu mystery was not unique; the old sayings settled my problems. 'Why should I keep myself worried about Kiambu District while there are many other districts which don't bother themselves with the Kenya freedom but who would be the first to enjoy that freedom? Never mind,' I said to myself, 'Jesus Christ died alone to save the world's people from sins—He freed all the people from the sins' slavery by his blood. Our blood, we who have volunteered, will free Kenya from colonial slavery and exploitation.'

Kahiu-Itina and Ndiritu returned. 'Are you all alone, Mr. Njama?' asked Kahiu-Itina.

'Yes, I have been tackling the Kiambu problem and I resolved that we must try and get them to aid us and if we failed we should go on, for I think if our volunteered *itungati* were well equipped they are sufficient to fight for Kenya.'

'You are quite correct, Mr. Njama,' said Ndiritu. 'We cannot get everybody to join in the fight, but we demand everybody's help.

Jomo Kenyatta and his colleagues are a sufficient army to fight for Kiambu. It isn't a wonder that *mundo mugo ndari ngumo rugongo rwake*. (That a medicine man is not as famous in his own region as he is in others.)'

'Don't be surprised,' remarked Kahiu-Itina, 'for we have seen that instead of Kiambu people fighting for Kenyatta, they became witnesses to convict him!'

I then told them my puzzling thoughts when they had left me alone in the hut and we spent much time discussing the same thing. It was at this time that a thought flashed in my mind which I did not tell my friends, as I thought that it might frighten them and endanger our position. I remembered that the educated persons had learned the history of the British wars. They had the knowledge of the colonial forces and powers. They believed that since we were neither armed nor trained it would be suicide to take a *panga* against a rifle, machine gun, jet bomber or the Lincoln bombers—which had been demonstrated to them either in army propaganda films or newspapers during the Second World War. The fear born out of this knowledge caused many educated men to seek security in the white man. On the other hand, the ignorance of the illiterate peasants of the enemy's power was our warriors' strength and courage.

Thinking it unwise to continue the topic, I dropped it off by introducing my desire to meet them at Karuri Ngamune and told how the enemy had dispersed my *itungati* on the way at Kariaini, thus causing my failure to attend the meeting. I told them all about the various camps I had visited, most of which were very disappointing. I told them how I had carried on my job in all the camps I had visited. They told me that Gathitu had collected all the data in that camp and had left for Nyaga's *mbuci* with Kimathi on the previous day. I asked them how I could get there. Kahiu-Itina replied that it was only forty-five minutes walk to get there. He advised me to write a letter to Kimathi telling him that I would be going there the following day so that he could make the necessary arrangements and appointment of receiving me. I wrote the letter and gave it to Ndiritu for dispatch. At six in the evening I received a reply from Kimathi saying that he expected me the following day before midday.

I spent a night in that camp, whose buildings and management were very good. Kimathi had previously issued ranks to many

itungati in that camp. The ranks were respected and reflected real
character. Each fireplace had a girl attendant who collected firewood, kept the fire burning and who was to be sent to and fro by
the owners of the fire. These fires, which were lit in every hut, were
grouped according to rank, [with the officers separate from the
itungati.]

After dinner, songs and entertainments which amused people
continued for a long time. Ndiritu told me that his camp had 13
new recruits who had escaped from the Nyeri Prison and that they
had been in that *mbuci* for three days. That had caused Kimathi
to leave the camp for not trusting all of them.

'One of them is Muthee Gatero,' said Kahiu-Itina, 'your old
friend who lived near your Muthuaini school and supplied you with
milk.'

I very much wanted to see him and he was called. When he
arrived, we first talked about personal affairs and then I asked
him whether it was possible to free the other prisoners. He said
that there were over five thousand detainees in Nyeri Prison and
that more than three thousand were accommodated sleeping outside the prison building in tents enclosed by a barbed wire fence.
He said there were armed sentries all along the fence at twenty
yard intervals. He said that the forest fighters could not succeed
in freeing the prisoners unless the prisoners cooperated in the planning, which was very dangerous for there were very many informers
who had been detained for the purpose of collecting information
and it was very likely that the plans would be known beforehand
by the enemy. He added that the prison was in a very bad location. The 3rd and 26th KAR had encamped to surround the prison
and the police H.Q. was only about 200 yards from the prison. It
was right in the heart of the town and surrounded by European
homes. We found it would be difficult to attack the prison so
abandoned the talk.

CHAPTER XVI

UNITY AND DIVISION

TOWARD the end of 1953 two events occurred which tended to reinforce the bonds of tribal unity among Aberdare guerrilla groups. Though it is difficult to assess the magnitude of their influence, there is little question that the formation of the Kenya Young Stars Association and the New Year's memorial ceremony held at Ruthaithi lent themselves to a strengthening of those wider loyalties to tribe, Movement and country which held in check certain divisive tendencies within the forest organization.

The Kenya Young Stars Association, to the extent that it was effective, functioned as a group which cut across the various territorial forest groupings and hence tended to weaken the narrower sectional loyalties based upon leader-followers-locality ties. As a loosely organized association of all Aberdare guerrilla fighters, laying great stress on the historical role and importance of the forest revolutionaries, it was received with considerable enthusiasm by the gathering of over eight hundred fighters and leaders from various sections of the forest at the New Year's Eve memorial ceremony.

The ideas which gave rise to this association, and to its name, are very interesting from an ideological standpoint. They reveal an important historical dimension not yet mentioned, an element which had as its central focus an almost urgent desire that the exploits, struggles and sacrifices of the forest revolutionaries not be forgotten or undervalued by future Kikuyu and Kenya African generations. This is clearly revealed in Karari's account of the discussion which gave birth to the Kenya Young Stars Association.

The second important unifying event was the New Year's Eve ceremony. Though difficulties in travel and communication kept attendance somewhat low, this was nevertheless the first general gathering of groups from the four Aberdare zones since the Mwathe meeting. As at all such forest gatherings, the collective participation in song, prayer and other activities tended to

strengthen the bonds of Kikuyu unity and bolster the fighters'
morale. Again, since the gathering was attended by most of the
important members and officers of the Kenya Defense Council—
the notable exception being Stanley Mathenge—and held under
its auspices, it tended to reaffirm the legitimacy, authority and
continuity of the Council as the central forest institution.

Perhaps it would be useful at this point to indicate some of
the strengths and frailties of the forest organization. As noted
earlier, the wider and more inclusive organization achieved
through the formation of the Kenya Defense Council and
military hierarchy was characterized, among other things, by a
decentralization of effective power and authority. While the
Kenya Defense Council had the power to formulate overall
strategy and policy, enact rules and regulations and sit as the
highest judicial body, the authority to implement and enforce
its policies and rulings rested largely with the individual leader-
members or section and camp heads. Kenya Defense Council
representatives, as we have seen, lacked the power to enforce
the Council's decisions, being limited in this regard to the use of
their individual persuasive abilities. Again, though Kimathi, as
Field Marshal of the Land and Freedom Army, could issue ranks
and tactical directives, he could not effectively demand compliance from other important leaders in the military hierarchy. The
latter, each commanding a personal following not dependent on
approval or legitimization from above, were in a position to
withdraw their recognition of Kimathi's authority at any time—
hence their continued support had to be solicited rather than
demanded.

These features of decentralization reflected the voluntary
nature of both membership in and recognition of the Kenya
Defense Council, as well as the prior distribution of effective
power among groups whose members were bound together by
strong leader-followers-locality ties and loyalties. Given this latter
condition, the creation of a strong central institution would have
been extremely difficult; it would have required a relatively
large-scale reorganization of forest groupings and led almost
certainly to a debilitating power struggle among competing
forest leaders. Put another way, the relatively weak central
council which emerged at Mwathe was advantageous since,
without significantly altering the existing distribution of power

amongst the various leaders, it allowed for a considerable degree
of cooperation among the latter in the planning and coordination
of policies, rules and tactics.

Another advantage of this decentralization lay in its allowing
for a very high degree of flexibility of maneuver and individual
initiative among the many forest sections. With rapid travel and
communication made extremely difficult by the forest terrain,
and military and logistic conditions necessitating the breakdown
of the former large groups into smaller sections and sub-sections,
it was important that each fighting unit achieve a considerable
degree of self-sufficiency and that section leaders be in a position to make day-to-day decisions regarding tactics and the
deployment of their men.

But what of the frailties? First, the Kenya Defense Council,
though continuing to function through the organizational work
of Kimathi and its field secretaries or representatives, was seemingly unable to meet when the occasion demanded in order to
consider changes in the overall mitilary situation, coordinate its
forces to exploit particular enemy weaknesses or endeavour to
reconcile differences of opinion or personal conflicts among its
members. While communications were sustained through letters
and messengers and numerous meetings took place between individual leaders, no meetings of the whole Council were convened
between August 1953 and the New Year's Eve ceremony at
Ruthaithi. Aside from the obvious difficulties of travel, the
primary reason for this failure to meet lay in the broadly representative composition of the Council itself. Comprised of a large
number of leaders, who were scattered widely over the forest at
the head of their respective sections, the Council was simply too
unwieldly to convene. Its officers, for the most part, were also
attached to particular sections and no arrangements had been
made at Mwathe for the establishment of a permanent headquarters camp or staff.

Another frailty emerges when we look at the opposing principles at work in the council system and military hierarchy. The
hierarchy of formal and informal councils, culminating in the
Kenya Defense Council, involved the principle of participation
in each council of all leaders under its jurisdiction. Again, at least
implicitly, it involved the traditional principle of discussion and
resolution of questions through consensus of opinion, with

unanimity being the objective. The military hierarchy, on the other hand, in which British army ranks were adopted, assumed a chain-of-command principle according to which orders from superior to subordinate officers were to be obeyed without question or discussion.

The difficulties here centered around two factors: (1) There was no clear-cut division of authority between the Kenya Defense Council and the military hierarchy headed by a Field Marshal; and (2) military ranks tended to parallel Council offices, with the President of the Kenya Defense Council, Dedan Kimathi, holding the highest military rank of Field Marshal, Stanley Mathenge, Chairman of the Ituma Ndemi Trinity Council, holding the rank of Commander of the Ituma Ndemi Army, etc. The problem thus arose as to whether, in particular situations, a leader was acting in his capacity as Council official or military officer, and, in the latter instance, whether his military rank justified the authority he had assumed. In concrete terms, as will be noted in Karari's account, this confusion tended to breed conflict between certain key forest leaders. Kimathi's 'right' to make certain decisions on his own was questioned and resented by Mathenge and certain other leaders who felt he was acting beyond his authority and without the necessary consent of the Council. This source of conflict, as we shall see, increases as the battle wears on.

Related to the absence of adequate enforcement machinery, the inability of the Kenya Defense Council to control or exercise effective influence over subordinate or marginal *komerera* groups constituted a third frailty. This was perhaps most important in respect to the relation of forest groups to peasant masses. The quest for food and other necessary supplies led to an increasing number of actions by guerrilla units which tended to alienate the support of the peasantry, particularly those living as squatters on European farms. Though most of these actions involved *komerera*-group thefts of civilian property, Karari's account reveals that some, at least, of the recognized forest groups also engaged in this type of raid.

A fourth frailty, already alluded to, lay in what might be called the vertical pattern into which effective power and loyalty were segmented. Based on the leader-followers-locality ties of the primary forest groupings (sections and sub-sections), and the territorial segmentation of the Land and Freedom Armies, several key leaders—e.g., Kimathi, Mathenge, Kahiu-Itina, Kimbo, Kimemia, Mbaria Kaniu—commanded the personal support and allegiance of numerous lesser leaders and the fighting units in their respective forest spheres. With subordinate leaders and the sections they commanded bound by greater loyalties to individual leaders than to the Kenya Defense Council, the forest organization was faced with an inherent danger that personal differences or conflicts between key leaders might result in its disintegration. And this danger was heightened by the fact that no single leader emerged who was able to rise above his particular territorial identification. Kimathi, who came closest to achieving a territorially detached position due to his constant travels and organizational skills, was nevertheless considered a 'Nyeri leader' by leaders from other districts, and a 'North Tetu man' by the other Nyeri leaders.

In the chapters which follow, we shall be able to observe the unfolding of the several tendencies mentioned above.

★   ★   ★

The following day, November 1st, I left the camp and, accompanied by Kahiu-Itina and Ndiritu and ten *itungati* including the four I had, crossed the river Chania and climbed its steep slopes on which Nyaga had built his *mbuci*. The guards had been informed of our visit and so we entered the camp easily. I learned that Kimathi had made a rule that no one was allowed to enter the camp he was living in without first being thoroughly inspected [i.e., searched] and could only see him at his consent.

There were only a few people in the *mbuci* as many had either gone to collect honey or to warm themselves by the sun's heat. Those who were in stood for us and happily greeted us. Colonel Gitau Icatha received us well. He led us into the officers' mess where we rested while he informed Kimathi of our arrival. After a few minutes, Icatha came for us and led us to Kimathi's office, about two hundred yards from the camp. We first met a dozen of Kimathi's strong bodyguards, parading outside the office. When they were called to attention by their commandant, Nguthiru Ngumo, brother-in-law of Kimathi, Kimathi and his colleagues came out and then the guards presented arms in our honor. The three of us saluted the guards and then inspected them. I had known some of his guards at Mwathe, such as Kirange (Gathuri Mukiri), Wanyee, Mbaka and Rwigi.

We entered the office—twelve by twenty-five feet. Three of its four-foot walls were well covered to protect [against] cold, while the fourth wall acted as a window with two and a half feet covered from the ground. The room had two long bamboo tables and one small table, all covered with pondo bark.

Kimathi had been preparing books in which Gathitu entered the data. Shamuli (Gathura Muita) had shifted from the hospital and had then become Kimathi's personal secretary. He was busy typing some letters from Kimathi's drafts calling leaders to attend cere-monial prayers ending the first year's fight in the forest to be held on December 31st at Ruhuruini Hill.

At first Kimathi was interested with my report which covered a long story since we parted. He very much wanted to meet Mathenge and Ngara. I told him that they had promised me that they would spend their Christmas in the Rift Valley between Nderagwa and Subuk. It was then difficult to send them letters inviting them to attend the annual ceremony. At any rate we hoped that they would be able to get the news in circulation before hand.

Referring to Kabuga's section, he commented that that *mbuci* should hold a cleansing ceremony for he believed that it had been contaminated by some evils.

Kimathi told me of his journey to Kiambu and how he was angry with the Kiambu people. I told him that we had talked the matter over on the previous day and hoped his letter might arouse the Kiambu people to join the war.

I then took out my record books and showed him the data I had collected. He told me that he had brought data from all the Murang'a camps and that was sufficient work to keep me in the office to the end of the year entering these data into the big books.

In the evening, Kimathi introduced me to our warriors in that camp. I gave a short speech to encourage our warriors. I pointed out that it was more than a year since the emergency was declared. The Kenya Government had agreed with General Hinde's forecast that he would defeat Mau Mau within 6 weeks. In fact, General Hinde was defeated and succeeded by General Erskine. I men-tioned that after travelling and collecting reports from many parts of Nyandarua, I had found that the last seven months of Harvard bombing—excluding nine deaths and ten casualties inflicted by the Police Air Wing early in March—only two persons in Kabuga's section had been killed and three injured compared with two air-planes that we have shot down, killing all aboard, plus petrol and bombs' cost and pilots' wages. In addition to that, these Harvards have helped us twice to kill their own forces, once at Kariaini where they killed forty-two and the other at Deighton Downs where a Government force camp was completely finished off by a jet fighter which had seen the camp fire at night.

'Without any doubt, [I said] one can see that God has protected us from the enemy fire poured from their planes with the intention to destroy us, but our God has destroyed them with their own weapons just as we had prayed.' I appealed to our fighters to per-severe and have confidence that we were going to win. Thereafter our warriors dispersed into their huts and the fires were lit. Colonel Icatha had ordered for my hut to be built; he took me there and then we moved to the officers mess where we sat around the fire talking on whatever flashed into our minds.

Maize mixed with *hatha* (a vegetable of the nettle family) was served to us for dinner, after which our *itungati* practiced drill, dancing and singing.

For the next three weeks I continued my office routine assisted by Gathura Muita and Major Vindo (Ndururi Gititika) and Gathitu Waithaka.

On one of the nights when we sat around a fire, Kimathi intro-duced a new idea saying that one day Jesus had spoken to his disciples saying: 'Ye are the light of the world...Let your light shine unto all.' 'We get light from the sun, moon and stars,' said Kimathi. 'Now, since the government has taken away our sun, Jomo Kenyatta, and the moon, all the other political leaders—and even all the big stars have been arrested—only the *young stars* are left shining over our country.

'The sun gives us its light for twelve hours a day. After sunset the moon takes over, but she is not faithful; sometimes she gives us her light for an hour only and then she leaves us in the darkness. When she is very sincere, she would give us her light for ten hours, The big stars are just like the moon, but the young stars abide with us from sunset till sunrise, giving us their little light; they are our sincere friends who will not abandon us when the troubles come.

As Jesus had told his disciples, I tell you. You are the KENYA YOUNG STARS; keep on shining till the Sun and the Moon are released.'

'Yes, Marshal,' I commented, 'that is a very important idea and should be conveyed to all our warriors, making each understand that he or she is a KENYA YOUNG STAR and that our lovely Kenya is longing for his or her light. By light I mean the leadership that would lead us to victory—to the promised Land and Freedom. This covers the power, knowledge and activities that are required right now by the Kenya people. By this I mean that we who are free to sit down and discuss, write our thoughts to our sympathizers or meet them or act according to what we think is right, should now take the country's leadership and all the responsibilities in our hands, command both the forest and reserve.

'I think that we have the right ideas, but communication has been made difficult by the enemy; it is sometimes difficult to communicate with other fighters, more difficult to communicate with the reserves bordering the forest and most difficult to communicate with other districts or provinces. Nevertheless, we must try all that we can do. At least we must organize here in the forest a Kenya Young Stars Association of which all fighters would be members. After the war this association should be registered and be recorded in the Kenya history as the "Light of Kenya During Kenya's Dark Ages".'

After a few comments of the same kind from Major Vindo and Gathura Muita we resolved that we should go on preaching the formation of the Kenya Young Stars Association to all our warriors.

It was November 17th in the afternoon when the whole of Nyandarua was first terrorized by the heavy bombers. A heavy rain had just stopped and we were in our huts warming ourselves and taking much care less any airplane sees the smoke of our fires. A heavy bomber dropped eight bombs consecutively at Ruthaithi about fifteen miles away. The airplane moved from north to south along the line bordering the black forest and the bamboo region in which the land forces had marked many of the deserted camps. Its noise grew louder and louder as it drew nearer and nearer. It became certain that the noise was not of the Harvard bombers but was of a passenger plane—then our fears disappeared [in the thunder of bombs]. Suddenly, it started dropping 1000 lb. bombs, eight of them consecutively at 200 yard intervals on the Chania Valley east of our camp. A great storm accompanied by both horrible thunderous noise and earth tremors knocked each of us down. This was over a hundred times stronger than any bomb's explosion we had experienced before. Some thought that the airplane had crashed down on us, others thought that that was an atomic bomb they had heard of. Some thought that the twigs which fell from the shocked trees were bomb shells. Fear and the airplane's speed did not give us any time to think. Though the plane was going away from us, it continued to drop bombs in Gura Valley, Kariaini, Mathioya and Maragua.

At about the same time, another airplane of the same kind started dropping bombs in the western side of the mountain bordering the Rift Valley. Before we could discuss anything of the new passenger bombers, another plane of its kind started bombing Mt. Kenya. These bombs were so thunderous that we could hear them clearly whenever dropped on any part of Mt. Kenya or the Aberdares. The airplane was slow in speed and its roars could be heard some fifty miles away.

Our warriors who had been collecting honey uphill arrived and reported that they clearly saw the airplane. 'It was not a passenger plane,' one of them said. 'It was a grey plane as big as the passenger planes but, unlike the passenger planes, it had a big *gikonyo* (i.e., protruding navel) through which it dropped the bombs.' This horrible bomber became known to us *nyagi-konyo*, the protruding-navel-bearer. Later on we learned that it was the Lincoln Heavy Bomber.

Kimathi and I, including many others, wanted to see the area destroyed by the bombs so that we could assess its strength. Many of us guessed that the bombs had been dropped between two and three hundred yards from the camp. We had walked about a quarter of a mile when we saw two big cleared areas on the other slope of the river Chania. It seemed to be more than a mile away. The soil from the holes made by the bombs seemed to have slid into the river and the big furrow was clearly seen.

We decided to walk further until we reached the place. On our arrival we were very surprised to see that the sliding soil from both banks of the river and their steep slopes had blocked the river Chania, making a very big dam. The bomb had made a hole about twenty yards in diameter and about thirty feet deep. Almost every tree within 200 yards radius had been injured by either the shells or the stones thrown by the bomb. A big *muna* tree with about seven feet diameter at its base had been completely uprooted and thrown some 200 yards away down the slope. One of the iron blades we collected was rough and sharp and weighed more than thirty pounds. The ground covering about a hundred and fifty yards in diameter was fully covered by the soil that had been thrown high up in the air by the bomb and had fallen to the ground. The bombs had destroyed more than a mile's length, which reflected a sorrowful scenery. It proved that the British had decided to destroy us.

'What makes the British use such strong and destructive bombs on unarmed people?' I asked.

'The answer is simple,' said Kimathi. 'The Europeans have seen that we are definitely winning while they are losing and that is why they have increased their powers so much. They are a strange people; they may try to destroy all the country and reduce the Africans to a less number in population compared to their own before they quit the country.'

'Have you forgotten that a European hates very much to see another person drinking out of a cup he himself has drunk of?' said Vindo. 'He would rather break that cup than to see it being used by somebody else, and an African in particular.'

'That is true,' said another *gitungati*. 'I have been a European's cook for twenty years and I have never seen them invite an African to dinner, no matter how long he has served or the quality of his service. I have gone on many *safaris* with them and I believe that they think an African does not feel hunger. And above all, he is so inferior that to treat an African as human would be [considered] an evil by a European.'

'I wonder how we shall live with them after acquiring our independence?' asked Gathura Muita.

'All the Kenya Europeans will have to quit the country when we get independence,' I said. 'Not because we shall chase them but many would be ashamed of their evil actions during the war, their utterances and their unrealistic promises they have given their children and wives that they are here to stay as masters in the White Highland. Many of them suffer from incurable gross superiority [feelings] and absolute selfishness. Many would be quite unwilling to work under the African Government as their superiority would lead them to disobedience. The fear that the Africans might revenge the inhuman treatment they have received from these

Europeans would definitely drive them all out of the country; but many more Europeans will come with full knowledge that they are visitors of the African Government which they would respect and obey as much as their own.

'Don't let the common statement that all Europeans are bad mislead you,' I continued. 'In fact there are very many good English men and women in Britain who share our feelings. They [would] like to see us freed and managing our own affairs. They are ready to treat us as equals. There are really little differences between white and black people considered as individuals under their own wills and feelings. You will understand it easier if you remember that probably the Home Guard you are fighting against is your real brother, sister or parent, while there are many Europeans in every country such as Germany, France, Italy, Poland, Russia and China, who very much share our feelings—they hate what we hate and like all that we like and if they were near they would help us in the fight to achieve our freedom. Those will come and we shall live with them as friends and partners in many enterprises. Mark that our real fight is not against the white color but is against the system carried on by the whites. What would be the difference between a white and a black European?' I asked.

'An enemy is an enemy,' replied Icatha, 'no matter whether he be your father or brother. Any one whose joy is your misery is your enemy!'

'*Ucio uri ho!*' shouted many *itungati*, in our colloquial terminology meaning 'That is true.'

'*Ucio uri ho?*' asked Kimathi.

'*Eei, ucio uri ho!*' replied the *itungati*.

'You can now be certain that our enemy is determined to finish us off,' said Kimathi. 'God is great, they will not be able to succeed; but woe to those who would surrender—there would be no hope for them to survive.'

Some heavy clouds had been spreading their thick grey blankets over the mountains and valleys and sending out signals of lightning and thunder, reporting that heavy rain was about to pour. Though we hurriedly ran back to the camp, by the time we arrived at the *mbuci* we were as wet as fish. *Nyagikonyo* had frightened our people and we had to wait for three hours before it became dark enough for us to light fires. Most of us had only the wet pair of clothes. We spent an uncomfortable night in both mental and physical conditions.

The following day Kimathi, myself, his clerks and bodyguard left for Ruhuruini Hill. After four hours walk we arrived at Gen. Abdullah's (Gitonga Muthui) *mbuci*. This camp had plundered some cattle from the reserve and we were served with cold roasted meat for lunch. Kimathi told Abdullah to send out scouts for selecting a campsite on Ruhuruini Hill where his section would be responsible for building the camp in which our fighters should perform the annual ceremonial prayers.

The following morning we left the camp in order to visit Ruthaithi area where lived many small sections. Soon after crossing Kinaini stream we came to Kabage road that goes to the Moorland. Our scouts spied the road reporting that there were no enemy tracks. We sent our bodyguards first and they took their positions in both directions of the road. We then passed between them taking much care that our footprints would not be seen by the enemy. We passed Kabage Forest Squatters' gardens, which then had big bushes growing in which large herds of elephants, buffalo, rhinos and various types of animals were seen here and there.

Soon we entered a large grassland area with small shrub bushes and very scattered big trees. 'This is Ruthaithi area, the center of the Mountain Royal National Park,' said Kimathi. 'See those trees? (pointing with his walking staff). That is where the Tree Tops Hotel was built. The whites used to enjoy the scenery and taking photos of the various animals which drink salt water in a small pool. The *Njeng'u* natural salt on the boundary of the reserve and the settled area is about two miles east of the Tree Tops. That salt, plus plenty of grass and warmth, makes this area the home of animals. This area, [being a salient] can easily be cordoned some three miles to the north, and one reaches the forest boundary both to the east and to the south. Ruthaithi is surrounded by the reserves.'

We could clearly see and hear people shout in the reserve. 'Mr Njama, I won't go to Kinaini to see the patients,' said Kimathi. 'You will go there and bring me the report before three in the afternoon. I have to return to Abdullah's. This place is not safe for me to stay.'

We continued our journey and soon came to a *mbuci*. It had no huts, the owners slept in tents during the rains only. Kinaini, the nearest river, was almost a mile from the camp. Colonel Wambararia (Wagura Waciuri), Kimathi's youngest brother, was the leader of the *mbuci* and Major Gathee Ngumo, Kimathi's brother-in-law, was the assistant.

We were served with cold boiled meat and honey after which I left with some strong escorts and a guide from that *mbuci*. After two miles walk eastwards, I arrived at King'ora Mutungi's small *mbuci* which had 18 warriors. He was very glad to see me. He called his wife and asked her to give us some cold well roasted mutton. While we were eating, he told us that his assistant, nick-named Blacker, had collected one of the mortar shells that were fired aimlessly into that area by cannon artilleries almost every evening. Since the mortar shell had not exploded, Blacker thought that if they opened it they could use the gunpowder inside for making hand grenades. He started opening the mortar while seven other *itungati* sat around him eagerly wanting to see what had made that mortar. All of a sudden it exploded, injuring six of them badly. 'Blacker has lost both eyes but he is getting better. Another *gitungati* has lost an eye; one of those we thought had lost sight started seeing yesterday. The others, with the exception of one *gitungati* who has two shells in his head, will soon recover.'

After eating, he took us to his hospital. My heart was full of sorrow and sympathy when I saw that those *itungati* had many dangerous wounds all over their bodies. I tried to speak to them for some encouragement but often my heart blocked my mouth whenever I tried to figure out the future of their disability. I told them of the blinds' schools and the various works that could be done by cripples out of which they could earn their living. I told them that people like themselves should be the symbol of the freedom price and that the African Government should honor and help all the cripples and would not let them move into the city and towns as beggars.

We left the hospital and, with King'ora accompanying us, took the report to Kimathi. After listening to the report, he warned us never again to attempt to open any shell. He showed that he felt great sympathy to the patients and wished, if such fighters could survive, [that they be] lined up under the National Flag on the freedom celebration day and let that blind man pull down the Union Jack for its last time in Kenya while another cripple would hoist the National Flag for the first time. We then talked on how our first Government should take care of all the disabled persons.

Kimathi then told me that he had split that *mbuci* into two—Wambararia, his brother, assisted by Capt's. Karau and Thia and his section of 40 *itungati*, while Gathee assisted by Capt. Binhalis would go to start a new *mbuci* of 33 *itungati*. Formerly, before it was split, the camp had 13 girls.

I pointed out to Kimathi that though we had named our armies we had never divided them into smaller units.

'Though it would have been better for you,' said Kimathi, 'to remain here and collect data from all these small *mbuci*, we will first go to Abdullah's *mbuci* where we shall divide the Ituma Ndemi Army into its various units, after which you will return and continue your job here.'

So we set off, arriving at Abdullah's at five in the evening. That night we spent much time dividing the Ituma Ndemi Army into Divisions, Companies, Sections and Sub-Sections, and roughly defining their areas of operation in both the forest and the reserves. Here is a sample of the results :

IDA 1st Division : commanded by Brigadier General Kahiu-Itina; North Tetu Location; four companies with three sections in each.

IDA 1/1 ....Gen. Ndiritu Thuita
IDA 1/2 ....Gen. Nyaga (Muriuki Gathure)
IDA 1/3 ....Gen. Abdullah (Gitonga Muthiu)
IDA 1/4 ....Gen. Jeriko (Mubia Mung'ongi)

IDA 1/3/1 ....Col. Wamthandi
IDA 1/3/2 ....Col. Wambararia
IDA 1/3/3 ....Col. Gathee

IDA 1/3/2/1 ......Capt. Karau
IDA 1/3/2/2 ......Capt. Thia

IDA 2nd Division : commanded by (General) Kihara Kagumu had four companies with four sections each; Othaya Location.

IDA 3rd Division : under (General) Njau Kiore; had six companies with three sections each; Mahiga Location. [Stanley Mathenge lived in this Division but was elected commander of the entire Ituma Ndemi Army.]

IDA 4th Division : under (General Gikonyo Kanyungu; three
companies with two sections; Chinga Location
and Muhito Location.

At about this time our fighters from Aguthi Location had moved
from the forest back into the reserve under Gen. Kariba. Plunder-
ing cattle from the reserve had become rather difficult due to
increased security forces and strongly fortified posts and the decrease of ammunition to our side. Carrying food on shoulders from
Aguthi Location, which is almost in the center of the district, had
become tiresome to those warriors. A habit of hiding in the reserve
for two days before returning into the forest was prolonged to a
week due to the fear of Lincoln bombers in the forest. Instead of
splitting and hiding in small numbers they stayed together in order
to strengthen their arms and ammunition in case they were forced
to fight. During the night Kariba's gang moved all over the reserve
and recruited many other fighters who might be sent from the forest
to join his company. In a short time his company had acquired
many arms and ammunition and ate the best possible food in the
reserve and enjoyed the girls as companions who served them in
the evenings. This was the beginning of the Kenya Levellation
Army in Nyeri. It spent the day in plantations [i.e., fields] and
small bushes and whenever discovered by the Government forces
it bravely fought many day battles . . . which we shall hear about
later.

We found that we could not divide the armies up into their
smaller units without the help of the leaders concerned. We postponed it to the end of the year during which time we could resume
it in the presence of the leaders we demanded.

I returned to Ruthaithi on the 1st of December in order to
collect the required data. This area had many small unorganized
komerera gangs with four or six fighters making a camp of their
own, taking much care on how and where to steal food and hide
their camp. During this period I visited nine camps in the area
[including] Wambararia's, Gathee's and Omera's (Ndiritu
Wang'ombe), which was unlike the others. This latter camp had
the best gunmaker. His homemade guns differed very little with the
manufactured ones. When I learnt that, I called Kimathi from
Abdullah's to come and see the ready made guns and arrange with
him [i.e., the gun-maker] how he could teach others and enlarge

the orders of the tools and equipment necessary. Omera had well organized some settler farm workers who regularly supplied his camp maize flour, coffee, sugar, medicine, money and clothing or any other of their requirements.

Next, I visited some *komerera* camps, Thuo's with ten *itungati*, Kiongi's with four and Lord's (Gicambira) with six. Unlike the other *komereras*, these leaders did not hide themselves. They liked to visit the big leaders and talk about their camps' activities as though they were of equal rank with the big leaders. They often presented gifts to the big leaders and cunningly evaded exposing how many *itungati* they had or whereabout their camps were, for they didn't like any leader to visit them.

After spending a night in each of the last *mbuci*, I visited Jeriko's *mbuci*, which had some eight *itungati*, and four hundred yards to the north was the Kenya Levellation Army camp under Montgomery, with some sixty [of the most] well-armed, clean and well-dressed fighters in the whole of Nyandarua. This is where the Kenya Levellation [sections] encamped whenever chased from the reserve; it was about one and a half miles from the forest boundary. Between the two camps was a small pond in which the rhinos, buffaloes, elephants and all the other animals drank. The two camps drank the same stagnant filthy water, full of animals dung and urine; frogs, toads, mosquitoes and various types of insects bred there. I felt that the water was unfit for drinking and when I pointed out to them that that water might infect them some diseases, they argued that there were no germs or diseases in the forest and that God had blessed everything in the forest to become food to our fighters and that he has allowed the warriors to lift all the taboos. They used the collecting of honey from beehives without the consent of the owners and stealing of bewitched food to illustrate their statement. In the end they rejected the idea that the water might be harmful.

These camps had plenty of meat to eat, which made one to feel thirsty frequently. I hated to drink that unboiled water which made them feel that I was too proud and wanted to live above their standard. As I was not pleased with life in those camps, I stayed two days in each and then moved to King'ora's camp. None of these camps I had visited in the Ruthaithi area built any huts. They used tents or slept in the open during the dry seasons.

On 14th December, King'ora asked me to go with him to a

laborers' village on a settler's farm near Mweiga. He wanted me to speak to the villagers so that they would be courageous enough to supply us with the things we wanted. Two house keepers, the farm supervisor and their families were the only ones in the village who had not taken the oath. The laborers wanted them to be initiated so that they could all help the fighters without anyone to inform the settler.

We left the forest at five in the evening, a gang of sixteen warriors, including King'ora and myself, armed with two rifles, one shotgun and five home-made guns. It was my first day to set foot out of the forest in six months.

We descended to an open grassland valley and by the time we had climbed its far slope we were one hundred yards from the main road and two miles from the forest. We could see Kenya Ng'ombe taking their ambush positions behind us in Hutchinson's farm where they had encamped. Six lorries and two Land Rovers carrying Kenya Ng'ombe and some KAR forces passed us. We thought that they were from Mweiga H.Q. and were going to ambush our fighters. I felt quite unsafe knowing that we were not well armed, and that only the long grass prevented us from being seen by the enemies. I knew it was difficult for me to run three miles to the forest without being caught. I then kept on praying Ngai to protect us from falling in the enemy's hands.

Before twilight we crossed the main road and the fencing wires and were walking along the farm's hedge among growing gum trees just about a hundred yards from the settler's house. Soon the farm owner arrived in his Land Rover. We saw two *askari* who guarded the house salute the settler. One had a rifle, the other had a shotgun. We sent some *itungati* to spy the village which was built next to the farm house on the eastern side and separated by a barbed wire fence.

At twilight our *itungati* entered the village and took guarding positions. A few laborers helped to collect the others into the largest hut. When they were all settled, one *gitungati* came for us. He said we could continue to give lectures to the villagers while awaiting for the two housemen and their headman who would leave their master's house at nine.

We first sent Kariuki Thandiku to administer the oath to the wives of those who had not been initiated. We told him to give them a simple oath consisting of meat, soil and blood pricked from

their own fingers, and to make them swear a binding promise of
not betraying us but of helping us.

When Kariuki brought the report that he had completed giving
them the oath, we entered the house in which about 60 people were
seated. Many of them knew King'ora, who introduced me to them
as the Chief Secretary of the Kenya Defense Council.

I told them that we took oath in order to achieve unity and
confidence between one another and among the African community. I told them that we were fighting for our lands which
Europeans had stolen some 50 years ago and in which they were
working as servants. I promised them that when we achieved our
victory that land should be shared unto them. The other thing we
were fighting for was freedom. I told them that we didn't want to
be ruled by the white community. We wanted to throw away the
bad rules and regulations which were enforced by the colonial
system. I told them that our aim was to form an African Government that would rule the country; that all the Africans were
welcomed with the exception of the traitors. I told them that there
was no difference between a traitor and an enemy. I told them
all the help we demanded from them.

The headman and his two men entered into the house after
being trapped by one of the villagers. Each of them at the guns
point were asked whether they were willing to take the oath or not.
As soon as they accepted they were initiated. Each paid 50 shillings
fine for their former activities. I repeated my speech and showed
them how they could help us to spy their master. We wished them
goodbye and then left.

We had hardly gone a hundred yards when the villagers started
whistling and shouting for help. Our tramps [i.e., walk] quickly
changed into loud pats as we ran away. The *askari* guarding the
house heard us and opened fire towards us. We quickly crossed
the main road and descended down into the valley. When we
started climbing the other slope of the stream, we saw many Land
Rovers and lorries going to that home for help. They used their
searchlights which showed us the way. When their lights struck us
we laid on the ground and walked on our knees and arms. Soon
we reached the forest boundary where we paused to have a breath
from the long run. I learned that we were only five persons. I wondered where the rest were. I was informed that they had driven all

the village sheep to our *mbuci* when I was lecturing. 'Some carried large luggage,' said one of the guards.

Before our sweat cooled down, the enemy started firing mortar which passed their red lights over our heads. We started to move again inside the forest, changing our direction in order to avoid those shells but they again aimlessly fired on our direction. Their firing angered some two rhinos who mistook us for firing on them and challenged us. Luckily, we all got up the trees and the rhinos disappeared in the darkness. We came down and slowly walked to our *mbuci*. We found the group that had sheep some 300 yards outside the camp. We all entered the camp at midnight and killed some 97 sheep. Since we could not slaughter them all, we split the abdomen and left them.

I was very much surprised when King'ora said that he wanted to see all the goods his *itungati* had collected from that village. I was ashamed to learn that our *itungati* had ransacked every house of our own sympathizers, carrying away much clothing, beddings and utensils. I asked King'ora why he had given such a command and he denied to have the knowledge. The *itungati* reported that they were ordered by Kariuki Thandiku, his lieutenant. I became very much angry with him for spoiling the lecture I had given and for making all those villagers turn away from us by stealing their property while I had sincerely advocated for confidence and cooperation.

'You must learn to act according to what you preach. To those villagers there is no difference now between you and Home Guards,' I shouted angrily. 'What you have done to them is exactly what the Home Guards do and you always complain and despise the Home Guards' activities.

'King'ora, I think it is advisable to return all this property to the owners. What is your opinion?'

'We should return only a letter of apology to the villagers,' said King'ora, 'and let our fighters use the clothing. Our *itungati* are fighting for those people! We have given out our lives for them,' he said in an angered tone. 'We are not fighting for wages but for the love of our people and country. They are still earning and cultivating—they are the state which should feed, clothe and supply everything to our fighters. How would the state [i.e., African Government and people?] expect us to continue the fight while we are hungry, starving of cold and with no supplies of any kind? Mr Njama, if you would visit that village next week, you would find that everything we took had been replaced by a new one. If we asked them to buy all these things for us the most we could get would have been less than a quarter of what we have, being supplied with many excuses. Could a million excuses satisfy our hunger? Don't you know that at this stage our living depends ninety-nine per cent on our personal strength and skill and not on our sympathizers' help? Since many of our sympathizers have lost their lives or have become cripples or are serving sentences in prisons, plus the ever increased supervision and information to the Government side, many are trying to escape us as much as possible though they are not helping the Government.'

'The country now is under the minister of war,' said Kariuki, 'and all its wealth and property is at the disposal of his warriors. During the war, no one should think that he owns anything, even his life.'

Though the two men seemed to out-vote me with their reasonable arguments, I warned them that our victory depended mostly on the mass support; that without the mass we would be easily defeated. To get the mass confidence on us would be our greatest weapon. Something must be done to maintain that confidence.

'Yes,' said King'ora, 'we must all the time let our sympathizers understand that whatever bad we do onto them is neither our intentions nor our will, but is always due to some circumstantial force.'

Though my clothes were badly torn, I did not accept any of the clothes obtained from that raid. We discussed the letter we should send to those villagers and then fell asleep at almost four in the morning.

The following day messengers were sent out inviting the surrounding *mbuci* to come and collect some sheep carcases as they would go bad, since that *mbuci* had only thirty fighters including the ones in the hospital.

Three days later I heard of another *komerera mbuci* and decided to spend a day searching it. I left the camp with four fighters. On our way we were challenged by a rhino, knocking down one *gitungati* by piercing its blunt horn through his thigh and making two other holes below the calves and many other bruises. We took our patient to Jeriko's *mbuci* and stopped our search of the *komerera mbuci*.

Four days later, on 22nd December, I visited our rhino victim with two escorts. I found that his legs were badly swollen and thousands of fly maggots were wriggling all over his body. At a close observation, I found that flies had bred in his septic wounds. When I turned him I discovered that the side he was lying on was rotten from the hip to the knee. It became clear that the patient had not been attended to for at least three days. Jeriko gave an excuse that they did not have any medicine left. I also had left my medicine kit and only carried my satchel. With salt, dissolved in luke warm water, I cleansed the patient's wound and removed him from the maggots into another hut.

On our return, we found that our *mbuci* had been found by the enemy and we did not know where our warriors had gone. We then went to Gathee's *mbuci*, arriving there at seven in the evening only to find that the camp had been deserted. We moved some four hundred yards from the *mbuci* and lit a big fire under a big tree surrounded by a small bush. We had neither food nor blankets nor anything to cover with. We spent a night of sorrow and worry.

The following day we went to Kinaini hospital. We found that the patients had greatly improved. The blind man had learned to walk to the lavatory some sixty yards and return to his own hut without being led. His senses of feeling and hearing had increased. I was very much amazed that the patient could describe the last thing he saw, and the hospital he was living in, though he had never seen it.

Soon after our arrival in the hospital, two *itungati* arrived from King'ora's *mbuci* to inform the patients' attendant that their camp had been raided by the foe. They suspected that the meat store might have been seen by the enemy and probably poisoned. They said that two scouts had been sent to make certain what things were destroyed by the enemy and which ones were not seen. They said that the enemy had surprisingly opened fire right inside the camp. One of the two *itungati* that were in the camp was still missing and the other had six bullet holes in his clothes but none hurt him. They told us where they had encamped. At midday we left for the new camp, arriving there in the evening. I found that my medicine kit was carried by the missing *gitungati*.

The following day I went to Warbararia's *mbuci*. After spending a night in his camp, he accompanied me with a dozen *itungati* and on the evening of 25th December we met Kimathi at Abdullah's *mbuci.* We spent that night telling each other what had happened since we parted.

The next day we visited the buildings where the annual ceremony was to be performed. A big meeting hall in the church fashion and tentatively called the Kenya Young Stars Association Memorial Hall was built 100 feet by 20 feet with three long rows of benches estimated to accommodate 500 people. Leaders' and *itungati* huts were still under construction.

On December 29th the Nyeri leaders started to arrive. In the late afternoon of the 31st two leaders from Gikuyu Iregi Army and nearly all the leaders of Mburu Ngebo Army had arrived. The only recognized absentee from the latter Army was Ndungu Giceru. The Mburu Ngebo Army leaders reported that Mathenge was in the Rift Valley and had given an excuse for his absence as not being invited. Though his letter of invitation had been written a long time ago, none of us knew whereabout his camp might be and so the letter was never dispatched. Leaders from IDA 2 and IDA 4 were absent. Wacira Gathuku and Gitonga Gicingu were the only leaders who represented IDA 3. All the leaders of IDA 1 and their *itungati* were present.

With my badly torn clothes, I looked very ugly amongst the leaders who were all well dressed. Kimathi noted that and nick-named me Huni Macaga, 'Raggy Johnny.' I told him that I had brought nine pairs of clothes with me to the forest of which I gave eight to some other *itungati* who dressed like me at the moment. Kimathi gave me his khaki long trousers and a woolen dark brown shirt. He also wrote a letter ordering clothes for me from his sub-location.

Kimathi and four other colleagues all dressed in Kikuyu elders' sheep cloaks. Each tied a Kikuyu sword around his waist, was bare-footed, [with] castor-oil smeared all over his body. They carried with them all varieties of the Kikuyu cereals, edible roots, bananas and sugar canes, Kikuyu slaughter knives, a gourd (*gitete*) full of honey and another one full of milk, half-gourds and pots. Kimathi, drag-ging a spotless all-black ram, departed from us heading to a big fig tree some two hundred yards from the camp under which they slew the ram and made fire by means of friction.

When we were called, about 800 fighters approached the cere-mony. Under the fig tree was a newly lit fire, burning slowly under a pile of wood. The five persons stood in a line by the fire facing

Mt. Kenya with Kimathi in their center. With the other leaders in the front row, we stood behind them. On their left side I could see all the apparatus that were used in the ceremony well lain on the ground. Kimathi, holding a small gourd in his right hand, began the prayer :

> Our forefathers' God, we beseech you to approach us and to hear our prayers. (We all together said 'Thaai,—'Peace be with us,' at every Kimathi's pause, with our hands raised high over our heads holding a little soil.)
>
> We are the sons and daughters and heirs of Gikuyu and Mumbi whom you created; your own creation whom you gave this green fertile land, full of mountains, valleys and many permanent flowing streams.
>
> Our forefathers for generations have enjoyed the products of this beautiful land of ours : meat, blood, milk, honey, cereals, roots and fruits.
>
> You taught our forefathers how to pray you and how to use the seven foodstuffs to your sacrifice.
>
> If we have offeneded you, Our Heavenly Father, by abandoning our prayers and sacrifices as you have taught our forefathers, we greatly repent and regret to have been ignorantly misled by the strangers; we humbly beg your mercy and forgiveness.
>
> In the whole fashion of our forefathers we approach your sacred place of sacrifice (moving forward, nearer the fire) offering you all that we have, as you did unto our forefathers. Oh God, respond our prayers !
>
> This is the ram's fat. (Pouring most of it on the fire from the gourd in his hand and the rest on the ground for the ancestral spirits. He passed the empty gourd on to the man on the right who put it on the ground while the man on the left picked another gourd and handed it to him.) Bless all the fat for us.
>
> This is bees' honey from both the hives and the wild hollow trees; bless all the honey for us. (He repeated the former procedure until the seven foodstuffs were finished.)
>
> Our Heavenly Father, we beseech you to accept our roasted sacrifice [i.e., sacrificial offerings]; we know no other God but you, Almighty Father; we have never worshipped any idols either of your own creation or men's handicraft in our forefathers' times.

We believe, Oh God, that the sweet smell of our offerings rising up with great smoke above this fig tree, which produces milk and which you showed our forefathers to be your chosen tree for sacrifice, will reach your Heavenly Home and your throne; we beseech you, our God, to hear our prayers.

Now, Almighty God, turn your face into our country and see that the white strangers you brought into our country have turned out to be our enemies; they have taken most of the best fertile lands and have enslaved us to work on the lands.

Our demands for our lands and freedom have been badly reprimanded; the white strangers have taken up strong arms through which they have poured pools of blood all over our country. Oh Merciful Father, hear the cries of widows, orphans, old aged parents who have lost their sons and daughters, and the perishing lives and the innocent blood.

Father, we do not accuse the white strangers alone for pouring the blood; we too, our hands are full of blood. Oh Merciful God, cleanse us and forgive us all our sins.

Our Heavenly Father, we have no arms and we have no helpers; we believe that your mighty right hand will deliver us from our enemies; lead us, keep us, guard us against the enemy day and night; let our enemies destroy themselves with their own arms.

Oh God, some of our relatives have turned against us through their ignorance; forgive them and let them understand our aims; convert them into our faith.

We pray for all our warriors who have died in this struggle of freedom; that their names may forever remain as heroes and that their spirits would abide with your glory forever.

Oh God, we pray for all our sympathizers who are starving under the oppression of the white strangers, either in the villages, towns, prisons or detention camps; save their lives so that your name would be praised by the Kenya people and the world.

We pray for all our leaders who are in prisons, detention camps, and in all the forests, that they may be guided by you as you did with Moses and many Israel leaders who delivered their people out of Egypt; give our leaders power and wisdom so as to lead us well. We place all our leaders under your protection.

We particularly beseech you for Jomo Kenyatta, our leader;

guard and guide him, glorify him with wisdom and power so that he may be able to lead the Kenya people.

We finally pray for our aims to be achieved; grant us our freedom quickly so that under your leadership we will come out of this forest victoriously; drive our enemies out of our country and let the faithful ones be our friends.

We thank you, Oh God, for keeping us alive throughout this ending year, in spite of all the dangers that have surrounded us; we thank you for our food, clothing and shelter. May the New Year break up with good news and our victory. Father, keep us alive so that next year we shall be able to praise your name again. *Thaai!*

Then Kimathie began the traditional anthem in a loud voice which we all joined :

Kimathi : *Huuuuu! Huuuu thaai!* ('Peace be with us !')
The fighters' chorus : *Huuuuu! Huuuu thaai!*
Kimathi : *Wiyathi thai!* ('Freedom and peace !')
Itungati: Huuuu thai!
Kimathi : *Tiri thai!* ('Soil and peace !')
Itungati: Huuuu thai!
Kimathi : *Andu thai!* ('People and peace !')
Itungati: Huuuu thai!
Kimathi : *Ciana thai!* ('Children and peace !')
Itungati: Huuuu thai!
Kimathi : *Mahiu thai!* ('Livestock and peace !')
Itungati: Huuuu thai!
Kimathi : *Kimera thai!* ('Harvest and peace !')
Itungati: Huuuu thai!
Kimathi : *Mbura thai!* ('Rain and peace !')
Itungati: Huuuu thai!
Kimathi : *Wiyathi thai!* ('Freedom and peace !')
Itungati: Huuuu thai!
Kimathi : *Thayu thai!* ('Peace, peace !')
Itungati: Huuuu thai!
Kimathi : *Huuuuu! Huuuu thaai!*
Itungati: Huuuuu! Huuu thaai!
Everyone (three times) : *Thaai, thathaiya Ngai thai!* ('Oh God, hear our prayers for peace !')

With that we ended our prayers and holding each others hands, we slowly walked in the darkness back into the camp. It was already eight o'clock when our cooks started preparing our dinner.

After dinner we all went into the big meeting hall at ten o'clock. The hall was illuminated by burning fires both inside and outside. We spent most of the time singing songs which had been invented to record our successes in battles, praising leaders, some encouraging songs, songs for warning the traitors, etc.

Kimathi delivered a speech to encourage our fighters. He referred to the prayers saying that God would grant our request according to [the sincerity of] our beliefs. He would hear only the faithful ones and not those who had doubts in their prayers. He stressed that we should be faithful to our God and take much care that we not violate our vows.

Kimathi introduced the Kenya Young Stars Association and asked the fighters whether they accepted the idea. There was a great applause of the fighters' approval of the association, and they started Kimathi's song : 'When our Kimathi climbed the mountain alone....' They were all glad to be members of the new association. The hall became a fashion to [i.e., model for] many other Memorial Halls.

I gave an account of our successful events, clarified all our armies and gave details of divisions in the Ituma Ndemi Army, and told them the different kinds of records that were kept for them. I told them that every individual's activity was recorded and that those records would form a book of history which would be read by our future generations. 'What you do,' I said, 'good or bad, is what they shall read of you.'

A few other leaders gave speeches after being introduced to the new *itungati*. At a quarter to midnight we started prayers in which two *itungati*, two leaders and two girls prayed and Kimathi ended and dedicated the prayers. The prayers were composed of thanksgivings, protection, forgiveness and God's guidance for the New Year. We finished our prayers at twenty after midnight and, being in a New Year, exchanged greetings and continued our songs to half past one when we went to sleep.

The following day, 1st January 1954, our fighters dispersed. Kimathi expressed his desire to visit the Mburu Ngebo Army and promised the leaders that he would visit them before the end of the month. Gen. Kimbo was left so as to have a chance of communicating with his people in the reserve. We then agreed that he would lead us to his camp as soon as he was ready to return.

Kimathi, Kimbo, Kahiu-Itina and myself, and many other leaders, left for Chania and Nyaga's *mbuci*. After our arrival, Kahiu-Itina and his leaders left and crossed the river Chania. Two days later Nyaga's *itungati* raided cattle in the reserve at about one in the afternoon. The armed Home Guards who were herding the cattle had driven them to a stream near the forest so that they could drink water. When our fighters opened fire, the Home Guards ran away shouting for help leaving the cattle behind.

Our warriors drove many cattle into the forest. They crossed the stream and as they were climbing the far slope they were spotted by KAR and Kenya Police who had come in Land Rovers to help the Home Guards. They opened fire on our fighters who were more than a mile away. The enemies' fire dispersed both cattle and our fighters as they were in an open area. At four o'clock some *itungati* arrived in the *mbuci* saying that they had some seventy-two head of cattle in the forest and that they had lost as many as three times that while fighting with the enemy who were still following them. Kimathi said that they should not bring the cattle in the *mbuci* but they should climb up the mountain until they came to the Mihuro area composed of all dry bamboo and make a new camp there. Some twenty armed *itungati* were sent out to help in the fight while the others drove the cattle.

One *gitungati*, nicknamed Mbaka, had been injured by an enemy's bullet from about a mile's distance. The bullet had struck his sword's sheath, making a big hole through his sword which he had hoisted on his shoulder, passing through the front bottom part of his stomach. As I was about to clean his wounds, Kimathi shouted that everyone was to take his belongings and quit the camp right then and head for Mihuro some seven miles away.

We quickly collected our luggage and left. We had only gone about a mile from the camp by the time the enemy opened fire in the camp we had left. We arrived at Mihuro at midnight and found some *itungati* killing the cattle. A few tents were pegged out for the leaders and the darkness prevented the *itungati* from building their own huts. Though we had fresh meat to eat, we spent a sorrowful night, for of some forty-eight fighters who had been left behind the cattle to fight the enemy, none of them had arrived to report the fight.

The following day, all our fighters arrived safely at midday and reported that they thrice exchanged fires with the enemy until it was dark. They told us that they had heard the enemy firing on the camp; they therefore did not know whereabout the [new] camp would be. They followed the cattle track but the darkness impeded their journey. During the night the elephants, buffaloes and rhinos followed the cattle track making it difficult for them to follow it.

In the afternoon, Mbaka, my patient, and I moved to Mihuro hospital with a bodyguard and two carriers. There were four other patients with four guards, one of whom treated the patients. One of the patients was suffering from pneumonia while two others had become very weak through starvation in the Moorlands where they had relied on trapping animals and collecting honey for some months. One of them, Ngara Mahihia, told me that during the month which they didn't catch any animal they had lived on water in which they boiled old bones and hide of a buffalo. The hard pieces of buffalo hide had become undigestable in their stomachs and had resulted to the death of two of their comrades.

For the next three weeks I spent my time treating my patients and recording. It was in this area that we built a book store for all the Nyandarua records. Together with the medicine I gave my patients, I urged them to eat much meat which was required for repairing their wounds. I was very much pleased when I got Mbaka healed within a fortnight. By the end of the month all the patients were completely cured. We moved from Mihuro to join Nyaga's *mbuci* at Thaina (Zaina) River, where we met Kimathi and Kimbo and many other leaders. Kimathi was very glad for the recovery of the patients. I told him that I had not finished the recording work and that I would continue it after our return from the Mburu Ngebo Army.

CHAPTER XVII

THE KENYA PARLIAMENT

IN EARLY February 1954, the unwieldy and largely ineffectual Kenya Defense Council was superseded by the newly formed Kenya Parliament. Comprised of Dedan Kimathi and twelve elected members, the Kenya Parliament hoped to establish itself as the legitimate interim African Government of Kenya. Its aims were (1) to establish its authority and legitimacy among Aberdare guerrilla groups, (2) to initiate a new military offensive, aimed at enemy property, (3) to separate itself from the military hierarchy and dissociate its members from particular sections or territorial groupings, (4) to demonstrate its national character and gain added military support by extending the revolt to other tribes and regions, and (5) to reorganize and assume authority over the civilian population in the reserves.

In contrast to the Kenya Defense Council, the limited membership of the Kenya Parliament enabled it to meet more easily and, in general, to react more effectively in the face of new situations and crises. On the other hand, the Kenya Parliament began with a somewhat narrower base of support as its members were drawn disproportionately from the various armies and forest zones. Thus, including Kimathi, the Ituma Ndemi Army placed seven men in the Parliament, Mburu Ngebo Army four, and the Gikuyu Iregi and Kenya Levellation Armies one each. More importantly, perhaps, a narrower breakdown reveals that six of the thirteen members were from North Tetu Division of Nyeri District, while three of the Rift Valley (Mburu Ngebo Army) members were originally from this area. Again, of the six officers elected, five were from the Ituma Ndemi Army and only one from the Mburu Ngebo Army. North Tetu held four positions, Othaya Division of Nyeri one, and the Rift Valley one.

In addition to the over-representation of Nyeri District, and North Tetu Division in particular, on the Kenya Parliament, it is significant that the majority of those elected had achieved some formal education and were, by forest standards, classed among the educated as distinct from the illiterate. As we shall see, both these features of Kenya Parliament composition were to become focal points of future conflict.

Events occurring outside Nyandarua during the first half of 1954 significantly affected Aberdare guerrilla forces and their relations with other rebel groups and supporters in the reserve, Nairobi and Mt. Kenya. The first of these began on 15 January with the capture of Gen. China (Waruhiu Itote), acknowledged leader of Mt. Kenya's 5,000-man guerrilla army. China's confession and ultimate collaboration with Special Branch officers led to an abortive three-month Government operation named Wedgewood, designed to bring about the surrender of forest forces through negotiation. Government military operations in the forest were temporarily suspended and contact was established with guerrilla leaders through leaflets and letters. The surrender talks, however, never extended beyond the Mt. Kenya leadership and ended (on a rather humiliating note for the Government) as all the guerrilla leaders save China managed to 'escape' Government custody and return to the forest.

As will become clear from Karari's account, the refusal of Kimathi and the other Kenya Parliament leaders to enter the proposed negotiations with Government until certain rather rigorous conditions were met was a reflection of both guerrilla strength and assumed Government weakness. Government's offer to negotiate was, in itself, interpreted among Aberdare leaders as a sign of weakness, and the prevailing circumstances did, indeed, seem to justify the belief that guerrilla forces were at least holding their own. It was certainly true that after almost a year and a half of fighting, and with vastly superior weapons, the Government seemed no closer to defeating the insurgent forces. In fact, guerrilla strength seemed to be growing, with Kenya Levellation Army units more active than ever in the reserve, a Nairobi Land and Freedom Army formed and very active, supplies flowing from the city into the forests, and Government apparently unable to launch a winning offensive against the guerrilla armies of Nyandarua and Mt. Kenya.

Government's position was thus assessed in the January 1954 Report of the Colonial Office Parliamentary Delegation to Kenya as follows:

It is our view based upon all the evidence available to us, both from official and responsible unofficial sources, that the influence of Mau Mau in the Kikuyu area, except in certain localities, has not declined; it has, on the contrary, increased; in this respect the situation has deteriorated and the danger of infection outside the Kikuyu area is now greater, not less, than it was at the beginning of the State of Emergency ... In Nairobi, the situation is both grave and acute. Mau Mau orders are carried out in the heart of the city, Mau Mau 'courts' sit in judgement and their 'sentences' are carried out by gangsters. There is evidence that the revenues collected by gangsters, which may be considerable, are used for the purposes of bribery as well as for purchasing Mau Mau supplies ... There is [also] a passive resistance movement amongst Africans, an example of which is a 'bus boycott' under which Africans have for several months boycotted European-owned buses ...

In addition to the visit of this Parliamentary Delegation, rumors were spreading that the Colonial Secretary, Mr. Oliver Lyttelton, was going to introduce a new constitution and form a multi-racial Government. The Aberdare leaders were thus optimistic and, while pressing their demands for land and freedom, were proud of the fact, as they saw it, that they had achieved more in a year and a few months of fighting than African politicians had managed in over thirty years of talk.

With the breakdown of the surrender talks, and putting the information obtained from Gen. China to good use, Government launched a two-pronged campaign to isolate the forest guerrillas from their sources of food and supplies in the reserve and Nairobi. Operation Anvil, commencing on 24 April 1954, was a major Government operation involving some 25,000 soldiers and police. It was intended to crush resistance in Nairobi and halt the flow of recruits and supplies into the forest. The entire African population of Nairobi, some 100,000 persons, were rounded up and driven into a huge field where 70,000 Kikuyu, Embu and Meru were sorted out and screened. Those suspected or identified as members of the Movement were segregated and sent by train to several specially constructed detention or concentration camps. Their families and dependent relatives were picked up and returned to the Kikuyu reserve. This operation was phased out over several weeks and the total number of those detained—mainly young men of warrior age between 16 and 35—reached almost 50,000.

There is little question that Operation Anvil disrupted organized resistance in Nairobi and significantly curtailed the flow of arms, ammunition, medical supplies, clothing and money into the Aberdares. It was followed by smaller-scale sweeps in Kiambu, Thika and Fort Hall and by a massive effort to cut the forest guerrillas off from the reserve.

A Government strategem called the "villagization program", initiated early in the year, was rapidly accelerated after Anvil. Used effectively by the British in Malaya, this program was an attempt to break down the traditional dispersed-homestead settlement pattern of the Kikuyu and place the Kikuyu peasantry in easily guarded, prison-like villages, located handily near the roads and grouped around Home Guard and police posts. Congested in these villages and unable to tend their fields due to dusk-to-dawn curfews and "communal" labor, the Kikuyu peasantry was hit ever harder by hunger and disease. By the end of 1954 over a million Kikuyu had been resettled in these village camps, which were constructed with Kikuyu labor and materials under the supervision of Tribal Police.

A similar program was carried out on the European farms and plantations of the Rift Valley, with field and house labor contained within fortified villages.

In addition to the "villagization program", a fairly wide trench, fenced with barbed wire, planted with mines and bordered by numerous military and police posts, was dug by forced peasant labor teams along fifty miles of the forest fringe which separated the Aberdares and Mt. Kenya from the Kikuyu reserve. Government, seemingly unable to defeat the guerrilla forces within the forest, was trying to starve them into the open, into security force ambushes or surrender. Though this Government strategy was not immediately successful, Aberdare groups were faced with an ever increasing problem of supplies and their relations with rural and urban supporters became more difficult and costly to sustain.

★   ★   ★

On 2nd February we set off to Mburu Ngebo Army led by Kimbo, together with all the leaders of IDA 1 and some of the *itungati*. Gen. Mbuthia of the Gikuyu Iregi Army and a company of Kenya Levellation under Gen. Rui accompanied our convoy of 210 warriors. It took us one and a half days walk to get to Kimbo's *mbuci* at Karathi's Mother area.

We were welcomed by Gen. Kirihinya (Ngunjiri) and Col. Kahii ka Arume (Wambugu Mwema). Kimathi had visited that area about a year earlier during which time our fighters were mobilized. Kimathi was very happy to meet those *itungati*, who cheerfully greeted him. Here we were joined by Aram Ndirangu from Kipipiri Hill bringing the data he had collected.

On the third day we held a general meeting. We met in a grassy open area under some big trees. About forty leaders and 750 *itungati*, representing mainly IDA and Mburu Ngebo Army (MNA), with four from Kenya Levellation Army and one from Gikuyu Iregi Army, were present. Kimathi introduced the meeting with a short speech and report on the Kenya Defense Council work and Kenya Young Stars Association.

When I stood up to speak, I first criticised the Ituma Ndemi Trinity Council under the chairmanship of Stanley Mathenge for its failure to hold meetings in order to discuss our *itungati* difficulties, to form plans, rules and regulations, and make arrangements on the supplies of arms and ammunition, money, clothes, food, etc., from Nairobi or district centers. I pointed out that the Council had never met since it was elected in May 1953, though its Secretary, Kimathi, had been very active in most of the forest affairs. I remarked that the Council had limited its duties to their own *itungati* and that it had completely ignored the management over the reserve people. Many leaders had taken power into their hands, each acting on his own, whereby our leaders presented plans and rules many of which contradict theirs, revealing to the reserve people that we are unorganized and showing our great weakness.

'The Ituma Ndemi Trinity Council,' I continued, 'was a small unit for Nyeri District only and could not organize the other districts. The Kenya Defense Council has met only once, in September at Murang'a, since its formation last August. Though this is a Council that could organize the whole of Kenya, it was wrong for us to admit that every leader was a member of the Council. The leaders do not feel as if they were elected to be members of Kenya

Defense Council—and in fact they were not elected. We only stated that all the leaders are members of the Council and since that happened a day before my arrival at the meeting, I did not criticise it then. The office bearers do not have a list of the leaders so that they can tell who were absent; even if the names of the leaders were available it would be difficult to get them together to a meeting. Each leader seems so busy with his own *itungati* that he can hardly spare any thoughts for *all our itungati*, or open his eyes in the reserves beyond where he is known and where his *itungati* operated.

'Broadly speaking, the Kenya Defense Council was mostly concerned on the military point of view. How could we be successful without the masses help? Who were to supply us with our needs? Since all the leaders in the reserve were either arrested or fled into the forest, there is no hope for the masses to organize themselves unless we organize them. We could not organize the reserves well unless we delegate that responsibility unto the hands of a few wise people who would understand that it is their duty to plan for the others.

'Our basic thought on forming the Kenya Young Stars Association led us to assume the African Government responsibility in our hands, but we lack a central organization. It surprises me when I realize that many of our leaders at present are working on either the locational or divisional level as the highest [level of] organization. The thing we lack is a Kenya central organization which should be the Government or the Parliament. I think it is high time we elected our Kenya Parliament members and let them run the country until the big stars, the moon and the sun will take over the rule. They shall praise us for not letting down our country during their absence and the little we would have done would be of great importance in Kenya's history, which will tell the Kenya Parliament was formed and maintained by uneducated warriors in Nyandarua for so many years. As the Kenya Parliament shall govern Kenya, the founders names shall live as long as the Kenya African Government shall live.'

My ideas gained support from many leaders and *itungati* and we then resolved that we must elect members of a Kenya Parliament. The first issue was the number of the members. After a heated exchange of opinions it was agreed that since Jesus Christ had only twelve disciples, whose preaching has reached all over the world, we should then elect twelve excluding Kimathi, the President of the Parliament. I supported the lower number because I felt the more members we had the less effective the Parliament would be.

The next issue was the qualifications of a member. I took the lead strongly and opposed election based on geographical regions, mere popularity, relative [i.e., kin] or friendship feelings—for these were our greatest weaknesses.

'I would like us to elect the best twelve persons we have in this forest so that we could have the best Government possible. Apart from education, we should look for the person's wisdom and ability, his courage and incorruptible character. It does not matter whether the twelve members were all real brothers or from the same village or district; what we would count on would be that they are the best we have, who will make the best we all want. We are not fighting for regions or clans or tribes. We are fighting for the whole Kenya, including our enemies as Home Guards and all the Africans employed in the enemy forces of KTP (Kenya Tribal Police), KAR and the police forces, for they will enjoy the freedom which will be so abundant that even if we imprisoned them, they would still enjoy the freedom we are fighting for in the prisons; for we have a song demanding freedom in prisons which you all always sing. One of its verses says : "Parents don't be frightened. A baby born dies. Tell the community we must persevere. Until color-bar is banned in the prisons."

'Be sure that freedom would be so abundant that there would be no competition of some people trying to get more freedom than the others. Just as the rain pours to the rich as to the poor, to the good ones as to the bad ones, to the lazy person's garden as to the industrious one's, the same will happen to the freedom. Some of us may seek privileges, but by the time we achieve our freedom you will have learned to share a grain of maize or a bean amongst several people, feeling selfishness as an evil; and the hate of oppressing others would be so developed in you that you will not like to become another class of "Black" Europeans ready to oppress and exploit others just like the system we are fighting against. And...'

'I have to speak,' shouted Major Windo, jumping in the center of the meeting. 'If oration or leadership were a dance, I would dance naked in order to attract you. I know more about dance and I can compete at it; but I cannot compete in firing a rifle, for though we can all fire exactly the same distance only very few of us would hit the target. I mean that everyone of us can stand here and speak in a loud voice demanding supporters for this election, but very few of us have the qualities that Mr Njama mentioned. We now want quality but we have much quantity. Any person who would cast his vote because of relation, friendship, neighborhood, is an enemy to our progress. It is better to vote for an absent person whom you have confidence in than....'

'No!' shouted Kahiu-Itina. '*Muti nduguagira mundu utari ho!* ("A tree never falls on one not standing under it!") If a bomb falls on this meeting it would kill us all but none of the people who are not in the meeting. It is wrong for us to elect a person without his personal approval for he might be unwilling or unprepared to do the work we elected him for. We better go on electing the people who are here on the understanding that the good they do will be for us all. If there happens to be better people absent from this meeting, I would say that it is not their day to be elected and that they would be better criticisers or advisers until their day of election comes.'

'Today,' said Ndiritu Thuita, 'the leaders are speaking as if this were their last opportunity, as though they are dedicating their final wills. One thing I am certain of is that I am a Kenya citizen. I will share all its goodness as well as its badness. So will every Kenya citizen. Since we all admire goodness and have the same ideas and objects, I am certain that we could achieve that more easily and quickly in the hands of a few of our best people than when we would call the whole Kenya to a general meeting on which unagreeable views, opinions and feelings would arise and increase. We need not waste more time on comments. I would like opposers to speak.'

As there were no opposers, Kimbo stood up and made more comments and, as an illiterate person, challenged the educated persons for abandoning the revolution and advocated that education not be regarded as a qualification in the election. He was opposed by 'Dr' King'ori who spoke well on behalf of the educated people. He said that without education, without making full use of our educated people, we were heading nowhere.

As a teacher I supported 'Dr' King'ori and stressed the import-ance of education, of both academic and cultural knowledge. I was certain that many of our fighters thought of the future in [i.e., as

a projection of] the past. In fact, the past was vivid while knowledge of the future was obstructed by the hatred of the white man
and his culture, and partly by our political leaders' failure in
informing the masses on the future of the country. I cut across this,
telling them that we would select all the good our forefathers
had and throw away any habit, custom or manner, or any traditions that would not suit us; and the same thing to the European
culture. We would accept all that we thought was good for us and
leave out what we thought did not fit us. We would then be able to
form a new Kenya on our own patterns like neither our forefathers' nor the Europeans'.

'Mind you,' I continued, 'that by modern progress we must learn
on the European side, for it contributes most of our modern needs
ranging from education to machinery, techniques and standard of
life. Though we feel that abandoning our customs and tradition is
a sign of defeat and going back to many of them already forgotten
is a traditional pride, it would be impractical to go back into our
forefathers' days as it would be impractical for anyone to go back
into his or her mother's womb. Every generation makes its own
customs, invents its songs and dances, makes its rules and regulations, which all die a natural death with that generation. Though
a few remarks of the outgoing generation may remain, nothing
remains forever, as man always continues to invent new and better
things than he has, which causes him to use the latter and abandon
the former.'

'You have now lost your path, Mr Njama,' said Kimathi. 'Let
me bring you back to the path. The issue is the Kenya Parliament
elections, which I wholeheartedly support. Since we have already
agreed on many points, I think the remaining question is how to
elect the twelve members. Should we name two dozen or more
leaders out of which we shall elect the number we want? Or just
name them and ask their supporters to raise hands or ask the supporters to stand behind the person they want so that we can count
how many persons support each candidate. Or if you know any
better method, stand and let us know.'

Shouting that I had a better method, I stood up. 'The best election all over the world is by secret ballots. Firstly, the people who
seek election are given a chance to speak to the people about their
ideas and leadership, and promises the electorate what they stand
for and what they would do for them. Here, after my speech, I

would like all those who want to be elected to stand up and see whether we could get a chance for each to speak. Secondly, comes the election itself. Every elector writes or marks the name of the candidate he wants to elect and then puts his card in a ballot box. Each candidate's votes are counted and then it is known how many persons have supported every candidate. When we raise hands, your friend sees that you did not raise your hand for him or you did not stand behind him. Some people are not sure who to elect and look for the person who seems to have more people and they would join there. Again. . . .'

'What about those who do not know how to write?' enquired one *gitungati*.

'In many countries they use pictures such as a cow, tree, car, airplane, etc., to represent the name of a particular person and after making a mark on the symbol one wants to elect, he then drops it in the ballot box. Here, today, I would suggest that we give each person a piece of paper and let him secretly write the name of the person he or she wishes to elect. One person only, and then drop it in one of these hats. For those who do not know how to write, they should secretly consult those who are able to write and ask them to write the name of the person [each] wants to elect.'

'Any further comments would mean waste of time,' said Gen. Muraya Mbuthia. 'Start now distributing paper. We have heard enough that will lead us in the best election I have ever heard of. It is already 3:30 p.m. and night would fall before we finish this election if more people are allowed to speak.'

'All those who want to be elected, stand up in the center,' said Kimathi. Thirty-three leaders, including myself, stood in the center of the meeting. Kimathi introduced all thirty-three, just mentioning their names, army affiliation, ranks, past activities, personal records, education, etc., while clerks were distributing pieces of paper to our warriors.

'Everyone here,' said Kimathi, 'including those who are seeking election, must write just ONE person's name; the best person you know. Make sure that you do not tell anybody whom you elect. When you finish writing, fold your paper and put it in one of the hats that are moved around by the collectors.'

After collection, a big sheet was laid in the center of the meeting. All votes were dropped on the sheet. Some thirty-three *itungati*, each holding a hat, were called in the center of the circle. Each hat had a piece of paper on which a leader's name was written. A group of clerks started sorting out the votes and putting each leader's votes in the hat bearing his name. After sorting, we started counting the votes. [Here are the results.]

Dedan Kimathi . . . President [By unspoken consensus.]

(1) Brig. Gen. Kahiu-Itina (Muruthi Mathi), IDA 1; most votes . . Vice Pres.

(2) Gen. Kimbo Mutuku (Theuri Mukua), MNA; 2nd . . . Treasurer

(3) Karari Njama, IDA 3/3; 3rd . . . Chief Secretary

(4) Gen. Ndiritu Thuita, IDA 1/1; 4th . . . Deputy Secretary

(5) Gen. Abdullah (Gitonga Muthui), IDA 1/3; 5th . . . Vice Treasurer

(6) Major Vindo (Ndururi Gitika), IDA 1/1; 6th

(7) Gen. Kirihinya (Ngunjiri), MNA; 7th

(8) Col. Kahii ka Arume (Wambugu Mwema), MNA; 8th

(9) Brig. Gathitu Waithaka, IDA; 9th

(10) Gen. Muraya Mbuthia, GIA; 10th

(11) Major Omera (Ndiritu Wang'ombe), MNA; 11th

(12) Gen. Rui, KLA; 12th

When all was over, we stood facing Mt. Kenya and prayed God, asking him to bless, guard and guide our Kenya Parliament members and grant them power and wisdom. It was already six when we finished prayers and we all moved towards the camp.

After dinner we amused ourselves with singing and dancing and military drill. We all felt happy and contented with the election. The following day all the elected members met and elected six office bearers, [indicated above.] We then discussed how we could reorganize the reserve in order to increase the flow of supplies. We decided to write letters to some known members in the reserves and ask them to find out what had happened to fees and dues at both the location and division levels. We wrote letters of appointment to some members who would reorganize the reserve as Divisional Officers. We told them that ammunition, medicine, clothing and stationery should be sent to the Kenya Parliament which would distribute them to our fighters. We suggested that if the old funds were not available then every man should contribute ten shillings and every woman, including girls, five shillings. We agreed that food supply would remain in the local leaders' hands and unchanged.

On behalf of our fighters, we concentrated our talks on 'attacking plans.' We agreed to instruct all our fighters to start destroying any enemy property by all means; to use fire to burn all the grass, corn fields, wheat and barley, stores and houses; to steal and spray the grass with cattle dip so that cattle and sheep will die of that poison; to use *pangas* or swords to cut down coffee, tea, fruits and any enemy property come across. We agreed that members of Kenya Parliament should not participate in any kind of raid and that it was both unwise and unnecessary [for them] to leave the forest for any purpose. All other leaders should satisfy all the personal needs of a Kenya Parliament member in any camp he might be.

We agreed that the first session of the Parliament should discuss rules and regulations and send out missions to all the bordering tribes and recruit them in order to increase our strength and refute the settlers' allegation that only the Kikuyu, Embu and Meru are struggling for freedom and that the other tribes didn't know what was freedom and they didn't like it and weren't in need of lands.

We resolved that the President and the Chief Secretary would be responsible for calling all the sessions, i.e., fixing the date and place of meeting, and dispatching information letters to the members which should include the agenda to be discussed. We also agreed that every member should send his proposed agenda to the Secretary at least a fortnight before the meeting date. The meeting then dispersed and all of us from Chania and Ruthaithi returned to our former *mbuci*.

On our arrival in the Ruthaithi area I departed from Kimathi on the account that I had to collect data from the Levellation Army company under Gen. Rui before they left the forest. On arriving at Rui's temporary camp, situated by a small stream close to the reserve, I was greatly shocked to learn that Gen. China was injured and captured on 15th January, in a strong battle in the reserve, while operating with the Kenya Levellation Army. Gen. China was the only man who had been sent by Kimathi in May 1953 from Nyandarua, as Capt. Waruhiu Itote, and ordered to organize all the Mt. Kenya fighters and take back the report to Kimathi.

During our discussion about China's fate, a *gitungati* interrupted our talk and said that a girl named Wanjiru from Aguthi Location was accused of being a police informer. I called a few leaders to assist me in hearing the girl's case. I ordered other girls to search her for any stamp, poison or document from the police. They didn't find anything in her possession that could make witness that she was an informer. The witnesses said she had lived in a police post for a month and all her companions were informers who had spied several of our Kenya Levellation fighters, who were all killed inside a hut at midday. Three of the captured girls had given all the names of other informers, including Wanjiru's, and had revealed that they all had taken a 'Kikuyu Musical Oath' administered by the police, binding the initiate to become loyal to the Government and an informer of the revolution. The witnesses concluded the police used poultry blood stored in bottles to administer the counter-Mau Mau oath but failed to explain how the oath was taken.

When I cross-examined the witness as to what they had done with the three girls, he replied that they had killed them. When I asked Wanjiru whether the witnesses were speaking the truth, she replied, 'Partly.'

'Then tell us the truth,' I said.

'I have stayed for a month at Kia Ruia Police Post in Aguthi Location,' said the girl. 'We were forced to take the Musical Oath which is generally administered while the others were dancing in the next room and we were forced to sleep with them. Our reluctance warranted our death. Some of us surrendered and became true informers, as the witnesses said, but a few of us only ensured our lives. I have been in Gen. Rui's company for one and a half months. In many occasions I have been asked to collect food, spy the enemy or be a sentry for a whole day. I have witnesses here who would say that they have seen me talking to police or Home Guards several times, yet instead of helping the enemy I have helped this company as much as I could. I would like my leader, Gen. Rui, to tell you of my activities.'

'Gentlemen,' said Rui, 'the girl has spoken what I think contains much truth, but I have no confidence in her for having stayed with me for almost two months without reporting that she had taken such an oath. Though it is difficult for me to comment about her, I would say that she is standing on the fence.'

'I will die with her!' shouted a *gitungati* armed with a Sten gun standing 30 yards away. 'And many of you will share her grave.'

'Get away!' ordered Rui.

'I mean what I say,' replied the *gitungati*. 'She is my lover.'

'We also love her,' said Rui, 'and have no enmity. Go away and await her in the evening.'

'Keep your word!' said the *gitungati*, turning away and disappearing.

I ordered the girl to be escorted by strong guards and kept away from hearing what we were saying. For a moment we discussed the *gitungati*, forgetting the girl. But before we resolved anything, the *gitungati* returned with other armed *itungati* saying: 'We won't accept that whenever a person is rejected by a girl he will accuse her of being an informer.

'For heaven sake,' I shouted, standing up. 'Have confidence in me, please! I am rightly conducting this case for your own sake without any favor. There is no secret about it. If I find anything significant, I shall ask these leaders, together with all the fighters in this area, to witness it.'

'Thank you very much,' said the *gitungati*. 'Please allow me to become her witness.'

'Yes, you will be allowed,' I said, 'if you stay away until you are called.'

'O.K. I would await for your call,' said the *gitungati*, going away.

Now the leaders felt insulted and distressed. We became sceptical whether the *gitungati* was inflamed as a petty lover or whether he and others might have taken the same oath. We resolved that while slow and strong investigation would take place, all our fighters should be informed of the oath and that each should be aware that Government might send its informers to live with us.

The girl was called and on her arrival was asked to explain the instructions given her by the police.

'We were all told,' said Wanjiru, 'to inform the police or Government forces where the fighters might be hiding and report their number and strength. Secondly, we were to trick a fighter, two or more, into the hands of the Government forces. Thirdly, we were each given five poison tablets by the corporal in charge. He told us that each tablet was sufficient to kill one of the top leaders when put in his food. Each of us vowed to exterminate at least five of the top leaders wherever they may be, in the forest, detention or prison, by using the poison. Some women have been supplied with the same poison after taking that oath so that they will kill their husbands.'

'What else did you swear?' asked Jeriko.

'I swore not to claim for land and freedom anymore and that the White Highland was for the whiteman; that I will never again help Mau Mau.'

'Can you confess all you have told us before all our *itungati*?' I queried.

'Yes,' replied Wanjiru.

'Do you know any fighter in this forest that has taken that Government oath?' I asked.

'No. Those who were converted to become true informers are all in the reserve,' replied Wanjiru.

'Would you show me those informers when we get there?' asked Rui.

'Yes,' replied the girl.

'Give me their names!' I demanded.

She gave me a list of seventeen women and girls and concluded that she did not know any fighter who had taken the oath though she knew police and Home Guards who had taken the oath. Gen. Rui carried the list of the informers so that his company would be able to check them as soon as it returned to the reserve.

We resolved to call all our fighters and get Wanjiru to confess before them. We asked Rui to keep an eye on the girl and her lover. After Wanjiru had confessed to all our fighters, I criticised the *gitungati* of falling into blind love and warned the others that girls had become the bait for trapping our fighters, mostly the Kenya Levellation Army in the reserve, basing my argument on Wanjiru's confession.

The *gitungati* confessed of his ignorant utterances. We cleared Wanjiru, though many of the leaders remained sceptical of her true stand.

The following day, Government airplanes spread in the air thousands of leaflets containing Gen. China's photo, and the airplanes appealed to our fighters through their big loudspeakers to surrender, taking green branches with us. The surrender appeal had become monotonous to our ears; it had started soon after the

Lincoln heavy bombers commenced bombing the forests—saying : 'Today, your food is being brought; it is the gift of bombs. Surrender today, carrying a green branch. Take the road leading to —— with your arms and you will be welcomed by the Devons.'

This imploring appeal by Government for our surrender only proved to us that the Government had been unable to defeat us in the fight and that was the reason why it insisted on entreating us to surrender. We held that if we did not surrender, then the Government would definitely surrender.

A warrior returned with one of the leaflets containing Gen. China's photo. It said that an important leader had been captured and that there was no use of our going on fighting. Rui and I discussed the leaflet, agreeing that it was another Government propaganda trick.

The following day, I left the *mbuci* with Capt. Binihalis and another *gitungati* heading to Binihalis' *mbuci*. The armed *gitungati* led our way through an animal path that was overgrown with scrub. Suddenly, we collided with an elephant which came into sight only five yards from us. The elephant blew its trumpet and we retreated, running at life's speed. We took another path, this time with Binihalis leading us. We kept on talking about the elephant and the difficulties each had when running. Feeling quite safe from the elephant, we talked loudly. Surprisingly, the enemy in front of us opened their Sten guns on us as Binihalis pulled away the shrub that lay between us and the enemy. Instead of retreating to our path as Binihalis did, the *gitungati* and I turned to the right and ran down into a small valley. We paused to listen whether we could hear Binihalis' movement. We didn't hear him, but we heard the enemy laughing and saying that our group must have casualties. We were both safe but were only worried about Binihalis.

We arrived in the camp in the afternoon and found Binihalis lying on the ground on his stomach, his nose touching the ground. His shirt on the back was full of blood. He asked me whether we were safe. I told him that we were safe, removing his bloody shirt. Through observation, a Sten gun bullet had entered his chest from his back making a small hole between the ribs. The bullet had stopped right inside his chest; he was puffing out froth containing blood which [made] me suspect that the lungs were injured.

I cleansed his wound by methylated spirit, dampened a clean cloth with diluted acriflavine and placed it well on the wound and then covered it with a piece of plaster. I moved with the patient into a new hospital which I used as my office while treating the only patient. His outer wound healed within seven days. On the eleventh day of his injury, I discharged the patient at his request and being satisfied that he was completely cured and as healthy as before—though the bullet had become a part of his body; it might form a cyst, I thought, and I remained sceptical of his future health; he might die of that bullet in the future.

Reports from all parts of the reserve continued to pour in congratulating the Kenya Levellation Army, which had become a strong and brave force and engaged in almost daily day battles with the Government forces right in the reserves and towns in most of which our warriors were very successful. The fights, which often took place in the eyes of women and children, increased encouragement to our sympathizers and [brought] great praise onto our side. As the women broke into cheerful songs praising our fighters, they angered the Home Guards who took drastic measures of revenge against them. A competition emerged between the Home Guards, assisted by the Government forces, and our Kenya Levellation Army which ruined our country. Firstly, the fountain of blood flowing from every Central Province ridge drowning thousands of lives to hell; secondly, the fires that consumed thousands of houses and property therein, set ablaze by the Home Guards under the supervision of their KPR officers [and destroying] all the houses surrounding the battle ground. Thirdly, clearing the reserve bushes, an order which regarded the crops in the gardens as bushes and cleared maize, millet, sugar canes, bananas, yams, etc., with the intention to accelerate hunger. Fourthly, strong curfew orders and restricting all movement, stopping all works including the collecting of some edible roots from the gardens or from the markets. The livestock were left uncared for as the Home Guards who were attending them became more engaged in the fight. Though the livestock turned to be the chief source of Home Guard food, thousands of them became weak and died just as their owners.

Some of the Kenya Levellation songs invented to record their battles might be useful to illustrate some of those battles.

(1) Listen and hear this story
     Of the Tumu Tumu Hill!
     So that you may realize that God is with us
     And will never abandon us.

     It was on a Wednesday
     We were in a village down the valley
     The enemy decided to climb
     In order to see Kikuyuland

     When it struck two in the afternoon
     Waruanja was sent down the valley
     Dressed like a woman
     In order to spy

     He brought back a valuable message
     That Kirimukuyu was guarded by security forces
     Down in the valley there were 400 fighters
     Whom the Government intended to surround

     Good fortune came our way
     In the form of a girl
     Named Kanjunio [who returned with Waruanja's message]
     Who saved a thousand lives

     When it struck two
     A thunderous noise was heard from atop the hill
     Bren guns were firing from every direction
     But God helped us and we descended safely

     Gakuru gave his own life
     To save the lives of his friends
     He lit a fire [i.e., threw a grenade]
     And the machine guns ceased their firing

     When we reached the valley
     We found parents in tears
     Coming down the hill
     To witness the death of their sons

The above song was invented by Gen. Kariba's group of the Kenya Levellation Army to commemorate their fight on the Tumu Tumu Hill in the Mathira Division of Nyeri.

(2) Who was in Timau
  When the children of Mumbi attacked
  The airfield at 'Thundani's'?
  The planes were their wonders

  Chorus : Listen and be told a story
     By the boys of the *mbuci*
     Who have seen a great deal
     Wherever they wander or roam

  When Thundani came
  He ran very quickly
  He was with his wife and her friend
  He wanted to surprise us

  We were fully prepared
  To enter Thundani's home
  A home fenced with stone
  Topped with broken bottles

  The Major stood to relieve the fears
  Of Mumbi's children
  He told them, 'Don't worry !'
  For Abdullah is going to lead you

  The Major also said
  'When you go in
  Break the cases and search
  Until you find the fire arms'

  Kenyatta's kingdom was blessed by his father, Gikuyu
  He will bang the tree with his head
  So that the children of Gikuyu will eat
  The fruit that falls to the ground.
  (The last verse is a Kikuyu proverb showing the great love
   of a parent for his children.)

(3)   It was on a Tuesday evening
In a house down the valley
The enemy decided to come up
And see the Kikuyu country

Chorus : Be happy ! Be happy, parents !
            The trouble is over in Kikuyuland

On our arrival in the valley
Our flag was hoisted
When the Government forces saw it
They took cover

Kariba said with his word
'All the whistles be up'
And when this signal was given
The bullets started pouring like water

Kariba said again
We'd better move from
The people's homes
And fight in the banana valley

When advancing very near
Ndungu's fig tree
The enemy was cautioned
By the sound of machine gun fire

When we arrived
At Ndungu's fig tree
Rongu long fired his machine gun
And scared away the Government forces

On 4th February Gen. China was sentenced to death and ten
days later, while I was still in Ruthaithi area, Kimathi received a
typed copy of a letter signed by China asking that he send two
men to represent the Nyandarua fighters in negotiations with
Government about surrender terms. Though I cannot reproduce
the letter exactly, the following is [what I recall of] the letter from
China to Kimathi.

Dear Kimathi,

You must have learned that on 15th January I was injured and captured. I am now writing you from the police custody. I have tried to present our demands to the Government through their interrogation. At this stage, I understand the Government is quite willing to put down arms and discuss our difficulties and if possible settle them in peace.

Firstly, I am very worried about the lives of our fighters for we are losing hundreds of lives daily. If you agreed with me we had better stop this bloodshed.

Below are questions which the Government has asked me. To answer these questions, I would like you to send two representatives from Nyandarua and two from Kirinyaga who will answer the questions and negotiate about the general surrender in which I would be a participant.

1. Why are you fighting?
2. What must be done so that all fighters will come out of the forest with all their arms?
3. What would you do if you fail to get land and freedom?
4. If you achieved land and freedom what would you do to 'thata cia bururi' (loyalists, traitors, Home Guards)?
5. Would you agree to suspend the fight during the talks, for the Government is willing and ready to stop the fight until the end of the talks.
6. Do you see this as a Government trap?
7. If you continue to fight to the last man's drop of blood, who would then be given land and freedom?

I have promised the Government that the talks will be successful and now I expect to come to the end of our fight and try peaceful talks to settle our demands; don't let me down on that account.

Yours,
(Signed) Waruhiu Itote

During the next few days 15 copies of this same letter, addressed individually to Nyandarua leaders, were brought to us by messengers from other camps. I saw Kimathi at Thaina and he asked me to write the 15 leaders and the members of the Kenya Parliament informing them of an urgent session. I enclosed my letter in China's envelopes and gave them to Icatha for dispatch.

While we were discussing China's letter with Kimathi, a girl named Wamu arrived from Mt. Kenya with a message from Gen. Tanganyika who had succeeded Gen. China. His letter said that the fighters in Mt. Kenya had been greatly upset by losing Gen. China, the leader they all had confidence in. Tanganyika said that he had not gained full control over the unsettled fighters and that he would like Kimathi to pay a visit to Mt. Kenya's fighters as quickly as possible so that he would be able to reorganize and advise them before they were downhearted.

After reading Tanganyika's letter we agreed we should visit Mt. Kenya as soon as the Parliament settled China's letter. Wamu, a Form 1 school girl, who had joined the fighters, had been staying with China. She was bright, expressive and fearless. She told us much about Mt. Kenya and the possibilities of meeting Gen. Ndaya of Embu and Gen. M'Inoti of Meru.

Four days later, the Kenya Parliament held its first session with Gen. Rui as the only absentee. Many other leaders were invited to the meeting. The session lasted two days, at the end of which Gen. Ndiritu Thuita and I were elected to attend negotiation talks with the Kenya Government whenever His Excellency the Governor of Kenya, Sir E. Baring and Gen. Sir Erskine, East African Commander-in-Chief will respond and agree to our requests in the letter we addressed to them, giving each a copy.

We answered the questions in China's letter and gave some conditions which had to be fulfilled in order to prove to us that the Government was willing to negotiate with us.

Answers to the questions :

1. We are fighting for our lands—the Kenya Highlands which was stolen from the Africans by the Crown through the Orders in Council 1915 of the Crown Lands Ordinance which evicted Africans from their lands at present occupied by the settlers or reserved for their future generations while landless Africans are starving of hunger or surviving on the same land as the cheap laborers to the settlers who were granted that land by the Crown.

2. Before we come out of the forest, the British Government must grant Kenya full independence under the African leadership, and also hand over all the alienated lands to Kenya

African Government which will redistribute the land to its citizens.

3. If we do not get land and freedom now, we will continue to fight till the Government yields or the last drop of blood of our last fighter is spilt.

4. If we achieve land and freedom, we would forgive all the *thata cia bururi*, for we are sure that they are either foolish or they have not other ways of ensuring their lives under your Government other than to kill and destroy as instructed by your officers. We have a battle song which says : 'Choose the whites, save the blacks, for they are working under their foolishness.' After all, we are certain that all these loyalists are our real brothers, sisters, parents, in-laws and our beloved friends. Blood is thicker than water. Our traditional beliefs cannot allow us to part with our relatives. The following Kikuyu saying will prove this to be true : '*Rurira rutithambagio rui*' ('The navel cord can never be washed away in a river'), meaning that one cannot under any circumstances deny his relative; even if one went to wash himself in a river he would still remain the same blood he is trying to denounce. Or a Swahili saying, *Mwana wa nyoka ni nyoka!* (The snakes son is still a snake). Now it is war time; and war means destruction of everything without recognizing children or their parents. War simply means taking away lives and wealth. The most civilized and advanced nations have failed to stop war as they believe that war is the only safeguard against slavery, oppression and exploitation by others. War seems to be a natural rule—the survival of the fittest to all creatures.

5. We are not going to stop fighting during the negotiation talks. Both will continue until an agreement is reached by our representatives in the talks who could only convince us to stop fighting.

6. Yes, we have seen that it is a Government trap, but we will throw a stick of wood in it and see its reaction. If we could release the spring we shall walk over it safely.

7. It is now almost one and a half years since the declaration of the emergency. Every day since then you have been trying your best to destroy us completely, using nearly 100,000 strong forces and dropping thousands of bombs on us from your jet fighters, Harvards and the heavy Lincoln bombers. All your

forces work day and night trying to finish us off, but our God is great and you have not been successful, and you will not succeed. Though you think we are unarmed compared to your strength, we stand for right and God will defend the right. We are confident of our victory. Even if you kill all the Central Province people, the now quiet Kenya tribes will still demand land and freedom—it is inevitable. You may lose your empire in the course of impeding Kenya's independence.

If you want us to negotiate with you, you must firstly disarm the Home Guards and remove your forces completely out of the Central Province where they are killing women and children, raping and robbing them and forcing them here in the forest to fight with us.

Secondly, demolish the newly established unsanitary villages, police posts and military bases and let every person return to his former homestead.

Thirdly, release all the revolution prisoners and detainees.

Fourthly, open all the schools you have closed down.

Fifthly, bring D. N. Pritt, A. R. Kapila and Ralph Bunch to the negotiation talks so that they will advise and draft our agreement.

Finally, we would like to meet Mr Jomo Kenyatta or his representative from Lokitaung, Mr Chief Koinange, Mr James Beauttah, Mr E. W. Mathu, M.L.C., Mr W. W. W. Awaori, M.L.C., and Mr W. Odede, M.L.C. We demand the signatures of all the persons mentioned in this letter confirming their participation in the negotiation talks. There will be no negotiations talks in the absence of the above mentioned people.

The letter was jointly signed by Kimathi and myself on behalf of the Kenya Parliament and was dispatched making sure that it would be posted in Nyeri the following day. The meeting ended. The nearby leaders left for their own camps, others promising to leave at sunrise.

The fighters who delivered the letter to the reserve returned the following day with a message that Gen. Tanganyika and three others fighters had been captured by the Government. They claimed that they had received China's letters asking them to go and negotiate about the surrender. After showing the police their letters, they were taken to Gen. China in police custody. The people did not know more than this.

The news was very distressing to me and Kimathi. We felt as if all the Mt. Kenya fighters might be induced by their leaders to surrender. We wrote an urgent letter addressed to 'All Mount Kenya Fighters.' We warned them not to surrender even if their leaders surrendered. We warned them not to participate in the false negotiation talks until it was fully proved by the leaders in Nyandarua to be worthy. We asked them to send some of their fighters through Gen's. Kariba and Rui who would guide and guard us from Nyandarua to Kirinyaga. We told them that we had formed a Kenya Parliament which would be responsible to all the fighters affairs. We promised them that if any talk will ever be held, the Mt. Kenya fighters will elect two representatives. We ended the letter by pointing out that we were very much distressed and suffered the same feelings as they did for the loss of the two prominent leaders. We hoped that their successors might be as good as the captured leaders.

We sent copies of the letter to Gen's. Kariba and Rui. In a couple of days we received news that Mt. Kenya fighters had sent four other fighters to the Government so that they could negotiate. The latter group told the Government that they had been sent by the fighters to get China and Tanganyika back into the forest to explain things to them. Their appeal to the fighters, at their own liberty, having been released from the police custody, would be a sufficient proof for the Mt. Kenya fighters to surrender.

The Government agreed to release Gen. Tanganyika and all his party except China to go back into the Mt. Kenya forest and convince all the other fighters to surrender. They were supplied with new pairs of clothings, shoes, watches, tinned foodstuffs, loaves of bread, and were driven back into the forest in a Special Branch Land Rover. They shook hands with the Government representatives and then disappeared into the forest.

The Government waited for the Mt. Kenya fighters to surrender but they did not. Gen. Tanganyika resumed his leadership in Kirinyaga. In a couple of days they had spent talking with Government's representatives, they had learned that the Government only wanted our fighters to surrender and that there was no real negotiations. We waited for the reply to our letter from the Government, but all in vain, for the Government never replied.

Toward the middle of March, Kimathi, his clerk and I were in Abdullah's *mbuci*, situated in the eastern dry bamboo area of Ruhuruini Hill facing Nyeri Hill. It was a bright sunny day and we were reading Napoleon's Book of Fate, consulting it of [i.e., regarding] our fates, when a gun bursted about 50 yards from us. As we started away, someone shouted for us to stop running. We paused and Kimathi angrily enquired who had fired it.

'It was an accident, Sir,' replied Wamuthandi.

As we returned to the place we were, we saw that many *itungati* had gathered where the accident occurred. Kimathi told me to see what happened. On my arrival to the gathering, I found a member of the Kenya Parliament, Gathitu Waithaka, lying on his stomach in the center of a circle. He had taken off his shirt and a very small Sten gun hole could be seen on his back just below the last rib on the left. He was not bleeding. I asked whether the bullet had gone through, and was informed that it had stopped in his stomach. I asked how it happened. Kimathi arrived while Wamuthandi was explaining it to me—how they were cleaning their guns and how the bullet accidentally bursted from the hands of a *gitungati* who had been cleaning his Sten gun. Kimathi said that he wanted all the persons who were there during the accident. The leaders who were there and Gathitu himself witnessed that it was an accident.

Gathitu stood up and said that he was going to meet an unfortunate death through no ones will. Expressing his feelings he said, 'Though I can speak and walk, I am afraid that the bullet might have touched my liver. Below the bullet's path I am feeling cold, almost freezing, while the upper part is very hot.'

We encouraged him that he was not going to die. Kimathi ordered that he be taken to a private place near the Kenya Young Stars Memorial Hall where we had held the annual prayers.

Kimathi sent me to Ruthaithi to wait for Gen. Rui so that his group would lead us to Mt. Kenya. A week later I learned that Gathitu Waithaka, our beloved member of Kenya Parliament, had died.

It was here, at Jeriko's *mbuci*, that I received a number of reports of what came to be known as the 'Kayahwe Massacre.' In the month of February some 2,000 fighting recruits left Nairobi to join our fighters in the Nyandarua forest. These recruits, fully uniformed and partially armed, made their way through Murang'a where they were received by Gen. Kago Mboko, then commanding six hundred experienced and well-armed fighters of the Kenya Levellation Army in the Kandara Division. Kago, being fully convinced that his men were able to attack Kandara Government base, which was a major military post in the Fort Hall District, decided to attack it at 10 a.m. When our fighters opened fire on the Kandara post, there was a little resistance at first; but when the Government forces learned that they were greatly outnumbered by our advancing forces they fled away. Many of them were killed when fleeing. Our fighters entered the post and set all its houses on fire.

After this successful attack, Kago split his group into small units in order to avoid being cordoned by Government forces and at the same time to be able to get a sufficient supply of food from other locations.

One of the groups of men from Nairobi encamped for the night in the bracken zone bordering the Nyandarua forest. The following morning, these recruits set off for the forest not knowing the Government had laid an ambush for them which resulted in the greatest single set-back we suffered in our struggles against Government.

It was at Kayahwe River in Forst Hall that Government surrounded 92 of the men and closed in to attack. Being inexperienced, the men, seeing that they were completely surrounded, raised their hands and surrendered. They were then told to put down all their possessions and take off their clothes. When this was over, the 92 men were shot in cold blood.

After the massacre of these men, the other forces which had encamped within the area entered Nyandarua safely under the leadership of Gen. Kago. The fate of the 92 men was only discovered when two of their group arrived a short time later, having been left by Government for dead with their 90 comrades. Their story was confirmed by our sympathizers who had been forced to accompany the Home Guards in that patrol and who witnessed the incident.

To commemorate this loss, a song was sung in the forests :

> Kayahwe is a very bad river
> Kayahwe is a very bad river
> Kayahwe is a very bad river
> This is where our heroes were exterminated

I'll go mother, I'll go
I'll go mother, I'll go
I'll go mother, I'll go
I'll go and see Kayahwe

General Ihura gets no sleep
General Kago gets no sleep
Our warriors get no sleep
They sleep not when remembering Kayahwe

Gen. Kago, an ambidextrous man who fired with his left hand, gained a reputation before his death [on 31 March 1954 in a daylight battle] of being one of our bravest fighters. He fought in the very dangerous areas of Fort Hall reserve and is said to have waged stand-up daylight battles against the security forces in the area. A verse from a song sung by his group proves his bravery : 'Kago s/o Mboko ordered the rifles removed from our shoulders and held in hands; and that we take firing positions and load our rifles. No *Iregi* [i.e., an early generation-set] exists, though they didn't take up arms.'

When Gen. Rui failed to turn up within two weeks, I left Ruthaithi and met Kimathi again at Chieni. He gave me a new pair of yellow corduroy pants, black shoes, a new watch, two fountain pens, a woolen shirt and a light black raincoat. I was very thankful for the clothings, which made me look like a leader.

Kimathi asked me to write letters to the Kenya Parliament members and ask them to attend the second session to be held at Nyaga's *mbuci* at Thaini River. When the leaders arrived, [toward the middle of May] we held our meeting under a rectangular rain-shelter in the thicket of bamboo. We sat on bamboo seats built all around the walls on which we leaned.

We opened the meeting with two minutes of silence while standing in memory of our deceased comrade, Gathitu Waithaka. I said opening prayers and then we all sat down. Gen. Rui and Wambugu Mwema were absent.

Kimathi opened the meeting by asking the members to elect a person who would replace Gathitu. After a short discussion, we found it difficult to elect or nominate anyone. We resolved that

Kenya Parliament members must be elected at a general meeting held annually.

I read the previous session's minutes. We resolved that China's negotiation was Government's lie, and a great attempt to capture the best leaders. China's talk was followed by the Nairobi Operation Anvil, [beginning on 24th April] which resulted to the arrest and detention of more than 40,000 persons, mostly young men who could join the fighting. In the reserves our agents were arrested and detained and many were killed. It followed that His Excellency the Governor of Kenya pardoned China's death sentence. This was the first fighter to be pardoned by the Governor, but I do not remember any other. We concluded that China must have revealed most of our secrets and plans to the Government which resulted in a complete destruction of our communications and supplies, and detention of about 60,000 great supporters (Anvil and Reserve operations). His attempt to convince our fighters to surrender or to trap them into the Government's hands had saved his life as a reward for assisting the Government to defeat us.

We learned that the Government had started using propaganda to defeat us. We agreed to start campaigns against Government propaganda and at the same time preach our propaganda. I then read the letters Kimathi had received. The first one was a copy of a letter written to Fenner Brockway by the Secretary, Kenya Parliament Nairobi. The letter accused the British Government of giving their forces and the Kenya settlers authority and arms to shoot the Africans. They were mercilessly shooting the Kikuyu people as though they were unwanted game. The letter claimed that the forces were paid five shillings bonus per Kikuyu killed. It had given a long account of robbing, raping, burning homes, destruction of wealth, closing of schools and trade centers, taking of vehicles owned by the Kikuyu, evictions and Special Areas, unsanitary villages, detention of parents leaving young children without hope, curfew orders, hunger and starvation. The letter requested Fenner Brockway and Peter Mbiyu Koinange to present our case to the United Nations Organization in the hope that the latter would help and settle our case. Copies of the letter had been dispatched to Russia, India and Egypt.

The second letter was a reply from Fenner Brockway, M.P. It read, [as I recall] :

Dear Kamau,

I am in receipt of your letter. I have read it with great sympathy. I have handed over the letter to Messers Ralph Milner and Johnston who will deal with the affairs in the Parliament.

Yours faithfully

(Signed) Fenner Brockway

The third letter was a reply to my letter to Prof. Motiwala, an astrologer in India; which I had sent a month ago. In the letter I requested him to predict my future. The aim of the letter was to check out whether we were able to communicate with other countries. We suspected the Government with censoring letters going to other countries.

Though we were happy about these letters, and very much longed to send out letters abroad, Operation Anvil and all the arrests of that month had completely blocked our means of communication. Nevertheless, we resolved that Kimathi and I must be very much engaged in the pen battle in such a way that our voice will be heard abroad.

Just before our meeting, the Colonial Secretary, Oliver Lyttleton, arrived in Kenya and formed a multi-racial Government of three European ministers, two Asians and one African, the first African minister, B. A. Ohanga. His attempt to quiet the African demands by banning color-bar, promoting the African to a high post in the Government, the preaching of multi-racial Government and co-operation, became the beginning of recognition and yielding to the African demands. This achievement was not through the Legislative Council politics, but through the admittance by the Colonial Government that granting some of the fighters' demands was the only sure way of restoring peace. This achievement was our pride. We used it to support our propaganda. We claimed that having defeated the colonial power in the fight, they were then inducing us to accept equality in a Government which they would lead, having all the powers. We then rejected the offer and wrote a letter to Mr E. W. Mathu, M.L.C., congratulating him for rejecting the ministerial post.

Being the majority in Kenya and having shown the colonial power that we had unreservedly revolted against their rule—and all the forecasts were that we were winning—we maintained confidence in our victory.

I informed the meeting of my intentions of going to Ethiopia. I said that if I got there, I could get help of arms and ammunition and the facility of expressing how our people were brutally destroyed in the course of obstructing them from rising to independence so that the Kenya settlers will continue to rule and exploit our people as very cheap labor. I demanded a dozen well-armed and equipped warriors and an average of 2,000s. each (26,000s.) for all the journey. I said that I had two fighters with me who had visited Ethiopia and they were willing to accompany me.

The other members said it was a good idea, though the Parliament didn't have money for the journey. There was a feeling objecting to miss twelve rifles. It was resolved that the Parliament will collect money from the leaders and buy all the necessary equipment I wanted and then prepare the messages I would take to the Ethiopian Government.

When we discussed the rules and regulations, we confirmed all the old ones and added that any *gitungati* who would run away from his leader and happened to lead other *itungati* into *komerera* gangs would face a capital charge.

The second day we were discussing how we could rebuild a bridge-system of supplies from Nairobi when two messengers arrived from Nairobi. They were Ndiritu Theuri and Joram Mwangi. They brought Kimathi a gift: a first grade khaki corduroy suit, leather jacket, wrist watch, fountain pen, a pair of half boots and 500s. They told us that the Nairobi Central Committee was not functioning well and that they had decided it wise to work on the district level in Nairobi so that each district could supply its fighters with their requirements while the Central Committee would supply the Nairobi fighters only. They said that according to information received in Nairobi from both Mt. Kenya and Aberdare, the divisional leaders in the forest were in a better position of distributing supplies to their division fighters rather than the district leaders, chiefly due to communication difficulties. They told us that they had been sent to make certain whether the goods sent from Nairobi reached Kimathi for distribution.

After a short discussion we found that a lot of goods had been sent from Nairobi directed to Kimathi and never reached him. We then resolved that the forest fighters should elect committees ranging from Sub-location, Location, Division and District (such as the Ituma Ndemi Trinity Council), with three leaders elected from each division [to serve on the latter.] On top of this should be the Kenya Parliament with members representing all thirty-three Kenya Districts. We agreed that we should elect representatives of the absent districts and that those persons should do their best to recruit the people of the districts they represented. We agreed that when the messengers returned to Nairobi, they would re-organize the bridge-system from Nairobi to the forests on divisional levels. We also agreed that another general election would be held before the end of the year in order to increase the membership to thirty-three. We wrote a letter to the Nairobi branch of the Kenya Parliament and asked it to collect 5,000s. from every district and supply clothing, medicine, water bottles and tinned food for my Ethiopian journey.

The messengers returned to Nairobi. The following day we con-tinued our meeting, this time arranging missions to send out; luckily, six leaders from Murang'a arrived including Macaria Kimemia, their head leader. They were invited to the meeting and after a long repetition informing them all that we had done, they congratulated our work and joined in preparing some missions.

The first mission was to Kiambu under the leadership of Major Kahiga, assisted by Gitekoba. Their main duty was to mobilize the Kiambu young men to join the fight. The second mission was to Gikuyu Iregi Army under Macaria Kimemia. This mission was required to encourage our fighters and if necessary to create and spread propaganda, teach our fighters some methods of attacking enemy's property, preach the leadership of the Kenya Parliament and finally issue ranks to our fighters. A third mission, and similar to the former, under my leadership was to tour the 2nd, 3rd and 4th Ituma Ndemi Army companies. General Abdullah and Makan-yang were to assist me. Kimbo and Ndiritu had similar missions to the Mburu Ngebo Army.

A fifth mission was under Capt. Rugani to Laikipia. Rugani resembled and spoke Turkana; he was to mobilize the Turkana and Suk. A sixth mission left for Londiani under Capt. Wanjeru in order to mobilize the Kalenjin tribes. Kimathi awaited a guide to Mt. Kenya while the other missions left.

I had not been issued with a rank officially and at that point I was going out to issue ranks up to General. Realizing this, Kimathi went into his office, discussed with a few members of the Kenya

Parliament, and returned with an envelope which he gave me in front of all the people a few minutes before we left for our mission.

When I opened this envelope, I found a hundred shilling note and a letter saying : 'Today Karari Njama has been promoted to Brigadier General and Knighted, for his service to the country, with the highest title—Knight Commander of East Africa.' It was signed by Dedan Kimathi on behalf of the Kenya Parliament.

I was very grateful for my promotion. I ordered a *gitungati* to take the hundred shilling note to my wife and ask her to share it with my step-mother.

It was already 8 a.m. when we commenced our journey. Kirangi (Gathuri Mukiri), one of Kimathi's strong old bodyguards was entrusted as our *muirigo* as well as a bodyguard. Our nine-man *safari* climbed the hill westwards up to the Moorlands, where the movement was much easier, and changed our direction southwards. Our chief obstacles were rain, mud, cold and swollen rivers. It was mid-May and we were at the height of the long rains.

We managed to cross the river Chania at a place where it had widened up to 120 feet and was only two feet in depth. On our approach to Gura River, we found it had so swollen that we could not cross it. We were forced to encamp there for the night, just about five miles from the river's source. This distance gave us much hope that the water might be low by the following morning, or we would have to go to the source of the river. We pegged our *safari* tents. Heavy rain started pouring as we were lighting fires. It put off the fires and we were unable to cook anything that night. Our tents flooded making it impossible for us to sleep in them. The night was terribly cold. All the water on the ground or on leaves formed thin layers of ice crystals.

Since the river had not changed, we made our way upstream crossing its tributaries until we were in a position to cross it almost a mile from the source. We changed our direction towards east and enjoyed the thin rays of the rising sun. Moving further, we arrived at a dead elephant. We guessed that it must have been killed by the heavy bombs. Hundreds of hyenas had enjoyed a great feast, leaving behind bones with little meat and two seven-foot tusks. We didn't remove the ivory but we agreed that we shall tell the nearest camp to collect them.

We continued our journey and were crossing a very small stream called Karimu that drains into Gura, when one of our *gitungati* sunk completely in it. We managed to save him but lost his luggage. The stream was only four feet wide and using a long bamboo to measure its depth, we found that it was eleven feet. Since Karimu flows in a grassland narrow valley, one wouldn't recognize that there was a stream until he was about twenty yards from it.

Kabuga's *mbuci* was only three quarters of a mile from the stream. We saw some animal traps which notified us that the camp was not far away. When we were observing and talking about the traps, the trappers were only twenty yards from us in their ambush. They had seen us coming far away but they were not certain whether we were foes or friends.

As they were leading us to their *mbuci*, they told us that their leader, Kabuga, had disappeared some three weeks ago in the upper Karimu stream. They had seen some people approaching as they were fishing and mistook them for friends. They only recognized them to be foes at a very close range when they opened fire on them. Since then Kabuga and three other *itungati* had been missing. They told us that they had spent much time searching for their corpses but all in vain.

We entered the camp in sparsely scattered bamboo just bordering the Moorlands. Here we were welcomed by Gitonga Caciingu, who had succeeded Kabuga, and Wacira Gathuku, who was advising him after the dissolution of a general hospital which was under his charge. His assistant Harrison Gathinji had joined the Kenya Levellation Army and was very active with Capt. Kihithuki operating in our location. Their clerk Julius Gathaiga s/o Mishek Matu had been injured in the knee and the bullet was still causing it to swell so badly that he could not walk. Gicohi Gitori was the acting clerk and he gave me all the data I wanted. In the evening, we were introduced to the *itungati*, though they knew me well. They were told of the mission I led under the Kenya Parliament authority. After greetings, we promised to hold a general meeting the following day commencing at two in the afternoon.

That night we ate animals meat from their traps; they had caught five bush bucks and had some remains of a buffalo they had shot. Though these camps obtained some food from either the reserve or Rift Valley, they had to carry the food for some twenty miles either way. The nights were very cold and we kept the fires burning almost throughout the night to keep us warm. The walls of the huts were well covered to protect us from the cold.

When the day broke, the leaders became very busy arranging the names of their *itungati* according to the ranks they were due to be granted. In the afternoon the meeting started and was attended by 97 fighters of IDA 3/3, including ourselves. I told them about the formation of the Kenya Parliament, its aims and works; read to them the letters from India, Nairobi and from Fenner Brockway. I gave them to their clerk and all persons who could read in order to prove to them that the pen battle in which I was very much engaged was as great as the rifle battle. Having convinced them, I was in a good position of forming propaganda for encouragement.

General Abdullah taught them the new methods of fighting—the destruction of the enemy's property. General Makanyanga talked to them about ranks and promised that they would be issued with ranks the following day. Kirangi warned them that though many people had [become] self-styled 'generals', none of those ranks would be recognized unless it was officially issued by an authorized person. He emphasized that the records in the books would be more reliable than any verbal claims. He said that every *gitungati* would not be able to present his service [record] to the first African Government but every *gitungati* expected his leader to speak for him. He then mentioned the disadvantages of *komerera*.

Their leader, Wacira Gathuku, told them that the ranks would be issued according to ones activities in the camp. The meeting broke up and we quickly went to warm ourselves.

The following morning, I stood between the two camp leaders on my left and my two assistants on my right and issued ranks to some 25 fighters, including their leaders Gen's. Wacira and Gitonga. We spent some 50s. on ranks—the highest getting 10s. and the lowest getting fifty cents.

The following day we visited IDA 2/1 which had encamped some two hours walk due south. On our arrival, we were welcomed by Elijah Kihara Gatandi and his assistant, Gicuki Mwii. We learned that Kihara Kagumu, the head leader of IDA 2, had been shot dead by the enemy at Kimbo's *mbuci* at Karathi's Mother. His successor, Gicuki Mugo, had been arrested while hiding in Nyeri European Primary School compound. I did not notice any difference between that camp and the former. We remained in the camp for three days during which we completed our program, ranking 22 of the 70 fighters.

We were given a guide to IDA 2/2, then under Kibira Gatu.

The camp was behind the old H.Q. at Kariaini facing Gikira River. Kibira Gatu had become very famous fighting with the Kenya Levellation in the reserve and returning in the forest while not attacking. The place was quite warm, between the black forest and the bamboo, compared to the freezing area we had been staying. After a thin maize-meal dinner, I feel in deep sleep. The next morning, I felt very tired and did not want to wake up.

At 8:30 in the morning I was still in bed and completely wrapped within a blanket when the enemy started firing at the camp. They had approached the camp unnoticed. I woke up, grabbed my satchel with one hand and my blanket in the other, leaving behind my shoes, raincoat and hat. As I ran, the blanket was held by a branch and knocked me down. I heard the enemy shouting : 'He is down ! See them run like cowards.'

I left my blanket there and, running barefoot, I fell many times while descending in a valley. As I was left behind, I managed to join three other fighters. I asked them to pause and listen. We did not hear our people but instead heard the enemy shouting in the camp. We learned that it was Kibithe's young boys from their shoutings.

We had not hope of joining our companions that day. The *itungati* suggested that we cross the Gikira River and visit IDA 4/3 led by Kahinga Wachanga. We managed to get there but the enemies had seen us going and followed us. They spotted some of Kahinga's fighters who had gone to collect honey and opened fire at them. When he heard the shots, Kahinga ordered his fighters to pack and move westwards to Githai area in the dry bamboo. The four of us accompanied him.

On our arrival at Githai, we were dispersed by another enemy force. The movement was very difficult there for one could not run over the fallen bamboo unless he followed an elephant's path. I found myself with a group of 18 of Kahinga's fighters and we encamped by one of the Gikira tributaries near its source. We found all of us had only one maize cob for our dinner. Some *itungati* searched for some edible vegetables but found none. The ones they found were very poisonous and if we ate them we would either run mad or become dumb. Our maize was roasted and each of us was given a dozen grains for dinner. I learned that Kahinga's section had lost the system of building a common food store and had substituted it by carrying on their shoulders all their belongings all the time.

The following day we vainly searched for the other companions. Night came and we encamped in one of Kahinga's old camps where Kahinga's *itungati* thought that it was easy for them to contact the other fighters. That night we had nothing to eat. The *itungati* discussion resolved that we would spend the following day searching the other fighters and that if unsuccessful by four in the afternoon, we would go to the forest edge and 13 of the fighters would enter the reserve to collect food and try to catch the other fighters there.

The next day we had no luck in the search. We went to the forest edge in the evening but met the enemy shelling the forest aimlessly from positions near the boundary. It would have been very dangerous to try and enter the reserve under those conditions so the 19 of us spent another hungry night without food.

The following morning we continued our hopeless search till noon. Being tired and hungry, we sat down for a rest. My soft bare feet had been badly pricked by debris, stumps, stones and were always wet, sinking under the black mud. I felt exhausted and did not want to walk any more. I asked the *itungati* whether they knew any other fighters' camp to which they could lead me. They replied that they did not know any other than the old deserted camps. The *itungati* suggested that we had better walk some ten miles to the edge of the forest where we would encamp for the night while some of us went to the reserve for food. I did not appreciate the idea and requested whether some of them would accompany me to the Moorlands where I thought I could catch other fighters easily. I learned that none of the *itungati* wanted to part from their companions.

In a horrified and worried state of mind, I took my small binoculars and started eagerly looking aimlessly for any people. Luckily, I caught some thin smoke rising up above a tall tree across the river Gikira to the northwest. I was unable to sight any person due to the hindrance of trees and bushes. I told the fighters that we had better catch the owners of that smoke, whom I thought to be our fighters who had gone round hunting for honey. One *gitungati* argued that it might be enemy's fire. At last they agreed and we walked to the tree.

On our arrival at the tree, we found that our other fighters who had made the fire while collecting honey had then left. We quickly followed their track, taking great care not to lose it. The track led us to IDA 4/1 under Gikonyo Kanyungu.

We were very happy to meet other fighters. I told Gen. Gikonyo that we had spent four days and three nights without food. He ordered that we be given as much elephant meat as we could eat. Though the Kikuyu tribe traditionally disapproves of eating any animal with one hoof [i.e., toe], like the horse, or with more than two hooves, and all clawed animals, a few Kikuyu hunters, 'Athi,' had started trapping and eating elephants, probably under the influence of Gumba and Nderobo some centuries ago. The Athi were sparsely scattered all along the borders of the forests surrounding Kikuyuland.

In Murang'a the practice of eating elephant had grown so that they almost ignored the taboo on eating such animals. They had influenced their neighbors in Gikonyo's camp.

Irrespective of any taboo and traditional beliefs, I personally believed that man could eat any animal, provided that it was not poisonous to him. I thought that God blessed all other creatures as man's food. This abundance had caused man to select which ones he liked according to their appearances and tastes.

With this in mind, I started eating the meat, weighing its taste and smell. The taste of the fried fat could not be differentiated from cattle fat. We ate much of the tender meat, which was as tender as pork. I noted that a girl and three other warriors had refused to eat.

After eating, I asked for *kiraiku*. I wrapped the tobacco well in a piece of paper in the form of a cigarette and heavily puffed it after lighting while I listened to Gen. Gikonyo telling me about his camp. He told me that his group had successfully exterminated a notorious headman and had readministered the oath to the Home Guards. He said that he was on very good terms with many Home Guards in Chinga Location. They were regularly supplying him with ammunition. He added that four of the Home Guards had joined his *mbutu* [i.e., section] with their rifles and ammunition supplied to them by the Government. He called them to come with their rifles. They stood in a line and presented arms to me. I inspected them and congratulated them for what they had done supporting the fighters. I told them their works should be recorded and that they were in a position of gaining high rank quickly and easily if they could bring into the forest some other Home Guards with their arms.

Turning to Gikonyo, I asked him whether it was possible to hold a meeting with his fighters. He said that some 88 fighters were in the camp, plus 25 who were at the forest fringe storing food for future use and twelve who were in his hospital attending three patients. One of the patients was his assistant leader, Munandi, who had shot the elephant but it caught him before it died and pierced its tusk right through his thigh and then threw him up on a bush. He concluded that if I wanted I could meet all the fighters in the camp. He said that he had better first consult his divining gourd as he was one of the medicine men, so as to know whether we were safe to the camp. I watched him counting his stones and seeds, whose numbers solved his questions. I very well understood that there was no truth in it but many of our fighters believed in it. After [he had finished] he said we were safe and called the *itungati* to a meeting.

After introducing me to his *itungati*, I told them of the mission I had led and how my men were dispersed by the enemy and the difficult life I had within the last four days. I started reading the letters and had not finished when I fell down on the ground in the center of the meeting like a person suffering from epilepsy.

When I rose up to speak, for a few seconds I was unable to maintain my balance. When I resumed my strength, I told the fighters not to think that I was suffering from any disease, as they might have thought—the fact was that I was suffering from hunger and exhaustion of energy in the long journeys. I took a New Testament out of my satchel, opened to St. Matthew, Chapter 5, and read verses 1–6.

> And seeing the multitudes, he went up into a mountain; and when he was set, his disciples came unto him. And he opened his mouth, and taught them, saying, blessed are the poor in spirit for theirs is the kingdom of heaven. Blessed are they that mourn : for they shall be comforted. Blessed are the meek : for they shall inherit the earth. Blessed are they which do hunger and thirst after righteousness : for they shall be filled.

I told them that Jesus was a great teacher and prophet and his prophesy would be fulfilled exactly as I had read unto them. I told them that it was just a matter of time and we would come to the end of the emergency, during which time our daily troubles would be changed in equal amount of goodness as the badness we had suffered.

'You all know that everything has its time, its beginning and its end,' I said. In order to witness my statement, I referred to one of the ancient great preachers, the Ecclesiastes, Chapter 3, verses 1–8.

> To everything there is a season, and a time to every purpose under the heaven. A time to be born, and a time to pluck up that which is planted; a time to kill, and a time to heal; a time to break down, and a time to build up; a time to weep and a time to laugh; a time to mourn, and a time to dance; a time to cast away stones, and a time to gather stones together; a time to embrace, and a time to refrain from embracing; a time to get, and a time to lose; a time to keep, and a time to cast away; a time to rend, and a time to sew; a time to keep silent, and a time to speak; a time of famine, and a time of plenty (my insertion). A time to love, and a time to hate; a time of war, and a time of peace.

'Though this is a time of war, the time of peace is just at the corner, coming,' I said. 'When it arrives, each of us shall receive happiness equal to the misery he or she has suffered in the forest, for God maintains the balance of good and bad and the lengths of their duration. Those who are happy now shall be very miserable when *uhuru* [freedom] comes, while we shall be very happy, balancing the suffering we are about to overcome.'

I then took the letter from Fenner Brockway, read it to them and then handed it over to them to witness that it had come from him. I told them that Mbiyu Koinange had succeeded in presenting our case to the UNO and that over 80 representatives of different countries (British Commonwealth Parliamentary Delegation) were coming to Kenya to hear our claims and collect reports from our leaders and settle our disputes with the settlers. I told them that I was making the Africans' difficulties known by the people of other countries and that soon we would get help. I promised them to issue ranks the following day and released them to collect firewood before darkness fell. Their leader thanked me and they seemed very happy as they left to gather wood.

By the time fires were made, I was as hungry as ever. I bewilderingly asked Gikonyo whether elephant's meat took the same length of time as cattle beef for digestion.

'The elephant's meat is very tender,' he replied, 'and takes less than three hours to be digested and absorbed in the body and very little of it is excreted. It doesn't matter how much one eats, for he will quickly feel hungry as elephants' meat is the easiest digestible form of food I know.'

He ordered his cooks to make *njima* for me (a hardened maize porridge) which I ate with meat and a nice gravy. After eating, I felt very sleepy. He gave me one of his blankets and asked one of his lieutenants to show me where to sleep. I was taken to a small rectangular hut with all the walls well covered and a nice fire was still burning. I wrapped myself in the blanket and soon fell into a deep sleep.

The following day, Gikonyo arranged the names of the fighters who were to be ranked and in the afternoon I issued ranks to 28 of them, including four Home Guards who had finished two months in the forest—each was made a sergeant. During the meeting I told them how to attack enemy's property and suggested for them to move from the reserves to the Rift Valley and in general tried to cover the mission's program, the Kenya Young Stars, etc.

After my speech, one *gitungati* offered me a pair of tyre sandals. Seeing that, Gikonyo promised me to order all my requirements from the reserve. The following day I visited the camp's hospital and found that all the patients were recovering. Munandi had two small wounds in the thigh through which the elephant had stabbed its tusk. They all witnessed that the hole was three inches in diameter and covered and filled with some elephant fat.

When I returned to the *mbuci*, I found four *itungati* from Gitonga's *mbuci* who had been moving from camp to camp searching for me. They told me that although my companions in the mission had been dispersed by the enemy the day we parted, they had later on all arrived at Gitonga's *mbuci* with the exception of me.

I made up my mind to join my companions the following day. Gikonyo told me that he would accompany me in order to be able to meet Kimathi. We left the camp in the morning with ten *itungati*, including his *kabatuni*. By noon we arrived at Kihara Gatandi's camp and he too wished to join my company on our way back to Chania. I learned that the enemy killed three of our fighters, injured two others and four others including myself had been missing for a week. I told the story of the three others and so cleared the worries. I rejoined my companions in the evening at Gitonga's *mbuci*. We were all glad to meet each other safely.

They told me that they spent two more days in Kibira's *mbuci*, held a meeting with all the *itungati* and preached all they could, mentioning the letters I had. They did not issue ranks. I in turn told them all that happened to me since we were dispersed.

After listening to my story, Wacira Gathuku wonderingly enquired whether our fighters would ever forget the miserable life we had experienced in the forest. Though the other leaders advocated that our fighters will never forget the emergency's difficulties, to me it seemed to be only hope based on their present feelings, while there was really nothing concrete to commemorate our misery. I then warned them that unless we had something concrete to commemorate our misery, it would become a forgotten factor in a very short time.

Wacira Gathuku then suggested that the day that the emergency will be declared over should become a public holiday and every year on that day we should pack our luggage in kitbags and make about twenty-five miles walk to the Moorlands and peg out our tents on the frozen areas, start hunting and trapping animals for dinner while our wives and children search for any edible vegetables (which is difficult to get in the Moorlands) and if we did not get any forest food we should then sleep without eating anything for that night. All people should be awakened by thunderous firing of every weapon that was used during the emergency. They should then walk back home.

Gen. Gitonga Gaciingu in support of Wacira's idea added that it should be a prayer day to be held on the mountains at midnight and that we should always sacrifice a goat to God before prayers.

I argued that though the idea was a good one, only the present fighters would carry it forward for a short time and then it would die with the fighters. I suspected that the future generations would not be willing to practice such hardships with neither fun nor interest in them.

'Though we would like to maintain the idea in the minds of our people,' I said, 'we could do so by building memorial halls or clubs and give them names symbolizing our miserable life. The buildings may live for many generations and people from other countries would see them and learn their names, keeping in their minds the memory.'

I suggested that we try to name those memorial hall or clubs. The following names were suggested: *Kari Iguru* (meaning the airplane is above), *Mwihugo* (Emergency), *Ruhati* (the hillside, created in the forest), *Ngai Ndeithia!* (God help me!), *Nyagikonyo* (Lincoln Bombers), *Bebeta* (Bren or machine gun), Nyandarua, Kirinyaga, *Mborabu* (Ice), *Ndia Ndarua* (Hides and Skins Eater), *Wiyathi* or *Uhuru* (Freedom).

Instead of suggesting any name, I first criticised the above titles. I pointed out that all the suggested names referred to forest fighters only—had omitted the civilians, detainees and prisoners, including our top leaders. I added that the name should also include both Mts. Nyandarua and Kirinyaga.

Wacira Gathuku, speaking on behalf of the others, demanded my suggestion, wanted to hear my ideas. I started mentioning the stages in which our people have suffered and which are worthy to commemorate. 'First, the Mt. Kenya fighters; second, the Nyandarua fighters; third, the Olengurone civilians' eviction, treatment and loss of property; fourth, the Kapenguria Trials of Jomo Kenyatta, by which we should commemorate all other trials which led to death by hanging for thousands of our supporters and long imprisonment to more than 20,000; fifth, Lokitaung Prison, in which leader Jomo Kenyatta and his colleagues were serving seven years imprisonment for leading the revolution. This prison should commemorate all other prisons and prisoners, detention camps and detainees.'

Our five stages have drawn people from the reserves. Our supporters in the reserves are in the same category as our fighters in many aspects. Since it would be difficult to have a club or memorial hall with five names, we should combine the five names into one name thus: putting together the first syllables of every name— *KE*nya, *NYA*ndarua, o'*LE*ngurone, *KA*penguria, *LO*kitaung—we would get the KENYALEKALO MEMORIAL CLUB.

My idea was approved by the other leaders and we resolved that our misery would be commemorated in big halls to be built in cities and towns under the name KENYALEKALO.

Before sleeping, we asked Gitonga to send some *itungati* to Kihara Gitandi and Gicuki Mwii very early the following morning

to take a letter requesting them to come and arrange our journey
to meet Kimathi in Chania.

The following morning, after the arrival of Kihara and Gicuki,
we agreed that we had to leave for Chania the following day at
seven in the morning. We asked them to pack their luggage and
come to pass the night with us at Gitonga's *mbuci*. When they came
in the evening we passed time by composing two songs to commemorate our mission and misery and praising the leaders. Some
verses of one song are :

> I left home
> And left my parents
> And promised them
> That I was going to fight for soil

> Chorus : Follow the young man
>   And remember
>   This soil is for blacks

> The man you see with a gap in teeth
> Is called Ndungu s/o Giceru
> He is the one who brings down airplanes
> When they come to disturb *itungati*

> Karari s/o Njama
> The hero of Mahiga
> Was willing to give his life
> To return the whites to Europe

> When I went home
> I found my parents
> Weeping, Oh our son
> Our homes were burned.

The following morning we started our journey to Mihuru with
a group of 35 fighters, including six divisional leaders of IDA 2 and
3. We took the same route back with the exception that this time
we managed to cross the river Gura at a point just above its water
falls where we had previously failed to cross. After spending a night

on the way, we arrived at Mihuru in late afternoon and met Kimathi in Nyaga's *mbusi* at the end of May.

I reported all about my mission and pointed out that I did not visit all the sections in that area because they were badly dispersed by the enemy during the previous month and, moreover, many of them were living in Rift Valley, including Stanley Mathenge. I told Kimathi about our idea of the Kenyalekalo Clubs, which he recommended.

After discussing with the six Othaya Division leaders, he advised us to return to Othaya and elect committees from sub-location location and division. After spending three days with Kimathi, the Othaya leaders left for Ruthaithi area where they said they would stay for a week. They would then collect me on their way back to Othaya.

Kimathi organized a visit to the reserve people in Icagaciru Village in North Tetu Location. We left the forest at sunset with 160 armed fighters who on arrival took up sentry positions along all paths leading into that village with the help of some civilians. We met in a home of three big huts on a farm whose owner had not shifted into the village. Each of the huts had at least 80 people— men, women and girls.

Kimathi, Abdullah, Ndiritu, Kahiu-Itina, Kimbo and I lectured to the villagers aiming at encouraging them and gaining their support and re-establishing communication links, bridge-system and a firm organization from the sub-location to the division. We elected some leaders in the reserve who would look after our affairs, told them about the Kenya Parliament, Kenya Young Stars Association and Kenyalekalo, and warned them of the Government propaganda, using bombing results and China's negotiations as examples.

After our long speeches we ate various types of food the women had brought to that home and our warriors carried bundles of raw food. One of the villagers took off his shoes and gave [them to] me. The sub-locational leader promised Ndiritu Thuita that he would send him all my requirements. It was already three in the morning when the meeting broke up. The villagers who had come from all parts of the location returned safely to their home and we entered the forest at dawn.

We held a similar meeting at Ihwa in the same location a week later. The Government was informed of our visits, and we too received that information, and we never again set foot or held any other meeting in the reserve.

During the two meetings we held in the reserve, we learned that Kimbo regarded himself as the representative of the Rift Valley and all the fighters who had made Rift Valley their homes before repatriation. Kimbo, who [seemed to] assume equal power with Kimathi, tried to gain his confidence [i.e., enhance his own status] by dividing Rift Valley fighters from the Central Province fighters. In his speech, Kimbo referred to *WE* (Rift Valley people both in the forest and in the reserve) and *YOU* (the Central Province people). He claimed that the Rift Valley people had lost all their property and were helpless. In his comparison he said that *HIS* people contributed more for land and freedom than the Central Province.

CHAPTER XVIII

THE TIDE IS TURNING

CONSIDERING the military, logistic and ecological difficulties confronting the Aberdare forces, the Kenya Parliament managed to achieve considerable success in implementing at least some of its policies and programs over the last half of 1954. Through its various missions, ceremonial gatherings and meetings, the Parliament was able to gain recognition and establish its authority—albeit largely nominal—over most Aberdare groups and several of the guerrilla units operating in Kiambu and the smaller forests. Its successes, however, were for the most part organizational and did not culminate in the new offensive thrust envisioned by the Parliament leaders. The tide, in fact, seemed to be turning against the guerrilla forces. In the forests they were becoming increasingly isolated and cut off from one another and from their major sources of supplies in the reserves and Nairobi. Related to this, and equally important, was the fact that guerrilla units in several areas were beginning to run critically short of arms and, especially, ammunition. The Kenya Parliament's proposed strategy of destroying enemy property, while sound in itself, was clearly insufficient to halt the steady depletion of weapons and ammunition. Military supplies simply had to be acquired from the security forces and it was here, if the revolt were to be sustained, that a new strategy—aimed at the enemy's weak points, utilizing the tactics of hit-and-run raid and ambush, capitalizing on the elements of surprise, mobility and coordinated action, and directed primarily toward the acquisition of arms and ammunition—was required. Instead, faced with a continuing build-up of Government forces, heavily armed guard and police posts, fortified villages, etc., the forest insurgents were using their dwindling supply of arms and ammunition ever more exclusively for food raids and defense. And, as the food quest led to raids on civilian stock and gardens, the support of the hard-pressed Kikuyu peasantry was steadily alienated.

Failure to sustain the military offensive was obviously related to the internal conflicts which rose to the surface among Aberdare groups and leaders during this period. The lack of significant victories, loss of forward momentum and increasing isolation within the forest tended to turn the Aberdare guerrilla forces increasingly in upon themselves, accelerating certain negative trends in the forest organization and heightening personal animosities between important guerrilla leaders. The tendency, for example, toward smaller and more numerous groups was accelerated by the mounting supply, travel and military difficulties and, as will be clear from Karari's account, it was these smaller marginal groups which deviated more grossly from Kenya Parliament policies regarding offensive tactics, treatment of civilian supporters, etc., and which adhered less closely to Parliament rules and regulations relating to discipline, respect for rank, division of labor, the role of women and defensive procedures. Again, it was the marginal and *komerera* groups which yielded more readily to the leadership of their seers or *mundo mugo*.

The Kenya Parliament's lack of adequate enforcement machinery, combined with the personal power maintained by individual leaders, also facilitated the defiance and non-recognition of the Parliament's authority by certain key Aberdare leaders, such as Stanley Mathenge, Kahiu-Itina and Kimbo. Coupled with the 'vertical' pattern of loyalties, this made the potential split within the Kenya Parliament threaten not only the loss of these individual leaders but also of the lesser leaders and followers attached to them. This segmentation, as noted earlier, was based upon the territorial criterion of recruitment into the various forest groups and was but a reflection of the fact that, for the most part, ties and loyalties based on kinship friendship and locality were strongest within the primary fighting units and towards sub-section leaders, and weakened progressively at each succeeding level of grouping and leadership.

As revealed in Karari's discussions with potential dissidents, there was also a growing tendency towards ideological polarization. In its strictly political dimension, 'victory' among the guerrilla forces continued to be conceived by all factions as the achievement of an independent, all-African Kenya government. Conditioned by the absence of a strong centralized form of government within the traditional Kikuyu political structure, as well as by the Kenya-wide administrative and political system imposed by the British over the preceeding fifty years, few if any Kikuyu thought in terms of secession or the formation of an independent Kikuyu state or nation. This Kenya-wide aspect of forest ideology was manifested both in the symbolic representation of Kenya's 33 districts in the reorganized Kenya Parliament and in the hoped-for participation of other tribes in the revolt.

Despite the general agreement concerning this political question, however, a polarization of ideological positions was developing with respect to the legitimacy of the Kenya Parliament, future rights to alienated land and the place of traditional beliefs and customs. The more acculturated, semi-educated leaders of the Kenya Parliament, such as Karari, expressed the view that all settler-held land should be apportioned among the landless by the first Kenya African Government. They also tended to accept a more or less syncretic version of Kikuyu and European religious beliefs and customs. Several illiterate leaders, on the other hand, questioning the legitimacy of the educated leaders' dominance of the Kenya Parliament, held that since the revolt was being fought by illiterate peasants, it should be led by the uneducated as well. They also maintained that the *White Highlands* should be turned over to the ex-Rift Valley squatters and laborers and that all mission influence should be purged from Kikuyu religious beliefs and practices.

As we shall see, Karari makes a valiant attempt to moderate this conflict and the Mihuro meeting in late November was devoted largely, and with some success, to bringing about a reconciliation between Mathenge and Kimathi and a reunification of Aberdare forces.

★   ★   ★

Kihara Gatandi and the Othaya leaders missed us and returned to Othaya. I followed them at the beginning of June and organized IDA 2, 3 and 4 and their sections—Othaya, Mahiga and Chinga Locations—which form Othaya Division. After each location had elected its sub-location and location committee members, the *itgunati* from the three locations met about one and a half miles west of H.Q. Kariaini and elected the Divisional Committee. Over 300 fighters met and elected [the following] persons, who also had to be members of their sub-location and location committees :

Chairman	Gen. Gikonyo Kanyunga	Chinga Location	IDA 4/1
Vice Chairman	Brig. Gen. Karari Njama	Mahiga Loc.	IDA 3/3
Secretary	Capt. Kunyukunyu	Othaya Loc.	IDA 2/2
Vice Secretary	Col. Wanjeru Kibiri	Mahiga Loc.	IDA 3/2
Treasurer	Gen. Kihara Gatandi	Othaya Loc.	IDA 2/1
Vice Treasurer	Gen. Gitonga Gaciingu	Mahiga Loc.	IDA 3/3
Committee Members:	Wachira Gathuki	Mahiga Loc.	IDA 3/3
	Mwaniki Gacoka	Chinga Loc.	IDA 4/1
	Kibicho	Othaya Loc.	IDA 2/3

After the election we drafted a letter to the Chairman, Othaya Division, Nairobi, and a carbon to the Nairobi Kenya Parliament branch. The letter which I wrote, under the instruction of the committee, reported the result of the election we had and requested that all our divisional supplies be sent to the Chairman via Chinga where the bridge system and communications had been re-established since Operation Anvil. We pointed out that we had no ammunition for attacking our enemies and that the little we had was only [sufficient] to fight for food for only a short time. We also mentioned that our fighters had started wearing skins due to lack of clothes and that we had no medicine left in stock. We also reminded them that we were still waiting for the help they would give for my journeys to Ethiopia. We enclosed specimen signatures for all the office bearers and warned them that all our letters would always be signed by three office bearers, each from a [different] location.

Apart from the election, I spoke to our fighters on many other points and wrote a letter to Kahinga Wachanga, IDA 4/3, who led the South Tetu Division and asked him to hold the same elections as we had and to accompany us, including his Divisional Committee office bearers, so that we could re-elect the Ituma [i.e., Nyeri District] Council at Chania.

In his reply he told us that his case was very easy since all his divisional fighters were not many and were living in one *mbuci* under his leadership. This division lacked the benefit of bordering the forest. It was the division [i.e., South Tetu] that was furthest from the forest. Its fighters had distributed themselves to Mt. Kirinyaga [Kenya], Fort Hall—Gikuyu Iregi Army, and most of them had been forced by subsistence circumstances to join the Kenya Levellation Army, leaving only about 80 fighters with Kahinga.

When Kahinga failed to come, we set off toward Chania with all

the Divisional Committee men. We met Kimathi at Chieni toward
the end of June. After reporting all about our journey, we learned
that Kimathi wanted each division to elect three of its members
and when they met they would form the Ituma Council. The
Othaya Division Committee resolved that it was bad for us to
elect any Ituma members in the absence of Stanley Mathenge, then
its chairman. Though very inactive, as he proved himself to be,
yet his popularity in the division was very great. Moreover, we
believed that it was bad to cast him out unknowingly and we
resolved that I had to go and meet Mathenge and try to bring
him at the Annual General Meeting when we would resume the
talk.

As we were about to break up our discussion, three *itungati*
arrived from Ruthaithi reporting that Wambararia (Wagura
Waciuri, Kimathi's brother) wanted to kill two *itungati* whom he
claimed had seduced his girlfriend. 'He grabbed a rifle from my
hands,' said one *gitungati*, 'and fired two shots at the *itungati*. One
of them was caught by a bullet in his knee. We were able to disarm him and he kept threatening to kill them.'

Kimathi wrote a letter to his brother and asked him to surrender
and peacefully go to present his case to the Kenya Parliament. He
warned that if he disobeyed his instructions he would forcibly be
disarmed and probably spoil his case. The letter was taken by six
armed *itungati* who were ordered to report the following day with
Wambararia.

Meanwhile, I wrote a letter to six members of the Kenya Parliament who were nearby asking them to come and hear Wambararia's case. They arrived the following day and the *itungati*
arrived with Wambararia, who was still armed with a rifle.
Kimathi spoke to him and he yielded his gun. Wambararia was released on his own word that he would neither run away or commit
suicide.

The following day, eight Kenya Parliament members (including
Kimathi) plus eight other leaders invited by Kimathi, sat down to
hear the case. Wambararia was accused of attempting murder. The
accused pleaded guilty and threatened that he would rather commit
suicide than be sentenced to death for his action. He claimed that
he had acted on bad temper. The girl and the *Itungati* who were
victimized by Wambararia swore that their talk had nothing to do
with sexual matters.

When Kimathi spoke, he defended his brother. He said, 'According to Kikuyu customary laws, there was nothing like "attempting murder;" all there was was "murder" or "wound," of which the penalty for the former was either 100 head of goats for a man or 30 for a woman or a revenge by killing the murderer or his relative. The penalty on wounding or assaulting another person was a ram for the medicine man who cleaned and purified the spilt blood, a very fat he-goat and a tin of honey as the compensation for serious injuries. I think Wambararia's case should be regarded as wounding a person and not attempting murder which is not our own law.'

Kimathi gained many supporters and his suggestion was accepted. I warned the meeting that Wambararia's case could not be unique and that our judgement, which would be recorded in our books, would become a pattern to any future cases.

Trying to find out the judgement, Abdullah suggested that according to Kikuyu customary laws, we should ask Wambararia to compensate the injured person by a billygoat and a tin of honey and in addition to that he should take much care to the injured person, especially in feeding and medical treatment.

Another person suggested that the two *itungati* be transferred from Wambararia's *mbuci* soon after recovery and discharge from the hospital. Both ideas were resolved as final, though the injured fighter received no better treatment than one injured by our enemy. Similarly, Wambararia had no billygoat or honey of his own, but instead would send his *itungati* to search them wherever they could find them and take them to the hospital—just what they do to other injured persons.

I later on learned from a few Kenya Parliament leaders that they were not satisfied with the judgement and blamed Kimathi for his fallacy. From the witnesses, the victims suffered for nothing and escaped death by mere luck. I shared their feelings but Kimathi's mood and activity of inviting stooges to hear the case had proved to me that peace could only prevail when his ideas succeeded.

Now July was approaching. I suggested to Kimathi that we should have a mid-year prayer day on 2nd July to commemorate our deceased fighters. By calculation I found that 2nd July was the mid-day of the year, so Kimathi asked me to write letters to all nearby leaders and tell them to meet at Ruhuruini Memorial Hall where prayers should be held at Gathitu's grave.

A few days later, some 400 fighters met at Ruhuruini Memorial Hall where we amused ourselves by songs, and hearing reports of missions. Our prayers started at a quarter to midnight inside the hall. The prayers were opened by Wang'ombe Ruga and said by two leaders, two *itungati*, two girl fighters and was dedicated by Kimathi.

Leaders of the various missions reported their journeys and those who were absent, we heard their stories from verbal messages by other people. I was the first to report on my journey, then Ndiritu Thuita reported about their tours in the Mburu Ngebo Army companies and praised them for their activities. He said that most of the Mburu Ngebo Army lived on settlers' livestock or wheat and other crops growns by the settlers and their employees. He said that some sections situated in Wanjohi Valley, Kipipiri Hill and the Moorland lived entirely on trapping and collecting honey.

We learned that Ruguni and two of his men were shot dead while crossing Nyeri-Thomson's Falls road and two others were captured by the enemy. Thus our failure to reach the Northern Frontier District Turkana and Suk.

Gen. Omera, a member of Kenya Parliament, had been badly injured in the right arm and captured by the enemy. He was known to be cooperating with Kenya Police Reserve at their H.Q. at Mweiga, where he was still receiving treatment after his hand had been completely cut off in hospital.

Macaria Kimemia had not returned but reports said that he was doing well in Murang'a. Kimathi read a letter written by Wanjeru while at Elburgon saying that his mission was forced to return as it had been very difficult for them to find any supporters who could lead them to the Nandi Reserve.

Major Kahiga, who was sent to Kiambu, was reported killed on his way back to Kiambu from Nairobi. His assistant, Gitekoba, had survived and was said to be in Nyandarua guiding some 90 Kiambu fighters to meet us.

I also learned that Kenya Levellation Army companies had entered Ruthaithi after the capture of their leaders, Gens. Hika Hika, Gaita Mbomu, Ngoma Kaigo and Montgomery. I decided to visit their sections and collect some data. When we dispersed the following day, I went to Ruthaithi and found some peculiarities in those sections. More than half of the fighters were girls; they acted according to the witchdoctors' will; a boy eleven years old had been made a general by their witchdoctors and they all obeyed him. The ways of prayers had changed; they started praying facing Mt. Kenya and then [turned toward] Mt. Nyandarua and finished their prayers facing the former. They did not want to eat or live with a person who had not been cleansed by their medicine man. They alleged that such a person would bring great calamity to their *mbuci*.

For a week I remained in Jeriko's *mbuci* at night and worked on these sections during the day. These Kenya Levellation sections refused to give me some *safari* food when I wanted to leave their camp, though they had promised me *safari* food, and while they had plenty of meat. When I arrived at their camp, the eleven year old camp leader told me that they had not held their morning prayers yet and that to touch food before would bring calamity to the camp.

I left their camp at 7 a.m. with three *itungati* and had gone hardly half a mile from their camp by the time their enemies opened fire. We sat down and astonishingly listened to the guns' echoes. We were afraid that they might be taken by surprise by the enemy for they did not keep any guards and the fact that we had left many of them still asleep.

We had only five maize cobs for our journey. At midday we came to a place where Lincolns had dropped bombs, killing two big bushbucks. We were very glad and thanked God for the gift. We slew the animals and each carried a heavy load of meat.

On my arrival at Chieni *mbuci*, I learned that Kimathi had gone to Mwathe (in the Moorlands) accompanied by two Kiambu leaders, a Kiambu elder and a dozen of their *itungati* who had been guided by Gitekoba. I also learned from Nyaga that more than 80 Kiambu fighters were in Gikuyu Iregi Army and that they would meet Kimathi at Mwathe. Some *itungati* had been sent to guide them to Mwathe. Kimathi had sent me a message asking me to go and meet the Kenya Inoro (Kiambu) leaders but I had not received the message.

On arrival at Mwathe, Kimathi introduced me to Joseph Kibe Kimani and Gathumbi and another leader of Kiambu fighters. They told me that they had received our message from Major Kahiga and Gitekoba and that Waruingi had received our former

message and had started fighting as early as January, but many of
their fighters had moved to Melili in Narok and were fighting under
Ole Kisio. They confirmed all that we had learned about Kiambu.

In a couple of days 88 Kiambu *itungati* arrived. Kimathi and
I gave lectures to the Kiambu fighters on our army registration—
telling them of the Kenya Inoro Army under which they were able
to register, various records, Kenya Parliament, rules and regulations, fighting tactics, food and supplies, camp life, etc. Due to
shortage of food supply in Nguthiru (Moorlands), we returned to
Chania and Nyaga's *mbuci*.

On arrival, I wrote letters to all nearby leaders inviting them to
come and meet the Kenya Inoro Army fighters. After their arrival,
they encouraged the new fighters in their speeches. We distributed
the Kenya Inoro Army fighters in IDA 1 companies 1, 2, and 3 and
told them that they had to learn for a month or two so that when
they returned to Kiambu they would have some experiences of the
life in the forest and be better equipped in how to handle their
own affairs. Meanwhile their leaders helped to send messages to
Kiambu fighters in Longonot, Naivasha and Suswa Hill. Most of
the time in August I stayed with the Kenya Inoro Army leaders
copying in their exercise books examples of the various kinds of
records required to be kept and instructing on rules and regulations, camp managements, Kenya Young Stars Association, Kenyalekalo Memorial Clubs, ceremonies, etc.

By the end of August, I went to Ruthaithi in Gathee's *mbuci*.
On my second day, I was awakened at 6 a.m. by gun blustering
about two miles away. Binihalis told me that Kenya Levellation
Army camps were being raided by the enemy. We quickly packed
and hid our luggage and kept sentries in all directions. Half an
hour later, a few fighters from the attacked camps arrived. They
were all badly scratched by thorny shrubs, looked very frightened
and breathed rapidly. Three of them were in pyjamas. They told
us they had been surprisingly attacked when they were all asleep
and could neither fight nor had they any chance of collecting their
belongings. They said that they must have lost most of their
property and even lives.

The following day I received news that seven of our fighters
had been killed in that raid and four others injured, and a good
number were still missing but were hoped to be in other camps. On
the third day all the fighters rejoined and resolved that there were

no more casualties but in the long run the enemy captured 19 guns, including ten homemade, clothings, blankets and camp utensils.

Informers at Mweiga told us that Major Owen Jeoffreys of the Kenya Regiment had led the raid that destroyed our fighters in the previous week. I asked Gathee to send scouts to Jeoffreys home. When the scouts returned they told us that Jeoffreys lived at Mweiga H.Q. and that sometimes he slept at his mother's house on a farm not far from his own farm. They told us that he had removed all his livestock from his farm, which was about five miles from the forest border, and that his house was being taken care of by two men and a boy about sixteen years old who were good supporters and shared their flour to our fighters. He always visited his house in the morning and evening, leaving between 6 and 6 :30 p.m. to join his comrades in their camp.

Major Gathee and I planned to raid Major Jeoffreys' home between 6 and 7 in the evening in an attempt to revenge for our fighters' property loss. We left the camp at 4 p.m. with 28 *itungati*, armed with a dozen homemade guns and six manufactured ones, plus Binihalis and myself. We crossed the forest border at 5 p.m. At 6 p.m. we were about half a mile from his home which looked very near as the crow flies. As we started descending the slope of a stream whose far slopes were his home we saw his car leaving the home.

We crossed the river quickly, climbing its slope and arriving at his house at 6 :45 p.m. His house servants welcomed us with *njima* and skimmed milk. After eating, Binihalis ordered the three house servants to have their hands tied with ropes. The head cook was asked to give all the keys of the home. Still tied, he led us into every room while the two sat down outside heavily guarded. We ransacked the house and took all his clothes, army uniforms, bedding, radio, hand sewing machine, new camera, medicine, tinned food, utensils, etc. In the sitting room I found one *gitungati* busy starting to tear books he had taken from his big library and I warned him and others not to spoil anything that we couldn't make use of but to take everything that we could use.

In the store we found two bags of maize flour and some other empty bags. We searched for guns and ammunition but didn't find any, instead finding two sets of compasses. I carried the pocket compass and left the big one which was floating in spirits.

When all was over, and our luggage well packed, Binihalis asked the servants to choose joining us or remaining there and serve their master. The head cook said that if they were seen the following day by their master, they would be called Mau Mau number one and it would be difficult for them to escape death.

I asked the head cook, 'Why haven't you already become *Mau Mau* number one, since the emergency was declared almost two years ago?'

'Because the European doesn't know that I help the fighters,' he replied.

"How do you help the fighters?' I demanded.

'I give them food and buy shop goods for them whenever they give me money or whenever I am sent by the village leader to buy some goods for the fighters.'

'And how do you help your master?' I requested him.

'I only help him in cooking his food and keeping his house,' he replied.

'You! Do you wear the *kanzu*, the woman's frock when cooking for his wife?' I asked.

'Yes, I do,' he admitted.

I angrily slapped him on the face. 'You woman!' I shouted. 'Your master calls you "Boy" and you keep comforting the European and giving them much hope for staying here! You really help the Europeans more than you help our fighters and claim credit on both sides. Give them good spankings!'

The angry *itungati* beat and kicked them for less than a minute.

'O.K. Stop!' I commanded.

'I am not a cook, I'm a driver,' said the other, 'but I have helped the fighters very much.'

'Shut up!' shouted an angry *gitungati*. 'It may be you are the one who drives the enemy when they come up in the forest or whenever they go to attack our fighters in other areas.'

'Have you taken the Second Oath?' enquired Binihalis.

'Yes, we have!' answered the head cook.

'And why haven't you obeyed it?' asked Binihalis.

'We obey,' said the head cook, 'and we have never betrayed any of your fighters. Some of you have visited here several times and we have never mistreated you. King'ora Mutungi is the only leader who knows that we are trustworthy people.'

'Your fighters were betrayed by a laborer who lives in Hutchinson's farm,' said the young boy.

"All right, good boy!' I said. 'You will tell us more when we get to the *mbuci*. Give them the heavy loads to carry. If any tries to escape just shoot him. Don't think that you are enemies. No indeed, we know well that you are our great sympathizers, but you are also European supporters.'

'*Muirigo!* Show us the way,' said Binihalis.

I sent one *gitungati* to call the sentries who were guarding the road coming to the house. Meanwhile Binihalis and I entered the store, poured paraffin on the plant that supplied light to the house. When all the sentries arrived, Binihalis lit the empty bags that we had poured paraffin on and we followed our people toward the forest. As we started climbing the far slope of the stream, the grass-thatched store blazed, casting light on us which showed us the way.

After crossing the forest border, we encamped some 400 yards inside. We opened tinned foodstuffs, cooked *njima* and enjoyed radio news. The three men repented and reported all the traitors and informers in Mweiga area.

The following day we set off very early in the morning and tried to hide our track as much as possible. We went far away from our camp, first passing it and then coming to the camp from the interior of the forest.

After our arrival in the camp, we selected the best army uniform and preserved it for Kimathi along with the camera. Gathee, the camp leader took the second best, Binihalis and I took khaki uniforms. All the other clothing were distributed to all *itungati*. The unshared camp property was handed over to the storekeeper for safe keeping.

When night came, I turned on the radio and listened to the news. There were many reports of Government forces colliding with our fighters. The worst news I gathered was the Government's plan for digging a deep trench all around the Nyandarua and Kirinyaga forests that would prevent the fighters from entering the reserve.

The following day, I wrote a letter to Major Owen Jeoffreys :

Dear Jeoffreys,

I visited your home on the previous night and found that you were absent. I had come for the 19 guns, clothing and utensils you took away from our fighters at Ruthaithi last week. Though I did not get the guns, I managed to get a radio, sewing machine, camera, utensils, clothings, food and medicine.

Your servants are now our active fighters. What I have done is just to make you feel what I and my colleagues felt last week for your actions. Your unfriendly action resulted in a revenge. I wonder how much you expect to live in Kenya while you spend most of your time and energy in destroying the Kenya Africans and creating enmity with us.

If I had revenged as I had been ordered by Kimathi, I would have put your living house on fire, but I spared it in order to prove to you that we are not so destructive as you might think. In fact, you must have seen that I stopped one warrior from tearing your books. All we want is freedom to form an African Government which will ban all discriminatory bars and extend individual freedom in movement, press and speech, give better pay and conditions to the workmen and most important eliminate European's selfishness and pride. We do not hate the white man's color, but we cannot tolerate seeing a foreign settler with 50,000 acres of land, most of which only the wild game enjoy, while thousands of Africans are starving of hunger in their own country. Nor can we accept the white man to remain as a master and the African as a servant.

Your only alternative is either cooperate with the Africans as equal human beings by creating friendship and good relationship which your bombs and guns will never achieve—for they only increase enmity, or quit Kenya and leave the African to manage his own affairs. I intend to make it clear to you through this letter that the more you fight the Africans, the more you endanger your future in Kenya. You cannot kill ideas by killing people. Since the declaration of emergency almost two years ago you have killed thousands of people, but you have neither killed the idea nor won the battle. Our battle is really between right and might. The six million Africans standing for right will definitely beat sixty thousand Europeans standing for the might, irrespective of your army strength. I am afraid that your Government had so many clever and wise men that are all blind to see the simple facts I have written you.

Your New Kenyan
Brig. Gen. Karari Njama
Chief Secretary, Kenya Parliament
September 1954

I addressed the letter and affixed the postage stamp and gave it to Kenya Levellation Army fighters who promised to post it the following day at Nyeri Station.

The following day I set off to meet Kimathi at Chania. My escorts carried Kimathi's uniform and camera—with no film— which I presented to him on arrival, reporting my activities. Kimathi told me that some more Kenya Inoro Army had come with six Masai (half-breed Masai-Kikuyu) from Melili Forest (Narok) bringing him a Masai sword and spear, being a gift from the Masai fighters' general, Ole Kisio. Kimathi ordered his spear be brought so that I could see it; his sword was still hanging on his left shoulder. He handed me the gifts which were very much decorated with beads and colors. I looked admiringly at them and told him it was a great honor from the Masai tribe and that many other gifts would come from all other tribes if they had a chance to communicate with us. The world had learned that Kimathi was the leader of the revolution, and it was bad for any other leader to compete for the leadership.

Kimathi introduced me to the six Masai, including their leader, Gen. Kibati, who told me that he was leading some 500 Kiambu fighters, formerly Rift Valley dwellers, in the Opuru Forest. He told me that Ole Kisio and Ole Ngapien were leading over 800 Masai fighters in Melili Forest. He said that he met 400 other Kiambu fighters in Longonot on his way to Nyandarua.

After talking with Kimathi, we decided to hold an extraordinary general meeting before the annual general meeting. The meeting was to be held at Mihuro in November 24-25. We arranged that all Kiambu fighters could return to Kiambu in order to mobilize and organize other fighters in their area. We believed that there was sufficient time for the Masai fighters to go and return to the general meeting. We informed the Masai fighters that they were registered in the Gikuyu and Mumbi Trinity Army. We asked them to send in the names of their fighters properly registered according to the patterns I gave them for every record to be kept. We wrote letters to leaders in Melili, thanked Ole Kisio and his army for the gifts and invited all the leaders to attend a general meeting which would prepare the annual general election for the Kenya Parliament Members and extend our movement to other Kenya tribes.

So we left Chania with Kenya Inoro Army fighters and parted

with them at Nguthiru [Moorlands]. Kimathi and I were to visit the Mburu Ngebo Army in the North Kinangop—Kipipiri, Wanjohi Valley and Subuk Plateau. We crossed the Nyandarua ridge a few miles west of its peak and soon came to a big tract of rocks and caves and scattered grass and shrub. Here we sat down on the rocks facing the afternoon sun trying to capture its warmth at 12,000 feet above the sea level. Though the weather was very bright, it was still cold and wet on the grass while solid rocks radiated some little heat.

Here was the best place I had ever visited for a geologist to study how the weathering process broke the hard solid rock into soil. The heavy rain water runs over the impenetrable rocks just on the old glaciers trails. The heat and cold, implementing expansion and contraction, have created many cracks in which mosses and lichens grow and slowly continue to wear away the rocks. The oxygen combined with water in basins or pot-like hollows causing rust has eaten away the rocks. The heavy water dropping on rocks 20-30 feet below making cavities and general decay process can be seen in layers of rocks where water has made a deep gully. One could see different type of rocks here and there.

While I was interested in the rocks, some of my comrades were interested in looking at the Europeans' farms with their large fields of green wheat and barley. Being busy in mind, we were approached by three other fighters whom we saw only a hundred yards from us. We recognized them to be our fighters and on the arrival we found that they were Ngara's *itungati* who had gone round searching for honey in caves and rock cavities. They showed us where their camp was situated far below in small shrubs. Observing the area with our binoculars, we saw the people. They had not found any honey but they carried fat and well-roasted meat which they gave us.

While we were eating they told us that many IDA 2 and 3 companies and their sections encamped in that area, including Stanley Mathenge, whose camp was another one and a half days' walk according to their estimation. Kimathi asked them whether they knew where any of the Murang'a fighters' camps were situated. They told us that they had parted with Gati's *itungati* a few hours ago who lived in a big cave, pointing to the southwest. They told us that Gati's *mbuci* was in touch with many others living in Kipipiri and Wanjohi Valley. Kimathi asked them whether they could lead us to Gati's camp. They agreed, suggesting the journey for the following day, giving an excuse that the *mbuci* was far away.

We descended slowly passing through grass, small bushes and into *lilishwa* bushes with scattered cedar and *pondo* trees. We finally arrived at Ngara's *mbuci* in the evening. There were no huts. They slept in tents or under the trees. On our arrival we were welcomed by Ngara and his *itungati*. After prayers, Kimathi and I spoke to the fighters. He told them all about the Kiambu and Masai fighters, the Kenya Parliament and its works, etc. I told them of the mission I had led and how I had missed them and then told them about the other missions.

That night we were served with roasted meat for dinner and broth. During our talks Ngara thanked me for my suggestion of taking his *itungati* to Rift Valley. He told me that though it was difficult for his *itungati* to get clothes there (they were all as dirty as garage men), he had found plenty of food and had restored his management and he could see a great difference between his camp and a *komerera mbuci*—though his *itungati* preferred to store personal rations in their kitbags which could last them at least five days if they were dispersed by the enemy.

We informed Ngara of the General Meeting to be held at Mihuro on 24th-25th November and asked him to keep it a secret from his fighters until the meeting was over. We warned him how bad it would be for our warriors if the Government knew when and where a meeting was to be held.

The following day we set off towards Gati's camp accompanied by Ngara. Walking on rocks and little grass we saw four *itungati* who wore bushbucks' skins only a few yards from us. The skin's color could not be easily differentiated from the background of rocks and stones on which they lay. After greetings, we sat on their cave and we did not know where their cave was until they told us.

As they were telling us about their cave and how we could meet other fighters, Gati and two other fighters arrived carrying two deers' meat. After exchanging greetings with Gati and his *itungati*, we entered the cave. It was big enough to accommodate more than fifty people and was situated among rocks and little grass. Inside the cave was a heap of bones of the animals they had trapped. They all wore animal skins and seemed to be professional trappers. Gati and twenty-one other *itungati* lived entirely on trapping and collecting honey. He gave us the names of the leaders in Kipipiri

Mt. and Wanjohi Valley. Kimathi wrote letters to seven of them asking them to meet us at Gati's cave on the third day.

While some *itungati* were cooking some meat for us, Gati told us of another cave about six miles away, pointing to the south. He said that it was big enough to accommodate a hundred persons but it had been surrounded at night by the enemy the week before who opened fire to sixty of our fighters who lived in the cave. Though none of these fighters knew the exact loss we had suffered in that cave, they knew that there were deaths, casualties and captives. Kimathi expressed his feelings, objecting to living in a cave.

Gati told us of a witchdoctor-prophet who lived in Kipipiri Mt. and claimed that Ngai used to speak to him at night in a dream revealing the future and all that he wanted the fighters to do. He said that one day he had called a big meeting on top of the hill and had conducted prayers and ceremony in which God sent him a book written in all the world's languages and writings [i.e., scripts] and which tells the future of our country.

Kimathi, though sceptical of the story, did not argue or comment on it but he said that he would be glad to meet Muraya and listen to his prophesy. After eating the boiled meat, we returned to Ngara's *mbuci*, arriving in the evening. On the way Kimathi told us that such false witchdoctors, who might mislead our fighters and yet were in a position of gaining confidence among our fighters, should be killed.

The following day Kimathi, Ngara and I visited Gicuki Wacira's camp. We met his *itungati* slaughtering cattle which they had raided jointly with Thiong'o's and Mamwamba's fighters. Kimathi, being suspicious that the enemy might follow their cattle enquired about sentries. He thought it was unsafe to stay in the camp and told the leaders that he would rather spend the day out of the camp in a private place.

We spent the day in the bush and in the evening we returned to the camp and talked to all *itungati* of the three *mbuci*, after which we enjoyed dinner of the fresh beef. We informed the leaders of the General Meeting.

The following day we headed for Gati's cave with Thiong'o and Gicuki joining us. We passed near Ngara's and arrived at Gati's cave at one in the afternoon. We found four of the seven leaders that Kimathi had written awaiting us. Three were unknown to me. I knew Gakure Karuri before, a prominent leader in the

Gikuyu Iregi Army. After a short talk with them, Kimathi told me
that Gakure would guide him to tour the Gikuyu Iregi Army
sections and that I should visit Mburu Ngebo Army sections and
try to bring Stanley Mathenge to the meeting. He remarked that
I should be at Mihuro Memorial Hall working in my office at least
a week before the meeting in order to see that my record books
were up to date and prepare a report on the Kenya Parliament
since it was elected.

I pointed out that I wanted to see the 100-person cave before
I lost the chance. Gakure said that he would lead us there and
tour in a nearby *mbuci*. Ngara decided to return and we started
our journey.

We arrived at the empty cave at four in the afternoon. The front
face of the cave had many grenade and bullet marks. A flock of
hyenas had visited and cleaned the cave, leaving some old bones
to be seen here and there. We entered the cave and, finding it
dark, became afraid of enemy mines and quickly walked out without a thorough investigation. We sat out on the cave which was
covered by grass on top and discussed about it. The old bones and
broken pots proved that the cave had been used by Dorobo and
probably by Gumban trappers and some old men said that Dorobo
were known to have lived in those caves at the beginning of the
twentieth century. That made me think of the myth told by the
Gikuyu people that the Gumba were known to disappear underground to their homes and reappear again some hundred yards
away, and finally they disappeared in those holes altogether; it
made me think that those caves were the holes referred to by the
myth. The disappearance of the Gumba, which is misrepresented
by the legend, was that Gikuyu people intermarried with the
Gumba and their offsprings were known as Dorobo or *Athi* in
Kikuyu (trappers or hunters). The Dorobo who lived far below the
cave in Kipipiri area were evicted by the colonial Government together with the Masai and moved to the Northern Province in
Mokogondu north of Nanyuki. A few Dorobo who had escaped
eviction because of living in the forests started seeking employment
from the Kenya settlers as herdsmen after the First World War.

Before leaving the cave we were told that two miles below that
cave was a steep 150 foot cliff on whose edge grows cedar trees.
In one of those trees were bees, living 120 feet high. A man who
had tried to get that honey many years ago, maybe a Dorodo fell

and stuck on the tree and remains of his bones were still hanging on the tree a hundred feet high.

None of the leaders could tell us the loss our fighters had suffered in that cave. It was getting late and we had not reached the *mbuci* we were going to. We left the cave and arrived where we were going at six o'clock. We found that the *mbuci* had been deserted. Kimathi objected to returning to Gati's cave. One of the leaders said that one of his trapping sections was living at Kiarucibi, right in the middle of Nyandarua and suggested that we'd better go there instead of searching a place for a night's camp.

At sunset we were in the middle of the Nyandarua plateau passing round a little lake which was clear and looked like water in a rock basin. Beside it were many different kinds of animals feeding on the high grass in large herds. Looking around, the nearest tree would be some three miles away. If any of the animals challenged us, there was no chance of running away from it, instead we would have to charge. Nevertheless, all the animals stood gazing at us, including the rhinos, while zebras, buffaloes and their families ran away. Among the flocks we saw two domestic donkeys which had joined the zebras and a cow that had joined a buffalo herd; they behaved as the wild animals did.

The darkness came before we got to the *mbuci* and the cold increased so that many of us started shivering. When we approached the camp we could smell their fire and hear our fighters speak. One of the Kipipiri leaders signalled by whistling and, at the return of his signals, he was asked to introduce himself. We then entered the camp. It had small huts and no kitchen. The eighteen *itungati*, happily and surprised, welcomed us. The visitors, eight leaders and 33 *itungati* could not be accommodated in the three small huts. It was night and we could neither build huts nor collect firewood. The tents we had were insufficient for our *itungati*. We still had plenty of fresh beef ready roasted. As we were eating and before we had gained sufficient warmth, all the wood in the camp got finished. I went in my tent and lay myself on the cold grass, wrapping in a blanket. It was a cold night.

The following morning was very cloudy and I forecasted possible rains. We parted with Kimathi. Thiong'o, Wacira and I made our way along the mid-ridge track toward the north. By midday we were at the mountain peak and hailstones were pouring on us. This was accompanied by a strong cold wind. A few minutes later, we

were as wet as fish in a river and as cold as a toad, and the hailstones formed an ice-sheet that covered the Moorlands.

We continued our journey on the open grasslands in spite of
those difficulties and two hours later we crossed the Nderagwa-
Deighton Downs jeep track which [now] brings visitors to the top
of the mountain. Here we learned that only little rain had fallen.
The rain decreased as we approached the forest.

We arrived in Thiong'o's *mbuci* at five in the evening. His
itungati were very happy to see us again after spending two days
and a night away. I cried for fire for I felt that my right arm and
leg were completely numb. In fact, it took me three days to regain
my strength on these limbs and aching pains continued in the
interior of my bones for almost a fortnight. Here I stayed during
the last week of September and twice corresponded with Stanley
Mathenge and arranged to go see him.

On October 1st I left for Njau Kiore's *mbuci* where I found
Stanley Mathenge who welcomed me. We first talked about *safaris*
and general events that had happened since we parted. We discussed as I told him about the formation of the Kenya Parliament,
China's negotiation talks, the election of local committees in
Othaya, the Kiambu fighters, the Masai fighters, the missions we
had sent to our fighters and other tribes, the letters we had sent
and received from abroad, the Kenya Parliament management, the
General Meeting to be held November 11th and the annual general
election for the Kenya Parliament membership.

I explained to him how Othaya leaders had confidence in him
and how we wanted him to rise and maintain his leadership position. I told him that Ituma Ndemi Trinity Council of which he
was the Chairman had failed to meet even once for a period of
sixteen months since it was elected. He claimed that the Council's
General Secretary, Dedan Kimathi, should also share the blame.

I agreed, but mentioned that Kimathi, as an individual, had
done a lot of work for Ituma's *itungati* and had visited nearly all
itungati in Nyandarua and had sent his management to other
fighters who had recognized him as the head of the revolution. I
told him that as head of Ituma, he had failed to visit IDA 1 since
they entered the forest, though he had only met a few of them by
chance at Kariaini H.Q.

He admitted his failures and told me that he had left it because
it was Kimathi's home and he believed that Kimathi had the right

to organize it and that Kimathi would be possibly jealous on seeing someone else organizing his home.

I told him that suspicion had misled him and that he wrongly thought that he could win people by being quiet and inactive while Kimathi believed in the contrary. I told him that activities proved abilities. I informed him that leaders and *itungati* wanted to see him in the general meeting. I warned him that his failure to attend the two proposed general meetings would lead to Ituma's general election which would cast him off his chair and probably he would have no chances of rising to that level again.

I asked him why he had failed to cooperate with Kimathi for the last fifteen months. In his reply he referred to the bullet in the fire incident and confirmed that he believed that any competition between him and Kimathi might lead to great hatred and possibly to the death of one of them.

I told him that their division was our greatest weakness and might help the enemy to defeat us. I confirmed to him that Kimathi realized the danger of their division and was all the time willing to discuss their differences and get it settled once and for all and in a brotherly way strengthen the unity of our team.

I told him that I had tried all I could to investigate about the bullet incident from the *itungati* who were in the camp the night of the incident. The truth was that the bullet was put inside bamboo while collecting firewood by Murang'a *itungati* intending only to frighten and astonish the leaders. Generally the bamboos store water in their hollow cavities between the nodes. When the water is heated, it boils and when steam tries to escape it always explodes like a bullet. You must have experienced this several times. The *itungati* thought it would never be discovered and the frightened leaders would only conclude that it was a very strong bamboo explosion. The *itungati* did not mean to harm anyone; to them it was just fun. But the leaders took the matter so seriously that the *itungati* had to hide the truth for their safety.

'In fact,' I said, 'it is still a fun to the *itungati*, for they laugh at your hatred and suspicions based on the bullet incident when neither you nor Kimathi was connected to it—to them, you are both fools.'

He said that I was so frank and helpful to him that I cleared away all his doubts. He expressed how he felt very sorry for blaming Kimathi and building a strong suspicion on a false assumption.

Before leaving him, he promised me that he would attend the Mihuro General Meeting.

I gave a speech to 128 *itungati* and leaders in the *mbuci* where Mathenge lived. He praised me and the Kenya Parliament work but complained that I had helped other divisions more than I had helped my own division. He criticized me that I had made North Tetu my H.Q. or home and toured my own division as a visitor. He praised the old days when I lived with him at Kariaini and welcomed me to live with them, saying that I should know that home is the starting point—village, then sub-location, location, division, district, province and then the Kenya Parliament. He said that it was difficult for a person to be elected as a Kenya Parliament member unless he was supported by his home constituency neighbors who would elect him from their region. He stressed that the Kenya Parliament membership should be based on regions.

I tried to tell them that one could become a popular statesman without seeking favor or election from his region. I told them that Kenyatta was not elected by the Kiambu people in order to become the leader of the Kenya African Union. I warned them that to become a statesman was a skill and not a favor as they thought. I quickly learned that they did not agree with my logic as they had been convinced by Stanley Mathenge that '*Kamwene Kambagio ira kari thongo.*' 'Ones own son first no matter his disabilities.' The saying had traditionally originated from *mundo mugos'* practices on [initiation] ceremonies whereby his son had to be the first initiated under all circumstances. The saying, however, has strong ties on self first and then next closest of relative or neighbor. This selfishness prevents one from seeing other people's interest and is a hindrance of national progress.

After spending a week with Mathenge in his *mbuci*, he accompanied me to tour the nearby camps. We first visited Gen. Makanyanga's *mbuci* where we were greatly welcomed. My speech in this camp mostly confirmed what Makanyanga had said before and the *itungati* were fully convinced of our victory and the Kenya Parliament managements. Many of the Makanyanga *itungati* were born and bred in the Rift Valley. They knew the Rift Valley so well that other *mbuci* from the Central Province Reserve depended on their guidance and scouting.

Three days later we visited one of the IDA 2 sections under Kibicho where we were guided by Makanyanga and his *itungati*.

Here we covered our program, moving on to another of Makan-yanga's sections led by Col Githengera, where we were greatly received and fed on very fat mutton from Fletcher's farm—a settler who owned more than 12,000 wool sheep (Merinos).

Most of the camps I had visited had no huts and only a few tents for shelters and many slept under trees in the open. Most of the *itungati* were dressed in oily dirty stinky rags. A few had started making animal skin coats, jumpers, caps and pants. Their hair, which had not been shaved nor combed for more than two years and which was generally smeared with animal oil, had grown long, curling and falling over their forefaces and ears. Many of the fighters had lost their weight and their bright faces had turned to be thin and black.

The general report from the leaders said that there was a general increase in *komereras*, whereby five or ten *itungati* ran away from their leaders in order to set up a camp of their own in the small forests and bushes right inside the settlers' farms. The reasons for this were to escape from both leaders' rules and the forest heavy bombing, lust for leadership in some *itungati*, and lastly to live as near as possible to the food supplies.

After encouraging our fighters, Mathenge and Makanyanga returned to the camps and I continued a day's walk to Kahiu-Itina's *mbuci* at Nderagwa. To my surprise, I found that Kahiu-Itina had greatly changed. He was against Kimathi, claiming that Kimathi had not given the other leaders chances of rising; he lived better than anybody else, ordered everyone to be inspected when entering his camp—thus showing that he did not have confidence in his people. He criticised the Kenya Parliament for being controlled by Kimathi during Wambararia's case and claimed that he had learned that all the uneducated members of the Kenya Parliament were merely stone walls which protected the educated members to carry on their plans and possibly to build on their future. He claimed that education and illiteracy could not work together. He said that all educated people were somehow affiliated to the religion and faith of the missionaries—which were totally against Kikuyu religion and revolution. He claimed that since the educated people had abandoned the revolution, it should then be led by the illiterate people who stand for it. The illiterate are in the majority in the country, he said, and since the educated persons chose to hide during the war, they should continue to hide during peace.

'We must see that our illiterate leaders here, in the reserve and in the future managements hold all the high positions in our Government,' he said. In general, he objected to being led by an educated person, saying that they were more Europeanized; no matter whether they were leaders in the forests, they rejected many of the old customs and tribal tradition which Kahiu-Itina and many others believed we were fighting for as part of our freedom. He claimed that Stanley Mathenge had been ignored by the Kenya Parliament because he was illiterate.

I argued that he was not ignored and that for the last two weeks I had lived with Mathenge and had been able to settle everything with him. He then said that Mathenge was a hypocrite and did not let people know his wishes or feelings. I learned that Kahiu-Itina hated all educated persons for he couldn't rise among them. His desire for power had generated the hatred.

I had weak arguments for defending the educated persons as my attempt would only make him mark me as an opponent. I explained to him the differences between literacy and religion, technical skill and wisdom, and supported him that the revolution had been carried on by the ignorant people who deserved some honor for their bravery and perseverance. I pointed out to him that it would be difficult for the illiterate people to lead the educated persons, as it is for the blind to lead one with eyes. But we could honorably put them in high Government posts knowing that their deputies and advisors are capable persons and that they would act according to their advice. Kahiu-Itina, who did not know the difference between a clerk and a secretary, was very pleased with my comment; he thought that deputy was another name for clerk.

Wishing to change the subject, I told him of the Kiambu leaders and their *itungati* and the six Masai who had brought gifts to Kimathi from Gen. Ole Kisio, and their promise of attending a general meeting to be held at Mihuro on 24 November and which I was going round telling all the leaders.

He told me that he would not attend the meeting as he intended to go to Dorobo (North Nanyuki) and recruit them, the Dorobo, after which he would convene a meeting of all the illiterate leaders and discuss their security and their future positions.

I tried to convince him to attend the meeting but he finally held his decision claiming that eight members of the Kenya Parliament were all from North Tetu Location, even though three of them (including himself) represented the Rift Valley where they were found by the emergancy.

I reminded him that during the election he was the person who defeated the others in votes, and that his failure to attend the meeting would be his failure to represent the *itungati* who elected him.

He replied that the *itungati* who elected him were still living with him and that they knew very well whether he led them well or not. He told me that his *itungati* had confidence in him.

Though I was neither satisfied with his reasons nor his intentions, I couldn't get any more information because he concealed the base of his dissatisfaction and the reasons for convening a meeting. Though I remained sceptical of his motives, I was certain that his section leaders, Ndiritu Thuita and Vindo, both solid members of Kenya Parliament, were not behind him.

Nevertheless, Kahiu-Itina allowed me to speak to the 48 *itungati* which he had—most of his *itungati* being in distant camps under Ndiritu Thuita and Vindo and a few of them had become *komerera* in the settled area. One of the things that I learned was that Kahiu-Itina had dropped most of the leader's privileges and was living almost at the same level with his *itungati* so as to enable him to preach equality in order to gain popularity by criticising the other leaders.

October 20th found me still with Kahiu-Itina. He suggested that the day should be a public holiday and also a prayer day to commemorate Kenyatta's arrest and the declaration of the emergency. I remarked that it was all right to make the day Kenyatta's holiday but the day was absolutely unfit to commemorate the emergency miseries. The end of the emergency would be more important than its beginning. Very little damage was done on that day and even some weeks after, but to commemorate all the emergency miseries the best day would be the end of the emergency. Though we did not resolve anything, we held prayers at midnight in the memory of two years of suffering.

On the 22nd I left Kahiu-Itina heading to Kimbo's at Ngobit in Lower Nderagwa or Deighton Downs. At midday, I and my three *itungati* found ourselves on a table-like level ground on which grew many scattered big trees and green undergrowth grass. Under one of those big trees, we found the remains of a waterbuck carcass. It seemed to have been killed by a leopard or a lion.

To our surprise, a very big lion lay twenty yards in front of us suspiciously looking at us. My frightened *itungati* commenced running away. I shouted to them not to run away. We planned how to deviate the sleeping lion. In the levelled forest which was only clear enough for one to see 100 yards under the trees, it became difficult for us to know which was east or west. I had offered Kimathi the little compass which I had obtained from Major Jeoffreys. We depended on guessing. We continued our journey and at four o'clock in the afternoon we found ourselves again at the lion's stored food. Though we didn't see the lion for a second time, we became very frightened of being lost and being under the mercy of the lion.

Fear drove us quickly from the scene and following our shadow cast by the setting sun we hurried due east. Night came; we were still in that black sea-like area. There was no sign of water anywhere near us. We chose a tree that could shelter us from rain and which we could easily climb if any animal challenged us. We collected a lot of firewood—old logs which would keep our fire burning through the night.

We roasted our meat and after dinner we felt as if we were going to die of thirst. We kept awake till morning and continued our journey as the sun rose and moved facing it as our guide. It was not long before we started climbing a steep hill following an animal path. When we came to the top, we were very glad to see Kirinyaga and many valleys which drain to the river Ngobit. As we descended the hill, we came across an animal path which was used by buffaloes going to *munyu mweru*, white salts, where they enjoyed the natural salts. Kimbo's *mbuci* was situated in this area.

We followed the path passing through grass and bushes, small bamboo bushes and finally in the thicket of bamboo arrived at Kimbo's in the afternoon. Kimbo welcomed me. I told him all about my journey and all that had happened since we parted. Instead of telling me about his *mbuci*, he asked my why I did not call any of the Mburu Ngebo Army members of the Kenya Parliament to hear the case of Wambararia.

I replied that the case was a matter of great urgency, that we could not wait for them. I added that though the eight members were sufficient to form a quorum, the case was not heard by the Kenya Parliament members [alone] for there were eight leaders who were invited by Kimathi to hear the case.

'That case made us think that Kenya Parliament was Kimathi's wall and power for achieving his ends,' said Kimbo.

I suggested to him that he should raise the matter to the Kenya Parliament members when they met at Mihuro. I hoped that he would receive supporters as there was a lot of complaints about the case.

He doubted of attending the meeting, but I told him of all the leaders whom I knew that had promised to come, including Mathenge. I mentioned that only Kahiu-Itina was not attending the meeting, partly because he shared his feelings and partly because he intended to leave Nyandarua forest.

Kimbo told me that he, Kahiu-Itina and a few others had talked and agreed to form a new association which would be exclusively organized by the illiterate leaders. I tried to persuade him to criticise the Parliament and to better it by any amendments within it. He told me that it was difficult for anyone to appeal Wambararia's case or to amend the Kenya Parliament under Kimathi without creating enmity.

I warned him that even forming another association would also create enmity. He replied that an enemy within its party had no defense but an enemy from another party would be defended by his party.

I asked him what were the real causes of forming another party, which would only divide our fighters, so that I could raise the matter to the Kenya Parliament for amendment. He told me that the reason was that Kimathi had ignored Stanley Mathenge the elected leader because he was illiterate and instead he was promoting the 'Yes, yes, men' who disassociated themselves with the revolution when it became red-hot, being afraid of death—while illiterate leaders were afraid of the same fate.

I told him that Kimathi had not ignored Mathenge, in fact he loved him and always tried to pull the reluctant Mathenge. I told him it was only three weeks ago since Mathenge promised me to attend the meeting so that they could settle their differences once for all. I told him that I would be their conciliator and I wished he could be at the meeting to witness for himself.

He told me that he would write Mathenge asking him whether he had promised to attend the meeting; if Mathenge was attending he would attend, and he would never attend any other meeting which would not be attended by Mathenge. He said that Mburu

Ngebo Army people were the owners of Rift Valley and that they wouldn't like to see a person from the Central Province becoming their master who would divide unto them their lands. They preferred to have a Rift Valley born and bred leader at the top.

After a week with Kimbo, I left his *mbuci* on the 30th October with his guides toward Ndungu's, whose camp was at Ruhotie stream. On our way we stopped twice to collect honey from beehives. At 4 p.m. we arrived at Ndungu's deserted camp. The camp seemed to have been raided by the enemy. We vainly continued searching their new camp till sunset.

We encamped for the night in one of the Amboni (Honi) River tributaries. The following day we continued our search up to midday. It became certain that we could not find their *mbuci*. Kimbo's *itungati* decided to return. I decided to continue my journey to Ruthaithi which I thought to be the nearest possible area for me to find other fighters. At sunset the four of us encamped at Thara stream that drains in Munigato stream.

The following day, November 1st, we continued our search for any camp down the stream. Luckily we found Major Gathee's *mbuci* at midday. Gathee and Binihalis were glad to meet me again. I told them all that had happened since we parted. Gathee told me that his *mbuci* was attacked at 9 p.m. by enemies who killed five of his *itungati*, captured two, injured four, and captured four manufactured guns and three homemade guns. The last two manufactured guns disappeared with four other *itungati* in the settled area about a week before. Whether the *itungati* had fallen into Government's hands or had become *komereras* was unknown.

'The enemy had seen us during the day,' said Gathee, 'and then hid themselves. As we made fires and started cooking, they approached our camp in the dark but they had the benefit of seeing us with lights of our fires. We finished cooking and dishing out food but when we started eating, the enemies opened fire at very close range, aiming at the persons who carried guns. We have lost eleven fighters since you left us and four others are in hospital.'

'Now they would be healed,' said Binihalis. 'I know that you have a good healing hand. We have medicine but we have run short of food. We have gone three days since we cut our rations in half. We are using a tea cup to measure daily ration, half of which is wild vegetables and some maize grains. Yesterday morning our *itungati* arrived from the reserve gardens with no food at all.

They said that beans were the only crops in the gardens, which would be ready in two weeks time.'

I told them that some of the *mbuci* I had visited lived on trapping, if they would go to Ruthaithi where the animals are so abundant they would have been happy. 'I know you do not have trapping equipment; you are inexperienced and you could not rely on traps. You should attempt to steal settlers' cattle as far as 20 miles inside the settled area where they wouldn't expect our fighters to go.'

Gathee remarked that the *itungati* had become scared for being poorly armed. Binihalis said that he would lead them to steal cattle but he would first consult the nearby *mbuci* so that they can jointly raid cattle with the help of their guns.

Three days later, Binihalis hadn't succeeded in convincing other *mbuci* to join him in a cattle raid. In spite of searching honey, wild vegetables and trapping small animals and birds, hunger was still increasing daily. I complained for the patients. Without proper feeding, it would be difficult for the patients to recover. Food was the basic medicine; a healthy body would be able to resist diseases and recover easily from wounds.

Binihalis led a group of eleven *itungati* to the settled area armed with only four homemade guns and another officer led ten *itungati* to the reserve gardens armed with only three homemade guns. The hospital had just one homemade gun to defend. In the camp there was only one fighter with a homemade gun to guard Major Gathee, four girl fighters and myself.

That night we had a few bites of wild vegetables, *hatha*. At about 9 p.m. thunderous heavy rain fell—the stormy rainy season had started and we only prayed that rain would be able to chase away our enemies from their ambushes so that our fighters may bring us food the following day.

At eight in the morning the reserve group arrived, each carrying a heavy burden of raw beans. Some had a few bananas, cucumbers, potatoes and arrow roots. They told us that they'd made fire and roasted bananas and potatoes for their dinner. They had nothing ready for us to eat. All the food they had could last the camp for only two days. The girls hid the food that had been brought and we all went to warm ourselves, sending the only rested *gitungati* left in the camp to guard the track of the reserve group.

At 10 a.m. Binihalis entered the camp with 27 fat calves, between

one and two and a half years old. Gathee and I quickly killed the
calves. The *itungati* had killed one calf for their dinner the night
before. They gave us the roasted meat to help ourselves. The
itungati who had come from *safari* were still wet, tired and sleepy.
I asked Gathee to post sentries to guard the calves' track lest the
enemies followed it; helped by the same rain that had helped our
fighters, it would be easy for them to see the foot marks in the
mud. He nominated two *itungati* to keep sentry. As I looked at
them, I became fully convinced that they were going to sleep in
the track which enemies had to follow. Their lives as well as ours
were still in danger. I asked them to return and help the others to
slay calves if they could. I said that I would keep the sentry and
asked for the best rifles. Binihalis offered me his gun with only two
bullets, .44 and .375; both could fit in the homemade gun which
was a pattern of the manufactured guns. He warned me that his
gun was loaded, as he had loaded it the night before. He showed
me a patch of grass on the other side of the Thara stream, saying
that I could see the enemy coming far from there.

After descending half the slope, I saw a good place for an
ambush. I sat down and continued to eat meat and watching the
far side of the slope in the grassland area. At midday, mist increased so that I could only see 50 yards. The weather changed
from warm to cold and I changed my position. I thought that I
was very near the camp and so I walked down to the stream. The
calves had crossed the stream at a buffaloes' crossing and drinking
path. The river bank gave me a very good strategy position. The
area was covered by bamboo mixed with coniferous trees.

At about two in the afternoon, two Kenya Ng'ombe officers
commanding a dozen well-armed African emergency soldiers
arrived at the river. They paused and their chief tracker, who
seemed to be a Samburi, pointed out where the calves had crossed
the river at a point about ten yards wide. His officer refused and
without talking signalled the others to move upstream. About 20
yards further the river had a big bend and a steep wall on my
side after which there was a good crossing point. He pointed where
they were to cross the river three people at a time.

I changed my position and standing less than ten yards from
them, I aimed so that a single bullet could pass through three of
them. I then pulled the trigger but failed to release my bullet. I
quickly tried a second time with failure. I changed the bullet and

by the time I was ready to fire, the first two men had crossed the river and were only seven yards from me and about three yards below me thus making it impossible for me or them to shoot one another. When the second group reached in the middle of the river, I pulled my trigger but it failed to discharge.

The noise made by the flowing water over stones prevented them from hearing the cracks made by my gun. Nevertheless two people on the other bank of the river became very suspicious, as if they had heard me. I ran down-stream some 20 yards away and stood against a big *muna* tree. I put a whistle in my mouth and blew it so that my comrades in the *mbuci* could hear me or the enemy firing.

When the enemy failed to open fire on me, I made off a hundred yards from them, climbing the hill. There, I paused and shouted as hard as I could in English, Swahili and Kikuyu, each time trying to create a different voice. I announced the number of the enemy, where they were, how they were armed and ordered a strong force to be sent to meet them down the stream. I said another group be sent to ambush them on their way returning home.

I became doubtful whether my propaganda had scared the enemy for they did not fire a single shot. I quickly ran to the camp and found that my comrades had gone. I carried a big piece of fatty meat and followed their track. After a short distance I lost their track for they had done their best to hide it. I continued searching them till six in the evening but all in vain. I made my mind to go to the hospital. I found that six persons in the hospital had nothing to eat. They were very glad when they saw me carrying about forty pounds of meat. We all ate to our fill and had a little left for breakfast.

At midday, I and the two *itungati* who attended the patients went to spy whether the enemies had entered the camp. We first went down to the river where I had left them. We found that they did not pass there. I had scared them with my propaganda. We followed their footsteps and became certain that they left the area.

We climbed the hill and entered the *mbuci*. We found our beef was still safe. We hung the meat on the trees and wrote a note saying that I was in the hospital. We carried as much meat as we could and returned to hospital. On our arrival at hospital, we found four *itungati* who had brought meat for the patients from the new

camp. As they were telling us where they were encamped, another
four *itungati* arrived. The latter had gone to spy the old camp and
had seen my note.

I started telling them what had happened during my sentry
time. The useless gun was still laying where I had dropped it the
night before. I picked it up saying that a club was better than it
was. It was still loaded and I pulled the trigger. It thunderously
bursted knocking me down. We all then started checking what had
been wrong with the gun. We resolved that rain water had entered
every part of the gun and had weakened the spring. The *itungati*
condemned the homemade guns as being inefficient but I encouraged them, saying that it might have been that the spring of that
particular gun was weak. Nevertheless, the *itungati* insisted that
many of the homemade guns behaved that way and sometimes
became a danger when exposing to the enemy; but they worked
pretty well during fine weather.

During my two weeks at Ruthaithi, I visited many camps in which
I learned that many *itungati* were no longer willing to serve their
leaders. This teaching, mostly from *komerera* and Kenya Levellation Army, had first been heard of in August in IDA 3/1 where
Joseph Mbaya, one of my location who had come from Nairobi,
was alleged [to be] instructing our *itungati* not to serve their
leaders. He claimed that our fathers had been enslaved by Europeans, carrying their *safari* food, tents and other belongings. He
had mentioned 'MacLoah,' who was well known in the early days
in Nyeri and Fort Hall, saying that he was carried on shoulders
by African servants from one camp to another. Mbaya had compared the leaders with MacLoah, accusing them to *itungati* that
they never went to war, but only sent *itungati* to die; that they
never went out to fetch their own food, [but] were fed with the
best food available at the cost of *itungati* lives. Their tents and
belongings were always carried by *itungati*; they never collected
firewood or made their own fires, yet they were the most famous
fighters. He had told the *itungati* that they were fighting for
leaders' slavery and not for freedom. He told them that the true
liberty was equality of all persons in which one was free from
anyone's rule. He'd cursed all the leaders' privileges and suggested
that *itungati* could socially contribute equally in all their per-
formances.

Mbaya surrendered quickly before I had a chance of meeting him. News reached us that he was cooperating with Kenya Ng'ombe at Naivasha. Some *itungati* who knew him confirmed that he sky-shouted from airplanes appealing to our fighters to surrender. His story made me think that he might have been sent by the Government to convert our *itungati* so that they would abandon their leaders.

Nevertheless, his teachings had caught our *itungati's* hearts, though only those who had heard of it. They started claiming that the best leader was one who led his *itungati* to get food, the one who didn't want any privileges and the one who felt that he was not a master but a sociable and equal person to any *gitungati*. In fact, the whole idea was to cast down the leaders. If the leaders were not to accept the idea, they would then have to strongly and cleverly challenge it in order to avoid being abandoned by the *itungati*.

I tried to prove to Lord Gicambira and his company (a *komer- rera mbuci* which had increased in size to be recognized) that there was no equality of persons on this earth in either height, weight or wisdom, but they claimed that man was the master of this earth and he could make changes to suit his desires. They claimed that we had a rule assuming that all people eat the same amount of food, for we measured our ration equally to all persons, forgetting that there were persons who liked to eat more than the ration we served. I remembered that people who were not well equipped with reasons hated and opposed any argument, they would either conduct their affairs secretly or use force if possible and do their best to get rid of their opposers as their hindrance.

I referred to the ration rule Lord had mentioned and admitted that though we'd all accepted it, it was not fair; but like many others it must have been based on the average or the majority. I warned them that right and equality were measured by might and majority will, which often hid justice and truth. I concluded that even if we adjusted our rules, they would still be imperfect. There was nothing in the world which would satisfy or please everyone.

I learned from King'ora Mutungi that one of Ndungu's sections under Nyahoro had been bombed by Nyagikonyo (Lincolns) and that six *itungati* were completely buried and that later they were unearthed by others; but the most interesting news was that none of them died, though they received small injuries. Another similar case had happened in Chania Valley in Ndiritu Thuita's *mbuci*, where a Lincoln bomber unloaded inside the camp at night while dropping bombs aimlessly. The result was that only two persons were killed without any other casualties. The fact that those powerful bombs did very little damage to our fighters cannot be interpreted that probably the bombs were inefficient, but that good luck was with us and according to our prayers and beliefs, God really defended us from bombing and in fact crashed the bombers and other planes from which we collected pipes and cranes for trapping animals.

On 11th November I experienced a horrible Lincoln bombers practice. It was two in the afternoon and a group of us were lying idly warming ourselves in Jeriko's *mbuci* situated on a gorge at the juncture of Thara and Muringato tributaries about two miles from the reserve. I saw a Lincoln bomber coming from the reserve about two miles away. Its flying line cut right across us. I saw the airplane dropping the first bomb from its big *gikonyo*, then the second and then the third. The bombs didn't fall to the ground instantly, they floated in the air current behind the airplane for some time while the plane drew nearer and nearer. If any of us tried to move it meant to expose ourselves to the pilot and certainly to our ends.

I ordered everyone to lie down and pray until the airplane had passed. Looking at the bombs, I became convinced that we were only under God's mercy, for the bombs were to fall on us. I pressed my chin to the ground and prayed, 'God, save my life so that I will witness to the world how God saved our fighters from the devil's fires; your powers...'

I had not finished my prayers when I heard the 1,000 lb. bomb blowing the air speedily as it was dropping to the ground. The whistling increased to a big wind and then into a storm accompanied by thunderous noise and earthquake almost simultaneously. The noise and storm followed the airplane west of us, while lumps of soil, dust, twigs and leaves fell amidst us. Raising my head, I saw some *itungati* running for better positions. Among them were seven Kenya Levellation Army fighters who shouted goodbye to us swearing never again to enter the forest and wishing to die in the reserve while exchanging gunfire with the enemy rather than to endure the unassailable Lincoln bombers.

I stood up still trembling of fear, wanting to see where the bombs had fallen. Looking around I could see only debris and lumps of soil and broken branches and dust-mist covering over us. I enquired whether there was anyone injured. Jeriko replied, 'everyone is certain of himself only!'

'Lie down!' shouted one *gitungati*. 'The airplane is coming again.'

I quickly ran into small bushes far from any big tree and lay down on my stomach. The airplane noise drew nearer. I turned my head and saw four bombs floating like big eagles under the airplane and a little behind. I pressed my chin to the ground, closed my eyes and ears and prayed God to forgive all my sins: 'God, let thy mighty arms by my armor. You are our General; deliver us from evil and from our enemies slavery! (Poooof! Poooof! Poooof!) God, thy will be done on earth as in heaven...'

Once again my heart came into my mouth and I could pray no more. When I opened my eyes and ears I saw a mist of dust high up in the air which proved to me that the bombs had been dropped on the southern ridge of Muringato stream.

In about three minutes time, the airplane was ready again at its offensive position this time dropping bombs on the Thara stream less than one half mile north. The airplane left after unloading 24 bombs each weighing 1,000 lbs. When Jeriko called all the fighters together, we found that a few had bruises caused by the lumps of soil but none was serious. In addition to that, 13 *itungati* were absent, including the seven Kenya Levellation Army fighters who had wished us goodbye. We concluded that they must have run away from the area and would return in the evening. Some *itungati* were still trembling when I started singing: 'Listen and hear this story, of Nyandarua Hill; so you may realize that God is with us, and will never abandon our cause....'

When we finished singing many of us had gained courage and confidence, but we realized that two fighters who were still trembling were suffering shock and couldn't use their voice. We tried to soothe them but all in vain. They later recovered at dinner time about midnight.

We went round to see where bombs were dropped. The first bombs had been dropped down in the valley near the juncture of the streams about 150 yards east in the grassland, and the second bomb 100 yards west amidst *Thaithi* trees, the next was about

200 yards further west, and so on. The second and third trips of bombing were about half a mile from us.

At night the airplane started bombing the same area at 8 :30–9 :30 p.m., during which time we stayed without fire and were terrorized every now and then by the great flashing lights of exploding bombs followed by the thunderous noise and tremor.

The following morning I left for Gathee's *mbuci* with the intention of leaving Ruthaithi for Mihuro. On my arrival at Gathee's I told him the bombing story. He said that the airplane was turning over their heads after dropping bombs. I asked Gathee to arrange and pack my *safari* food so that I could leave the following morning. I had written Gathee [earlier] telling him to order his *itungati* to dry meat for me and my three *itungati* sufficient to keep us for at least two weeks during which I would stay at Mihuro lonely in the office. I asked him now to give me two more *itungati* for the *safari*. He agreed and reminded me that Nyaga's *itungati* were supposed to be in Mihuro for repairing huts and building a memorial hall. I wished Gathee's *itungati* farewell and in the evening slept early, for I had not slept the night before because of airplane disturbances.

I left Gathee's *mbuci* on 14th November with five *itungati* equipped with dry meat to keep us for two weeks. I spent a night on the way, arriving Mihuro the following day in the afternoon. We cleaned two of the old huts, took our ration into the store, and collected firewood. The next day I went to the bookstore and carried all the books I wanted to the camp. For the next seven days I was busy in record books, entering data, history and reports and preparing a general report of the Kenya Parliament's works since it was elected.

On 22nd November Kimathi and a group of Gikuyu Iregi Army arrived [at Mihuro] from Fort Hall with twenty-six leaders and 304 *itungati*. Kimathi introduced me to them and pointed out the twelve who had been elected by their fighters to become members of the Kenya Parliament. Kimathi told me of the power conflict between Macaria Kimemia and Mbaria Kaniu over the leadership of the Gikuyu Iregi Army. Macaria told me that their quarrel was so great that they almost opened fire against each other but a general election settled that Macaria Kimemia was the head leader of the Gikuyu Iregi Army. But Mbaria Kaniu, who was

very popular to North Kinangop inhabitants originally from Fort
Hall, moved back to his area and went on claiming to be the leader
of Murang'a as well as the leader of Mburu Ngebo Army. I learned
from Kimathi that Gikuyu Iregi Army fighters had ruled that
Macaria Kimemia was their leader and Mbaria Kaniu was the
leader of the Mburu Ngebo Army, the section that belonged to
Murang'a people.

I told Kimathi of Kahiu-Itina and Kimbo's ideas and after
balancing it, we found that it had originated from power envy and
could result in personal enmity or split the Rift Valley from the
Central Province and possibly cause our *itungati* to urge for personal rewards, as some of these leaders had started deceiving their
itungati by falsely allocating the settlers' farms to some *itungati* so
as to win them. But since envy was not evil and nothing dangerous
had happened yet, we left the matter out [of the agenda] but
became aware of it.

On 23rd November, I spent most of the time collecting and
recording a general report from Murang'a, Masai, remote areas of
Rift Valley (Il Doigan Hill in North Nanyuki, Naivasha, Dundori
and Elburgon), and within Nyandarua. I had to explain Kimathi
all this before I took it to the General Meeting.

I learned from Kiarii Mubengi, the head of the Kenya Inoro
Army, that their armies were still rising up in numbers and
strength and were in a very good supply of arms from Nairobi,
especially Waruingi's companies. The Rift Valley sections under
Joseph Kibe Kimani were still active but they were badly dispersed by the enemy at Longonot Hill by an air raid while the
foot soldiers surrounded the hill. Some of them had entered Nyandarua and others were still in the settled area.

Gen. Kibati reported the sad news on the Gikuyu and Mumbi
Trinity Army (Masai fighters mostly), saying that their chief leader,
Ole Kisio, was killed at the end of August. His successor Ole
Ngapien, was captured three weeks later. The dispersed and dis-
heartened fighters were under Ole Ngare. This seemed to be a very
great blow on our side.

Wanjeru had returned from Elburgon via Dondori. His mission
had failed to enter the Nandi reserves. He said that there were
fighters in nearly all the small forests in the settled area but they
were not getting support from the settlers' employees—mostly due
to the repatriation of Kikuyu and their jobs being taken by the

tribes who did not know our aims and who were regularly fed by the Government propaganda which really meant to ostracise the Kikuyu under the allegations that they had taken an oath urging them to kill, rob and rule other tribes. Wanjeru claimed that when an informer was killed the Government's propagandists took the incident to witness the vows taken and used it to build mountains of tribalism and hatred.

Ndiritu Kimani from Il Doigan Hill said that he had two sections there and that a third section had arrived under Kahiu-Itina. He said that Dorobo, Samburu and a few Turkana in the area were very sympathetic to the Movement and a few had taken the traditional oath.

News from the reserves was not pleasing, for Government had greatly increased its forces and arms, forced all people in the Central Province into villages which were strongly supervised as prison camps. We had been cut off from Nairobi supplies and communication and worse still from our supporters in the reserves. For the last two months I had noted and notified our Nairobi base that the [little] ammunition we had could only be used for defending or fighting for food. We couldn't make any more offensive attacks. Over 30,000 Kikuyu, Embu and Meru had become loyal Home Guards to the Government, most of whom were previously our strong supporters. After their surrender they accused other supporters whom they beat and tortured badly until they confessed and became converted in their faith. In addition, our *itungati* who had either surrendered or were captured had given the enemy sufficient information about the forest fighters and, worst of all [some] had joined the enemy's pseudo-platoons and had become their guides to our *mbuci*. In fact the wind had changed, this time against us.

By the evening I learned the attendance situation—1,500 fighters had arrived, mostly from Ituma Ndemi Army, followed by Gikuyu Iregi Army, Mburu Ngebo Army (sections under Mbaria Kaniu, Makanyanga and Thiong'o's section, which reported his death), and Kenyo Inoro Army. Kibati and his assistant plus six fighters were the only ones who were in touch with Masai fighters at Melili Forest, but they had failed to bring Masai leaders as Ole Ngare had not been able to hold meetings with his fighters due to enemy harassment.

One of the most interesting things of the meeting was that Stanley Mathenge had arrived together with four other sections and their leaders who had attended the meeting under his influence. The other interesting person was Mbaria Kaniu. Both were strong enough to split Ituma Ndemi Army and Gikuyu Iregi Army. Up to this stage, Mathenge, who had many possibilities of competing with Kimathi, had not really motivated any campaign for competing with Kimathi. One thing certain was that Mathenge was not satisfied to be under Kimathi; again, he had no intentions at all of getting other fighters under his rule apart from his own Division, which he had assumed responsibility for and which he didn't like Kimathi to interfere with, so that he could maintain his security. In fact he had no objections to Kimathi's rising to power provided that he maintained his position—which I thought was fit for him, for he had no ability of rising above division level, which was even difficult to his brain power.

In addition to this, it was clear that Kimbo, Kahiu-Itina and Mbaria Kaniu had started to motivate Mathenge to rise against Kimathi and took him as their leader. Taking into account the criticisms given to me by both Kahiu-Itina and Kimbo, and reasons for seeking a new party under illiterates, I could clearly see that the main division was what one stood for : Kimathi who stood for Kenya's revolution was on top of those leaders hats, while they, far below, stood for tribal tradition and customary laws as they were before European civilization as the goal after victory.

Now, turning to the Kenya Parliament members attendance, it was as follows :

PRESENT
1. President, Dedan Kimathi
2. Chief Sec., Karari Njama
3. Dep. Sec., Ndiritu Thuita
4. Vice Treasurer, Abdullah
5. Major Gen. Vindo
6. Gen. Muraya Mbuthia

ABSENT (under boycott, 1-4)
1. Vice Pres., Kahiu-Itina
2. Treasurer, Kimbo
3. Ngunjiri
4. Wambugu Mwema
5. Gen. Rui (never attended any meeting of Kenya Parliament)
6. Gathitu (dead)
7. Omera (captured)

The six Kenya Parliament members met after dinner to discuss the report to be issued out the following day. The first thing to be noted was that the Kenya Parliament attendance had fallen below half, which showed some weakness. One possible way of strengthening it was to increase its members. Learning from Kimathi that Gikuyu Iregi Army had elected their twelve representatives in the Kenya Parliament, including Muraya Mbuthia an old member of K.P., and the fact that they were all in the same camp, made us conclude that they were to participate as members of the Kenya Parliament the following day. Among them were Macaria Kimemia their head, Mwangi Gicimu their chief secretary, Kimani Waweru and Mutuota.

The Kenya Inoro Army had four elected members to represent them in the K.P. We accepted them and agreed that they should elect five more who should join us at the Annual General Meeting on 31st December at Mihuro.

General Kibati, speaking as the Masai representative, said that any journey to Narok or Melili Forest was very difficult and dangerous. Our fighters, [he said] had to walk over large grassland areas at night and sleep during the day. Sometimes they had to hide themselves in small grass which could not at all cover them from either footmen or air patrols. He suggested that they needed rules and regulations, plans and general organization, to enable them to manage their own affairs without attending the Kenya Parliament meeting. His suggestion was accepted.

Now since the other armies had done their elections, only Ituma Ndemi Army was left to elect its members. If we held the election in the absence of Kahiu-Itina and Kimbo they would get grounds to justify their split, claiming that they had been ousted by the K.P. Looking at the attendance, we thought that Mathenge might lose the election as he had not many of the fighters; who were aware of his negligence of duty. So we decided to introduce Mathenge to our fighters as the elected head of Ituma and ask him, as chairman of Ituma, to call a general meeting for Ituma which would elect its new leaders. It seemed impossible to hold another general meeting before the Annual General Meeting for all the fighters, so we concluded that we would make it clear to Mathenge after discussing the matter with him. We decided that we had better nominate seven additional leaders to strengthen the five old K.P. members of the Ituma Ndemi Army until such a time as we were able to hold a general election and study the motives of Kahiu-Itina and company. We then nominated the following persons to become members of the Kenya Parliament :

1. Gen. Gathura Muita; IDA 1/2 and Kimathi's personal clerk
2. Gen. Makanyanga; Mburu Ngebo Army
3. Gen. Kihara Gatandi; IDA 2/2
4. Gen. Wacira Gathuku; IDA 3/2
5. Gen. Gitonga Gaciingu; IDA 3/3
6. Gen. Gikonyo Kanyungu; IDA 4/1 (absent from meeting)
7. Gen. Kahinga Wachanga; IDA 4/3 (absent from meeting)

Qualifications for the above nominees were cleverness, national feelings as opposed to tribal, leadership ability and regional representation in Nyandarua. We had learned that success in a general election depended on either popularity or deceitful propaganda and not on merit.

The question of the settled area in the Rift Valley being represented by leaders who claimed that it was their land was the one which could bring about a split between all other fighters and the Rift Valley fighters. Rift Valley was the land we all were fighting for and it was then ridiculous for some fighters to claim it to be theirs for the reason that they were born there or had lived there for a long time. That would definitely create mistrust among the fighters and mostly destroy the fighters' spirit, losing confidence in the land he was fighting for. We resolved that we had to make it clear to all our fighters that Rift Valley did not belong to the settlers' employees or squatters as they were being deceived by some leaders who claimed that they were sharing land to their *itungati*, but in fact that it belongs to all Kenya Africans and could only be shared at the consent of the Kenya African Government.

Before closing the meeting we resolved that the New Kenya Parliament, 28 members present, would meet the following morning before the General Meeting began. We sent out Gen. Muraya Mbuthia and called on Mathenge so that we could discuss his differences with Kimathi, a matter only for the Ituma Ndemi Army. It was already a few minutes after midnight when he arrived. This took place in an informal talk in which both denied hatred or dislike against each other when we interrogated them. Mathenge, in an effort to prove his good will, repeated the story of the bullet in the fire saying that I had completely cleared his suspicions and doubts about the incident by telling him what had happened and convincing him that Kimathi was always sincere to him and had demanded his cooperation. Mathenge concluded that he had nothing more other than suspicion of the bullet in the fire.

Kimathi then suggested that they should both take an oath binding them as brothers, vowing never to kill or cause [injury] in any form to each other and never to undermine each other or degrade each other to their *itungati*. Though they did not take the oath they promised before us to work together. Kimathi ended by cursing himself and calling God to witness that he will never hurt Mathenge, who said the same.

We then told Mathenge our plan of introducing him to all the *itungati* and giving him chances of speaking and calling a general meeting so that all our Ituma *itungati* will know him before a general election of its leaders. Mathenge was very pleased and promised to call a general meeting early at the beginning of the year. The date was to be fixed at the Annual General Meeting. It was already three o'clock in the morning and we went to sleep.

The morning of the 24th November all the new members of Kenya Parliament, 28 of them, met in a big memorial hall 120 feet by 20 feet with three rows of seats and a platform for the Kenya Parliament members. Guards had been properly posted in all directions at least three miles in radius.

I opened the meeting with prayers which were dedicated by Kimathi. The first thing was to get to know each other and Kimathi did all the introduction work. Second was to tell the new members the duties and policies of the Kenya Parliament, the work done by the K.P. since it was elected, general report on our armies. Courage and unity to our fighters and supporters was to be adopted as our greatest weapon, being now unable to attack the enemy due to lack of ammunition.

Our inability to make gunpowder became our greatest weakness and we resolved to ask our fighters what gunpowder was made of. We then arranged the order of our speeches : who was to speak, his subject and time allowed. Kimathi was to control the meeting, introduce and keep time for every speaker. Gathura Muita was to call out the next speaker from the prepared list and tell the audience what they were to hear from the speaker. The President and Chief Secretary were allowed to speak without any fixed time until they covered the required ground. I was to record everyone's speech as it directly came from his mouth. The other 16 speakers were allowed ten minutes only, including Mathenge and Mbaria though they were not members of the Parliament. The meeting ended at lunch time and we walked out for lunch—a cup of boiled maize.

The General meeting was to start at two in the afternoon with an opening ceremony of the Kenyalekalo Memorial Hall. Wang'-ombe Ruga, the only reasonable *mundo mugo* we had, was standing with Kimathi at the hall's entrance, each holding a *gitete* of diluted honey and a flywhisk. Wang'ombe had another *gitete* of uncooked gruel—*githambio*, a fermented mixture of millet flour and water—which he poured on the entrance and on either side of the hall as he said his prayers asking God to bless the site, the hall and the army. After a short prayer in the memory of all our miserable life since the coming of the Europeans, Kimathi poured honey on the same places, sprinkled the hall with honey and cut the string across the entrance and declared Kenyalekalo Memorial Hall open in the memory of the miserable life of our Mt. Kenya and Nyandarua fighters, the O'lenguruoni eviction and all the evictions, the Kapenguria Trial and all other trials in which thousands of people were sentenced to death, deportation, imprisonments ranging from one year to life or indefinite detention, Lokitaung Prison where our leader Jomo Kenyatta and his five colleagues were serving their sentences to represent all prisons and detention camps and all our sufferings in general.

He then entered the hall, pouring honey all the way to the platform and followed by Wang'ombe who was pouring *githambio*. Then they came out and started cleansing 1,400 fighters by sprinkling them with honey from his flywhisk while Kimathi was blessing them by sprinkling honey on them as they entered the hall. The Kenya Parliament members were the first to enter—and Kimathi poured a little honey on our heads—followed by the other leaders and lastly by the *itungati*, who were sprinkled from the flywhisk. The hall could hold only 700 fighters and the rest had to stand against the walls both inside and outside.

Kimathi opened the meeting with two minutes of silence for the dead and short prayers. He then introduced all the K.P. members and prominent leaders. He mentioned the names of absent members without apology for them and informed the audience that we had nominated seven other leaders whom we thought were fit so that they could lead until we held a general election, possibly before the end of the year. He mentioned the Kenya Parliament's works and asked the Chief Secretary to read the general report of the K.P. work since it was elected.

When I stood up, I told the audience how and when the K.P. was formed and the qualifications for election and then explained how we first dealt with China's surrender negotiations, then correspondences inland and abroad—reading either the reply or the letters sent—missions and tours in and out of Nyandarua, Kenya Parliament's sessions, discussing rules and regulations, plans of attacking and defending, discipline, cases heard. I warned them on pseudo-platoons and informers within the camps, read recordings of lost property, lives of fighters and supporters, enemies, supplies, finance, history, songs, activities in camp, battle activities, issuing ranks, Kenya Young Stars Association, Kenyalekalo Memorial Clubs and Halls.

Achievements up to this stage were that the Colonial Government had sent a Royal Land Commission in 1953 in an attempt to adjust our land complaints, whose findings were unknown to our fighters and which we believed was kept secret in order to cover Government's face from shame. Though it was right for the Government to return the lands to the Africans, it would have been interpreted as a great defeat of the settlers and we thought that their request was to be given time to defeat us in the battle and then issue out land to the survivors. Some Government officials had in many cases promised the Loyalists that the Government would return lands to them when they defeated *Mau Mau*, for the Government didn't want *Mau Mau* to prove to have fought for right.

In April 1954, a Commonwealth Delegation arrived in Kenya for the first time in history. We claimed that they had come to settle our case versus settlers and wanted to accept our country on their equal status as a member of the commonwealth. At about the same time, [a month after the Colonial Secretary, Oliver Lyttelton, visited Kenya] the Colonial Government had changed a policy. Kenya was no longer a colony in the old sense but a multiracial Government recognizing the African as equal for the first time and promoting him to ministerial post. The Kenya Legislative members had been increased, a Commission for Wages appointed, many of the KISA schools reopened under the missionaries or the District Education Board.

Our two years fight had made Kenya Government run bankrupt,

causing its Finance Minister Mr. E. A. Vassey to borrow almost £30,000,000 from Her Majesty's Government, and in spite of that the Colonial Government had failed to defeat us. In fact it had shown its weakness by asking us to surrender. I had also learned from *East African Standard* that the European migration from Kenya was so great that the Government had to do all it could to stop them from running away and to enable it to do so, the Government had to regulate the service leave from Kenya. That made us proud of having succeeded in chasing away many Kenya settlers and increased our hopes that by the time we achieved independence all the Kenya settlers would have left the country.

I warned the audience that the Government had succeeded in cutting us completely from our supporters anywhere outside the forest by putting all the people in village prison-like camps. There was a decrease of both arms and fighters from our side and a great increase to the Government side—but [during] the two years of our fight, the Government had failed to defeat us [though] doing their best daily, using 100,000 soldiers, including Home Guards, all equipped to their best, lorries, Land Rovers, planes—Police Air Wing, Harvards, jets, Lincoln bombers, of which our Almighty God had crashed about eight of them.

I stressed that our defeat would be lack of supplies and food. The enemy's patrols and operations here in the forest had done very little compared with the fight for food. It seemed that the Government was now aiming at preventing us from getting food so that we would die of hunger or fall into their food traps. But since there were plenty of animals in this forest which we could trap for food or clothing, we could then live in the forest for many years. Though we had not lifted the rule preventing us from killing the animals, many fighters were already living on animals. I suggested that the rule should be amended that... 'No one should kill an animal which he was not going to eat, unless it be for defending reason and only when attacked.'

'*Ucio uri ho!*' shouted the fighters in cheers saying that was right.

I enquired which animals couldn't be eaten and received different replies mentioning the ones unfit to be eaten, but the replies from Kipipiri fighters were peculiar and laughable :

'I would eat whatever would be caught by my trap,' replied one fighter. 'When I lay my trap I do not choose which animal is to be caught. All I do is pray God to give me meat, whatever he thinks fit for me and I. . . .'

'Would you eat a monkey or leopard?' asked another *gitungati*.

'Yes, in fact some of us have eaten them!' replied the *gitungati*.

Laughter increased and the whole hall was filled with noise, one talking to the other. Kimathi rose to quieten the people, commenting that he would also eat whatever he found in his trap.

'Yes, that's right!' shouted the audience.

'No! Would you eat a hyena?' asked Nyaga.

Kimathi sat down without answering the question. I managed to quieten the meeting. 'Every creature you know,' I said, 'is eaten by some other people,' giving some examples: 'the Akamba eat birds, even the smallest ones, the Giriama eats the tortoise, the French eat the frog and snake-like fish, the Turkana eats donkey, dog, ostrich, etc., the Kitosi eat locusts and the flying ants of which the Gikuyu people do not eat. The Luo and Baluhya eat porcupine, etc. God created and blessed all the creatures to be man's food. He only chooses which to eat because of their abundance and appearance and in a few cases by taste.

'Apart from the animals we have plenty of honey, vegetables and fruit in this forest which can keep us alive for years. You should then try to obtain food anywhere you wish and by any means—and make sure that the enemy wouldn't defeat us on the food issue.

'The last and worst of our defeats would be disunity among ourselves—*komerera* leaders seeking power, disobedience to our leaders, discouragement, lack of confidence to our victory, and being unable to persevere to the last man and minute. We have bravely fought the battle and we have scored more goals than our opponents and if the referee blows the whistle now to stop fighting, we would definitely win the battle. We have all the chances of winning if we persevere. Don't be worried about the Home Guards or surrenderees. The Kenya settlers are in a worse situation than ourselves in unity. Up to June 1953, the Aberdare Electoral Union was the only settlers' political union and it wished to rule Kenya forever under the leadership of Michael Blundell. Its final petition to Her Majesty's Government during Her coronation ceremony, demanding independence for the white man in Kenya, was completely rejected and Blundell was warned that the settlers had only one chance and that was to form a multiracial Government,

THE TIDE IS TURNING 421

which they are experimenting with at present. If it failed, Her Majesty's Government promised to grant the Africans independence and [said] that it was for the Kenya settlers to fit themselves in the African Government.

'When Blundell returned here, he told his party that Her Majesty's Government had thrust an arrow right in the heart of their party's aim. He warned that they were pushing their heads against a brick wall. That there would never be a white man's independence in this country. That multiracialism was the only chance they were given and, provided that they were the strongest, wealthiest capitalists and the cleverest, they would lead and control that multiracial Government. And that now their main problem would be how to gain cooperation from the majority of Africans in the multiracial Government.

'On hearing this, the Aberdare Electoral Union split into the Federal Independence Party under Humphrey Slade, demanding Kenya be granted autonomous provinces, the United Party under Blundell, the Upcountry Party and another party under Mr. Baxter and Major Day claiming that the European supremacy in this country must prevail. With these different parties voicing their policies at liberty, the Europeans are weaker than ourselves, for the Home Guards and surrenderees were created by security reasons and force. If there were no such force then there would be no more Home Guards or surrenderees or disunity or different aims as it has happened with the settlers.

'Time is almost ripe. Freedom is just around the corner. The referee will soon blow his whistle for the change over. The result will be an "about turn!" The first will become the last. The last will become the first. The servants will become the masters. The ruled will become the rulers. The miserable will become the happiest. This would be the reward for perseverance. Are you ready to persevere to the last minute?'

'Ei. Yes!' roared the audience. 'We are ready!'

'Then shall we all sing together?'....

The children of Gikuyu live in the forest
Under the pouring rains
With much hunger and cold
In quest of their land

(chorus) Woeee! Woeee! Woe-eyae!
          Will you persevere death
          Continuous pains and troubles and
          Often imprisonment for the love of your land?

Who are those singing aloud
And living beyond the sea
Praising Jomo and Mbiyu
As seekers of right and justice

Some Gikuyu separated themselves
And betrayed the others because
They thought we could never win
Our House of Mumbi, we have won!

Our fighters sang happily and bravely. It was getting late for them to collect firewood before nightfall. Sitting down, I promised to tell them more at night. Kimathi, commenting on my long speech, asked them to cheer up and adjourned the meeting so that we could get a chance of collecting firewood and cooking. He told the audience that there were sixteen other leaders who would speak to them at night after dinner and ordered that every one should be in the hall before 10 p.m.

As the *itungati* left the hall, I sat down on the platform next to Kimathi and lit my *kiraiko* to smoke. Many leaders came to shake my hand and congratulate me for my long speech. They said that I had covered a large ground and given encouragement to the fighters. When the fires were lit, we dispersed to our huts to warm ourselves while awaiting dinner.

At 9:30 p.m., singing sounded like ringing church bells calling everyone to attend. The warriors who had finished eating were already awaiting leaders in the hall and were entertaining themselves by singing. At five minutes to ten the Kenya Parliament leaders entered the hall, which was lit by burning fires inside and outside which also supplied warmth.

Gathura Muita asked me to do the calling of the speakers as he didn't know them well enough to introduce them properly. He said he would record their speeches. The leaders spoke on courage, unity, obedience, perseverance, fighting tactics, Home Guards, surrender, trapping, camp life, *komerera* jealousy, settlers' history, wealth (ivory, precious stones, etc.), Kenya's African Government, leaderships, etc.

Mathenge, who spoke on many points, drew audience attention on unity, obedience, courage and perseverance. He warned the meeting not to be misled by any propaganda that he and Kimathi hated each other; neither should they be worried for him not being a member of the K.P. He warned the warriors against suspicion and fallacious propaganda. He said that suspicion was the source of evil and confessed to have wrongly suspected Kimathi of the Murang'a bullet incident. He confirmed that he would support Kenya Parliament and any person who did any good work for Kenya. He said that if the devil was to save Kenya, he would then support him. He claimed that the leader who will lead the fighters victoriously out of the forest would automatically become the leader of the revolution. He warned the leaders against jealousy and false pride. He said that we were all in the middle of a big river crossing and we could easily be drowned with our jealousy and pride before we managed to cross.

He told a story of a people who were engaged in a similar fight as ours. Their army was living in the forest just as we were. Their opponent knew neither their number nor their strength. As the years passed by, the enemy's bombs and foot soldiers killed the forest fighters and only one of them survived. This brave warrior refused to surrender and fought as if he was the whole army. He took from the deceased warriors different kinds of weapons. He kept on ambushing the enemy using his different weapons as though there were many warriors. At night he did a lot of distruction by using fire and poison to the animals. He changed his position daily, moving from one side of the forest to the other. The enemy believed the forest was still full of fighters, and then [finally] surrendered. When his people were released from prisons and detention camps and formed the first Government, they then called their fighters who were living in the forest to march from the forest to the national flag where they would receive their honor for bravery and perseverance and their willingness to free their people and their country at the cost of their lives. Though the people were very happy for their achievement, they were very much surprised to see only one warrior carrying many different kinds of weapons, which he defeated the enemy with, marching and beating his big drum in the big street towards the city center.

At first the people wondered, thinking that the whole army was still in the forest, but then he told them that there were no more fighters in the forest and that he was the only man who defeated the enemy; he had fought for more than a year all alone in the forest. Amidst cheers and cries for the dead, the brave courageous and persevering fighter received the greatest honor that was to be granted to all the country's fighters.

'Hold on! Keep up!' concluded Mathenge. 'He who surrenders loses what he had fought for. He who perseveres wins. You can decide to surrender now, and [soon] after your enemy surrenders. It is all just a matter of perseverance, as Mr Njama has said. The last man *will* become the first!'

Whenever a speaker sat down, we sang one of our songs to awaken people and keep them alert. Usually we chose a song that corresponded with the speakers news. A song of praise, a song of courage, a song of recording events, a song of degrading the enemy and Home Guards, a propaganda song for spreading the Movement, etc.

At five minutes to midnight we commenced our prayers in the memory of the dead, injured and captured comrades, their torture, and our miserable life. We prayed God to defend us and fight for us. We prayed for unity, courage and perseverance, and asked God to grant us power to defeat envy, jealousy, hatred, diseases and climate. We prayed for leaders so that they could rightly lead us. Two leaders, two fighters, two women spoke our prayers, which were concluded by Kimathi.

We continued our program until we realized, about 3 a.m., that most of our *itungati* had fallen asleep. Kimathi dismissed the meeting, saying that there would be no general meeting during the day, but that the leaders would meet. Another general meeting would be held the following night.

The next morning, being certain that sentries had been posted, I slept up to 9. At 10 a.m. the members of the K.P. met to discuss what matters were likely to be raised at the next Annual General Meeting. Apart from New Year's prayers, we agreed that such a meeting was the best way through which we could encourage, unite, discipline and educate our fighters, through lectures and challenges from distant leaders on the bad points and habits. We then invited other leaders in and asked them what each would like to tell our fighters that night. We made up the program of their speeches similar to the one we had the night before. We broke for lunch, after which I recorded all the previous night's speeches in the minute book, keeping me busy till evening.

After dinner we entered the hall and continued our program. Nearly all the leaders praised the K.P., its leaders and the effort they were putting in propagating the Movement to other tribes and making our troubles known abroad. Finally, I called for any fighter who wanted to speak for or against what we had preached. Hundreds wanted to comment and praise the leaders, of whom I allowed only 3 to speak. I gave allowance for anyone who wanted to criticise what we had preached to speak, but none volunteered. The meeting ended at half-past 1 in the morning.

We wished everyone farewell and hoped to meet next time whenever our leaders fixed the date and place. We did not want our fighters to know when the next general meeting would be held. We then went to bed.

CHAPTER XIX

PRIME MINISTER DEDAN KIMATHI

D u r i n g the early months of 1955, several attempts were made to strengthen the forest organization and heal the rift between leaders which threatened a split. External pressures and events, however, playing upon the internal tendencies toward fission, made this an extremely difficult, if not hopeless, task. The General Annual Meeting of the Kenya Parliament, which was to commence on 31 December 1954, coincided with the opening of Government's greatest assault on the forest guerrillas since the revolution began. 'Operation Hammer', as it was called, lasted almost three weeks and threw over a division of infantry into the Aberdares. They began by clearing the moorlands, then moved in staggered, coordinated patrols toward the eastern fringe of the forest where a line of heavily manned ambushes had been set up. Considering the massive nature of the operation, guerrilla casualties were relatively light, numbering, according to Government sources, 161 dead, captured or surrendered. Nevertheless, Government did succeed in badly dispersing the forest forces, hampering their movement and destroying Mihuro camp, thus forcing the Kenya Parliament to twice postpone its general meeting and the important Ituma District Committee elections.

Operation Hammer, a military failure from Government's point of view, was followed on 18 January 1955 by a new campaign designed to bring about the surrender of forest guerrillas by offering a general amnesty for crimes committed during the emergency. While very few fighters surrendered during this period, it is clear from Karari's account that the dire conditions prevailing in the reserve, the Government amnesty offer and their own plight in the forest, resulted in widespread demoralization amongst Aberdare fighters. The Kikuyu peasantry, it seems, had for the most part lost both the means and the will to resist. The villagization and communal labor schemes combined with bad harvests to produce widespread hunger and a mounting toll of deaths from starvation among children and the aged. Cut off from the fighters in the forest and seeing no chance of winning, a growing number of Kikuyu peasants, therefore, yearned only for an end to the struggle.

The Chieni meeting in early March was designed, at least in part, to bolster the sagging morale of the forest *itungati* by consolidating the rapproachement between Stanley Mathenge and Dedan Kimathi. The latter would be promoted to the new post of Prime Minister while Mathenge and Macaria Kimemia (Commander of the Gikuyu Iregi Army) would contest for the vacated post of Field Marshal in a Kenya Parliament election. In this way, the military hierarchy would be separated from the political hierarchy of councils and, it was hoped, the areas of conflict between Mathenge and Kimathi reduced. Kimathi, as head of the Kenya Parliament, would be responsible for the proper functioning of the Parliament and district committees. Mathenge, or perhaps Kimemia, would take over all of Kimathi's duties regarding the management of military affairs and forces. Both men would thus be satisfied and the dissident leaders could, in all likelihood, be persuaded to return. As we shall see, an unexpected turn of events was to dispel these hopes and plans.

The formal ceremony described by Karari, in which Dedan Kimathi was made a senior elder of the highest rank and elevated to the post of Prime Minister, is a significant illustration of the manner in which both traditional practices and statuses and British ranks, titles and offices were utilized in an effort to sanctify and legitimize the Kenya Parliament and forest organization. While traditional aspects of the ceremony underscored the Parliament's claim to legitimacy as a Kikuyu institution, and sanctioned the intended separation of political and military offices, the British features tended to support the Kenya Parliament claim to legitimacy as a Kenya-wide governing institution, representing the interests of Kenya Africans as opposed to European settlers. Here again, in terms of both organization and ideology, is an illustration of that conjunction of Kikuyu and Kenya 'nationalisms' so frequently exhibited by the forest guerrilla forces.

★ ★ ★

When the day broke, our fighters dispersed from Mihuro in many directions. Kihara Gatandi, one of the seven nominated Ituma members of the K.P. and Gicuki Mwii joined the Kiambu fighters on a mission to encourage the fighters around Naivasha and Opuru Forest. I joined Mathenge's company to Subuk and stayed for the next month in Gicuki Wacira's section, up to the 28th December, when we left for Mihuro in order to attend the Annual General Meeting. We slept two nights on the way and arrived in the afternoon of 30th December.

I was glad to meet many of my friends from whom we had parted a month ago. Reports from various directions were that there were a lot of enemies in the forest who had been seen in many areas. We became suspicious; suspected that the enemy might have known that we were to hold a general meeting. Kimathi forbid singing or making loud noises. About 500 persons had arrived and the poor attendance also made us suspect that many of our fighters might have been dispersed by the enemy.

Very early the following morning, Kimathi ordered that the sentries be posted all around the camp, within three miles radius, and that they must keep their positions until sunset. To ensure our safety, 350 *itungati* were sent on guard, leaving only 150 persons in the camp.

The attendance was very disappointing for none of the Kenya Inoro Army had turned up. From the Gikuyu Iregi Army only six members of the Kenya Parliament had arrived. From the Ituma Ndemi Army, Kahinga, Gikonyo and Kihara, who had accompanied the Kenya Inoro Army, had not arrived. From Mburu Ngebo Army only Makanyanga had arrived. Total attendance— fifteen members of Kenya Parliament out of thirty-three expected. We spent the day in fear and worry, knowing that the enemy was within [i.e., around] us and not knowing what had happened to our warriors who had not arrived. Learning from Makanyanga that the enemy was sweeping the whole forest, the sooner we dispersed the better for us.

Nevertheless, we trusted our guards and sat down to plan our program. If no more members of the Kenya Parliament turned up, we couldn't hold an official session with less than half the members, but we could give lectures to our fighters. Mathenge had arrived and had kept his promise. Kahiu-Itina had not returned from Il Doigan Hill. Kimbo had not changed his mind; in fact he was reported to have toured some Mburu Ngebo Army sections preaching against the Kenya Parliament.

By nightfall some 300 more *itungati* had arrived with their leaders, but no more members of the K.P. showed up. From the echoes of the enemy's guns, we learned that we were surrounded and became very much afraid that some captives might tell the enemy of the meeting they were going to attend and probably lead them to Mihuro. Nevertheless, when our great ally, the darkness, arrived, we became brave enough to sing and shout hard. We covered our program and held prayers for the New Year.

Mathenge talked to the *itungati* and promised them that he would call the first general meeting for Ituma Ndemi Army under his chairmanship sometime early in February. The leaders would inform their *itungati* of the date and place later on. All the leaders had to keep the meetings secret, but it was to be at Mihuro on 7th February 1955. The Kenya Parliament session, which had failed, was postponed to the same date. The Ituma Ndemi Army election was postponed until Mathenge was in a position to organize the election in order to convince the ones who had threatened a split.

Very early the New Year's morning we dispersed after our prayers for our journeys and God's protection. I joined IDA 3/2 and before our arrival at Gura Valley we four times narrowly escaped enemy collision. The camp was situated in the black forest dotted with very few bamboo on the northern Gura slopes just above the old Kigumo gardens. The water sprung up a few yards from the camp and then the stream went underground some thirty yards below the spring. Two hundred yards to the east were two big bomb craters. Our guards could see the enemy three-quarters of a mile below moving down the valley in the old gardens. Casting my eyes on the opposite steep slope, I could see a wide 'road' made by the sloping soil from a bomb crater almost vertical to me. The camp benefited from having a good view of the Gura Valley, which enabled us to see the smoke from enemies' camps in the mornings and evenings and their airplanes dropping them food. The other benefit was that there was no known water nearby, which proved to the enemy that the area was unfit for camping.

In this quiet camp, not even known by other fighters, I lived with Wacira Gathuku, Gitonga Giciingu and Wambugu Mutiga, who had been given the whole camp's management by Gitonga. The eighteen *itungati* in the camp were brave fighters and men of goodwill. They cleverly managed to harvest maize from the reserve gardens which we dried in the sun, for January is the driest month.

On the 15th January, our *itungati* returning from the reserve reported some interesting news that Government forces had withdrawn from the forest. The following afternoon I went fishing down the Gura River. On my way I crossed many enemy tracks which showed me that they had left the forest. At twilight, I returned to the camp with nine trouts, which enabled us to have a change in our maize meals for the first time in a month.

On 18th January Wacira, Gitonga, two escorts and I went to visit Gicuki Wacira who lived on the same slope about one mile from the forest fringe. On our way, we heard an airplane skyshouting an appeal for us to surrender. As it passed us following the forest border, we saw it dropping thousands of leaflets. I sent one of the escorts to get me a leaflet. It read :—

GOVERNMENT PROMISE!

The Kenya Government has offered all the fighters a chance to come out of the forest and return to the normal peaceful life. His Excellency the Governor of Kenya Sir Evelyn Baring has given a general amnesty to all persons who have committed crimes during the emergency up to today, the 18th January 1955. Save your life now! Surrender with all your fighting weapons and you will not be prosecuted. You will be detained and receive good medical treatment, food, clothing and general care.

(Signed by) Sir Evelyn Baring
His Excellency the Governor of Kenya
Gen. Sir George Erskine
Commander-in-Chief, East Africa

'No matter whether this is a Government propaganda,' I said, 'one thing I am certain of is that these are their real signatures and although forgery is possible, whether this letter comes from the senior or junior officers, the fact is that this is the Government's statement. It is a fair proof that the Government is defeated and instead of yielding to our demands it appeals to us to surrender.'

'If we surrender, we would lose what we have fought for at the last minute of our victory. On the other hand the Government offers us to become its detainees or prisoners. Oh no!' cried Gitonga, 'We have declared the fight to the end.'

'Though it may be true,' I said, 'that no one would be taken to a magistrate for prosecution, at the same time it warns us of being detained indefinitely—possibly detention throughout their rule, which would mean that we could only be released when Kenya gets independence.'

'It is foolish to place oneself willingly under the enemy's mercy,' said Wacira. 'Forget all about it and persevere and you will find that the Government has completely surrendered.'

We continued our journey and soon arrived at Wacira's *mbuci*. It was similar to ours and had a good view of the Kigumo main road and the reserve as well. Standing here I could see Munyange Village in which was the strongest military base with over 700 Devons plus a police camp and Home Guard camp. I could count any persons entering the forest in that area within a mile or two in the reserve. I could still see my garden one and a half miles away; my fruit trees and the remains of the unroofed house I was building before the emergency. This *mbuci* could see the enemy making their ambushes in the evenings and knew well when they had abandoned their ambushes.

Gicuki told us that the enemy's plans of fighting us had greatly increased. He said that the Government had dropped all its forces in Nguthiru [the Moorlands] where they started their sweeping operation down the streams, valleys, slopes and on the ridges, so distributed that they moved in almost parallel lines less than half a mile apart. Our trick of encircling behind the enemy wouldn't have worked this time for they were moving in three groups. The second group was to search the same area for the second day that had been covered by the first group and sleep in the same camp. The third group was to search the same area for the third day and sleep in their already established camp.

They continued their slow and thorough sweep toward the forest boundary where their comrades laid in ambushes all the nights. Since it was dangerous for our fighters to run away toward the forest boundary, they always tried to move across [i.e., laterally] which was impossible to move more than half a mile before colliding with another enemy force. The only way was to move up the mountain but having passed the first group and coming to its camp, our fighters thought it to be safe, while the second group was ready to charge. Their next escape would just put them into the enemy's third group's trap. Though we didn't know the exact damage caused by the enemy to our fighters, it must have been great for fighters could only run away instead of ambushing the enemy as they used to do. This was all due to lack of ammunition.

I told them that I had tried to make gunpowder and had found that elephants' tusks burned the same way as gunpowder, but I had failed how to light it. By examining different forms of gunpowder, I had concluded that it was made of elephants' tusks, charcoal, phosphorus and some alkali acid. I could see a lot of phosphorus staying as parasites on many decaying logs but I was unable to get acid. My inability to make gunpowder, or any other of our fighters, proved to me that we had a lot more to learn from the European's technique. We rediscussed the Government's surrender offer and resolved that it was a mere propaganda and we shouldn't listen to it. In the evening we returned to our *mbuci* with confidence that there was no enemy near us.

On the 20th January 1955, I received news that Ngara was encamping near us on the rocky slope area. I arranged with Gicuki to lead me there. On arrival Ngara told me that his section was chased by the enemy from the Rift Valley across the Moorlands, where he lost seven fighters including his youngest brother. He told me that his *mbuci* in Rift Valley was very close to Makanyanga's and that they had made their escape together. The enemy had caught up with Makanyanga in the Moorlands and he had no doubt that Makanyanga had fallen into the enemy's hands, but whether dead or alive he didn't know for the enemy opened fire at very close range in the open grasslands. He said that every camp in the Rift Valley must have been raided.

On 5th February, Gitonga, Wacira, Gicuki, fifteen *itungati* and myself started out for the meeting. We spent a night on the way, arriving at Mihuro at about four in the afternoon on 6th February. To our surprise, we found that our Kenyalekalo Memorial Hall and all other huts had been burned up by the enemy. In the center of the camp was a little note, stuck in a planted bamboo. It said: 'You will find us at Chieni,' signed Kimathi. We could also see a big track of our other fighters who had attended the meeting.

Gitonga and I left the others in the camp ruin and went to check the bookstore. We desperately, hopelessly followed an old enemy track leading to the bookstore. On our arrival, we found that all the books had been taken and the store was completely destroyed.

We sadly returned to the camp and quickly started for Chieni. Night came before we arrived at Chieni and we encamped about three miles away.

The following morning we arrived at Chieni to find that only Kimathi, the section leaders of IDA 1, Mathenge and three Murang'a leaders had arrived. The attendances were eight members of Kenya Parliament, plus 420 warriors, including other leaders. IDA 2 was absent; IDA 3/1, thirty-six warriors including Mathenge, and IDA 3/3, nineteen warriors, had arrived. Twenty-one fighters had arrived from Mburu Ngebo Army—Makanyanga's section now under Githengera.

The attendance was so poor that we could not carry on our intended plans. The enemy had dispersed our fighters so badly that some were forced out of Aberdare to the bushes and small forests in the Settled Area. I learned from Kimathi that the Government had collected three sacks full of books from our store. We only had the incomplete book which I carried.

We decided to write many letters to Ituma Ndemi Army leaders under the name of Mathenge, its Chairman, and inform the leaders to attend a general meeting to be held at Chieni on 6th March 1955 in which IDA leaders will be elected. We also resolved that the twice postponed Kenya Parliament session should meet the same day in the same camp.

We also agreed that in that session we would promote Field Marshal Dedan Kimathi to be Prime Minister and that Macaria Kimemia and Stanley Mathenge would be voted for by the Kenya Parliament members, whereby the winner would become the Field Marshal and he will be responsible for all our armies and we would expect him to carry on all Kimathi's duties. After promotion, Kimathi would have little to do with the armies so that the other leaders would be able to practice their ability. Kimathi's concern would be the K.P. only. The District Committees would be under the Kenya Parliament. The rest of the armies would be under the Field Marshal. A special anointment ceremony would be performed to indicate these promotions.

After encouraging the few fighters who had attended, and being proud and thankful to God for keeping us safe after such a strong sweep, we dispersed. My group returned to our *mbuci* in the Gura Valley.

The rest of February, the Government forces did not enter the forest and instead of fighting against us, they instructed our parents, wives, friends and the Home Guards to do all they could to convince us that the Government had really given us an amnesty and they wished us to stop fighting in order to save our lives and release them from Government's punishments and enable them to return to a peaceful life.

In order to achieve this, the Government forces stopped guarding the villages and the forest boundary and instead sent our wives and mothers in the forest to take food to the forest fighters and have time to discuss our surrender with them. Learning from Gicuki Wacira, who had attended such a meeting with women from the reserves, I understood that the women showed great love and sorrow to our fighters and always shed tears whenever our fighters rejected the surrender offer. A few fighters who surrendered at the request of their relatives were set free in their villages to move and talk to the people without any supervision in order to induce the other fighters.

I warned Gicuki that our fighters should be stopped from attending such meetings as it would result in weakening our fighters' spirit and possibly many would fall in the surrender trap. Gicuki replied that it was difficult to supervise such a rule. He felt that our fighters were suffering from homesickness and they very much desired the nice food brought them by the women, and the other supplies such as clothings. He believed that our fighters would try to hide in order to make such meetings. He suggested that leaders should attend such meetings and talk to the women in order to convince them that our victory was just about to be announced and that the women should encourage our fighters to persevere and not to surrender. He said that such meetings would give our warriors a chance to strengthen the women's spirits and warn them that they have all the time been fed by the Government's misleading propaganda.

Though I did not agree with him, his suggestions were to be continued. I very well understood that the love of our fighters to their relatives and the country was very great and very sympathetic. To me, I had recorded that love sympathy was the greatest weakness to the revolution loyalties. No one can serve two masters. In order to become a strong faithful warrior who would persevere to the last minute, one had to renounce all worldly wealth, including his family; for if one caste his eyes to his family and wealth, which were in a very detrimental condition, his love and mercy would be drawn to them and he would forget the fight in an attempt to rescue them. This could only lead to surrender and defeat. The Government thought that our feelings were tied to our property and it had destroyed homes or confiscated livestock and even land so that our fighters would feel sorry to lose their lands. The Government claimed that one only could save his land from being confiscated if he surrendered. But knowing the trap, I and other leaders continued to preach that thoughts on family and wealth were strings tying us so that we wouldn't be able to achieve our aims. After all, we were starving of food and cold and had failed to support ourselves. How then could one support his family. We had no money to send them and couldn't take any care of them.

In fact, I had said goodbye to my wife. In a letter I had sent to her enclosing 100s., I had warned her not to expect any sort of help from me for at least ten years time. I had instructed her to take care of herself and our beloved daughter. I had trained myself to think of the fight, and the African Government; and nothing of the country's progress before independence. I had learned to forget all pleasures and imagination of the past. I confined my thoughts in the fight only—the end of which would open my thoughts to the normal world.

I had learned that danger in my early days, when my teacher comrades, my pupils, loss of my job, amusements, love of my wife and our baby, were still flashing in my mind. Those days were long past and I had become accustomed to my way of thinking. In fact, that part of the world was out of my mind. I knew I was different to many others. Up to this stage I had never felt sex desire with the girls in the forest, though I had seen that many had been returned to the reserve where they could be taken care of at maternity, or even at villages, for no child could survive in this frozen forest.

A few days later, Wambugu, one of our fighters from the *mbuci* where I was staying, told me on his return from the reserve that he had to fight his own mother, aged over 60, who hugged on him crying and cursing him not to return to the forest again. He added that the women had started trapping our fighters inside houses where they were entertained with food while other women went to call Home Guards who only forced our fighters to surrender at the points of their guns. The women's trick became known to our fighters who learned to enter the village with great awareness of many friendly traps conducted by wife or mother or even the children.

Though our fighters were still willing to persevere and continue the fight, more than half the people in the reserve had become tired and longed only for peace. They had experienced dreadful torture, collective punishments, disgraceful and miserable life in the concentrated and insanitary camps in which hunger starvation was decreasing our population at Government's supervision. The civilians were forced to labor daily without pay or food. They were highly oppressed and had no means of resistance. Sons and daughters were being shot in cold blood in front of their parents. The parents were rebuked that death was the only freedom their sons were seeking. Thousands of our killed warriors were often taken to the villages for the parents to witness the harvest for demanding freedom.

Radio sets were distributed to all villages in order to propagate the Government's propaganda from the General Information Office, Nairobi. In addition, vernacular propaganda papers were freely distributed to all the civilians, even the illiterate ones, and they were forbidden to read any other newspaper. Both the radio and the vernacular papers—among them *Uhoro wa Ma, The True News*—were completely anti-(Mau Mau) revolution. They branded the revolution as *Mau Mau* and referred to our fighters always as *spivs, thugs, ruffians, gangsters, thieves, murderers, mad outlaws, atavism barbarics, terrorists, bandits* and *greedy enemies of peace.* They always referred to the Government forces as *security forces, defenders of peace, peace restorers, Home Guards* and *loyalists.* They referred to the civilians as the *law abiding citizens, Kikuyu loyalists* or *Government servants.*

Generally, my tribe is industrious, agriculturist, clever and quick at learning, good imitators, well organized in its own affairs, brave fighters and peace lovers, proud of good humane honesty, lovers of giving and helping and haters of begging and bowing and, above all, proud of good fame and of being independent. The Government's propaganda, which was broadcasted at least three times daily, defamed and destroyed the good name of our tribe and degraded it to the lowest abyss. The starving, suppressed and oppressed KEM tribes suffered the greatest humiliation from the propaganda—with many practical illustrations—and felt the pain right in their hearts.

The missionaries, at the Government forces supervision, challenged the civilians as having revolted against God . . . the Kikuyu Supreme Being whom our tribe has honored and obeyed since creation. They referred to the revolt as 'atavism, barbaric,' a draw back, setting back the tribe, etc. The missionary referred to the fight as 'the fight against God'—God the Son, Christ. The missionary claimed that God had given his people—Christians—forces and powers to punish the rebels. If the rebels failed to repent, God would cause them to be finished off. But our people would never like to fight against the unassailable God, lest the tribe perished.

Over 75% of the 100,000-man Government force was African, comprising over 30,000 Home Guards (KEM) 10,000 Regular Police, 8,000 Kenya Police Reserve, plus 4,000 Tribal Police. The rest were regular soldiers in East African (KAR), the Kenya Regiment and the British troops (four battalions). The Government had drawn its African forces from Akamba, Nandi and Kipsigis, Luo and Luhya, Kisii and Tende, Turkana and Somali. Most of these, soldiers who had either been badly trained or had not been trained at all, insulted, scorned and despised the whole Kikuyu tribe. They said :

'You Kikuyu want to expel the Europeans so that you will rule us ! Why have you taken an oath to kill others ? To rob Europeans their lands and property ? To steal other peoples' property ? So you want *uhuru* (freedom) to kill and rob others ? Do you think that Kikuyu alone will manage to free all other tribes ? We do not like your freedom ! We will beat you until the oath goes out of you ! You claim to be the rulers of Kenya ? Death is the only freedom you will get ! You will see; you will be ruled by the smallest and uncivilized tribes (which was absolutely true then) ! Your oaths have only caused complete destruction of your own people, homes, livestock, crops, trades, progress and happiness. You Kikuyu have lost your morality and dignity and you have become maniacs !'

These were some of the questions and phrases frequently uttered to our supporters by their brothers who were supporting the Europeans. When the Kikuyu were mourning for the loss they had suffered for African freedom, their African brothers—who represented their tribes in their interpretation—not only scorned, despised and taunted them, but they beat, tortured, robbed and mistreated them in every way. Yet the Kikuyu were willing to give their lives as ransom for all Kenya peoples—excluding the settlers who were not wanted in the country.

In addition to the bad treatment, shame and guilt senses created by the Government's propaganda, the chiefs, the headmen, the churches, the traders, the educated Africans, the African Representatives in the Legislative Council, the Kenya African Union leaders, free or detained, were continuously denouncing and disassociating themselves from the revolution. Jomo Kenyatta, the symbol of the revolution, and his five other colleagues, were now serving their seven year sentences passed on 8th April 1953 under the charges of managing or assisting to manage Mau Mau. Ever since, they were completely cut off from the public and the lack of their communication became their lack of leadership and ability at the time when it was greatly needed. But Kenyatta's name was branded by Government's propaganda; [he was] the 'leader of darkness and death,' an evil man, opportunist, etc. The revolution had lost a spokesman, apart from its leaders in the forest who were also handicapped on communication bases. I remember to have shed tears at the regret of my inability to transmit my thoughts to the public; in spite of how hard I shouted, my voice could only be heard a few yards from me in that dense forest.

It was at this crucial period that I first heard of willing confessions in the villages, which were reported to have unearthed skeletons of informers and traitors who were assassinated two and a half years ago. All this news really shocked me. It made me think that our people had lost the way and were moving in the darkness to the Government's surrender-offer trap. If we lost both the battle and our claims, it would take us at least another twenty years to be able to motivate people to another revolt, but I was too optimistic and concluded that we could lose the battle and achieve our aims if right and justice ever prevailed.

Since the Government forces had not interfered with our movements in the forest, our fighters had been able to communicate and learn whereabouts the other fighters were situated. On the 2nd March, 155 fighters and leaders of IDA 3/2, 3/3 and 3/5 and I set off for the Ituma general election and the promotion of Kimathi. We arrived at Chieni late the following afternoon. Our arrival coincided with the arrival of twelve Kenya Parliament members from Gikuyu Iregi Army. We were all glad to meet each other and Kimathi forcasted a successful meeting since there were no enemies within the forest.

'Mind you, the enemies are not asleep; they're planning what to do next,' I remarked.

'Whatever they will do, they will leave us in this forest,' said Macaria Kimemia. 'Their last sweep operation left us here.'

'We are God's people. They cannot defeat us,' said Kimathi, leading us to the Kenya Parliament meeting room.

We sat down and exchanged reports from various parts of the forest, while arriving *itungati* built new huts. Among the topics was the Government's surrender offer. We resolved that if it were not a propaganda, the Government would have asked for our representatives in order to negotiate a peace treaty.

Kimathi told us that he had not received all the paraphernalia for the ceremony which caused Nyaga, Ndiritu and Abdullah to be very busy sending out their *itungati* to the reserve in order to collect the ordered paraphernalia. The *itungati* returned safely with all the requirements.

On 5th March, the twenty K.P. members spent some time enlisting agenda to be discussed the following day and planning how the ceremony would be conducted. By nightfall, Kihara Gatandi, Gikonyo Kanyungu, with their sections IDA 2/2 and 2/3 and IDA 4/1 had arrived with more than 130 fighters. Our worry increased for the absence of Mathenge, the Chairman of the meeting. We resolved to wait for Mathenge until midday; if he failed to turn up then we would put the matter over to all the fighters and discuss whether it would be possible or not to hold the general election. The attendance was 800 fighters. Nobody had turned up from the Kenya Inoro Army and only one section of the Mburu Ngebo Army and the Kenya Levellation Army had arrived.

After asking all the leaders questions which helped me to estimate the number of our fighters, and taking into the consideration many camps which I knew very well the losses they had suffered, I concluded that about 35% of our fighters was still at large—of which nearly 5,000 were in Nyandarua. Then I told Kimathi my estimates : over 22,000 fighters all over Kenya killed, 800 captured while in action, 700 surrenderees. Taking an average death rate of 200 persons daily up to the end of 1954 killed by both Government and our forces, this would mean at least 150,000 persons killed, taking into account death by starvation or diseases in the unsanitary villages which, of course, swept thousands of children and old aged persons. It was obvious that thousands of our supporters and sympathizers had been killed in the reserves, which had become the battleground on the fact that all KEM people had revolted.

Kimathi, agreeing with my estimates, asked me whether I had seen Gen. Erskine's report. I replied that I had not seen it. He pulled a copy of the *East African Standard*, gave it to me to read and warned me not to tell anyone else about the figures or our estimates. As far as I can remember, by the end of January 1955, Gen. Erskine reported : 8,000 killed, 700 hanged, 880 captured injured, 300 captured unhurt, 888 surrenderees, against 68 Europeans, 21 Asians, 1,800 Africans killed by our forces.

We concluded that these figures were not correct. Though Government was not willing to announce the truth, it did not know how many people it had killed, either in the forest or the reserves, nor did it know how many people had been assassinated before July 1953.

'Nevertheless, this is the price of Freedom,' said Kimathi. 'Kenyatta asked us whether we had the blood to pour on the Freedom Tree so that it can grow.'

'Yes, we all promised to pour our own blood so that the Freedom Tree would grow,' I said, 'but Kenyatta also promised us that he would hold the lions jaws so that it wouldn't bite us and asked us if we would bear its claws.'

'Though Kenyatta is still holding the head, as he said,' said Kimathi, 'we have suffered from the claws more than we expected.'

'Did he really know that this is how it would happen?' I asked.

'Yes,' replied Kimathi. 'Kenyatta is a very wise man, in fact he had predicted many of the emergency events. He is a prophet chosen by God just like Moses, who God chose to deliver the Israelite nation out of the Egyptian slavery; so is Kenyatta chosen to deliver the Kenya people out of the colonial slavery.'

'I wonder whether Gen. China has informed Mr Kenyatta of the ruthless slaughtering of our people by the Government forces, the starvation conditions created, our fight against a large well-equipped army, with unassailable air bombers and artillery cannons against poorly armed fighters?'

'Yes, he must have told him,' replied Kimathi. 'Though I do

not have confidence in China; conditions have greatly changed since his arrest more than a year ago, for Government has increased brutality, strength and methods of defeating our people more than what China could tell. You see, China had only less than ten months experience of the fight in the forest during which time the Government was quite ignorant of the Movement, and of our secrets, and had no knowledge of the forest it has now from both experience and surrenderees who have greatly supplied the Government with information.'

'I still doubt whether Kenyatta knows the situation of the people he leads, for it is absolutely true that our tribe is like a flock of sheep without a shepherd. But Kenyatta is a good shepherd and he wouldn't keep quiet knowing the loss of property and lives of an unarmed people in the reserves who are shot like unwanted game. I think that if he knew, he would appeal to his people and surely the Government would allow him, for it knows that he is the leader.

'I remember Kenyatta saying that he could make Kenya a football match, and also there were a lot of rumors at the beginning of the emergency that Communists would help us, but now this is the third year of our fight and there is no one who has come to help us, nor have we received any supply of arms from the Communists.'

'It is all true what you say, Mr Njama, but you should remember that expectation is better than realization, and also it is very easy for anyone to utter impossibilities as though it was as easy as his speech.'

It was dinner time and we moved to join the other members of the Kenya Parliament at the mess hall. While we were eating, Kimathi enquired us how the ceremony was to be conducted. After a long discussion on many suggestions, we decided to call Wandere, an elder over 70 years old, to advise us.

After a long talk with him and accepting his advice, we resolved that the ceremony must be traditional, one which was performed in order to promote a man to the top hierarchy council of the elders, i.e., *Kiama kia Mataati*, the Council of Peace. Traditionally, to qualify for this promotion one had to pass through many other ceremonial stages ranging from birth, circumcision, warrior, an officer of the Council of War, marriage, junior elder, *Kiama kia Kamatimu*, i.e., Council of Elders, and finally *Kiama kia Mataathi*.

Age was also considered in the promotion. A sheep or two goats were given to the higher rank as a fee and in the case of becoming a member of a *kiama* one had to brew beer of pure honey which was a part of the feast in which the initiate would invite his age friends. We tried as much as we could to copy our old pattern.

Kimathi was fully prepared for the ceremony. He had brewed beer of pure honey and had a *gitete* full of undiluted honey. He had stored in his hut every type of food that was required. He had three sheeps to be slaughtered, sheep fat and castor oil, [as well as] warriors weapons—spear, sword, club, bow and arrow, a head-dress (*thumbi*) and a walking stick, shaped like an upside-down 'L'. He had ordered Elders' equipment—walking staffs (*mithegi*), *mataathi* (leaves of *mutaathi* tree used by the elders as their hand-kerchiefs), *munyeni* headdress, sheep cloaks, hyrax and monkey cloaks to be worn after the ceremony.

We agreed that the ceremony had to start at sunset the following day. But the participants and the administrator were to be elected the following morning by the K.P. before the meeting commenced. Being quite late, we retired to bed.

At 9 a.m. on the 6th March 1955 the Kenya Parliament met. Kimathi nominated Gathura Muita and Ndururi Vindo to be in charge of his feast to be held in this hut in the evening. He nomi-mated Abdullah as his companion in the ceremony. He classified his guests according to Members of Parliament, age-group (*riika*), friends, elders divided into *Mwangi* and *Irungu*. The former, *Mwangi*, would receive his father's honor [i.e., blessing]. Each group was to be entertained separately in the surrounding huts.

Now, who was to hand over to Kimathi the *muthegi*, *mataathi*, the rank of Prime Minister, anoint and bless him and his suc-cessor and conduct the ceremony? The administrator was to be elected by the Kenya Parliament, but Kimathi remarked that since the administrator would become his godfather, he should be allowed to nominate at least five persons out of whom the Kenya Parliament would elect the administrator. The nominees were Ndiritu Thuita, Vindo, myself and two others from Gikuyu Iregi Army. The next qualification was generation-age, *Mwangi* or *Irungu*. Two persons who were found to be *Irungu* were dis-qualified, for they were of the same age with Kimathi and the administrator had to be *Mwangi*—Kimathi's father's generation— so that he would be able to bless him.

In order to save time and get rid of any favor, I wrote on a piece of paper in capital letters, 'ADMINISTRATOR' and the other two 'NO'. I folded the three pieces of paper. We then stood to pray God that the best and the right person be chosen by Him by giving him the lucky chance of picking the right paper.

We then sat down; I threw up the pieces of paper so that they would fall in the center of the circle. As I was not interested in participating in any kind of ceremony, I was the last to pick my paper from the ground. When I opened it, to my surprise, I was to be the administrator. I made excuses that I didn't know what was required to be done and they all insisted that Wandere would instruct me. We made amendment that Abdullah was to assist me, while Vindo would accompany Kimathi and Nyaga was to take care of the feast with Gathura.

In addition to our traditional ceremony, there was another plan to anoint Kimathi as the head of our Government. Traditionally, no such ceremony could be performed if the initiate was unmarried, for his wife had to stand on his left hand during the ceremony. Kimathi's wife and legal daughter were still living in Nairobi under the care of our supporters. It was impossible to get her to attend the ceremony. Up to this stage, Kimathi had been living with a girl about four months before abandoning her and taking another from the recent arrivals from the reserves. Wanjiru Wambogo daughter of Waicanguru Wanarua, pretty, brown, healthy, medium girl, had by now completed over six months living with Kimathi. Their love had grown so that Kimathi did not hesitate accepting Wanjiru as his wife. Since Kimathi was the head of our Government, Wanjiru was to be the head of the women and the mother of Mumbi's children. She was then to be awarded the highest women's rank, colonel, and knighted with Knight Commander of the Gikuyu and Mumbi Empire.

Who was to succeed Kimathi as Field Marshal? It was now midday and Mathenge had not yet arrived. Over 800 warriors were lying idly awaiting him. It was his general meeting, under his Chairmanship, and yet he had not yet attended. We were certain that there were no enemies in the forest who might have brought inconveniences. His qualifications were—very popular, inactive and incapable, unfit for such a post, for he had spent most of his time hiding, even from other fighters, afraid of touring other camps, had no plans, suggestion, advice or organization.

And now, what about Macaria Kimemia? Uneducated but very clever, could read and write in vernacular, very industrious, sagacious and active, very brave and with a high commanding tone, had toured many camps in the whole forest, lecturing to our fighters on methods of fighting, getting food, unity, obedience and courage, etc. In general, a very auspicious person. Macaria Kimemia would become second to Kimathi and let Mathenge remain with his chair as the head of Ituma Ndemi Army in order to avoid a split until such a time as the fighters from Othaya Division could recognize that Mathenge was inactive—for he had tied himself with them on regional thoughts. We agreed not to tell the general meeting our decision and let the warriors decide themselves whether to hold the election or to postpone it.

We walked to the general meeting with nothing concrete other than what the general meeting would decide. Wang'ombe Ruga said the opening prayers and we all sat down on grass surrounded by bamboo clusters. Kimathi was the first speaker :

'I greet you all, leaders and *itungati*. First thing, I am very sorry because our Chairman, Mr Mathenge, is absent. I do not know what has happened to him for he should have arrived yesterday in order to organize the meeting for today. Before I continue any further, you should appoint a temporary chairman for today's meeting.

'You are the chairman,' replied many voices, though there was a little opposition on doubts that temporary might be permanent.

'No,' said Kimathi. 'According to the election twenty months ago, I was elected to be the Secretary of Ituma Ndemi Trinity Council, which is [holding a general] meeting here today for the first time since its election. Remember that our last month's meeting did not become successful as our fighters had been badly dispersed by the enemy. It is impossible for me to become both Chairman and the Secretary. You must find someone else.'

We finally agreed that Abdullah should chair the meeting. Kimathi then proceeded by giving the names of its [other] officers, of which only Wacira Gathuku was present. He said that the elected leaders of Ituma Ndemi Trinity Council had completely failed to do their duty to their fighters as a council, but as individuals some had helped their *mbuci*, location or division at the most, with the exception of himself who had done his best for Ituma Ndemi Army and the other armies of Kenya and, in fact, for all the warriors in Nyandarua, Kirinyaga and even Narok. He pulled his sword, the gift from Masai fighters, and showed the meeting as witness for his leadership and command over a large area. He admitted that as the Secretary of the Ituma Council, he should share the blame of their failures, which their Chairman Mathenge should carry the most.

He accused Mathenge for not calling his officers even once to discuss what was wrong or what to do for the fighters, what advice or suggestions to give them. He had even failed to call a general meeting and report that his officers had failed to accomplish their work; he had not asked for a general election that might give him new, able and active leaders. In general, he had failed. He then asked the meeting whether it wanted to renew the council and elect new officers.

The answers from the audience split the meeting into Othaya Division and North Tetu Division, while the few Mburu Ngebo Army [fighters] tried to be mediators. By the attendances, the North Tetu outvoted Othaya together with Mburu Ngebo Army. The Tetu IDA 1 and its sections demanded an election be held right there. The Othaya sections of IDA 2, 3 and 4 were splitting again, some supporting the election while others shouted that they would not participate in the election during Mathenge's absence— giving only one condition, if Mathenge was to remain Chairman.

The meeting split into three sections. I attended the Othaya meeting and warned our warriors not to favor a person because of popularity, regional representation or a symbol. 'We should like someone because of his ideas. If our popular person has no ideas, when he dies we would also die with him on our thoughts for he would leave nothing for us to follow. When a man of good ideas dies, his people continue to follow his ideas. If he had become popular for his activities, then as long as his actions remain in sight and mind of the people, so will his name remain. Learn to love the truth a man represents apart from his physical personality in which most of you have fallen.'

Though I gained a few supporters, the Othaya Division concluded that there would be no election in Mathenge's absence unless it was agreed that he would still be the chairman of the new council.

When we all gathered together again, each group reported its decision. Kimathi stood up and ruled that in order to avoid a split, and to achieve good cooperation and unity amongst ourselves, there would be no election without Mathenge. He then appealed to Mathenge's supporters to make sure that Mathenge called a general election for Ituma Ndemi Trinity Council or forget that there was such a council, as in fact it was a dead council under the names of living persons.

'I wouldn't like to be called Secretary of such a council which creates shame, irresponsibility, incapability and laziness on its leaders. Actions speak louder than words. I and my colleagues will continue to act what we say and do what we think is good for our fighters, supporters and the whole country. Tonight we have a ceremony which Mr Njama will tell you about and in which one of the most active and industrious leaders would be promoted to Field Marshal rank. But such a rank cannot be given to lazy, inactive persons or even to one who is never punctual to a meeting.'

Kimathi, who had spoken in an angry tone, sat down. When I stood I said : 'Exactly a month ago, just in this very place, seating more than 500 fighters, including Mathenge, all agreed that we shall hold a ceremony today in which we shall promote Field Marshal Dedan Kimathi to become the Prime Minister of our Government. This would mean to anoint and symbolize him as the head of the revolution—the head of the Emergency Government. We have then been preparing to accomplish our ceremony for a long time. The day has arrived, we too have arrived; it is now about an hour before we start the ceremony.

'Though we have postponed today's election because of Mathenge's absence, which was fair because it was Mathenge's meeting, I don't think that there would be any such reasons that would confront our ceremony in the last hour. Though we would all have liked very much to see Mathenge with us in the ceremony, it is obvious now that we are to do without him unless he arrives in the last minute... thus the saying, *Nyanja imwe nditiragia itega*. "The absence of one calabash cannot stop one from sending beer to an organized feast," will have to be fulfilled. The main importance is that when we are to do any ceremony, we must always approach it with goodwill, taking much care not to spoil our ceremony by taboos or having an ill-will to other persons or contaminating it with any impurities that might disqualify the ceremony in the eyes of God. You should always approach any ceremony with a humble, honest and clean heart, with a true cooperation with others, and good faith. I now appeal to you to forget all your differences of the day's talk and get together to accomplish the ceremony, knowing well that it is through unity, cooperation and understanding one another that we can settle our differences. Tonight, instead of our daily evening prayers, we will hold the ceremony at twilight.'

With this, we dispersed and soon started preparing for the great drama. In a short time all the required apparatus were brought. We entered in my hut and dressed. Abdullah and I dressed like elders. We took off our clothes, remaining with undershorts only, and smeared all over our body with castor oil. I then put on a sheep cloak, tied a sword around my waist with its bright red sheath, put *munyeni* on my head—a feather- or fiber-made beret, rattles on my legs, rubber sandals, an elderly leather satchel under my left shoulder, a black honorary walking staff—*muthegi*, made of *mungirima* tree—in my right hand, together with *mataathi* leaves—elders' handkerchief—a fly-whisk and a traditional three-legged stool in my left hand.

Being fully dressed, we walked out of the hut pretending to be really old men. We had so greatly changed that our comrades could not recognize us. Amid cheers and laughters and doubts, we went to Kimathi's hut and found that he and Ndururi had dressed like ourselves, but didn't have *muthegi*, *mataathi*, flywhisk or satchel, for they were juniors. We exchanged greetings : '*Wanyua*,' '*Wanyua*'—father, *Mwangi*, to son, *Irungu*. '*Wanyua wakine*,' was exchanged between persons of the same [generation] age.

While sitting down, Kimathi took his *ndahi*—a little gourd half the size of a glass—and filled it with the pure honey beer which he had brewed. After each of us had drunk one *ndahi*, we filled two *itete* with beer to be used in the ceremony and the rest we put in *nyanja*, gourds for storing beer. Wang'ombe Ruga took one *gitete*, a little gourd with sheep's fat, blood and abdominal dung, and went at the main entrance where he stood cleansing all the fighters as they entered the ceremonial hall.

When Wang'ombe sent a report that he had cleansed all the fighters, Kimathi and his wife to be, followed by Ndururi Vindo and Macaria Kimemia, entered the hall. When they were all seated, Abdullah and I, Wandere my advisor and two other elders who carried the paraphernalia required, entered the hall. All the warriors stood up as we slowly walked the 120 feet along the narrow path between the standing columns. On our arrival at the platform, I filled a horn with beer from the *gitete*, purposely letting it flow over to the ground. I held the horn in my right hand and the little fat gourd in my left. Facing Kirinyaga, I asked the audience to attend prayers :

Our Heavenly Father, I beseech you; draw nearer and hear our prayers. (*Thaai*! audience) Our merciful Father, forgive us all our sins and wash our hearts, hands and minds as it satisfies thy will, so that we may be clean in your eyes. (*Thaai*!) Oh God! defend and guide us for we are your children, your own creation. We believe that you are our leader, general and King of Kings, and we humbly pray you to lead and supervise our ceremony. (*Thaai*!) I now present to you fat and honey (pouring a little to the sides and front), our best produce, your own choice, and which you have instructed our forefathers to present to you in all ceremonies.

Now God, I pray you power and wisdom to enable me to accomplish this ceremony in your name, Father, I present Dedan Kimathi to you, the man you chose to lead us in this forest. We have gathered here today to pray you to glorify Kimathi, fill him with power and wisdom, defend and keep him, and let him lead us to victory in your home. (*Thaai thathaiya Ngai thaai*— three times)

All sitting down, Kimathi and his party standing, I turned to Kimathi and, pouring fat and honey on his head, I said : 'May this be the sign that we all here accept and witness Dedan Kimathi as the Head Leader of all our armies. May God bless this head, fat and sweet honey help it to grow and rise above all heads in the name of our god. *Thaai*.'

I sipped the beer and made a spitting gesture on my both shoulders and sipped again, spraying Kimathi and his girl with it from my mouth. I said : 'May you have power to defeat the enemy, long life, many children and popularity.'

Handing over the horn and the gourd to my assistant, I took an envelope out of my satchel and holding it together with my *muthegi* in my left hand and the flywhisk in my right, I addressed the audience : 'We all know the work done by Dedan Kimathi in our struggle for Land and Freedom. He was the Secretary of the Kenya African Union Thomson's Falls Branch during which time he preached and motivated the desire to fight for our freedom to thousands of people in Thomson's Falls, Ol Kalao, Leshau and nearly half the Nyeri District. He administered oaths to such an extent that his head was valued at 10,000s. by the Government nearly two and a half years ago. Thousands of people who want to sell this head to the Government have not succeeded for God has really protected him, and you his bodyguards, for you too are defended by Ngai.

'In the reserves Kimathi has organized how our fighters can be supplied their requirements. In the forest he has organized eight armies, has helped to instruct leaders how to keep differents kinds of records. He has planned many attacks, has led Kenya Defence Council, Kenya Parliament, and founded the Kenya Young Stars Association. He has appointed leaders and issued ranks, has toured nearly all the camps in Nyandarua preaching unity, courage, obedience and discipline, has sent various missions in and out of Nyandarua, has spoken to the Government through letters and even to people abroad. His actions have made his name to be advertised to the world in both newspapers and radios as the leader of the war. Actions speak louder than words. Kimathi has never advertised himself as the leader of the revolution but his actions have made him well known all over the world. Has Kimathi stopped any leader from advertising himself to the world in his own words or actions? Why then are some leaders infested with jealousy and envy at Kimathi's success? (cheers and great applause).

'Kimathi, my son, for your good service to your country, your willingness to sacrifice your life for your people, your bravery, your industriousness, your good conduct and leadership has made the Kenya Parliament, which is the people's eyes, to promote you today, 6th March 1955, to become the first Prime Minister of the Kenya African Government (amid cheers) and knight you Sir Dedan Kimathi, Knight Commander of the East African Empire. Here (handing him the envelope containing a letter and 500s.), in the name of Gikuyu and Mumbi and the Kenya Parliament's authority. You will now be leader of the leaders, an elder of the first order who only advises and settles down quarrels. Let another warrior rise as much as you have done in the army. This is the elder's honor (handing over the *muthegi*, *mataathi* and flywhisk) which marks that you have passed the warriors stage (shaking hands and exchanging greetings—"*Wanyua*," "*Wanyua wakini*").

Wang'ombe Ruga comes with wet skin ribbons, dipped in blood and the stomach contents of a goat, *ngwaru*. He puts these bracelets on Kimathi's right wrist and also on his four companions on the platform, telling them that they had officially joined the elders' class.

I then turned to Wanjiru : 'Wanjiru d/o Waicanguru has been with us since we entered the forest. She has shared and tasted the bad cold weather, hunger; has managed to run away with leaders' heavy burdens of clothes and utensils and has never thrown away leaders' property so as to make it easy for her to flee. She was very trusted by Gen. Makanyanga who was living with her. Her good conduct and service has made the Prime Minister to choose her in this great historical event whereby you see her standing by the Prime Minister's left hand. As the queen receives the king's honors or the wife receives her husband's honors, may it be so with Wanjiru. I therefore declare Wanjiru to be our foremost lady and hereby issue her with the highest women's rank (handing her an envelope), Colonel Wanjiru, Knight Commander of Gikuyu and Mumbi. I would appeal to you to address her now forthwith as an old woman of your mother's rank. (Laughter.)'

I took from Kimathi his walking stick, sword, spear and club. 'These are the warriors' weapons. They should not be kept by an elder like Kimathi or myself but should be kept by the brave, industrious and energetic warrior who is ready to use them rightly at all times. The warrior to whom I'm going to hand over these weapons is not the one I like for being my relative, neighbor, or friend; neither because he belongs to my division or district, nor is it because he is popular, but for the reason that his actions have spoken and proved him to be a hero who is ready to serve the fighters and his country and the one who doesn't hide and wish only to be served by our fighters'.

'*Ucio uri ho*! That is true!' shouted the fighters.

'Your eyes, the Kenya Parliament, has seen that Macaria Kimemia of the Gikuyu Iregi Army is the right person to take over Kimathi's post as Field Marshal. This proves that Kenya Parliament has no favor other than one's own merits. There are only sixty warriors from Murang'a in this hall out of more than 800. If it were a matter of your votes, you would definitely have voted for your own leader or the one who is fully acquainted to you regardless of the qualifications. You cannot expect excellent

work from an unqualified person. Macaria Kimemia has never
failed to attend any meeting and has always been punctual in spite
of long distances, dangers of the enemy and bad weather. He has
all the time cooperated with Kimathi and the Kenya Parliament.
Gikuyu Iregi Army has elected him as its head leader. They know
his actions better than we do.'

Calling Macaria Kimemia, who dressed like a general, to stand
up, I exchanged warriors' weapons with a horn of beer and the
fat gourd. I poured the sheep's fat (oil) and the beer on his head
saying : 'May this fat and honey soften this head and let it grow
above other heads. May your head and hands be fitted with wisdom
and power. May God bless, keep and guide you, and grant you
with power to defeat the enemy. Macaria, your good work has
been well recorded in our books and, more important, in the minds
of those who have seen your actions. Kenya Parliament has decided
to promote you to Field Marshal and knight you, Sir Macaria
Kimemia, Knight Commander of the East African Empire.'

Amid cheers, I handed him an envelope in which we had enclosed 300s. and a letter. 'This is a spear, a sword and a club. They
are the warrior's weapons which you must use to defend your
country and people from any attackers. This is Kimathi's walking
stick, you must herd our fighters with it. You must be a good
shepherd. All our fighters are now under your command. If you
work hard you will be promoted again. You are to start your work
right from this minute.'

Macaria sat down. I filled the horn with beer and drank it and
then addressed the audience : 'As we had prayed God to guard and
guide us through this ceremony, we have come to the end very successfully, more than I had expected, and for this I thank God
once again. I know that many people are very much worried about
Mathenge's position. There are many positions awaiting him and
any other leader whose actions will prove him fit. Some of you
might be thinking that we have given Macaria a good name, but it
is not a name, it is work we have given him—very difficult and
tiresome work. If he thinks that we have given him a good name
and fails to do his job properly, then his Field Marshal rank will
not be any different from 'Major' or general nicknames of the
boys at dances. Be sure that our ranks are real and should be
respected.

'Though Mathenge was absent, we cannot do all at the same

time. Today was the day for the two promoted; tomorrow may be Mathenge's, and maybe he will get a better post than the others—but at present we cannot say more. Don't you go and deceive him that he is neglected or degraded. You all know how much we love him and that we all have spent the whole day waiting for him. If you are feeling like me, I am very unhappy about it. Think about it this way : if Mathenge had been awaiting us all the day to attend his meeting and by evening he found that he was all alone, what would he think? What would you think if you were Mathenge?'

Replies from various people were : 'I would think that you all hate me.' 'I would think that you have no confidence in me.' 'I would think that you are all against me.' 'I would think that you have all fallen into danger,' etc.

'His failure to attend his own meeting has caused the same kind of feelings and doubts in me. I would now like the Prime Minister, Field Marshal, Wandare, our advisor in this ceremony, and one more leader to say a few words before we go to make fires.'

Kimathi, like an elder, started greeting the audience according to their generation ages, male and female separately : 'I am very glad and thank you for your attendance and every effort you have rendered me to make this ceremony so successful that it has made us all happy. I am proud of my own works, which have placed a record in your minds, and that my record in our history up to this stage is very clean and admirable. I have no doubts I shall be able to finish it the same way. You are all leaders, show your effort now and when we achieve independence we shall know where to post you and which part of Kenya to send you to lead. It is only through obedience, perseverance and unity that you can learn and develop your talents. I will continue to advise you.'

'I am glad for the responsibility you have given me,' said Macaria Kimemia. 'I promise you that I will try my level best to maintain it at all costs. I will unreservedly and mercilessly smash any hindrance of our progress, even [from] within. I will be very strict on obedience and I will sentence you just as Thacker sentenced Kenyatta. If you would like to nickname me Thacker, all the better, but I am willing to die for you !'

The other two leaders stood up to comment on the ceremony. It was now 8 :15 p.m. and the last speaker was Wandare, the old man. Just when he started commenting on how successful the ceremony had been, Mathenge entered the hall holding a *gitete* of pure honey and a flywhisk in his left hand and his walking staff in his right hand and, after greetings, sat in the front row with the audience.

I addressed the audience again : 'I am glad because Mathenge—whom we have been waiting for all the day long—has arrived safely, but I regret to say that he has been so late that the train has already gone, leaving him. Nevertheless, if he will be punctual he can board the train next trip. Referring to the meeting you called us to, Mr Mathenge, we couldn't hold the election without you on the chair. This proves that we still have confidence in you. Kimathi is now Prime Minister and Macaria the Field Marshal. We were just about to leave the hall when you arrived, having completed all we had to do or say. I know that all our fighters are very anxious to hear you speak; you have five minutes to speak.'

'Greetings,' said Mathenge. 'I am sorry for being late and I would ask all of you who have really been waiting for me to excuse me. I was late right at the beginning for I confused the dates. I thought that the meeting would be on 7th March, tomorrow. I only remembered yesterday that the 7th was the date for the last month's meeting. I then hurriedly started my journey. I would have arrived here before sunset, but unfortunately we missed the way for some time. It is all right that you have successfully completed the ceremony but *"Thutha wa arume nduoyagwo ruoya,"* "You cannot find feathers along other men's paths" (a saying related to birds' feathers which were used by men as ornaments for headdresses in dances. It was then certain that a man picked all or the best feathers he found on his way and if he left any, then they must be of a low or poor quality.) I very much doubt of whatever good might come after, but *"Ngari nditunyagwo maara mayo,"* "You cannot rob a leopard of his spots." Everyone will take his inheritance—mine is mine. The one who will lead us from the forest will be the leader. The one who will take us to freedom will be the leader and all people will follow and obey him. I will call you for the election whenever I think it fits. You are all my fighters, I hate none. I was prepared for the ceremony and this is the honey I had brought. (He started pouring the honey on the ground and on his flywhisk, spraying all the fighters in the hall, saying :) May God bless, keep and guide you forever. May you have power to defeat the enemy. Peace be unto you all.'

With that we ended the ceremony. Any person who wanted to

give Kimathi a gift for his great day was to take it to his hut and see Gathura Muita who was recording all the gifts.

Leaving the hall, those of us involved in the ceremony were entertained by Kimathi as his guests of honor in his hut, where a big feast was conducted. Singing and dancing continued until very late at night. Before retiring to bed, the Kenya Parliament, including Mathenge, agreed that he, Mathenge, and all the leaders of IDA 2, 3 and 4, would build their Memorial Hall at H.Q. Kariaini and that Kimathi and all Murang'a leaders of the K.P. would open the hall on 18th March on their way to Murang'a where they would be opening the H.Q. for the Gikuyu Iregi Army on 20th March at Karuri Ngamune. All the fighters in the areas concerned should attend the general opening and supply the K.P. members with food for *safari* to Murang'a.

Early in the morning, 7th March, we dispersed, returning to our former *mbuci*, and being accompanied by Mathenge on our way back to Gura Valley. On the way, I weighed in my mind what we had accomplished in that long ceremony. Firstly, we had created Kimathi the symbol and head of the revolution beyond any doubts. No other leader might think of competing with him and we had successfully achieved our aim. Secondly, we had created room for other leaders to rise—maybe we would appoint a Field Marshal for every army so as to get Mathenge in this rank in order to avoid splits and conflicts. But for most of the time, the inactive Mathenge had not sought support from other armies apart from his own division, in which he was building a wall to mark his boundaries. Since Mathenge was a person of my sub-location, I had learned that the whole of Chinga Location was against him, a third of Othaya Location and a quarter of Mahiga, his own location. I thought that a split would be slight, for Mathenge could only be supported by a few Mburu sections under Kimbo and only the section of IDA 1 under Kahiu-Itina. Nevertheless, if the split were to arise, we should settle it by making Mathenge a Field Marshal of the Ituma Ndemi Army.

CHAPTER XX

CLEAVAGE AND DISINTEGRATION

B Y M A Y of 1955, the rift between forest leaders had become a deep cleavage between openly hostile segments of the once unified forest organization. The dissident leaders under Stanley Mathenge formed a new central council, the Kenya Riigi, which set itself in opposition to the Kenya Parliament and undertook a lengthy series of surrender negotiations with Government representatives which ended in failure on May 20th. Karari's account vividly depicts the events which led to this open conflict —capped by the Kenya Parliament's arrest of Mathenge and other Kenya Riigi leaders and the latters' eventual escape—and lays bare the pattern which this cleavage took.

Once the split was crystalized amongst top-ranking forest leaders, it is not surprising in view of the vertical patterning of loyalties discussed earlier that lesser section and sub-section leaders, and the followers under them, tended to continue or withdraw their support of the Kenya Parliament largely in terms of their allegiance to particular territorial leaders. Thus, reflecting the strong leader-followers-locality ties characteristic of the forest organization, Othaya groups and leaders aligned themselves for the most part with Mathenge and the Kenya Riigi, while Kimathi and the Kenya Parliament retained the support of North Tetu leaders and followers. Kahiu-Itina, a North Tetu leader allied with Mathenge, was able to hold the support only of *itungati* under his personal command. The Fort Hall groups and leaders under Macaria Kimemia remained steadfastly behind Kimathi and the Kenya Parliament, while Mbaria Kaniu carried the support of Fort Hall sections of the Mburu Ngebo Army under his command. A vertical pattern of segmentation thus emerged as dissident Kenya Riigi leaders were, on the whole, able to retain the support of subordinate leaders and their followers.

With the escape of the dissident leaders and the development of openly hostile relations between the Kenya Parliament and Kenya Riigi, each of these forest bodies claimed legitimacy for itself while challenging that of the other. The Kenya Parliament, though failing in its original efforts during the trials, continued for a time to regard the Kenya Riigi leaders as individual renegades and refused to consider their *itungati* as enemies. Claiming sole authority over Nyandarua fighters, the Kenya Parliament hoped to apprehend and try the Kenya Riigi leaders while at the same time it sought to contact the Government agents so as to assume its rightful position in the negotiations.

The Kenya Riigi, on the other hand, claiming to represent the majority of illiterate Kikuyu fighters, attacked the Kenya Parliament as a body dominated by Kimathi and a few educated members who favored North Tetu and sought only personal power and reward at the expense of the illiterate. Though its base of popular support among Aberdare fighters was somewhat narrower, the Kenya Riigi claim to legitimacy was greatly enhanced by its position in the surrender negotiations, the cease fire it had agreed to with the Government, and by the Kenya Parliament's inability to apprehend its leaders.

With the breakdown of the surrender talks, Government resumed its land and air attacks on the forest and, perhaps more significantly, intensified its efforts to isolate and starve out the remaining guerrilla fighters, whose numbers had been reduced to around 5,000. A tight control over both Kikuyu 'villages' and the forest fringe, combined with a Government food denial policy requiring that cattle be kept in guarded enclosures during the night and prohibiting the peasant cultivation of food crops within three miles of the forest, forced the forest units to utilize their dwindling supplies of arms and ammunition exclusively for food raids and, where absolutely necessary, defense.

★ ★ ★

On arrival at Tusha stream, Mathenge paused a little on the way and told me to go ahead for he was following us. After two hours walk, without seeing Mathenge and his men, we arrived at Ngara's *mbuci*. I told Ngara about the ceremony. He then asked whether we had met Kahinga's *itungati* on the way, taking a Government message to Kimathi which was brought to the forest by four surrenderees. Ngara said that they, the surrenderees, had left his camp about 2 p.m. in the afternoon with a guide from his *mbuci* to Chieni. I asked Ngara whether he had inspected the Government messengers. He replied that his clerk had told him that they had a good letter from Kahinga and that the known *itungati* from Kahinga's *mbuci* spoke well for them.

Thinking that the Government messengers might hurt Kimathi, I hurriedly wrote a letter to him :

The Prime Minister, Sir D. Kimathi,

On my arrival at Ngara's mbuci, 3 :30 p.m., I learned from Ngara that Kahinga Wachanga is keeping four surrenderees with a Government message for you in his *mbuci*. One of them with three other *itungati* from Kahinga's *mbuci* passed at Ngara's *mbuci* at 2 p.m. on their way bringing the Government message to you. For security reasons, get these people thoroughly scrutinized and interrogated by junior officers before you meet them. In case they fail to arrive there by the following morning, please send information to all IDA sections that surrenderees working for the Government are amidst us and every *mbuci* should beware of them, their intentions, motives, etc.

I think it advisable to strengthen the inspection of all in-comers to an *mbuci* in order to avoid a spy from entering your camp unnoticed. I expect to be in Kahinga's *mbuci* within two days time for further investigation.

Your loving father,
Brig. Gen. Sir. K. M. Njama
Chief Sec., Kenya Parliament
7/3/55   4 p.m.

Giving the letter to two of our *itungati* and two of Ngara's, I ordered them to run as quickly as they could on the same way we had come and take the letter back to Chieni. I told them that they had to overtake Kahinga's messengers and try to reach Chieni very early the following morning.

When night came, we learned that Mathenge had not followed us, but more likely had stopped at Kahiu-Itina's section, whom we learned, from Ngara's *itungati*, had returned. The following morning I crossed the Gura River and arrived at Kariaini at midday in Kibira's *mbuci*. He told me that the surrenderees in Kahinga's *mbuci* wanted our leaders to go and negotiate with the Kenya

Government how to put the fighting to an end. He told me that they were being supplied with food and other requirements. 'In fact, the Government has started supplying Kahinga's *mbuci* with bags of maize flour, etc. Kahinga's *itungati* have been accompanying these surrenderees when they meet their European officers on the Chinga road. Their last meeting was reported that the Europeans agreed to hand over their Sten guns to Kahinga's *itungati* in exchange for our *banda*, just for a short time to look at and check our homemade guns. They then shook hands with Kahinga's *itungati* and bade them goodbye, promising to return on the 17th March.'

I was very surprised with the news for I couldn't understand what kind of friendship Kahinga had with the enemies—living with them in his camp, being supplied with food and clothing.

I took out my Challenge notebook, put carbon papers in, and drafted letters to all leaders of IDA 2 and 3 in Kariaini and Kigumo areas and asked them to attend a meeting at Kariaini to discuss about the surrenderees in Kahinga's *mbuci*. The other items for discussion would be the planning, organizing and distributing labor for the building of our H.Q. Kenyalekalo Memorial Hall to be opened by Kimathi on the 18th March—all the IDA 1 section leaders and the Gikuyu Iregi Army leaders would be present on their way to Murang'a where they would open a similar hall. The meeting would be held in Kibira's *mbuci* on 13th March.

The following day, I toured King'ora's and Kibico's *mbuci* and learned from many *itungati* that they had gathered from Kahinga's *itungati* that the Government messengers in their camp were always talking of how the Government was ready and willing to forgive and let all by-gones be by-gones and settle our problems peacefully. I asked them whether they would like to shake a Gicakuri's (European's) hand. They all rejected the shaking of hands but [said they] would like to witness that really the Europeans had stopped entering the forest and shooting our fighters and were only willing to talk the matter over. When I asked them what they thought Government's intentions were, they told me that it was to induce us to stop fighting.

With a six-man-strong escort, I arrived at Kahinga's *mbuci* on 11th March. He received me warmly and introduced me to the Government messengers—Ndirangu Kabangu, a person whom I knew before as a *gitungati* in Kahiu-Itina's sections under Ndiritu

Thuita, and one Mung'ata Kiguta, from Kirinyaga. He told me that Kariuki Wambugu and Wambui d/o Wanjau, a girl, had gone to Mt. Kenya and would rejoin them on 17 March. I asked Kahinga which Government messenger had taken the letter to Kimathi. He answered that only his *itungati* had taken the Government letter. I asked him what was the contents of the letter. He replied that it was a Government appeal for a peaceful negotiation for putting bloodshed to an end. The Government wanted our representatives for the negotiations.

'Who had signed the letter?' I demanded.

'The Kikuyu-written letter was signed by Mr Windley, the Chief Native Commissioner, and General Heyman.'

Sending the Government messengers away, I asked Kahinga how he first met them and how he came to live with them. He told me that he had met them at Mihuro on 10th February. [He had gotten lost] on his way to attend his first session of the Kenya Parliament on 7th February, since he had been informed that he had been appointed to become a member. He had then lived with the Government's messengers for exactly a month. Kahinga told me that the four messengers were forest fighters who had surrendered and they were not intending to spy our fighters but only wanted to see that our leaders will get in touch with the Government and arrange how to end the fight.

I asked Kahinga whether he had ever inspected them or interrogated them. He replied that he had interrogated them but had never inspected them. I told him that I wanted to inspect them thoroughly and interrogate them.

I started with their leader, Ndirangu Kabangu—ordering my guards to inspect them. He was stripped naked and scrutinized thoroughly, but we found nothing dangerous in his possession nor any peculiar mark. After dressing, I had him swear with soil, in the name of God, that he would tell me only the truth. He admitted that he had surrendered because our fighters were poorly armed and couldn't by any means defeat the Government forces in the fight. He said that he had learned that our fighters were only decreasing daily in numbers and arms and ammunition while the Government was increasing daily.

'The decrease of your *itungati*,' he said, 'means perishing of our people, the fighters as well as the civilians. If we continue the fight until we are finally defeated or all our fighters have perished, we would be in a worse condition than today while the Government still recognizes us as brave fighters and while the forest fighters' efforts are regarded seriously by the Government. It would be easier to achieve our aims at this stage for we have proved to the Kenya Government and world that we are men. Had we a supply of arms, the Government could not defeat us. Nevertheless, I would like to make it clear that the mass of our people in the reserves are so oppressed that they are now only praying for an end of this miserable life. Be sure that all our people are now Government prisoners in the villages and cannot fight anymore; neither can they get anything to help you with, nor can they get means of contacting you any further.'

'Do you know that within the last month our fighters have managed to enter villages and get supplies?' I asked.

'Yes, I know,' he replied. 'But the people in the reserves are so poor that they cannot afford their own clothings or food. It may surprise you to hear that they are eating sweet potato leaves like sheep, and many other leaves that you have never heard of being eaten by man in history. One of the facts I haven't told you is that the Government has let your fighters enter the villages because it wants you to come out of the forests and go back into the reserve. The Government knows that when your fighters go into the villages, they would be convinced by their parents and relatives to abandon the fight.'

'Are you sent by the masses or by the Government?' I asked.

'We are sent by the Government to call you for negotiation talks that would end the war.'

'Which Government officer sent you?' I queried.

'Firstly, the Special Branch officer, Mr Ian Henderson, asked me whether I knew Kimathi and whether I would be willing to convey a Government message to him. I told him that I knew Kimathi very well and I could take the message to him, but I was afraid that Kimathi might order his *itungati* to kill me for being a Government stooge. Mr Henderson told me that for one and a half years I had lived in the forest, that I was willing to die in order to save my people—and that made me Government's enemy. Finally, he said, I surrendered into the enemy's hands but instead of the enemy killing me in a revenge, they treated me well in food, clothing, housing, etc. This is because the Government had changed its mind. It had learned that it cannot settle our problems by killing people and even if it were able to kill all the fighters, the demand for land and freedom would recur in the future. The Government believes, he said, that it could settle the matter with you once for all. It is on this ground that the Government has built hopes on me and my colleagues that I will be able to convey this valuable message to you fighters and I am glad that I am talking to the Chief Secretary of the Kenya Parliament, a person who I know loves his people. I know that once you have received the message it will reach Kimathi in a short time.'

'Is Henderson the Government officer that has sent you?'

'No, I am only working with him. When I agreed to bring the message to you and declared that I did not fear to be killed by my own people in my attempts to save thousands of lives and bring this war to an end, he took me to Mr Windley, the Chief Native Commissioner, in the Government's Secretariate Office. There, when I admitted to carry the message to Kimathi, His Excellency the Governor of Kenya, Sir E. Baring, came to see me. I repeated my promise to him. He said that he would be very glad if I took that Government message to Kimathi. The message, which was signed by Windley on behalf of the Governor and Heyman for Gen. Erskine, was handed to me by Mr Windley in Nairobi. That message left here on 7th March with Kahinga's *itungati* who were to deliver it to Kimathi.'

'How much are you paid for your service to the Government?'

'Not a penny, apart from food and clothing. I am doing it for the love of my people and at the risk of my own life—from both the Government and my own people.'

'What does Government do with surrenderees and captives?'

'Formerly, as you know, many of the captives were shot in cold blood right on the spot; others were shot for refusing to give the enemy any information that might endanger others or enable them to be taken to the court where death or long sentences were the only answers. Others were killed by Home Guards because of personal hatred based on lands, women, revenge, etc. The Home Guards and their KPR's used to put ammunition in the pockets of a captive so that he could be sentenced to death for being caught with it. From 18th January this year, the Governor and Gen. Erskine have appealed to their forces not to kill any more people. Detention camps have been established for surrenderees and captives at Thika where they are given food, clothing and medical treatment and are well protected. The Governor has promised all the people that no one will be prosecuted for any crime committed from the declaration of the emergency up to 18th January 1955. I hope you have read this from the leaflets dropped by the airplanes.'

'Do you think that we are fighting for the food, clothing and detention promised by the Government?'

'No, I know that we were fighting for land and freedom, but this could only be resolved in the negotiations I am calling for.'

'Doesn't Government know where Kenyatta and the KAU leaders are so as to negotiate with *them* about our land and freedom?"

'You should bear in mind that Kenyatta and the KAU leaders have all the time denied their knowledge of the fight. They have all denied membership, leadership and, worse still, they neither support the fighters nor show any sympathy to the revolution. Their general comment is "Government should deal with control and discipline all the criminals." It is on these grounds that the Government has decided to negotiate with the war leaders, whose country's peace rests in their hands for they are the only ones who can stop or continue the fight.'

'Do you know that we learned during China's negotiations that the Government only wanted to trick us into a trap?'

'Yes, I know. But this time I trust it is not a trap but a true negotiation, for I have seen the Governor and he promised me that it is a true negotiation.'

'If I ask you to return to your section and continue the fight as you vowed, would you agree?'

'Yes, I would agree if you could arm me and supply me with ammunition, food and clothing, and do the same for our other *itungati*. How can you win while you are fighting against four strong enemies—clothes, food, arms, and Government forces—each strong enough to defeat you?' asked Ndirangu.

'Do you know that you have violated your vows by surrendering?'

'Yes, I know. I have done what I could and left what I could not. For one and a half years I had been waiting for my death every minute, but the merciful God spared my life. During that time you acted as a leader and you know very well that I have received no reward for my service and I very much doubt whether

I shall receive it. My heart is with the dead and I wouldn't like any more of our people to die, for none of the dead shall ever rise to fight again for this country, but surrenderees like myself will fight again for the country when we would be better equipped for the fight. But remember, that I have come here to link you with the Government with whom you can peacefully settle what you are fighting for. I have not come to spy or trap you into the Government hands. You have a lot of power in your hands. You can kill me. You can refuse the negotiation and continue the fight until you realize the defeat and by that time you will not be able to bring the dead to life again. Their widows and orphans will always curse you.'

'How do you know that the Government is not trapping us?'

'I am sure that the Government is not trapping you because according to the Governor's promise it is not killing people but is only healing the injured ones. The Government has run bankrupt, it cannot maintain all of you in prisons or detentions, feeding and clothing you and paying thousands of warders. In fact, the surrenderees who are found not dangerous to the public or those who have not hatred with the *kamatimo* are not at all detained, but are returned to their villages and set free, restricted to their villages. The Government does not want the fight and in fact everybody in the country is praying for peace.'

'Would you also pray peace from me?'

'Definitely yes!'

'Then go in peace and wait to hear more from me today or tomorrow. Don't you be afraid if you are confident of your stand.'

As Ndirangu left, I told my guards in his presence not to guard him any more. Being now more confident than before in the possibility of negotiation, and satisfied that a negotiation was necessary, my first duty was how to find out that the Government was not laying a trap for us. I called for Ndirangu again later. On his arrival I asked him whether he could take my message to the Government and bring me a reply. He said that Mr. Henderson (Kinyanjui) was coming in that forest area once a week to collect messages from the forest fighters and bringing them replies from Government—but the main thing was not to establish a correspondence with the Government. 'Since this would be a part of both introduction and negotiation it would be all right. If you sent me I would take your letter to Nyeri tomorrow or wait until Henderson comes on 17th March.'

I asked Kahinga to call the other surrenderee for interrogation. I repeated my procedure and asked the same questions. I learned through their answers that while Mung'atu Kiguta had surrendered for personal security and had turned against the revolution, Ndirangu was very sympathetic to the suffering of other people.

I spent the night in Kahinga's *mbuci* in order to be able to observe the cooperation of the surrenderees and the rest of Kahinga's *itungati*. Kahinga Wachanga, who had nicknamed himself the 'Colonial Secretary of the States' when he was a clerk to Thiong'o Watoria and Gicuki, in the early days when Kariaini was strong, had become weak in body and mind. I suspected that he might surrender and possibly influence his *itungati*.

I asked Kahinga what he had done or told the Government. He replied that [he had done] no more than inform the Government of his efforts to convey the message .... apart from writing a letter, a copy of which he showed me, asking the Government to show its willingness to end the fight by releasing detainees and captives, stopping communal forced labor in the reserves and, finally, withdrawing its forces from the reserve.

I congratulated him for what he had done and asked him not to write any more letters on his own to the Government. I told him that Kimathi was coming in that area to open a Kenyalekalo Memorial Hall at old H.Q. Kariaini on the 18th and that he would be accompanied by all the leaders of IDA 1 and Gikuyu Iregi Army members of Parliament. It would then be possible to discuss the message he sent to Kimathi from the Government. In addition to this, I notified him of the meeting I had called for all the leaders in that area to consider the building of the Memorial Hall. I warned him, on the question of keeping surrenderees in his camp, that their influence could lead to the surrender of his *itungati*. I told him that I completely disagreed with him for being supplied with food by the enemy and keeping them in his camp, that he should have made a rendezvous where he should be meeting with Government messengers and by all means not in his camp where his *itungati* were slowly falling to surrender. I told him that Ndirangu had sufficient power of ideas that would convince them to surrender.

The following day I visited Kihara Gatandi's section and told him all about Kahinga's section. He agreed with me in all points. We were to talk over the matter at a leaders' meeting the following day.

On 13th March, sixteen section leaders and five members of the Kenya Parliament from Kariaini and Kigumo areas met. Mathenge and Ngara, though invited, didn't turn up. Kimathi was still at Chieni. Though many of them knew much about the surrenderees from their *itungati*, they did not want Kahinga or his *itungati* to know the whereabouts of their *mbuci* in case the surrenderees might direct the enemy to the surrounding *mbuci*. In fact, they were glad that Kahinga had not turned up in the meeting.

The meeting resolved to draft a letter to the Government in favor of the negotiation and set forth conditions. It condemned the harboring of surrenderees or Government messengers done by Kahinga. All *mbuci* were to shift in new sites unknown to Kahinga's men. Some *itungati* were to be sent to Kahinga's daily so as to find out what was being done there. We agreed that each section was to send ten *itungati* to the old H.Q. and they should start building the Kenyalekalo Memorial Hall on the 15th and all building work should be completed on the 17th, including leaders' huts and *itungati* shelters. Wacira Gathuku would supervise the building work and the site should be a few hundred yards west of the old hospital. By the evening of the 17th all the food contributed by each *mbuci* for the leaders who would visit us, including their *safari* food to Murang'a, should be handed over to the Divisional Treasurer, Kihara Gatandi. All the leaders must be at the hall by that evening in order to check that everything was perfectly done before midday, 18th March, the opening day.

I then drafted the following letter to the Government :

His Excellency the Governor of Kenya
Sir E. Baring
General Sir G. Erskine
Sirs,

I met your messengers on the previous day. As a result of my talk with them, I called an urgent leaders' meeting from the nearby area under my chairmanship—fifty sectional leaders and five members of the Kenya Parliament including myself. We have learned from both your message and messengers that the

Kenya Government is willing to put an end to the bloodshed and that you are ready to meet our representatives for negotiation. We all here at this meeting congratulate you for your intelligent human decision. If this be true we shall put our effort to make it a success. But we do not want to mix up your 18th January 1955 surrender offer with the negotiations.

Meanwhile I have forwarded your message to Kimathi and at the same time have called a Kenya Parliament session to be held on the 18th March in order to discuss your request.

We demand a written proof that this is a true negotiation and signed by you both. Secondly, we suggest to you that in order to prove to us that you don't want to continue the fight, you can start it by releasing detainees and captives, withdrawing your forces from the reserve, disarming the Home Guards, dissolving the villages, stopping communal forced labor, and opening the closed schools and trading centers.

Our representatives are ready, they were elected during China's false negotiations. Be sure that our representatives would only come when we received your signatures and not from any other officer, lest it be a trap.

Stop bombing the forest, as this would disturb our meetings.

Yours faithfully,
Brig. Gen. Sir Karari Njama
Chief Secretary, Kenya Parliament

On the 15th and 16th I assisted Wacira Gathuku at the building of our H.Q. Memorial Hall and visited Kahinga's *mbuci* on the 17th morning. I read the letter to him and asked him which of his *itungati* were going to meet Henderson so that I could give them the letter. He told me that he was one of those who were going. I tried to stop him from going for I was afraid that he would be interrogated by Henderson and give him wrong impressions and ideas, for Kahinga had not attended a single Kenya Parliament meeting and didn't know its policies.

He insisted on going and at 10 a.m. he left me to meet Mr. Henderson and his group of surrenderees. He promised me that he would return to the camp about 1 p.m. At 2:30 p.m. Kahinga's *itungati* returned to the *mbuci* with news that Kahinga, two other fighters, and Kahono Githu, who was to become his clerk, had left for Nairobi in a Special Branch Land Rover.

Being very disappointed with Kahinga, I left for H.Q. arriving
there at 6 p.m. My anger increased when I found that the attendance was very poor. From Kigumo only Gitonga's and Gicuki's
mbuci had arrived bringing leaders' food. Around Kariaini, IDA 4,
under Gikonyo Kanyungu, had the best attendance, then IDA 2/2
under Kihara Gatandi, then IDA 2/3. Nevertheless, we passed the
night talking about Kahinga and also what might be the cause of
some leaders and *itungati* failing to turn up and do their duty.
Leaders' huts, which were supposed to be built by Ngara's *itungati*
were still not touched since they had not arrived. We spent the
whole day of the 18th building huts, cleaning the compound, etc.
Mathenge, who was supposed to organize the opening of the hall
had not even arrived. All we knew about him was that he was
at Kigumo.

At two in the afternoon, Kimathi arrived with a group of 148
persons including sixteen members of Kenya Parliament. Kimathi
told me that he and his party had lodged at Mathenge's for the
previous night and they were badly treated by Mathenge.

'Mathenge did not want to talk with any of us,' said Kimathi.
'He had forbidden all his *itungati* to give us any welcome. Though
we encamped by his *mbuci*, they completely refused to give us any
help. Mathenge himself refused to accompany us. Since he did not
want to talk to me last night, I cannot tell what he has in his
mind. I can only guess that he became angry when Macaria was
promoted instead of his being promoted.'

'Things have started going bad,' I told Kimathi. 'Mathenge
might cause a split at this stage.' I told him all that had happened
since we parted. Kimathi and all the members of the Kenya Parliament became very angry for they could not trust Kahinga to
represent the fighters, for they knew him as a person who boasts
for nothing, and his failures to attend Kenya Parliament meetings
and any other meetings, apart from the Mwathe General Meeting
in 1953, made him lag behind our policies.

'Kahinga has elected himself our representative just the same
way he had self-styled himself "Colonial Secretary of the States,"'
said Kimathi angrily. 'Maybe he is trying to find a way to surrender or gain fame—but I would expect nothing good out of him.'

Many leaders commented and the talk continued for a time. By
sunset only 368 persons had arrived. We learned from Gitonga's
itungati that Mathenge had sent a message to the fighters in the

Othaya Division warning them not to attend any meeting led by Kimathi. He had told them that he would open the hall when Kimathi was at Murang'a.

Kimathi opened Kenyalekalo Memorial Hall, the H.Q. of IDA 2, 3 and 4. He stood at the entrance with Wang'ombe Ruga who cleansed the *itungati* while Kimathi blessed them and wished them best of luck.

My main speech in the hall was 'unity is strength and division meant defeat.' Kimathi condemned all over-ambitious men. He said that those people were the source of evils and dangers to a society. He warned our fighters not to fall in the Government's trap of the surrender offer. He promised that he and the Kenya Parliament would attend the matter carefully whenever he got in touch with the Government.

Wacira Gathuku read a verse in the New Testament: 'Then if any man shall say unto you, Lo, here is Christ, or there; believe it not. For there shall arise false Christs and false prophets, and shall show great signs and wonders; in so much that, if it were possible, they shall deceive the very elect. Behold, I have told you before. Wherefore if they shall say unto you, Behold he is in the desert; go not forth; behold he is in the secret chambers; believe it not.'

Wacira said that we were about to the end of our fight and that many leaders, knowing that fact, had started blowing their own pipes aiming at greatness. He pointed out the dangers of disunity and the false statements and promises made by the leaders in their attempt to win followers. He warned our fighters that there would be no other organization than the Kenya Parliament.

Macaria Kimemia, commenting on Wacira's speech, said that any person who would be found acting on his own and not through the Parliament would be prosecuted. When I stood up again to sum up the speeches, I told the audience that if a person stole a police uniform and wore it, he would be a policeman to those who did not know him; but he would hide from the real policemen and from all those who knew him, his friends, his relatives, his parents and even from his children. He would not like them to see him in a uniform which he had got in a wrong way. He would be proud to all if he had got it in the right way and at the right place. Those who had self-styled themselves in ranks were thieves and did not like to appear to the Kenya Parliament in case they may be asked why they stole the ranks. In the same way, those who were stealing our *itungati*, misleading them into Government traps, were great thieves and whenever caught they should be prosecuted.

We walked out for dinner and returned for singing and giving the other leaders opportunity of speaking to the *itungati*. We agreed that Kihara and Gitonga were to stay at H.Q. in order to learn what Mathenge was planning to do and also to check on Kahinga's movement after his return from Nairobi. After all the entertainment, we slept.

Early the following morning we started for Murang'a, a party of 178 warriors. We climbed due west to the Moorland in the dry bamboo, now with new shoots not more than five feet high. On our arrival at Nguthiru, having passed the sources of many streams in order to avoid descending and ascending their valleys, we turned due south moving up the slopes of the second highest peak of Nyandarua. After crossing North and South Mathioya rivers, with their many tributaries, we encamped for the night in one of the deserted camps. From sunrise to sunset we had only half an hours rest; we had gone more than fifty miles. After eating my half-ration dinner, and feeling very tired, I fell asleep.

The following day we continued our journey, crossing Maragwa River and climbing its far slope, crossing a big ridge path and then moving into a dense bamboo forest on level land. Moving behind the long convoy with eight strong guards, I arrived in Karuri Ngamune at 5 p.m. to find over 1,200 warriors who had come for the opening of Karuri Memorial Hall. Kimathi had arrived an hour before me and was now lecturing the big audience.

A large group of men and women had been invited from the reserves. Karuri Memorial Hall was the biggest of all our halls—150 by 30 feet. Our fighters seemed very happy and proud when Kimathi told their parents : 'You have always been deceived that there were no people in the forest—that they were all killed by bombs; but this is only a small part of the Gikuyu Iregi Army. Do you now believe that the Government doesn't tell you any truth?'

'*Ei*, Yes!' they shouted.

'Go and encourage all other parents that we are alive, strong and healthy. As you can see, we are poorly clothed and armed. When you return to the villages send us clothes and ammunition.'

Kimathi then called all the members of the Parliament on the platform, blessed them by pouring diluted honey on their heads and introducing us. Then two old aged persons, a man and woman from the reserve, smeared ram fat on our forefaces, hands and joints, and laying their hands over our heads, prayed and blessed us and wished us the best of luck. This was followed by special prayers for those leaders by all. When all was over we continued covering our program by allowing each leader to speak to the audience.

The meeting dispersed just before twilight. The leaders were left in the hall with the parents and mothers who presented us with the food they had brought. We ate while talking with them. They confirmed to us that they had been defeated by the Government propaganda and its punishments. They promised us that they would tell the civilians that there were many thousands of fighters in the forests. We dispersed and resumed at 10 p.m. for singing and entertainments, after which we retired to bed.

The following day, the parents and the fighters from far away *mbuci* left in the afternoon, after we had issued ranks to some fighters. We remained in the camp for three days during which we resolved that the Gikuyu Iregi Army should give the Kenya Parliament eighty well-armed fighters and fifty carriers who were to be stationed at Kariaini H.Q. for guarding the Kenya Parliament during the time which it would negotiate with the Government and discipline all the leaders who seemed to brag for disobeying the Parliament, for acting on their own—whereby they had let us down many times and even our supporters, by presenting many contradictory ideas and rules which only proved that we were an unorganized body.

On 24th March we left for Kariaini H.Q. We ascended the steep ridge path due west and by eleven in the morning we were climbing the second peak of Nyandarua on its southern end. At midday we were on its top. Though this peak is marked at 12,816 feet, the eyes consider it to be the highest—possibly because it is sharp and the other is flat—and with the best view on all the sides. Here, one can see an iron-bar cross standing about twelve feet high and being cemented on the ground by Catholic padres in 1910. Lake Naivasha seemed very near down below on the western side.

We descended its grassy slopes due north just above the source of the Gura River into the small thorny and bamboo bushes. In the afternoon we changed toward the east. Night fell when we were still in the Moorlands. We hadn't sufficient tents and we could not build huts for 280 of us. The long rains had started; we only prayed

Ngai to save us from rain and cold. Though there was heavy rain on Mt. Kenya that afternoon, it ended in the northern end of Nyandarua.

We arrived Kariaini at about 5 p.m. Kihara Gatandi had arrived to meet us. We learned from him that Mathenge had called all the fighters from Kigumo and Kariaini area to come and open the H.Q. under him. With a good attendance, he had conducted an opening ceremony in the same hall. This proved that Mathenge was not satisfied with Kimathi's prayers and the opening of the hall. On the other hand he was doing it to show his followers that he had equal powers with Kimathi.

In his speech, Mathenge had told his audience not to obey Kimathi and his Kenya Parliament, and had instructed them to give their allegiance to Kenya Riigi (riigi = old Kikuyu doors made of interwoven thin sticks mostly from climbing plants)—a league under his leadership in cooperation with Mbaria Kaniu, Kimbo, Kahiu-Itina and many non-yes-yes leaders. He told his audience that Kenya Riigi had been formed in order to oppose the Parliament and express the voice of the majority of fighters who are illiterate and who were led and controlled by a handful of 'yes yes' leaders. He remarked how cowardly and selfishly the educated men had abandoned the fight in the hands of the illiterate peasants. He complained that the Kenya Parliament had neglected him on the account that he was illiterate. He asked whether education helped one to fire his gun a longer distance than the others or aim better than them.

On the other hand, Kahinga had returned from Nairobi with replies of my letter to the Governor, signed as I had requested. He had interviewed Mathenge and they were planning to continue the negotiation with or without the Kenya Parliament help.

Filled with this disgusting news, the Kenya Parliament held a session on 26th March in which a resolution was passed that Mathenge and all the Kenya Riigi leaders must be disciplined, firstly by showing them that they have no powers of their own other than the powers granted by the Kenya Parliament. Secondly, they must be shown all their mistakes and, where necessary, punished for intentionally wrecking our fight and misleading our itungati for their personal ambition—which could turn out to be the betrayal of the revolution. Thirdly, they must be instructed on the right way to approach the Government, our supporters, rules and policies. All complaints must be brought to the Kenya Parliament. They had to realize that K.P. was both the eyes and the voice of our fighters all over Kenya. We could not let anyone act on his own outside the Parliament's organization.

The resolution said that arrest warrants [were to] be issued to twenty-one leaders, including Mathenge, Kahinga and his self-styled delegates to Nairobi. The Kenya Parliament issued arrest warrants to all these persons under the procedure that each had to (1) surrender his arms, (2) be inspected by the guards, (3) have his hands tied together, (4) be brought in guarded, and (5) bring all their camp record books. If any ran away or refused, he was to be shot. The warrants were signed by Kimathi and I.

Meanwhile, the Kenya Parliament organized itself into a British-type court in which Ndiritu Thuita acted as the Head of Police and the Chief Prosecutor. Macaria Kimemia was the Chief Judge, helped by an advisory committee; Kihara Gatandi and I were the recorders of the cases and four members were appointed to become jurors. Abdullah became the Minister of War and Vindo became the Commissioner of Prisons.

I drafted a letter to Kahinga and informed him that the Kenya Parliament was holding a session and was anxiously awaiting to hear his reports from Nairobi. I reminded him to bring with him all his recorded documents and that the Parliament wished to see the other delegates.

Having supplied our guards with sufficient arrest warrants, they left early morning on the 27th March. During the day the Commissioner of Prisons, Major-General Vindo, built his prison camp one hundred yards away across a swampy stream southwest of the main camp. At the same time the Parliament prepared charge sheets for every accused leader listing all his offences.

At midday, Kahinga and his companions arrived. He told the Parliament how he met the Government messengers and how he went to Nairobi to confirm to the Government that the forest fighters were preparing to send representatives who would negotiate with the Government. He said that he met and talked with Mr. Windley, who represented the Governor, Gen. Heyman, who represented Gen. Erskine, and B. A. Ohanga, African Minister of Community Development. Asked whether their speeches were recorded he replied that Kahono Githii, pointing at him, had recorded all their speeches. He was asked to hand over all the books to me.

Opening Kahinga's satchel, I found two new big size *Challenge* duplicate books and copies of a photograph in which Kahinga and his party were photoed together with the Government representatives.

When asked to mention the points they had agreed on, he said that they had not agreed on any points but that their talk was a form of interrogation in which they asked him many different questions. Asked who had sent him to Nairobi, he replied that his going to Nairobi was the result of his talks with Ian Henderson, who complained that his messengers had lost one and a half months in Nyandarua and that not even one leader had gone to see him and that he was finding it difficult to convince the Government that he was doing something to make the negotiation a success.

Reading from Kahinga's documents, we learned that he had deceived the Government that he was the elected representative of the fighters. The questions and answers were well recorded:

Windley: Why do you live in the forest?

Kahinga: Because your forces chased us from the reserve.

Heyman: Why then haven't you accepted our amnesty offer?

Kahinga: Because we think it is a trap and moreover you haven't promised us land and freedom in that offer.

Windley: There cannot be such a thing as freedom while you continue to fight. If you stopped fighting there would be time to discuss freedom.

Kahinga: We are fighting for land and freedom and if you grant them the war would be over.

Windley: If you are not given land and freedom, would you accept His Excellency's amnesty offer?

Kahinga: We are going to consider it because we do not want to live in the forest, we are only forced to.

Ohanga: Why do you keep such long shaggy hairs?

Kahinga: Because we do not have any means of shaving. You can see that we have grown weak in body because of lack of food and bad weather. (Kahinga expressed how ashamed he felt for being very dirty.)

Ohanga: The Colonial Government has already shown that it is willing to grant you freedom in a multiracial Government.

Why should you continue your fight while the Government has met your demands?

Kahinga: We are going to consider your request, but land and freedom would be the answer.

Though there were other good points of Kahinga in the negotiation, the above answers and his activities were sufficient offences—which caused his remand awaiting to answer his case.

Then Gen. Ndiritu Thuita called the guards, inspected Kahinga and his comrades, and took them to our prison awaiting for their cases to be heard after perusing all their documents. By the evening, all our *itungati* returned safely bringing all the persons on the arrest warrant list. Mathenge had surrendered his automatic pistol but our *itungati* had accepted his request not to tie his hands.

Three armed sentries were to guard the prisoners for three hour periods all the time. During the night the prisoners' hands had to be tied together, but untied during the day. On 28th March, we spent most of the time studying Kahinga's, Mathenge's and the other leaders' record books. From Mathenge's books, which were written by his clerk Ndung'u Mathenge, we learned of the formation of the Kenya Riigi and its officers—whose main task was to oppose the Kenya Parliament. Another resolution was passed extending arrest warrants to 20 more officers of the Kenya Riigi who were living in the Moorlands, Kipipiri and Subuk, mostly Mburu Ngebo Army fighters from Murang'a under Mbaria Kaniu.

On the 29th our *itungati* left to arrest the Kenya Riigi officers in the Moorlands and Kipipiri Mt. We decided to start hearing the light cases of junior officers. We heard three cases and released them in the evening, free under their promises to obey and cooperate with the Kenya Parliament. The *itungati* who were being led by the captured leaders had arrived to witness what would happen to their leaders. Kimathi addressed them, warning them that all fighters were under Kenya Parliament and there was not any other organization to lead the fighters. He promised them that nothing bad would happen to their leaders apart from finding our differences and strengthening our unity, cooperation and obedience to the Kenya Parliament. He appealed to all the *itungati* to obey the Kenya Parliament, to which they agreed. Later, those *itungati* were to be posted to guard their leaders, and were sent to fetch food in the reserve for the Kenya Parliament.

On March 30th three more cases were heard. All were released, two being fined 25s. each and the third one set free. Our *itungati* returned from Kipipiri with eight arrestments [i.e., prisoners]. They reported that the others had fled away on seeing them and believed that they must have had some information about the arrest of their comrades.

I wrote a letter to Mr. Henderson, signed by Kimathi, telling the Government that our representatives would be meeting the Government's in a week's time.

On 31st March, we heard six cases and passed no judgement. I generally visited the prisoners in the mornings and evenings, asked them their complaints, encouraged them to have no fear over the Parliament's motives, told them our intentions were only unity, cooperation and obedience to the Kenya Parliament.

In the evening our *itungati* returned, having failed to meet Mr. Henderson at Chinga road. I was awakened by a bullet's thunder and shouting at four o'clock in the morning. 'All the prisoners have run away!' cried the guards.

I ordered a girl in the officers' kitchin to make me a bamboo torch. With the light of my torch I walked a hundred yards to the prison camp. Kimathi and the other officers had arrived a couple of minutes before me. 'Any casualties?' asked Kimathi.

'We have only one prisoner left?' said the guard. 'He awoke me when he pulled my gun. I firmly held my gun and he badly bit my fingers—and I fired for help, scaring the other two prisoners who were the last to leave.'

'So you were asleep when they escaped?' shouted Kimathi.

'Yes Sir,' replied the guard, 'but the other two guards were awake. We had arranged that one of us could sleep while the others were on guard and . . .'

'Where are the other two guards who were on duty?' demanded Kimathi.

'I think they must have escaped with the prisoners for they were the prisoners' *itungati*,' said the guard. 'Instead of guarding the prisoners, they untied them and have run away with the guns issued them by the guard commander.'

'What are the names of the guards?' asked Vindo.

'Samuel Wahihi and Mwangi(?),' replied the guard.

Waweru Ngirita, the only prisoner in the camp, caught in his attempt to rob the guard's gun and who had badly bitten the guard's fingers, was strongly held down by a group of guards and was appealing for mercy to Kimathi.

'Forgive me Kimathi. Spare my life. Ohhh ...'

'Who poured that blood?' demanded Kimathi.

'I was trying to release myself, but forgive me ...'

'Waste no time Kimathi,' interrupted Macaria Kimemia, 'order the guards to strangle him.'

'O.K. Guards! Take him away!' shouted Kimathi, going away. Waweru cried for mercy but the guards covered his mouth. By this time hundreds of fighters had arrived at the scene. Without talking to anyone, I slowly walked back to my hut with my heart beating high and very much worried of what was likely to happen. It was now dawn, and the beginning of a declared split among our fighters, which could easily turn to be a real fight between ourselves, giving the enemy all the chances to defeat us. How shall we contact the Government? Wouldn't Kahinga and Mathenge send their representatives to negotiate with the Government—and then the two delegations, and possibly a third from Kirinyaga, each independent from the other, would present its different case to the Government? Wouldn't that reveal our weakness in our organization—our hatred, ambition in leadership and lack of confidence in one general leader? Shall we ever be able to cooperate again with the lost leaders?

Kimathi came into my hut and found me wrapped in my blanket. He informed me that he intended to move from the camp in case Kahinga may bring the Government forces to the camp accusing us of opposing and preventing the negotiation. 'On the other hand, Mathenge and his officers, driven by fear and suspicion that we wanted to kill them, may return here well armed for a fight; they may even ambush us just like the enemies. The sooner we quit the camp the better.'

I went for Gen. Gikonyo Kanyungu; he came with me to my hut. Kimathi told him that he was to show us a good place for camping where his *itungati* could easily take our message to Mr. Henderson. I called the Guard Commander to announce orders.

'Attention! Everybody! You must pack all your luggage now. We are leaving the camp by sunrise!'

April 1st 1955 we dispersed. The *itungati* who had helped their leaders to escape were already gone. The others returned to their camps. The K.P. and its forces followed Gikonyo's *itungati*, IDA

4/1, climbing due west on a ridgeway to Muthuri Hill where we stopped for a rest. We sent a dozen *itungati* to shoot elephants for food.

By midday we had arrived at Gikonyo's old camp at Itwe and our *itungati* were busy building new huts. At two o'clock our gunning team brought news that they had killed one big elephant and that it had fallen about a mile east of the camp. I accompanied over 150 *itungati* who rushed out to carry meat. At first I was surprised to see Murang'a fighters eating raw marrow just as one chews a piece of sugar cane. Later on that evening I joined them in chewing the elephants raw marrow fat obtained in the bones. The IDA 4/1 quartermaster stored the eight-foot ivory tusks.

Our intentions now were to contact the Government through Mr. Henderson, and to find out where the runaway leaders had encamped and their motives. If they had run away on fear of punishment that might be inflicted on them we would then be able to seek their confidence by getting only a few of them at a time, instruct and warn and release them and prove that we did not want to kill any of them and that a split would be our defeat. On the other hand, anyone who refused to accept that friendship offer and really stood for opposition to the Kenya Parliament leadership would be charged and tried as a traitor on all accounts and unless he changed he would meet his death.

The following day we sent our *itungati* to take the letter to Henderson. They returned in the evening, having failed again to meet him. They said that Land Rover trails indicated that he had come on the previous day. We sent out two other groups, one to Gitonga's and Wacira's sections, led by assistant section leaders Kiongo and Wanjeru Kibiri. The second group was sent to Kihara Gatandi's section. They were to find out what the runaway leaders were doing.

The following morning, Kiongo and Wanjeru returned badly beaten and deprived of one rifle by their own *itungati* under Mathenge's command. Their good luck was their success to run away in the darkness. Some shots fired after them had missed them. They had swollen bruises all over their bodies. They had spent a cold, hungry and painful night.

It was now certain that Mathenge and his supporters had classified the Kenya Parliament and its supporters as enemies. The Kenya Parliament would do all it could to see that these people obeyed. Wanjeru told us that Mathenge and company were preaching to their *itungati* that the Kenya Parliament had sentenced all of them to death, but that a girl who was working in the Parliament's kitchen foretold them and saved their lives.

Among our fighters was Wambui—Mathenge's girl—who was now to stay with Wacira Gathuku. Since Mathenge's arrest Wambui had been working in the Parliament's kitchen. She had confirmed her loyalty was not to a person but to the Movement. [Wanjeru's comment] caused Wambui, the only suspect, to be interrogated. But there was no proof to the story. It was an invented story to justify their case and escape.

Since the beginning of our fight we had never had a prison, simply because we could not afford to feed and guard the enemies and worse still, they could be freed by their forces or manage to escape. We had kept Mathenge and company in our first prison for five nights, feeding and guarding them simply because they were not our enemies but our disobedient fighters who only deserved discipline and instruction. To our sorrow, they had identified themselves as enemies. But this had to be taken as an individual case regarding the leaders and not as a group case including the *itungati* who were being misled. We did not want to fight against a group but we had to fight against a person who misled our fighters.

We wrote another letter to Mr. Henderson, signed by Kimathi, asking him to change his rendezvous to Kabage road if he wanted to negotiate with the Kenya Parliament. The letter directed him where he should post the reply in a tree trunk hole of a big tree by the roadside. We instructed him that we would collect his message there. We warned him that the Kenya Parliament had disassociated with Kahinga's negotiation because he had elected himself and was deceiving the Government. We concluded that the Government could communicate to the Kenya Parliament by any means in North Tetu area—north of the River Chania.

We instructed our messengers to plant the letter in the middle of the road hanging on a thin bamboo stick a few yards below the meeting place. Our messengers returned reporting that they had planted the letter. Gathuru Muita had twice been appointed as the spokesman of our messengers in case they were to be interrogated by Mr. Henderson.

On the 8th of April the Parliament and its guards left Gikonyo's *itungati* and arrived at Ndiritu Thuita's *mbuci* at Mutanga Riua Hill facing Chania slopes. The court heard two cases of *komerera* leaders. They were both sentenced to be caned 20 and 25 canes [i.e., strokes] and promised good conduct onwards.

On 15th April, the court moved to Chieni. Our messengers had not received any response from the Government on behalf of the negotiation. We sent a copy of that letter to the Government; this time the letter would be taken to the village and would be stuck in bamboo by our supporters just inside a Home Guard post.

At Chieni the court heard a dozen cases of the *komerera* leaders, among which one of them was sentenced to death after admitting that he had administered a strange oath to some *itungati* compelling them to abandon their leaders and never again to serve any leader who did not participate in fetching food and firewood, building his hut and carrying his own luggage.

Inside the Kenya Young Stars Hall, I read his case to over 400 fighters. He was caught leading four others in the settled area. Fourteen of his *itungati* had been killed in his *mbuci* which was witnessed by the survivors to have been built about 400 yards from a settler's house. I asked him to confess before the fighters, after which the Chief Judge Macaria Kimemia announced his death sentence, asking him whether it was fair according to what he had done in undermining leaders and wrecking the revolution. The accused spoke bravely, accepting his sentence as being fair. Kimathi ordered the guards to strangle him far away from the camp in the bush. The court released one and ordered the others to receive a dozen canes.

The court left the hall after the last accused had received the canes. Later in the afternoon the guards reported that the sentences had been fulfilled. That afternoon Kimathi called on Joseph, one of the three remaining accused *komerera* leaders and started interrogating him in his hut. Kimathi, Kimemia and three *itungati* left for a stroll with Joseph. When Kimathi returned in the evening he told us that he had saved us a day or two of hearing Joseph's case. He said that he had heard the case within five minutes, after which he took his pistol and ordered Joseph to lead the twenty-one dead *itungati* who had died in his *mbuci*.

Joseph, a *komerera* leader of the Mburu Ngebo Army, was arrested in the settled area leading two almost naked *itungati* of IDA 3/3. One of them, Maina, was to become my books carrier.

They told us that whenever Joseph went out with some three others in their attempt to look for food, he always returned alone to the *mbuci*, saying that he was the only survivor. He would then enter Nyandarua and persuade three or four more *itungati*, taking them back to his *mbuci*.

Nevertheless, though Joseph might have been proven guilty by the court, it was a bad report to hear that Kimathi's hands killed him before he was tried. The propaganda based on that incident would increase hatred, enmity and proofs to the runaway leaders. Kimathi's action would definitely be interpreted as Parliament's action, for Kimathi generally acted for the Parliament—but this was wrong. 1 did not want to share Kimathi's blame. That night, filled with a lot of grief, I convinced half the members of the Parliament that we should have a by-law which controls the powers and actions of our President.

'It would be very bad,' I said, 'if we became his wall to protect him in such actions of personal killing which would only increase hatred and enmity among ourselves. We shouldn't allow the President to dictate the Parliament in such a way for he can easily turn out to be a dictator. He should accept our advice and criticisms, of which I am sure that he does not appreciate. If we do not have such by-laws we may find ourselves increasing enmity with other fighters, and worst of all it is a sign of weakness in our leadership; in other words, there would be no Parliament, but Kimathi would be the Parliament—a dictator.'

Having convinced half of the 22 members [present], we arranged to put forward the following motions : (1) The President should accept both the advice and criticism resolved by the majority of members in either a session or in private discussions—by K. Njama. (2) President's powers and activities on behalf of the Parliament should be limited and defined by our written laws and rules—by Major Gen. Ndiritu Thuita. (3) Ministerial posts should be created and be granted to various members so that each would be certain of his job and stick to it—by Maj. Gen. Vindo.

In our discussion over the first two motions, Kimathi became very angry and twice banged the table, left his chair and walked out; he shouted, complaining of being insulted and betrayed by his members—chiefly myself. Nevertheless, we passed both motions.

We then resolved to grant Ministerial Posts and, after casting ballots, we found that I was elected to be Minister of War. The result hurt Kimathi. He did not want me to take that post. He left his chair and stood in the center of the meeting to address us. In his argument he claimed that the Parliament could not get a person of my standard in the secretaryship, which he thought to be of more value than the Ministry the Parliament had given me. He claimed that the election must be done again, in a few days time.

Wacira Gathuku accused Kimathi of being impatient, quick and bad tempered, relating his case to the shooting of Joseph, banging table, throwing pencil, leaving the Presidency chair in anger, and of his will to dictate the Parliament. The discussion only increased Kimathi's anger. We adjourned for lunch.

When we resumed the meeting in the afternoon, Major Gen. Vindo turned to Kimathi's side and withdrew his motion of ministerial posts. This split the Parliament in debate, Othaya versus North Tetu, and Murang'a as moderator. Kimathi said that he had all the information of how I had conducted a meeting at night in which only he and Kimemia were absent. He accused me of trying to lead and control the Parliament without him. He suggested that a law be made that 'The Kenya Parliament will never hold any meeting in the absence of the President.' He said: 'I have learned that I am living with enemies within the Kenya Parliament.'

With threats and fears that Kimathi might accuse some of us of betrayal and perhaps have us strangled, his motion was passed with only one vote over a majority. Myself and nine other members failed to raise hands. Any further arguments were to split the Parliament into his and my loyalties. This would definitely put me directly against him and that would mean venturing into great dangers.

Night came before we had solved anything. We dispersed in a state of confusion and worry. Fear that Kimathi or his envoy might hurt me kept me awake through the night. When we resumed the following day, we heard the case of two arrested persons. More than half the members showed no interest in the cases and by lunch time both were set free.

At this stage, the five Othaya Division members, including myself, decided that we should return to Othaya, find Mathenge and the runaway leaders and our *itungati* and prove our sincerity to them. We didn't want to be cut off from our people by Kimathi; we wanted to moderate and prevent the split from getting worse.

We called Kimathi and informed him that since the Government had not replied our letters, we should all go back to Othaya and find out what Kahinga and Mathenge might be doing about the negotiations. We could easily get in touch with the Government there. He agreed and we arrived Gikonyo's *mbuci* on 13th May. We found that his *itungati* had not changed the *mbuci* nor had they known whereabout the other *mbuci* were.

We sent Gikonyo's *itungati* to find out where Mathenge's and Kahinga's *mbuci* were and whether they were still negotiating with Government. They returned the following day reporting that they were still negotiating; Kahiu-Itina, Mbaria and the other officers of the Kenya Riigi were negotiating with the Government.

On 16th May, we sent Gicuki Wacira, a person whom we thought could easily be accepted by them. But on his return, Gicuki told us that he arrived at Mathenge's *mbuci* and when one *gitungati* shouted that the Kenya Parliament had arrived, the whole *mbuci* dispersed as if it were invaded by enemies.

Being very disappointed by recent events, Kimathi and the twelve Gikuyu Iregi Army members of the Kenya Parliament left for Murang'a on 18th May 1955. The five of us Othaya Parliament members decided to correspond to Mathenge through Gikonyo's *itungati* until we could clear their fears. Though we believed that the Parliament had the best leadership, we repented for having unknowingly created such hatred with our own people.

On 20th May we sent two *itungati* to Mathenge to take him a letter requesting him to arrange that the five of us would meet all the other leaders and discuss our differences. About two in the afternoon, a big airplane flew around the mountain dropping more general amnesty offer copies and sky-shouting: 'Today your leaders have ended the negotation with the Government. The fight is to go on. Surrender now with all your arms and save your life...'

In the evening our messengers returned saying that they only found many deserted camps.

On 22nd May, the enemy forces were two miles from our camp following Kahinga's and Mbaria's track, who had been seen by our sentries passing by our camp on their way to Kinangop. By midday the Government forces were less than a mile from the camp. Gikonyo and I and his 82 *itungati* carried some of our belongings and left the camp moving due west then turning south to the source of North Mathioya River where we encamped for the night.

The following afternoon we learned that the airplanes were dropping food to their troops very near us. We moved due east, passing the enemy's camps and intending to go to the forest edge where the enemies were certain that they had chased away all the fighters. We unknowingly encamped near the enemy, but we were lucky that they did not notice us. We finished our last bite of elephant's meat and decided to split up into small groups to enable us to hide our tracks.

As we dispersed in groups of fifteen or so, on the morning of the 24th, two of our groups were fired at. We escaped very narrowly. We decided to go to the dry bamboo area where we could see the enemy at long distance. There were eleven of us—four K.P. members (Gitonga, Kihara, Wacira and I), three section leaders (Gicuki, Wanjeru and Kiongo), and four *itungati* including Wambui. Being afraid that the forces would see us moving, we spent a day and a night with neither fire nor food. The long heavy rain was still pouring.

Just as we were able to detect the enemy's camps, the enemy had seen us and awoke us with their fire at sunrise. Like many of my comrades, I lost my tent, blankets and shoes. We ran eastwards to Kariaini Forest behind the H.Q. arriving at a Government force empty camp. Thinking that we had passed all enemy troops, we rested a few hundred yards from their camp and kept watching it. At two in the afternoon another enemy group arrived in their camp. We quickly entered the black forest and by 4 p.m. we were in Kariaini old gardens. Here the forces' tracks seemed three or four days old. The footpaths made by Mathenge's *itungati* leading to their *mbuci* were very big. It seemed that three months without being chased by the enemy forces had caused them to forget to hide their tracks. We passed many of their abandoned camps. We collected some wild vegetables in the gardens enabling us to have three bites for the night.

The following day we crossed the River Thuti and looked for any camp on its slopes. Seeing no trace of our people, we decided to cross the Kariaini road due north. On our arrival we found that Government forces were still entering the forest. We paused and twenty-one of them passed only thirty yards from us. Before we had all crossed, another group arrived passing between us. We had many chances of attacking, but how could we do it with only two rifles, a banda, and ten rounds of ammunition.

When we'd all crossed, we decided not to move any further in order to avoid collision with the enemy. We spent the day less than 400 yards from the road and less than a mile from the forest boundary. By 5 p.m. our sentry reported that over 800 army personnels had left the forest. Knowing that the Government forces were now resting in their camps we walked about two miles and looked for a place to encamp. At 6 p.m. we sent two *itungati* and two junior leaders into the reserve to search food for our group of eleven persons.

They returned at 7:30 p.m. reporting that there were very many security forces ambushing all along the forest border. We spent the fourth night without any food. How could three *itungati* be able to carry food for eight leaders including a girl? Surely some leaders had to serve others according to their order of ranks. In the morning we moved for a better camp knowing that our comrades, who returned to the camp at night, had left a track leading to our camp. Arriving at Thiathiini forest gardens we spent the day and in the evening the same four persons left for food in the reserve. That night we at *marerema*, a type of wild vegetable.

Our men returned the following morning, 28th May, with some vegetables, a few bananas, potatoes and some arrowroots. My group had lasted three days on under quarter-rations and the last five days with no food at all. We were all glad of something to eat and ate enough that night. We went on half ration for the next two days. On 31st May we sent five persons to search food in the reserve and they returned on the 1st June with the same kind of food.

I remembered my plans of escaping to Ethiopia and rediscussed them with my comrades and found that conditions were now forcing us to leave the mountain. We resolved that Kihara Gatandi should take 50s. to his wife who would buy the maize and *safari* food for us which would enable us to cross the enemy area of the Rift Valley and enter the Northern Frontier Province and make our way through the semi-desert west of the Lake Rudolph.

Gen. Kihara Gatandi, Gen. Gitonga Gaciingu (both members of Parliament) and Maina, my books carrier, left for the reserve on the evening of 3rd June. I gave Kihara my watch so that they would be able to check the time of security forces maintaining ambushes. The following day I became worried about my books, for I did not know where Maina had hidden them. In the evening, Wacira, Gicuki and I spent some time vainly searching for my books.

On 5th June, after morning prayers, I informed my comrades that if our people in the reserve did not arrive before midday—they should have been back by 7 a.m.—we had to desert the camp. I warned them not to hide our belongings but stay with them ready to go at any time. I told Wacira and Gicuki my dream—I had dreamed that we were crossing the Nyeri-Thomson's Falls road in an open grassland area when we collided with a police lorry and we were all held captives. A Mkamba Sergeant Major who led the troop was my school mate and he stopped the others from mistreating us. They gave us bread and tinned beef and when the lorry started moving toward Nyeri I woke up.

At 7 o'clock we continued an hour's search for my books. We concluded that if our men didn't turn up by midday, they must be captured and the books were lost and we had to leave the camp in case one of them brought the Government forces to our *mbuci*. The three of us returned to the camp and found that the five others had gone to warm themselves by the sun some 100 yards from the camp in an old cleared garden. We crept along our path through tangled thicket bush extending some 30 yards, after which we arrived at the cleared area. It was already nine in the morning and the sun was shining brightly. We stopped to catch the warm rays of the sun. I told Gicuki to go and check the guards and make certain they were properly posted.

I stood leaning on my *muthegi* and Wacira Gathuku on his walking stick, both puzzled and worried about what had happened to our people. I heard a [twig] crack and bent in order to be able to observe our path. Twenty yards from me I saw Maina creeping, holding his gun. He saw me too. I was glad and stood telling Wacira that our people had arrived. Bending again I noticed another gun and informed Wacira.

They were still approaching us in the tangled thicket bush. When Maina was less than ten yards from me I noticed the face of a European and shouted to Wacira, 'There's a European!'

Before I could move a bullet had entered my ankle. Turning away in order to escape, another bullet caught me, cutting three-quarters of my tendons behind the ankle. Running amidst hundreds of automatic bullets, I fell some eighty yards away being caught by a bush. Wacira fell on me. Now, out of the enemy's sight, but their bullets only missing us narrowly, we struggled through a strawberry bush and managed to enter the black forest where one could easily run. I saw Wacira running due northwest and our people disappearing to the north. I ran to follow them, crossing a stream and climbing its slope.

Arriving at a ridge-way, I found that some people had passed along it entering the forest. I followed their path thinking it to be our comrades' path but soon found that it was the enemy's track. A blood trail was clear behind my path. I was in danger of being followed by the enemy. I descended half way down a stream's slope and decided to stay there till evening, then to make my way to Kigumo where I would look for any camp.

Looking at my wounds, I learned that one bullet had passed through, cutting about three-quarters of my tendons behind the left ankle; the other bullet was still in my ankle and had cut the artery causing my blood to jet out as my heart strongly pumped it. I tore my vest to make bandages and a pad which I used to press the artery in order to stop the bleeding. I lit *kiraiko* and smoked, thankful for having learned first aid as a Boy Scout.

Many thoughts flashed at the top of my head—sorrow for Kihara and Gitonga, anger at Maina's betrayal; why had God given the enemy power to injure me? Could my survival be God's warning? How shall the bullet in me be removed? And what about the broken bones? Shall I ever manage to go to Ethiopia? Should I surrender? I should first search any of our *mbuci* for at least three days.

Oh! I had so tightly tied the artery my foot had become paralysed. I untied and tied it again but it did not get any better. At about three in the afternoon I noticed a Government troop about 100 yards from me moving along the stream toward the reserve. I crept slowly, ascending, and to my surprise another enemy troop about fifty yards ahead was walking toward the reserve. I lay down and prayed Ngai save me. I raised my head a little to watch their movement. Thank God they passed without seeing me.

At about four o'clock, another Government troop arrived down the stream and started cutting trees and preparing their camp just below me. I walked up to the ridge path, and started moving along it toward the reserve, intending to go to the forest boundary and watch the enemies' ambushes in the evening. I would then walk at night in the Special Area and enter the forest again at Kigumo where I knew I was likely to find our fighters.

Walking through bushes in the path, I suddenly met two Home Guards who came in sight only a few yards from me. Instead of running away I greeted them with '*Muriega*,' (Hello) and, to my surprise, they answered my greetings in a startled way: '*Ei, muriega*, is that you Karari Njama?'

'I am Karari, and I know you Gathithi s/o Ndarathi and Ndiritu s/o Mbai.'

'Are you injured?' asked Gathithi.

'Yes,' I said, showing him my wound and telling how it had happened in the morning.

'Let us take him to the camp,' said Ndiritu.

'Oh no! He would be killed right here in the forest,' said Gathithi.

'Then we'd better hurry up. We have one and a half miles to walk to Gitugi Village,' said Ndiritu.

I paused, unable to walk or comment.

'Don't worry Karari,' said Gathithi, 'you are safe; God has blessed you. The Governor has forgiven everybody.'

My day had come, I thought, and I preferred to die in the village where many people would witness my death rather than there in the forest, unwitnessed by a fighter or by any of our supporters.

*   *   *

After Karari's capture conditions in the forest continued to deteriorate. As militant resistance in the reserve and Nairobi was broken and the Aberdare fighters became increasingly isolated from outside contact and supplies, more and more forest groups began to live entirely on honey, edible nettles and the rewards of their traps and snares or move into small wooded areas of the Rift Valley where food raids were easier to carry out. Thus, another of my informants, Kahinga Wachanga, has stated that:

In September, myself and a few other fighters were able to live for a whole month without being noticed in a small clump of trees about 200 yards from a settler's house and 400 yards from a military camp. We got water from a tiny stream which ran through the woods and we raided settler farms at night for animals and wheat. After a raid we started off toward the forest, walking a long way before returning to our *mbuci*. The Government patrols sent out the next morning followed our tracks, but were misled by the fact that we returned to the forest walking backwards. The area between the forest and the Kipipiri Hills was very flat and our scouts, climbing high up in the trees, could see for miles around. We were often amused watching the security forces go by into the forest; they never believed we would set up our *mbuci* so close.

It was during this period that Government increased its use of surrenderees or captured and 'converted' fighters in what were called pseudo gangs. A Special Forces H.Q. was set up in Nyeri where teams of ex-fighters were formed under Europeans. Subjected to various forms of persuasion, and often unexpectedly happy to have their own lives spared, a number of ex-forest fighters thus lent themselves to Government's efforts to track down and destroy their former comrades.

To a considerable extent, these psuedo gangs both reflected and exacerbated the hostilities between forest-group leaders. The conflict between Kenya Riigi and Kenya Parliament leaders was exploited, at first inadvertently, by the Special Branch. Some of the Kenya Riigi supporters, such as Gati and Hungu of the Mburu Ngebo Army, found it relatively easy to assist Ian Henderson in his 'Hunt for Kimathi' in exchange for their lives. Though the number of ex-fighters used in these psuedo gangs was never very large, reaching a maximum of 90 by June 1956, their presence in the forest greatly increased the suspicion and hostility already existing between opposing leaders and groups.

The Kenya Riigi, which had emerged at the onset of the negotiations with Government and was to a large extent sustained by its participation in these talks, ceased to function soon after the negotiations broke down. At its last meeting in June 1955, the leaders decided to remain on the Rift Valley side of the range where food was more easily obtained and some of the pressure removed from their people in the reserve. They also agreed that surrender was an individual matter and that those who feared losing their *shambas* could return to the reserve if they wanted. Government had earlier proclaimed that all fighters who failed to surrender before the termination of the amnesty offer on 10 July would forfeit their land in the reserve. At this final meeting of the Kenya Riigi, no resolutions were passed regarding future policy or military tactics.

By the time fighting was resumed, most of the sections and sub-sections attached to the Kenya Riigi were scattered in the North Kinangop, Kipipiri Hills and Nderagwa regions of the forest. In September, according to Kahinga Wachanga, the Kipipiri groups under Mbaria Kaniu decided to leave the Aberdares and try to make their way out of Kenya. Some are said to have succeeded in reaching Ethiopia or the Sudan. Mathenge also disappeared at this time and is the only major forest leader still unaccounted for. By the end of 1955, then, those groups formerly integrated by the Kenya Riigi retained only a loose, informal relationship to one another. The highest level of leadership at this time was reduced to the section leader, who led his own unit and one or two attached sub-sections.

The Kenya Parliament also failed to survive 1955. Just prior to Karari's capture, as we have seen, new conflicts emerged within the Parliament leadership which resulted in a further split. As Kimathi left with his supporters for Fort Hall, the five Othaya members, including Karari, decided to rejoin Mathenge and seek a reconciliation. Three of the latter were captured in June and before the end of the year several other Kenya Parliament members had fallen and only about 1,500 fighters remained in the Aberdare Range. While Kimathi remained as the leader of several strong North Tetu sections, and was not captured until October of 1956—whereupon he was tried and hanged—the Kenya Parliament failed to meet again after July 1955 and, with the dispersal of those forest groups which remained at the end of the year, leadership was reduced to the level of section leader.

As the central forest institution first split and then collapsed, so likewise did the hierarchy of ranks and statuses created and legitimized by this institution cease to possess any meaning. With the loose military chain-of-command broken and the hierarchy of committees inoperative, forest leaders tended, despite their former positions, to assume more or less equal statuses as the leaders of their respective sections. Power, in the sense of the number and strength of fighters under their command, had become the sole remaining basis of legitimacy and respect.

In the latter part of 1955, with no legitimate institutions existing beyond the section and sub-section heads, there ceased to exist any coordination between the various individual sections. No longer functioning as parts of a larger network of guerrilla units, and considerably reduced in both size and strength, forest groups sought various and independent solutions to the situations they faced. Some chose to surrender, others to flee the forest or colony and, perhaps the majority, to remain in the Aberdares. The latter groups, no longer capable of offensive action beyond the occasional raid for food, lived almost entirely off of the forest. They developed great skills in trapping forest game, utilizing the skins for clothing and avoiding detection. Fearful of psuedo gangs and other hostile groups, they tended to remain within circumscribed areas of the forest, within which, however, they were forced to be extremely mobile. Camps became less and less elaborate, often consisting of little more than a few lean-to shelters.

Under these circumstances, it is not surprising that the rather complex division of labor and differentiation of statuses and roles achieved earlier was greatly reduced and simplified. For the most part, the only status distinction made was between leader and followers, and the various tasks of trapping, honey collecting, cooking, standing guard, etc., were shared by all with no clear-cut division of labor. As no hope remained for a military victory and concern was centered more and more exclusively on mere survival, the role of the *mundo mugo* took on increasing importance. The dreams and prophesies of the seers became the sole remaining basis for hope among those of the forest who survived 1955.

Accompanying the collapse of the Kenya Parliament and the general organizational breakdown which occurred during 1955, there was a disintegration and cessation of those associations and activities—such as the Kenya Young Stars and the Kenyalekalo Memorial Hall ceremonies—which had previously operated to reinforce Kenya and Kikuyu national sentiments and tribal unity by cutting across the more parochial and territorially based loyalties of the various forest groupings. As hostile relations developed

between competing forest leaders and groups, and were intensified by a lack of inter-group contact and the activities of
Government pseudo gangs, tribal sentiments and the Kikuyu
national aspect of forest ideology tended to be displaced by considerably narrower loyalties to individual leaders and sections,
and by a growing belief and feeling of betrayal by other forest
groups, the Kikuyu peasant masses which had abandoned them
and the non-Kikuyu tribes which had sided with Government.

Both the Kenya African and the Kikuyu tribal aspects of
nationalist ideology, then, tended to wither and, with forest
conditions steadily deteriorating and rational means of military
success gone, greater and greater stress was laid on the hoped for
divine intervention of Ngai. Thus, Kahinga Wachanga states of
this period that:

> ... we prayed continually that Ngai would intervene on our
> behalf and repeated over and over again the old saying: 'Justice
> must be sought first with gentle hands and only then by force;
> when both fail it remains only to pray Ngai's assistance.' The
> prayers we were saying went like this: 'We pray you Ngai,
> please rid us of our enemies. You are our only defender, we have
> no other. The whites came and took the land left us by the man
> Iregi. We ask you now to remove them, as there is nothing more
> we can do. This is the time they should go, for they are killing
> innocent women and children; starving them and working them
> to death. The whites rejoice when our people die and so we
> beg you to come to our aid. The whole of Kenya is full of tears,
> shed by those who wonder when their freedom will arrive.'

The growing concern with survival as such, and the felt necessity for divine intervention, tended to override all other ideological dimensions and practical considerations. Disintegration
and defeat had, for the most part, destroyed the collective and
positive tenets of the old forest ideology.

Around the beginning of 1956, the revolution popularly known
as 'Mau Mau' came to an end. The forest groups which remained
in the Aberdares after this time were no longer part of an
organized, active revolutionary movement. As small, largely
isolated, poorly armed groups, constantly harassed by Government forces, the forest bands of 1956, having developed a fantastic expertise of the forest, were concerned only with staying

alive. Their numbers steadily decreasing, these remnant gangs of the once proud and hopeful Land and Freedom Army were, in 1956, simply endeavoring to conceal and protect themselves from the forces of 'law and order' they had earlier confronted with considerable success.

The revolt of the Kikuyu peasantry lasted for more than three years. Though defeated militarily, few objective observers would deny that there was more than mere coincidence in the fact that the official end of the State of Emergency in January 1960 occurred while British colonial officials at the Lancaster House Conference were agreeing to an African majority in the Kenya Legislative Council and eventual independence for Kenya under African rule. The lowering of the Union Jack in Kenya on 12 December, 1963 was unquestionably the culmination of political forces set in motion by the 1953–56 peasant revolution called 'Mau Mau'.

GLOSSARY

Aanake—Senior warriors in the traditional Kikuyu age-grade system.

Ahoi—Tenants of an *itora*.

Athamaki—The lowest sub-grade of senior elders, for which a man became eligible when his first child was ready for circumcision.

Athi—The Kikuyu term for forest trappers and hunters.

Banda—Forest guerrilla terminology for home-made guns.

Batuni Oath—Also known as the 'Warrior Oath' and the 'Platoon Oath'. This second oath was originally designed for those males who were about to enter fighting units attached to the elders' councils.

Bebeta—Derived from the Swahili term *pepeta*, meaning to winnow or sift; it was the forest term for Sten gun.

Bhangi—A drug highly prized by the Somali.

Bururi—'The countryside'; the territorial scope of the *kiama kinene* or *kiama kia bururi*.

Comba—Pronounced 'chomba'; the Kikuyu term for Europeans.

Eeei—Yes.

Gakenge—A very small child.

Gatheci—Literally, 'sharp instrument'; it was a forest term for Home Guard, derived from the fact that Home Guards were initially armed with spears.

493

Gathugo—Literally, 'a throwing weapon'; forest term for Home Guard.

Gatimu—Literally, 'small spear'; forest term for Home Guard, derived from the fact that Home Guards were initially armed with spears.

Gatua uhoro—Literally, 'the decider'; forest term for big game shooting guns ranging from .375 to .450.

Gicakuri—Singular of *icakuri*; meaning 'heavy pitchfork'; forest term for any Government personnel or European.

Gikonyo—Literally, 'protruding navel'; forest term for British bombers, derived from the impression conveyed by the open bomb doors.

Gikuyu—The mythical founding ancestor of the Kikuyu tribe, along with Mumbi, his wife. Also often used instead of Kikuyu.

Gikuyu Gitungati Ngereneva Thingira-ini—An unregistered boys' association at Alliance High School which Karari attended. The name literally means 'receive reward at the elder's hut', and signified Kikuyu servants or the rear guard. It was both political and educational in its aims.

Gikuyu Iregi Army—Murang'a District warriors under Gen. Macaria Kimemia; called Gikuyu because legend instructs that the Kikuyu tribe originated in Murang'a. Iregi was one of the Kikuyu ruling generations which is believed to have radically revised tribal law; it literally means 'innovator' or 'rejector'.

Gikuyu na Mumbi—Mythical founders of the Kikuyu tribe; a term also used for the underground movement by its members.

Gikuyu na Mumbi Trinity Army—All unorganized Kikuyu who sympathized with and/or aided the guerrilla fighters. 'Trinity', following Catholic theological notions, refers symbolically to the 'unity of all in one'.

Gitete—A small gourd.

Githaka—The land held by a Kikuyu *mbari* or sub-clan.

Githambio—A fermented mixture of millet flour and water; employed by a *mundo mugo* in his purification rituals.

Gitumbeki—Term for the kitbag carried by forest fighters.

Gitungati—Singular form of *itungati,* used to refer to all forest fighters other than officers.

Gituyu—A large forest rat with a two-foot, whip-like tail.

Hatha—An edible nettle.

Hiti—Literally 'hyena'; used as a forest camp password.

Ihei cia mihitu—Literally 'forest boys'; forest term for warriors.

Ithanji—A reed used for thatching the roofs of dwellings.

Itora—A dispersed village traditionally containing, in addition to sub-clan members, a number of attached dependents and tenants.

Ituma—First word of Ituma Ndemi Trinity Army, whose letters are significant. 'I' stands for *Itungati,* 'Warriors'; 'T' for North and South Teu divisions of Nyeri District; 'U' for Uthaya division of Nyeri, and 'MA' for the Mathera division of Nyeri.

Ituma Ndemi (Trinity) Army—Nyeri District warriors, under General Stanley Mathenge. *Ndemi* refers to an old Kikuyu ruling generation who were the founders of smith work and hence militarily of great importance. *Ndemi* literally means 'arrowhead'.

Itungati—Warriors (see *Gitungati*).

Itwika—The traditional 'handing over ceremony', which formally marked the accession to power of the junior generation-set when the elders of the 'ruling' generation decided to step down or retire from active political life.

Kaana—A young boy still too small to help in herding the family stock.

Kahi—A young lad, old enough to help in the herding of his family's sheep and goats.

Kamatimo—Lowest in the traditional hierarchy of elders.

Kamatimu—Home Guards and other traitors to the revolution.

Kamwaki—Literally, 'small fire'; a forest term meaning pistol.

Kanzu—A frock frequently worn by servants.

Karai—A metal basin.

Kariiguri—Literally 'it is up'; a forest term meaning that an airplane was approaching.

Yenya Inoro Army—Kiambu District warriors, under General Waruingi. Inoro, literally a stone used for sharpening knives, spears, etc., here referring to the fact that the Kenya Teachers College, Githunguri, in Kiambu, was sharpening the brains of the Kenya Africans.

Kenya Levellation Army—All persons fighting on the side of the revolution in the reserves. This 'army' lacked a central command, with outstanding individual leaders emerging in each of the various districts. *Levellation* was derived from the English 'level'; Home Guards and other traitors were regarded as stumps in a field, to be levelled or gotten rid of.

Kenya Ng'ombe—Forest term for Kenya Regiment personnel; derived from the fact that *ng'ombe*, meaning cow in Swahili, was the Kenya Regiment symbol.

Kiama—A council of elders.

Kiama kia bururi—'Council of the countryside'; another name for *kiama kinene*.

Kiama kia itora—Village council of elders, which performed a wide range of judicial, religious and social functions.

Kiama kia mwaki—A neighborhood council of elders, administering a *mwaki* and comprised of elders representing the lower level village councils.

Kiama kia rugongo—A ridge council, made up of senior elders selected by the councils of the constituent neighborhoods; held jurisdiction over all religious, judicial and military matters which affected the entire ridge.

Kiama kinene—'The Big Council'; a body of elders which convened whenever matters arose involving two or more *rugongo*. Its members included representatives of all the involved *rugongo* and, on certain very special occasions, senior or leading elders representing all of the ridges within the territory of a particular sub-tribe.

Kiama Kiria Kiracoria Wiathi—Literally 'The Council Which Is Searching Freedom'; referred to the Freedom Seeking Council, a name used briefly by the new Nairobi leadership.

Kiambo—The name of Karari's grandfather's spear, which was also the latter's nickname.

Kihi—A young boy approaching the age of circumcision and initiation into manhood.

Kihumo kia Uiguano na Ngwataniro ya Agikuyu—Literally, 'The Beginning of Unity and Cooperation of the Agikuyu'; an organization of students of which Karari was Vice-President. The initials, KUNA, mean 'true'. The aim of the organization was to deplore the differences and conflicts among the Christian sects.

Kipande—A combined identification and employment card which all African males over 16 years of age were obliged to carry on pain of arrest and imprisonment.

Kirinyaga—The Kikuyu term for Mount Kenya.

Komerera—A term normally used for persons or criminals in hiding from the law; especially employed in the forest to refer to men who wished merely to escape army discipline and avoid clashes with Government forces. A *komerera* usually spent his time hiding in the forest or reserve, occasionally stealing peasant crops and raiding supporters' stores and shops.

Kuri hono-i ndirara?—Literally, 'It is cold, where shall I sleep?' A forest signal to camp guards signifying that one was not an enemy.

Makara—Literally, 'charcoal'; a forest term for ammunition.

Makumi mana—Forty shillings.

Marerema—A type of wild vegetable.

Mataathi—Leaves of the mutaathi tree, used by elders as hand-kerchiefs.

Matemo—News.

Mau Mau—A Kikuyu colloquial meaning 'greedy eating'; popularized by the Europeans as the name of the revolutionary movement.

Mbari—A traditional Kikuyu sub-clan; the largest localized kinship unit; a landholding group ranging as high as 5,000 persons and comprised of the male descendents of a common ancestor, together with their wives and dependent children.

Mbuci—Forest terminology for a camp; derived from the English word 'bush'.

Mburu Ngebo Army—All Rift Valley fighters, under General Kimbo. *Mburu*, derived from *MBUtu cia Ruguru*, meant 'Army of the West', or 'Rift Valley Army'. *Mburu* was also the name of a Kiambu age-group, and was frequently used in reference to

Dutch settlers in Kenya. *Ngebo* means 'level' and symbolized being level to the ground when fighting so as to avoid the enemy's bullets. The implication was that this army was to fight as strongly as the Dutch settlers in the Kenya Regiment and Kenya Police Reserve.

Mbutu—A forest term meaning group or fighting section.

Mei Mathathi Army—Mount Kenya warriors, under General China. Mei was derived from *M*eru, *E*mbu and *I*kamba, who made up the majority of Mt. Kenya fighters. *Mathathi* refers to an ancient ruling generation believed to have discovered red ochre and its use in painting hair, shields, etc. Literally, *thathi* means red ochre.

Mihuni—Songs created in 1939-40 by youths which prophesized the coming scarcity of food and property, and the bravery and death of thousands of Kikuyu.

Mikorobothi—A tree bearing bitter leaves.

Miraa—Leaves of a certain tree having an intoxicating effect when chewed.

Mucii—Kikuyu term for 'homestead'.

Muciriri—President of an *njama* or judicial council.

Mugwanja—The Kikuyu term for 'seven'.

Muhimu—A code term for The Movement, meaning 'Most Important' in Swahili.

Muiguithania—The name of a vernacular KCA newspaper, literally meaning 'the unifier' and used sometimes to refer to the underground movement.

Muiko—A wooden sword carved for use when dancing the *muthuu*.

Muingi—Literally, the 'community'; a term used by members of *The Movement*.

Muirigo—Literally, 'a clear forest path'; used of persons with great knowledge of the forest.

Muiri—A variety of tree.

Muma—A term employed by members of the Movement when referring to the 'Oath of Unity', *Muma wa Uiguano*, and also frequently used to symbolize the movement as a whole.

Muma wa Ngero—'Oath of Violence or Crime'.

Muma wa Uiguano—The 'Oath of Unity', by which members were initiated into the underground movement.

Mumbi—The traditionally acknowledged female founder of the Kikuyu tribe.

Mumo—A junior warrior in the traditional Kikuyu age-grade system.

Mundo mugo wa ita—A war magician who utilized his art to bless and cleanse warriors and to determine the propitious time and place for raids. Used in the forest to refer to religious practitioners and seers.

Munyeni—An elder's headdress, like a beret.

Munyu mweru—'White salts'; a place where animals came to lick the natural salt earths.

Muriega—'Hello'.

Muthamaki—Spokesman of a *kiama* who was chosen from among the council members and, being responsible to them, carried out any talks or negotiations which might be necessary with 'outsiders' or foreigners.

Muthamaki wa bururi—'Leader of the Countryside'; a prominent political figure.

Muthamaki wa cira—'Leader in Law'.

Muthamaki wa ita—A 'Leader in War'.

Muthegi—A black honorary walking stick, used by elders and made from the mungirima tree.

Muthuu—A youth dance invented in 1942 in which the dancers referred to themselves as Germans or Japanese and proclaimed their will to fight.

Mwaki—A 'neighborhood' or 'fire-linked unit' within which members from the included villages could call upon one another for assistance in domestic tasks and situations of need.

Mwembaiguri—A creeping plant considered lucky by the Kikuyu and used by *mundo mugo* in preparing warriors for battle.

Mzungu Arudi Uingereza, Mwafrica Apate Uhuru—Literally, 'Let the European return to England so that the African may get freedom'. A suggested source of the term 'Mau Mau' which its initials spell.

Mzungu wa Njama—Literally, 'Njama the European', in Swahili. Used by a Boer settler who spoke little English to refer degradingly to Karari who, because he spoke English, was considered a 'Black European'.

Mzuri—'Good', in Swahili.

Nakombora—Literally, 'the destroyer'; a forest term for Bren gun.

Ndahi—A small gourd, half the size of a glass.

Ndemi—In Ituma Ndemi Army; literally 'arrowhead', refers to an early generation-set believed to have invented the art of metalworking and made the first metal-tipped spears.

Ndio, Abandi—'Yes, Sir.' A Swahili expression.

Nduma—'Arrowroot'.

Ngai—The Kikuyu term for 'God'.

Ngarango—Fried fat crisps.

Ngata—The bone which connects the head and the spinal column of the goat and contains seven holes. It played an important part in the 'Oath of Unity' ritual.

Nguthiru—The moorlands of *Nyandarua* or the Aberdare Forest.

Ngutu—A traditional club for uninitiated boys.

Ngworu—The stomach contents of a goat, employed in purification ceremonies.

Nindakwirire utige kunora mukuha na mbari cieri, ugagutheca— 'Don't sharpen the Kikuyu needle at both ends, for it will surely prick you', meaning that the Europeans should not give the Kikuyu education, as it might endanger the formers privileged position in Kenya.

Njama—A traditional Kikuyu council sitting as court of law.

Njama ya aanake a mumo—'The Council of Junior Warriors'.

Njama ya ita—'War Council'.

Njamba cia ita—One of the forest terms for 'warriors'.

Nyagikonyo—Literally, 'the bearer of a protruding navel'; a forest term for the Lincoln heavy bomber.

Nyanja—Gourds for storing beer.

Nyomu Nditu—Literally, 'the heavy animal'; a forest term for 'Mau Mau'.

Panga—A long, curved knife, sharpened on one side; introduced by the Europeans.

Rŭgi—Literally, the traditional doors made of interwoven thin sticks or reeds.

Riika—Named age- or generation-sets in the traditional Kikuyu social system.

Rugongo—A 'Ridge' generally comprised of several *mwaki* and covering an expanse of land lying between two rivers and extending some 25 to 30 miles.

Sauti ya Mwafrica—The African Voice, a Swahili newspaper, originally the official paper of the Kenya African Union (KAU).

Shamba—'Garden', or 'acre' in Swahili.

Simi—The double-edged traditional Kikuyu sword.

Thaai—'Peace'; a means of signing a letter.

Thaai, thathaiya Ngai thai—Meaning 'We praise Thee, oh Lord', or 'God's peace be with us'; used to end certain Kikuyu prayers.

Thabu—A poisonous stinging plant leaf of the nettle family which causes great pain and swelling; employed as a device to torture and extract information from Mau Mau detainees and suspects.

Thumbi—A traditional Kikuyu headdress.

Tie-ties—African white collar workers; a pejorative term for Europeanized Africans who were least likely to assist in the revolutionary struggle for land and freedom.

Timamu Abandi—The meaning of 'finished, fulfilled, done, or complete, Sir.'

Togotia—A wild edible vegetable.

The Townwatch Battalions—The forest term for all those who fought in the towns, most of whom carried on their normal jobs during the day and fought at night.

Ucio uri ho!—'That is true'.

Uhuru—'Freedom' in Swahili.

Uiguano wa Muingi—Literally, 'The unity of the community'; an expression used by members for the underground movement.

Ukuri—The traditional term for highest rank of senior elder.

Uma Uma—'Out, Out'; suggested by some as the source from which 'Mau Mau' was derived, with the intended meaning that the Europeans should leave Kenya. The change for *Uma Uma* to Mau Mau is thought to have been arrived at via a children's game similar to our Pig-Latin.

Utuku wa Hiu Ndaihu—'The Night of Long Swords'.

Wamana—The nickname for Karari's father, Njama Karari, it literally means 'of forty' in Kikuyu.

Wanyua—A respectful mode of address meaning 'Father'.

Wanyua wakine—Greetings exchanged between persons of the same generation, age.

SELECTED BIBLIOGRAPHY

AARONOVITCH, S. and K. *Crisis in Kenya.** Lawrence & Wishart, London, 1947.

BALDWIN, William. *Mau Mau Manhunt.* E. P. Dutton & Co., Inc., New York, 1957.

BENNETT, George. 'The Development of Political Organizations in Kenya'. *Political Studies,* Vol. 5, No. 2 (June).

BENNETT, George. *Kenya: A Political History; the Colonial Period.* Oxford University Press, London, 1963.

BOYES, John. *King of the Wa-Kikuyu.* Methuen & Co., Ltd., London, 1911.

CAGNALO, Fr. C. *The Akikuyu.* Mission Printing School, Nyeri, 1933.

COROTHERS, J. C. *The Psychology of Mau Mau.* Government Printer, Nairobi, 1955.

CONGRESS OF PEOPLES AGAINST IMPERIALISM. *Press extracts: Diary of the Kenya Crisis.** Unpublished papers, 1955.

CORFIELD, F. D. *Historical Survey of the Origins and Growth of Mau Mau.* Her Majesty's Stationery Office, London, 1960.

DELF, George. *Jomo Kenyatta.* Victor Gollancz Ltd., London, 1961.

DILLEY, M. R. *British Policy in Kenya Colony.** Nelson, New York, 1937.

EVANS, Peter. *Law and Disorder: Scenes of Life in Kenya.** Secker & Warburg, London, 1956.

FARSON, Negley. *Last Chance in Africa.* Victor Gollancz Ltd., London, 1951.

GANN, L. H. *and* DUIGNAM, P. *White Settlers in Tropical Africa.* Penguin Books, 1962.

HAILEY, Lord. *An African Survey.* Revised 1956. Oxford University Press, London, 1957.

HENDERSON, Ian *and* GOODHART, Philip. *The Hunt for Kimathi.* Hamish Hamilton, London, 1958.

HEYER, Sarjit S. *Development of Agriculture and the Land System* *in Kenya, 1918-1939.** Unpublished Master's thesis, University of London, 1960.

HOLLINGSWORTH, L. W. *The Asians of East Africa*. Macmillan & Co., Ltd., London, 1960.

HUXLEY, E. *White Man's Country*. 2 vols. Macmillan & Co. Ltd., London, 1935.

HUXLEY, E. *and* PERHAM, M. *Race and Politics in Kenya*.* Faber & Faber Ltd., London, 1954.

INGHAM, Kenneth. *History of East Africa*.* Longmans, 1962.

KENYA GOVERNMENT PUBLICATIONS

1908–1926 *Annual Reports of Kenya Colony*.

1913   *Report of the Native Labour Commission*.

1918   *Report of the Land Settlement Committee*.

1950   *Geographical and Tribal Studies*. East African Statistical Dept.

1948   *East African Census*

KENYATTA, Jomo. *Facing Mount Kenya*. Secker & Warburg, London, 1938.

KENYATTA, Jomo. *Kenya: The Land of Conflict*.* Panaf Service Ltd., Manchester, 1945.

KILSON, M. L. 'The Land and the Kikuyu'. *Journal of Negro History*, 1955.

KITSON, Frank. *Gangs and Counter-gangs*. Barrie and Rockliff, London, 1960.

KOINANGE, P. M. *The People of Kenya Speak for Themselves*.* Kenya Publication Detroit, 1955.

LAMBERT, H. E. *Kikuyu Social and Political Institutions*.* Oxford University Press, 1956.

LAVERS, Anthony. *Kenya During and After Mau Mau*. Press Office, Office of Information, Nairobi, 1957.

LEAKEY, L. S. B. *Mau Mau and the Kikuyu*.* Methuen & Co., Ltd., London, 1952.

LEAKEY, L. S. B. *Defeating Mau Mau*. Methuen & Co., Ltd., London, 1954.

LEYS, Norman, *Kenya*. Hogarth Press, London, 1924.

MAIR, Lucy P. 'The Pursuit of the Millenium in Melanesia' (Book Review). *British Journal of Sociology*, Vol. 9, No. 2 (1958).

MAJDALANEY, Fred. *State of Emergency*. Longmans, Green & Co. Ltd., London, 1962.

MIDDLETON, John. *The Kikuyu and Kamba of Kenya.** International African Institute, London, 1953.

MONTAGU, Slater. *The Trial of Jomo Kenyatta.* Secker & Warburg, London, 1955.

PARKER, Mary. *Political and Social Aspects of the Development of Municipal Government in Kenya with Special Reference to Nairobi.** Unpublished manuscript : Makerere University College, 1948.

ROBERTS, G. *The Mau Mau in Kenya.* Hutchinson, London, 1954.

ROSS, M. *Kenya from Within.** Allen & Unwin, London, 1927.

UNITED KINGDOM GOVERNMENT PUBLICATIONS

1923   *White Paper of Indians in Kenya,* Cmd. 1922.

1930   *Native Policy,* Cmd. 3573.

1933   *Report of the Kenya Land Commission,* Cmd. 4556.

1956   *East African Royal Commission,* 1953–5, Report, Cmd. 9475.*

WELBOURN, F. B. *East Africa Rebels.* SCM Press Ltd., London, 1961.

WORSLEY, Peter. *The Trumpet Shall Sound.* MacGibbon & Kee, London, 1957.

INDEX

Abaluhya Association, 28

Abdullah, General (Gitonga Muthui), 312, 314, 363, 447

Aberdare forest, 144-6
  guerrilla forces, 170, 375, 376
  (see also Forest groups)

African Independent Pentecostal Church, 38

African Legislative Council, 39

African Orthodox Church, 38

Africans, the, 29
  educated, 28-9
  poverty of, 27

Alliance High School, 88, 96, 97, 99

Apartheid, 25

Baluhya Tribe, 23, 24, 30, 31

Baring, Sir Evelyn, 350

Batuni Oath see Warrior Oath

Beecher, Rev., 77

Beecher Report, 77-8, 112, 122

Blundell, Michael, 420, 421

Bombing of the forest areas,
  by Harvard bombers, 190, 203, 267
  by Lincoln bombers, 211, 308-10, 408-10

Boran Tribe, 23

British Commonwealth Parliamentary Delegation, 368

British East Africa, formation of, 23

Brockway, Fenner, 129, 357, 363

Buffs and Devons, the 39th Brigade, 212

Central Province Committee (CPC), 62, 63, 125, 171

China, General (Waruhui Itote), 170, 255, 258, 340
  capture, 330

tries to negotiate surrender, 349

Christianity, 38, 100, 101, 201

Chuka Tribe, 43

Collier, Mr. (District Education Officer), 111, 112, 113

Colonial Office Parliamentary Delegation, report, 330

Colour Bar, 29

Convention of Associations, 25

Crown Lands Ordinance (1915), 33, 36, 350

Danile, M. P., 82, 84

Delamere, Lord, 32, 109

Detention camps,
  reported torture, 209

Devons, the
  fighting in the Aberdare forest, 204, 206, 215, 216, 220

Domestic and Hotel Workers Union, 28

East African Association (EEA), 36, 37

East African Census (1948), 24

East African Trades Union Congress, 40

Embu Tribe, 23, 43
  withdrawal into forest, 71, 149-53

Erskine, General, 211, 306, 350, 440

Ethiopia, 23, 39, 359

European population, 24

Forest groups, 153-6, 158, 170, 213, 301, 375-6
  open rift between leaders, 455

Forest Reserve, 33, 80

Francis, Mr. E. C. (Principle of Alliance High School), 99

MONTHLY REVIEW

an independent socialist magazine
edited by Paul M. Sweezy and Harry Magdoff

Business Week: ". . . a brand of socialism that is thorough-going and tough-minded, drastic enough to provide the sharp break with the past that many left-wingers in the underdeveloped countries see as essential. At the same time they maintain a sturdy independence of both Moscow and Peking that appeals to neutralists. And their skill in manipulating the abstruse concepts of modern economics impresses would-be intellectuals. . . . Their analysis of the troubles of capitalism is just plausible enough to be disturbing."

Bertrand Russell: "Your journal has been of the greatest interest to me over a period of time. I am not a Marxist by any means as I have sought to show in critiques published in several books, but I recognize the power of much of your own analysis and where I disagree I find your journal valuable and of stimulating importance. I want to thank you for your work and to tell you of my appreciation of it."

The Wellesley Department of Economics: " . . . the leading Marxist intellectual (not Communist) economic journal published anywhere in the world, and is on our subscription list at the College library for good reasons."

Albert Einstein: "Clarity about the aims and problems of socialism is of greatest significance in our age of transition. . . . I consider the founding of this magazine to be an important public service." (In his article, "Why Socialism" in Vol. I, No. 1.)

Selected Modern Reader Paperbacks